The Affirmative Discomforts of Black Female Authorship

The Affirmative Discomforts of Black Female Authorship

Rethinking Triple Consciousness in Contemporary American Culture

Nahum N. Welang

LEXINGTON BOOKS
Lanham • Boulder • New York • London

Published by Lexington Books
An imprint of The Rowman & Littlefield Publishing Group, Inc.
4501 Forbes Boulevard, Suite 200, Lanham, Maryland 20706
www.rowman.com

86-90 Paul Street, London EC2A 4NE

Copyright © 2022 by The Rowman & Littlefield Publishing Group, Inc.

All rights reserved. No part of this book may be reproduced in any form or by any electronic or mechanical means, including information storage and retrieval systems, without written permission from the publisher, except by a reviewer who may quote passages in a review.

British Library Cataloguing in Publication Information Available

Library of Congress Cataloging-in-Publication Data on File

ISBN 978-1-66690-714-8 (cloth)
ISBN 978-1-66690-716-2 (paper)
ISBN 978-1-66690-715-5 (electronic)

Contents

Acknowledgments	vii
Introduction	1
Chapter One: Triple Consciousness	19
Chapter Two: Popular Literary Culture: Roxane Gay's Bad Feminist and Difficult Women	49
Chapter Three: Popular Music Culture: Beyoncé's Lemonade	93
Chapter Four: Popular Television Culture: Issa Rae's Insecure	157
Conclusion	203
Bibliography	213
Index	231
About the Author	243

Acknowledgments

It is only appropriate that I begin by thanking Professor Lene M. Johannessen, my mentor, colleague and friend. I am infinitely grateful for her meticulous contribution to this manuscript over the last four years. Not only did she go through every chapter with a fine-tooth comb, but her limitless expertise in the field of American literature and culture also affirmatively challenged me to deepen the historical nuance, rhetorical scope, and critical vitality of my ideas and thoughts. None of this would have happened without her support. *Thank you!*

I am also indebted to Professor Asbjørn Grønstad, who was the first person to see the potential of this manuscript, back when it was still an incoherent sketch. I am grateful for his foresight. Most importantly, his extensive knowledge of philosophy and visual culture sharpened the multidisciplinary threads and theoretical substructure of my analysis, allowing me to make insightful connections between genres and disciplines. *Thank you!*

I must also thank the University of Bergen for a generous Research Fellowship, which enabled me to write this manuscript comfortably and securely. I never took this opportunity for granted. *Thank you!*

Holly Buchanan and all the wonderful people at Lexington Books deserve recognition for being great communicators and collaborators. *Thank you!*

And finally, to my parents, Samuel and Pauline Welang, for the gift of education and imagination. *Thank you!*

Introduction

In our current multimedia era of diverse storytelling techniques and platforms, I have noticed the emergence of a group of popular Black American female artists who are exploring an understudied but momentous rupture in the intermediate realm Black women often inhabit between racial and gendered identities.[1] This rupture represents an unresolved sense of identity that seeks to uncover new knowledge systems beyond the constraints of hegemonic dogmas and practices. In this book, I unpack the implications of this rupture by using a multidisciplinary approach to, first, highlight how systemic institutions of American patriarchy create and propagate master narratives, which have historically supplanted and skewed Black female self-expression. Moreover, the historical tendency to prioritize white women's interests within and beyond mainstream feminist spaces produces comparable master narratives by sidelining and silencing the interests of Black women. Due to unfolding eras of reformism and the manifold avenues of expression available in our contemporary time, a diverse group of Black female artists are now using novel and dynamic approaches to confront racial and gendered forms of marginalization, legitimize their intermediate existence, and explore the affirmative possibilities of counternarratives, revelations, and insights that reject strict adherence to hegemonic knowledge systems.

My manuscript works through the exploration of these possibilities by rethinking triple consciousness theory (TCT), a contemporary amendment of W.E.B. Du Bois's famed double consciousness concept.[2] Although double consciousness characterizes collective Black consciousness as an existential rift between American citizenry and the Black experience (Du Bois 1994, 2–3), the Black female perspective, scholars argue, remains supplanted because Du Bois's theorization of the Black experience is often informed by patriarchal sensibilities (Smith 2004, 38). Contemporary African American feminist writers such as Danielle Moodie-Mills and Sara Lomax-Reese have addressed this limitation in their writings by using the concept of "triple consciousness," a philosophical attempt to redesign the Du Boisian framework by underscoring the gendered perspective in a newly enacted third consciousness. In brief, triple consciousness argues that Black women view themselves through three lenses and not two: Blackness, America, and womanhood.³

I problematize this existing triple consciousness framework by arguing that in the works of writer Roxane Gay, popstar Beyoncé, and writer/actress Issa Rae, there is an exploration of a new kind of gendered third consciousness that is not an extension of Du Bois's double consciousness. What makes this novel third consciousness unique, and not largely reliant on other recognizable "thirdness" concepts like postcolonial scholar Homi K. Bhabha's hybridity, is its primary focus on the individual's efforts to affirm their right to difference by simultaneously embracing and rejecting hegemonic notions and manifestations of culture. While the works of these Black female artists sometimes echo the racial and cultural tensions embedded in Du Bois's double consciousness paradigm and Bhabha's hybridity of cultures, they are fundamentally and philosophically engaged with a plethora of other vantage points such as the hegemonic mandates of Black hypermasculinity, power imbalances within the African diaspora's syncretic religious practices and an institutional tendency, both within and beyond the African American community, to characterize the Black experience as a monolithic ethnic identity. The radical nature of these engagements, I believe, has not been properly or sufficiently addressed by contemporary scholarship. My motivation to write this manuscript was thus inspired by a desire to investigate and amplify the theoretical depth and richness of contemporary works by these popular Black female artists.

I attempt to accomplish this objective by rethinking ubiquitous interpretations of triple consciousness. As a reimagined theoretical concept, TCT acknowledges, accommodates and works through this novel interpretation of the third lens, a new imaginary that uses its awareness of intersectional knowledge systems to splinter entrenched paradigms of Black identity and explore the possibilities of counternarratives. I characterize this exploration of possibilities as a new kind of agency, not because it is necessarily tied to power or liberation but because it is a unique form of expression that has not been broadly represented in ordinary philosophical language. This unique expression of rupture, an audacious celebration of racial and gendered experiences that are affirmative but also contradictory, unsettling and ultimately unresolved, problematizes hegemonic notions of identity and boldly moves toward a potential shift, a shift on the cusp of profound rethinking and reimagination.

The gatekeepers of traditional academic research have historically regarded popular culture as a form of "low culture," arguing that the broadness of its appeal and the perceived simplicity of its discourse lack the specialized aesthetic sophistication of classical works of "high culture" such as literary fiction, painting and philosophy (Gregorio-Godeo and Ramón-Torrijos 2017, 5). These perspectives began to change when Stuart Hall, a Jamaican-born British sociologist and cultural theorist, appeared on the academic scene in the 1970s and was later able to bridge the traditional gap between "high culture" and "popular culture" by making a case for the scholarly vitality of popular activities (Gregorio-Godeo and Ramón-Torrijos 2017, 5).[4] Hall argues that "widely distributed forms of popular music, publishing, art, design and literature, or activities of leisure-time and entertainment, which make up the everyday lives of the majority of ordinary people" reveal "the 'way of life' of a people, community, nation or social group" (1997, 2). Thus, by studying the meanings individuals attach to popular activities, popular culture can be described as the study of "shared values" (Hall 1997, 2).

My reworked triple consciousness model examines the contemporary works of three popular Black female artists (Roxane Gay, Beyoncé, and Issa Rae) across four disciplines (history, literature, music and television), paying particular attention to the rupture that develops when these works simultaneously resist and embrace the hegemony of shared values. The ability of these artists to challenge and rethink collective knowledge systems is largely predicated by their status as popular artists. The artistic productions of these women are widely consumed, celebrated and condemned by the masses, imbuing them with the agency to reflect, influence, and even redirect, trends in contemporary popular culture and academic discourse.

In order to illuminate the philosophical depth of contemporary works by Gay, Beyoncé, and Rae, TCT uses concepts by French philosopher Gilles Deleuze to solidify its theoretical substructure. I must emphasize here that I am neither positioning myself as an expert in Deleuzian philosophy nor am I attempting to cover the philosophical expansiveness of Deleuze's ruminations. My manuscript solely focuses on the Deleuzian concepts of "foldings" and "becoming" because their emphasis on a counter-actualizing mechanism, which affirms the individual's infinite right to difference by resisting external interference, speaks directly to the tension in contemporary Black female authorship between an individual's right to difference and community's preference for conformity.[5] These specific concepts of Deleuzian philosophy are thus the most apt framework for my manuscript because they can identify and conceptualize the tension that orients momentous moments of rupture in the works of Gay, Beyoncé, and Rae.

Unpacking the varied dimensions of this tension requires additional theoretical support, so I use concepts such as idioculture, aesthetic imaginaries and everyday aesthetics to problematize the existential practice of simultaneously embracing and rejecting shared identities. The complexity of this practice takes on different elastic shapes and forms, making the prospect of arriving at a tidy conclusion, both in terms of ideology and identities, impossible. However, I argue that by using my reimagined triple consciousness framework and its theoretical inspirations to interpret the artistic creations of Gay, Beyoncé and Rae, the reader develops a more profound understanding of momentous moments of rupture, episodes that encapsulate the unresolved existential tension between an affirmative right to difference and community's fondness for conformism.

My manuscript is divided into four chapters. Chapter 1 traces the origins and development of TCT by examining the nature, implications and shortcomings of the "double consciousness" described by its progenitor W. E. B. Du Bois. The goal of this chapter is to make a case for TCT's relevance by underlining the limitations of the application of double consciousness in contemporary scholarship. In chapter 2, I discuss writer Roxane Gay's essay collection *Bad Feminist* (2014) and the short story collection *Difficult Women* (2017). In both works, Gay's third consciousness strives for pluralism in contemporary feminism and reorients the moral epicenter of Black narratives by authenticating the authority of an individualized female-centric perspective, a perspective that is both chaotic and affirming. Gay ultimately rebels against ingrained perceptions of womanhood by emphasizing an affirmative right to difference, a right to exist and thrive beyond the expectations and constraints of enclosed communities and hegemonic mandates.

Chapter 3 problematizes Gay's notion of an affirmative right to difference by foregrounding the function of community in *Lemonade* (2016), a visual music album by pop star Beyoncé. In *Lemonade*, Beyoncé's third consciousness uses Afrofuturist tropes, indigenous African spirituality, and Southern Gothic imagery to demonstrate how community concurrently destroys and affirms individual agency. In other words, *Lemonade*'s primary source of tension is community's conflicting role as both ally and aggressor; the community responsible for Beyoncé's metaphorical death is the same community responsible for her existential salvation. I move to the realm of television in chapter 4 by addressing the ordinary but subversive aesthetic of writer/actress Issa Rae's HBO television series *Insecure* (2016–2021). Although Rae explores familiar tensions between the individual and the community, her third consciousness adopts a distinct aesthetic, which subverts television tropes and gendered stereotypes by reimagining Black womanhood as extraordinarily ordinary, the antithesis of the ubiquitous #BlackGirlMagic hashtag. Unlike the thematic and aesthetic spectacle of Gay's *Bad Feminist* and *Difficult Women* and Beyoncé's *Lemonade*, *Insecure*'s subversive affirmations reside in the quietude of everyday traditions, locations, and objects such as having dinner with a friend at a restaurant and buying a couch. My manuscript ultimately argues that in *Bad Feminist*, *Difficult Women*, *Lemonade*, and *Insecure*, Gay, Beyoncé, and Rae employ different aesthetic approaches that not only redefine skewed master narratives of Black womanhood but also contend with the self-affirming yet unresolved aftermath of rupture.

In order to grasp the radical nature of this rupture in the contemporary, we also have to see where it is coming from. The embrace of rupture and the subsequent exploration of counternarratives in the works of Gay, Beyoncé and Rae are direct consequences of earlier ruptures and explorations in American history and culture. Thus, I will provide essential contextualization by examining three pivotal periods in American history. I have termed these pivotal periods "John Hancock moments" because they echo the revolutionary resistance of American founding father John Hancock, a resistance that irreversibly changed the destiny of America. These John Hancock moments span from the late eighteenth century to World War II to our contemporary period and, I argue, they reveal an oppressed-oppressor paradigm, which effectively functions as the preferred interpretive lens to read the historical genesis and augmentation of rupture in contemporary works by Black female authors.

THE FIRST JOHN HANCOCK MOMENT

On July 4, 1776, upon signing America's Declaration of Independence from the British crown, American Revolution Patriot John Hancock audaciously declared, "There! His Majesty can now read my name without glasses" (Meyers 2005, 26). This saga, historicized in works like Jay Fliegelman's *Prodigals and Pilgrims* (1982) and David Lowenthal's *The Past Is a Foreign Country* (1985) as a revolt against patriarchal authority, was the genesis of an ideological shift that forever changed the political landscape of what would become America. The British crown, in the preceding century, was commonly regarded as an omnipotent parent with a divinely ordained mandate over its colonial subjects (Boyd 2009, 247). This notion was influenced by the patriarchal authoritarianism of traditional households (Lowenthal 1985, 106). Because fathers were thought to possess a lifelong authority over their offspring, colonial subjects owed the British crown, their sovereign father figure, the same unhesitating compliance (Lowenthal 1985, 106). As a result, "Britain . . . treated colonials as infants dependent on their elders and subject to their whims" (Lowenthal 1985, 107). From early to mid-eighteenth century, however, English philosopher John Locke momentously reimagined the parent-child framework that shaped America's relationship with the British crown. The mind at birth, Locke argues, is a tabula rasa, a blank slate that matures by acquiring, over time, the knowledge of human experience. Locke states,

> Let us then suppose the mind to be, as we say white paper, void of all characters, without any ideas; how comes it to be furnished? Whence comes it by that vast store which the busy and boundless fancy of man has painted on it, with an almost endless variety? Whence has it all the materials of reason and knowledge? To this I answer, in one word, from experience. (1836, 51)

If the mind is a blank slate at birth, then its maturation process, the imprinting of ideas and character through experience, requires a great deal of tenderness and nurture. Authoritarian parenting is therefore ineffective because it employs dogma and fear to subjugate its offspring. In *Two Treatises of Government*, first published in 1689, Locke cautions fathers against keeping their offspring in a perpetual state of dependency and subjugation (1998, 2T 55).[6] In well-ordered homes, the father is responsible for imparting reason to his children, and as they age and acquire valuable life experiences, they "come to the use of Reason, or a state of Knowledge, wherein they may be supposed capable to understand that Rule, whether it be the Law of Nature, or the municipal Law of their Country they are to govern themselves by" (Locke 1998, 2T 170). In other words, children attain freedom by eventually understanding and participating in the legal discourse governing their societies. Because Locke's disrupting philosophies emphasized to American society the necessity of filial rebellion against patriarchal authoritarianism (Holden 2010, 10), Hancock's audacious "There! His Majesty can now read my name without glasses" moment can thus be characterized as the materialization of America's filial uprising against the patriarchal tyranny of the British crown.

This first John Hancock moment incentivized the American Revolutionary war that began in 1775 and finally secured independence from the British crown in 1783. Locke's influence, American studies scholar Jay Fliegelman argues, extended beyond the Revolution. George Washington, the first president of the United States of America (1789–1797), embodied the antipatriarchal indulgent parent who replaced "patriarch with benefactor" (Fliegelman 1982, 210). Unlike the British crown, Washington shunned absolutism and demonstrated through his leadership style that "sovereignty and power were no longer glorious in and for themselves. Rather, they were glorious . . . only as opportunities to do good" (Fliegelman 1982, 210–11). While there is some truth to this assertion, the patriarchal tendencies of pre-Revolution America were very much present in post-Revolution Washingtonian America. This is evident when one observes the discrepancy between ideology and practice. The founding fathers of the American Constitution were concerned about the abuse of power; after suffering through the despotic reign of George III, they had to endure the overindulgences of state legislatures in post-revolution America (Vile 1999, 6). In order to curb these undemocratic governmental excesses, they created a constitution that separated "parts of government . . .

by balancing them against each other" (Vile 1999, 6). The twin doctrines of checks and balances and the separation of powers thus became the cornerstone of the American Constitution (Vile 1999, 6).

This new American political experiment was unquestionably, in theory, more egalitarian than the authoritarian government of the British crown: "We hold these truths to be self-evident, that all men are created equal, that they are endowed by their Creator with certain unalienable Rights, that among these are Life, Liberty, and the Pursuit of Happiness," the Declaration of Independence proudly asserts. But the usage of "men" here, as we now know, did not refer to all men (i.e., human beings). The white men who overthrew the British crown and took control of the new American nation did not grant natural rights to women, people of color, and economically disadvantaged individuals. In 1776, the year the Declaration of Independence was signed, Black people were still legally classified as property, Native American communities still had no sovereignty over their own land, women could not vote or own property, and white men could only vote if they were property owners. Because these discriminatory practices continued over the next century and beyond, the Declaration of Independence might as well have said, "We hold these truths to be self-evident, that all *white men with property* are created equal, that they are endowed by their Creator with certain unalienable Rights, that among these are Life, Liberty, and the Pursuit of Happiness."

Fliegelman and Lowenthal do not adequately engage with the reasons why the alleged post-Revolution antipatriarchal ideology did not grant natural rights to women, people of color, and poor white men. However, Lowenthal does debunk the notion that post-Revolution America was not deeply influenced by its pre-Revolution past. He states, "the past many nineteenth-century Americans claimed to have left behind was still a baneful living presence . . . the New World could not afford to be corrupted by nostalgia, but Americans were nostalgic all the time" (1985, 113–14). Lowenthal discusses several reasons for this nostalgia. There was, first, the yearning for the rich and textured history of old-world antiquity (1985, 114). The so-called newness of America's landscapes and architecture felt unfinished, lacked associations to established traditions, conjured no memories, and bore no tangible traces of any meaningful historical events (Lowenthal 1985, 114). This complaint is of course rooted in Eurocentrism because Native Americans, I am certain, have never considered the cultural richness of their ancestral land as "unfinished." America did have an illuminated past, but because this past did not specifically illuminate the presumed cultural superiority of European heritage, it was discarded.

The legend of the founding fathers also elicited nostalgia. These were men revered for plotting and orchestrating the liberation of America from the paternal shackles of the British crown and because the infant American nation was naturally in need of guidance, these men "offered ideal, indeed inescapable, paternal models" (Lowenthal 1985, 117). They, as a result, quickly became veritable superstars; they personified "Revolutionary immortality," and they were venerated as "thorough-going modernists" who bravely shunned "earlier precedent" (Lowenthal 1985, 118–19) and forged a new liberated path for America. Steadfast devotion to the paternal authority and legacy of the founding fathers ironically revealed the deeply entrenched filial adjurations of American society. Americans, it seemed, were not ready to let go of the parent-child framework that had shaped their relationship with the British crown. Post–Civil War immigration equally contributed to feelings of nostalgia. After the Civil War, there was increased immigration from eastern and southern Europe (Lowenthal 1985, 121). Because these new immigrants did not share an Anglo European heritage, their so-called alien languages, family structures, religions, and character traits "seemed unassimilable and dangerously un-American" (Lowenthal 1985, 121). The backlash to this cultural "contamination" was a profound yearning for the moral "purity" of British paternalism (Lowenthal 1985, 121).

Missing from Lowenthal's list of reasons for nostalgia in post-Revolution America is what I consider the most obvious one: the child growing up and eventually craving the power his father possessed. One could argue that the founding fathers resorted to paternal models because, during their infancy, they craved the omnipotent power of the British crown, their sovereign father figure. This argument has its basis in the psychology of oppression. In *Pedagogy of the Oppressed*, philosopher Paulo Freire argues that, within the context of liberation struggles, "the oppressed, instead of striving for liberation, tend themselves to become oppressors, or 'sub-oppressors'" (2018, 45). When the oppressed are birthed and raised in spaces governed by the misguided morality of their oppressor, their perception of selfhood is skewed by their immersion in oppression (Freire 2018, 45). Because the existential configurations of the oppressed reflect the inhumanity of their oppressor, both parties develop a profound attachment, a bond Freire describes as "adhesion" (2018, 45). Revolutions, thus, are not always about liberation. Rather, they often reveal the oppressor's existential identification with the power possessed by their oppressor and an opportunity for the former to claim this power and replicate familiar oppressor-oppressed dynamics. This partly explains why, I argue, natural rights were not extended to women, people of color and poor white men in post-Revolution America. The white men who overthrew the British crown existentially identified with the power possessed by their equally white oppressors, wealthy aristocrats who symbolized the hegemony of the British crown. After acquiring the power formerly exercised by their oppressors, and ratifying the Second Amendment, which guaranteed their right to bear arms and defend their interests, they firmly established a familiar pre-Revolution oppressor-oppressed dynamic. In the so-called new America, this replicated dynamic functioned as a patriarchal pyramid that safeguarded the hegemony of wealthy white men. Throughout the 1820s and 1830s, however, this patriarchal pyramid would begin to curtail its classist prejudices (while retaining its racial and gender bias) by eliminating the property ownership voting requirement for white men only (Kenny 2003, 101).

THE SECOND JOHN HANCOCK MOMENT

Over 155 years after America's independence from the British crown, during the apex of World War II, the stage was being set for the second John Hancock moment. Despite the booming wartime economy and the increased demand for labor in semiskilled and skilled occupations (Wynn 2010, 67), Black Americans still endured widespread discrimination in the labor market: "employment offices either refused to register the black skilled workers or did not provide them with employment advice. . . . The Government carried out 4,630 programs, of which, only 194 admitted blacks" (Zhang 2002, 101–2). And then there was the issue of segregation in the army. Segregationist policies at home followed Black soldiers everywhere they went. At some army camps, German prisoners of war were granted access to drinking fountains that Black soldiers were prohibited from using (Zhang 2002, 101–2). What is the point of fighting for freedom and democratic values abroad if you lack freedom and democratic values at home? Black Americans began to wonder. In the words of civil rights activist Roy Wilkins, "the fight against Hitlerism begins in Washington, D.C." (Wynn 2010, 40). The dissemination of this sentiment emboldened Black American political consciousness and, as a result, facilitated the historic achievements of the civil rights movement such as the Civil Rights Act of 1964 and the Voting Rights Act of 1965 (Zhang 2002, 101–7).

Traditional domestic roles were also shattered during the war. In order to address the labor deficit created by enlisted men, women were actively encouraged to keep the war economy afloat by taking historically male jobs (May 1996, 128). Between 1940 to 1944, "manufacturing alone accounted for more than three million more female workers . . . rising from 21 to 34 percent of total female employment" (Rose 2018, 673). The profound sense of fulfillment American women gained from mobilizing and running key sectors of the war economy was quickly lost after the war when patriarchal structures, in an attempt to reinstate the status quo, decanted women back to domesticated work (Wilford 1994, 268). This loss, both profound and existential, emboldened feminist consciousness and laid the groundwork for second-wave feminism (Wilford 1994, 268).

The systemic success of the civil rights movement served as a blueprint for second-wave feminism (Freeman 2014, 220), and while the commonly endorsed narratives of both movements touted a united front against white-dominated patriarchal institutions, within their respective groups, the reality was far less sanitized. Black women including Ella Baker, Septima Poinsette Clark, Fannie Lou Hamer, Vivian Malone Jones, and Dorothy Height greased the organizational and legislative wheels of the civil rights movement in the 1960s. Although these women raised funds for alternate transportation during bus boycotts, educated the masses on voter registration, protested at segregated establishments, fed volunteers, and marched on Washington, their contributions were often sidelined in favor of the movement's Black male leaders (Associated Press 2005). A major reason for this sidelining was the leadership preference at the time. Scholarship on the civil rights movement, from the 1960s through the 1980s, originally used principles like resource mobilization theory (RMT) to rationalize the necessary connection between charismatic leadership and material resources (Delinder 2009, 987). Scholars pointed out that the charismatic leadership of mesmerizing male orators like Martin Luther King Jr. and Malcolm X was responsible for inspiring the masses and generating substantial material resources for the movement (Delinder 2009, 987). This "politically centred" characterization of the civil rights movement as an implicitly masculine and intrinsically patriarchal movement reflected the reality of its time (Delinder 2009, 987–88) and explains why the unique interests of Black women at the intersection between race and gender were often ignored (Martin et al. 2015, 103).

The white women at the helm of second-wave feminism intellectualized the movement within the framework of first-wave feminism and the civil rights movement, "both of which failed to think through the intersections between race and gender" (Henry 2004, 78) and produced, as a result, a "damaging theoretical blind spot" (Henry 2004, 78). Moreover, second-wave feminists, when conceiving their manifesto, ignored the contributions of first-wave Black feminists and whitewashed America's history of feminist activism (Henry 2004, 78). Leslie Tanner's *Voices from Women's Liberation* (1970), for example, only contains one essay by a first-wave Black feminist, "The Women Want Their Rights" by Sojourner Truth (Henry 2004, 78). Furthermore, key figures of the second wave, such as Canadian-American feminist Shulamith Firestone, inadvertently minimized the racial aspect of feminist activism by claiming that "racism is sexism extended" (Henry 2004, 80). According to this perspective, because male supremacy is the fundamental element of gendered oppression, all forms of female subjugation are more or less identical. In a 1971 essay published by the *New York Times*, "What the Black Woman Thinks About Women's Lib," writer and Black feminist Toni Morrison refuted this ideology by pointing out its failure to recognize the distinct intersectional experience of Black women as marginalized entities in both categories of race and gender, and its refusal to acknowledge the privileges white women innately have access to by virtue of being white citizens in a white-dominated society. The marginalization of Black women in the civil rights movement and second-wave feminism reinforces Freire's argument in *Pedagogy of the Oppressed*. In both movements, Black men and white women existentially identified with the power possessed by their patriarchal oppressors, and, as a result, replicated familiar oppressor-oppressed dynamics. bell hooks aptly articulates this phenomenon in *Feminist Theory: From Margin to Center*:

> White women and black men have it both ways. They can act as oppressor or be oppressed. Black men may be victimized by racism, but sexism allows them to act as exploiters and oppressors of women. White women may be victimized by sexism, but racism enables them to act as exploiters and oppressors of black people. Both groups have led liberation movements that favor their interests and support the continued oppression of other groups. Black male sexism has undermined struggles to eradicate racism just as white female racism undermines feminist struggle. As long as these two groups, or any group, defines liberation as gaining social equality with ruling-class white men, they have a vested interest in the continued exploitation and oppression of others. (2014, 16)

To recapitulate, I am using the above John Hancock moments to historicize and contextualize the intersectional entanglements of Black American women. The first John Hancock moment represents filial maturation and rebellion against England's patriarchal authoritarianism. This rebellion might have espoused egalitarian values on paper, but in reality, it sought to use the power of its oppressor to fashion a new kind of patriarchal order, a system that safeguards the hegemony of white American men. The second Hancock represents filial maturation and rebellions against white patriarchy's authoritarianism. These new waves of rebellions (the African American civil rights movement and second-wave feminism) might have espoused egalitarian values on paper but in reality, they too sought to use the power of their oppressor to fashion new patriarchal and feminist orders, systems that safeguard the hegemonies of Black men and white women respectively. The third Hancock moment is arguably the most dramatic, and its story begins with the backlash to unfolding eras of postwar reform.

THE THIRD JOHN HANCOCK MOMENT

After the Civil War, during the Reconstruction era, America's political institutions strongly rebelled against the emancipation of former slaves and the granting of suffrage rights to Black Americans (Fobanjong 2001, xv). This rebellion was manifested in discriminatory regulations like Jim Crow laws and literacy tests, regulations that sought to restrict the natural rights and upward mobility of Black Americans (Young 2015, x). A century later, the accomplishments of the civil rights movement, such as the Equal Rights Amendment (ERA), led to what historians called "Second Reconstruction" (Young 2015, x).These dramatic changes challenged the hegemony of white-dominated patriarchal institutions in an unprecedented fashion and, once again, there was a formidable backlash: "the dismantling of welfare and other social programs, the wars on crime and drugs, mass incarceration, and the violent, heavy-handed policing of Black neighborhoods in America's cities were all part of the white backlash to the successes of the civil rights movement" (Young 2015, X).

This backlash snowballed into the 2000s. The economic insecurity that plagued the start of the third millennium provoked an almost apocalyptic sense of anxiety among working-class Americans (Gusterson and Besteman 2010, 8–9). The American dream, the promise of achieving upward social mobility through nothing else but hard work and determination, is tied to an ominous sense of anxiety. Sociologist Michael Kimmel is one of the many scholars to examine this phenomenon: "just as you could rise as far as your aspirations and talents could take you, you could also fall off the cliff" (2017, 19–20). The pursuit of prosperity coexists with the prospect of failure, however big or small. The patriarchal establishment, ever since America's inception, convinced white men that ownership of America's abundance was their "God-given right" (Kimmel 2017, 18). This claim is supported by the decision, after the 1820s, to afford natural rights only to white men (Kenny 2003, 101) and the consistent efforts over the past centuries to disenfranchise people of color and women (Young 2015, x). A grave sense of existential anxiety is therefore provoked in white men when the procurement of America's abundance seems out of reach. Kimmel calls this historical sense of entitlement over America's resources "aggrieved entitlement" (2017, 18). While participating in a show titled "A Black Woman Stole My Job," Kimmel confronted three "angry white males" (2017, 17) who believed they were unfairly losing economic opportunities to Black women even though white men, based on median hourly earnings, still outearn Black women, Black men, Hispanic men, and women of all other racial groups (Patten 2016).[7] Kimmel recalls,

I asked the men to consider just one word in the title of the show: the word *my*. What made them think the job was theirs? Why wasn't the episode called "A Black Woman Got *the* Job" or "A Black Woman Got *a* Job"? Because these guys felt that those jobs were "theirs," that they were entitled to them, and that when some "other" person—black, female—got the job, that person was really taking "their" job. (2017, 17)

This lashing out at Black women adeptly encapsulates the concept of aggrieved entitlement, the sense that "those benefits to which you believed yourself entitled have been snatched away. . . . You feel yourself to be the heir to a great promise, the American Dream, which has turned into an impossible fantasy for the very people who were supposed to inherit it" (Kimmel 2017, 18).

To make matters worse, in our contemporary time, aggrieved entitlement provoked by economic insecurity is coinciding with profound social displacement. The crusading of progressive groups such as fourth-wave feminists, the Black Lives Matter movement, and LGBTQ activism is turning American society on its head by directly challenging the foundational pillars of traditional society. These profound social changes also coincided with the political ascendancy of Donald Trump, a billionaire businessman and television personality who unapologetically rebuked left-leaning politics and promised to Make America Great Again. His usage of "Great" is loaded with subtext. Make America Great Again, superficially, promises a return to the lost era of American economic prosperity. Trump intentionally never specifies the dates of this lost era because he is exploiting a vague nostalgia for simpler times. By simpler times, I am referring to the so-called white-picket-fence epoch of the mid-twentieth century, a time when patriarchal structures reigned, minorities lacked basic civil rights, and white middle class families had secured jobs and owned homes behind white picket fences. Thus, when Trump talks about Making America Great Again, he is arguably talking about reestablishing traditionalism and the hegemony of white-dominated patriarchal institutions. This message effectively assuaged the anxieties of the white voters in battleground states, and they voted devotedly for Donald Trump as the forty-fifth president of the United States of America.

I must emphasize that I am not discrediting or downplaying the severity of the domestic and global economic anxieties that preceded Trump's presidency. I am also not insinuating that all Americans who responded to these anxieties by supporting Trump are gatekeepers of white patriarchy. For fiscally anxious white voters who prioritize economy over social issues, Trump's grandiose promises to restore the former glory of the American economy made him the most viable candidate, not white patriarchy. What I am pointing out here is Trump's characterization of economic insecurity as a consequence of dismantling the systemic structures of white patriarchy and his worrying tendency to seduce anxious white voters by peddling this misguided logic.

The political victory of Donald Trump in 2016, and its reverberations, marks the third John Hancock moment. I have deemed it the most dramatic of the three because it vehemently discarded, on a national stage, the pretense of a unified front by women and minority groups and signaled instead a kind of rupture, an unraveling termed "America's Great Divide" by the PBS investigative series *Frontline* (PBS 2020). This divide, according to *Frontline*, escalated when the promise of unity by America's first Black president, Barack Obama, "collapsed as increasing racial, cultural and political divisions laid the groundwork for the rise of Donald Trump" (PBS 2020). Trump's presidential campaign and eventual victory, they argue, exploited these divisions and "unleashed anger on both sides of the divide" (PBS 2020). One of the most buzzed about postelection stories was the overwhelming support Trump received from white women:

> There is a 53 percent problem in American feminism. According to exit polls, that is the percentage of white women who voted for Donald Trump. Whose votes helped land the presidency to a man who said women who have abortions should face punishment and bragged that he grabs women "by the pussy." (O'Neal 2016)

From the *New York Times* to Fox News to the *Washington Post*, the mainstream media either cheered or was left aghast by the revelation that white women willingly supported a presidential candidate who is often characterized in the press as an unapologetic misogynist.

Readers of Black feminist scholarship were certainly not shocked by the exit polls. As mentioned earlier, Black feminists including Toni Morrison and bell hooks have spent decades discussing, in great analytical detail, the intersectional complexities and entanglements of mainstream feminism. Even self-identified socially liberal feminists must navigate the confounding dimensions of their varied identities. It is therefore no surprise that the racial politics of Trump's message, a shrewdly conceived rhetoric that venerates, and seeks to reward, the heteronormative white family unit, also appealed to some heterosexual white women who may consider themselves feminists. The surprise, I think, should be the scope of the "53 percent" coverage. The institution of feminism was being attacked, discussed, and dissected from all corners in an unprecedented fashion; it was unlike anything one had ever witnessed in contemporary popular culture. Such dissections of feminism used to be a fringe activity by radical feminists and their allies, but overnight, everyone, across a plethora of media platforms, was either applauding Trump for galvanizing the support of white women or critiquing the whiteness of mainstream feminism and the problematic alliance between white women and white patriarchy. As the illusion of feminist solidarity unraveled, epitomized by Black women disassociating themselves from mainstream "almost all white" (Tolentino 2017) feminist movements like the Women's March on Washington, emboldened Black feminists were getting ready to draw the same level of national attention to another historical trend: the marginalization of Black women within the Black community.

When the #MeToo movement kicked off in 2017 as an anti–sexual harassment crusade founded in response to the repercussions of infamous Hollywood producer Harvey Weinstein's sexual assault allegations, there was a great deal of discussions about "men's behavior towards women and power imbalances" (Khomami 2017). The origins of the movement can be traced back to 2006 when Tarana Burke, a Black American activist, created Me Too, an activist group with the aim of empowering survivors of sexual abuse and violence (Brockes 2018). Twelve years later, in the wake of the Weinstein scandal, Hollywood actress and activist Alyssa Milano used Burke's #MeToo phrase on her social media as a "rallying cry against sexual harassment" (Khomami 2017). Milano wrote, "If all the women who have been sexually harassed or assaulted wrote 'Me too' as a status, we might give people a sense of the magnitude of the problem" (Khomami 2017). As the #MeToo movement grew, Hollywood actresses and female filmmakers reacted by creating TIME'S UP, an organization that seeks to amplify sexual harassment awareness and raise a legal defense fund to support low-wage-earning women pursuing justice for sexual harassment-related injustices in the workplace (TIME'S UP 2021).

The reverberations of #MeToo became a watershed moment for women, and Black feminists smartly exploited this newfound agency to take on R. Kelly, an R&B legend who has been plagued for decades by allegations of using his power and influence to abuse underage Black girls and women. On April 30, 2018, the Black women of the TIME'S UP movement, consisting of actresses, activists and filmmakers like Kerry Washington, Shonda Rimes, and Tarana Burke, invigorated the #MuteRKelly campaign by releasing the following statement: "We demand appropriate investigations and inquiries into the allegations of R. Kelly's abuse made by women and their families for more than two decades now.[8] And we declare with great vigilance and a united voice to anyone who wants to silence us—their time is up" (Read 2018). This was a bold and unprecedented move because Black women have historically been socialized to yield to Black patriarchal authority, especially in the public sphere of civil rights activism (Delinder 2009, 987). Although Black women are integral to the success of these social justice movements, they are usually expected to support and succumb to the masculine rhetoric of "organizational leadership and community organizing" (Eaton 2010, 1).

The agency procured by #MeToo's reverberations, however, is causing a profound shift in gender relations within the Black community. Across social media, blogs, and a surfeit of other digital platforms, Black women are now having candid conversations, both personal and scholarly, about the gendered impact of Black patriarchy and hypermasculinity. Despite decades-long attempts to prosecute R. Kelly for his alleged crimes, the outcome of the #MuteRKelly campaign (a scathing docuseries on his alleged sexual offenses called *Surviving R. Kelly*, more attempted prosecutions, concert cancellations, radio boycotts and the eventual arrest and detainment of the R&B legend) arguably represents the first time in Black America's history that Black women have publicly, decisively, systematically and effectively gone after a prominent Black male celebrity for inflicting pain on Black female bodies. As #MuteRKelly's founder Oronike Odeleye stated, "Someone had to stand up for Black women" (MuteRKelly 2019).

Set against the backdrop of these John Hancock moments, my manuscript emphasizes the unique intermediate existence of some Black American women at the uncomfortable intersection of race and gender. As I pointed out earlier, Du Bois's double consciousness does not sufficiently engage with the unique experiences of this intermediate space. As a result of this shortcoming, contemporary feminist writers have coined the phrase "triple consciousness" to describe and emphasize the three folds of the African American female experience: America, Blackness and womanhood. To reiterate, my manuscript views this third dimension not as a settled sense of identity or a definite consciousness but as a manifestation of rupture, an audacious fragmentation that subverts established epistemologies in order to explore the possibilities of chaotic yet affirmative counternarratives. I develop TCT as a way of imagining alternate ways of being, a new imaginary to accommodate and assist with the exploration of this novel reading of triple consciousness, as illustrated in the contemporary works of three Black female artists: Roxane Gay's *Bad Feminist* and *Difficult Women*, Beyoncé's *Lemonade*, and Issa Rae's *Insecure*. The ability of these women to reach a wider and engaged audience by exploring the possibilities of counternarratives on a plethora of multimedia platforms reveals the wielding of a new kind of agency, an agency that is rejecting past paradigms and developing a new language to articulate the uniquely affirmative but unsettling experiences of Black womanhood in American history and culture. In order to elucidate the contemporary necessity for TCT, it is imperative to examine the origins and historical endurance of its predecessor, double consciousness. Thus, chapter 1 of this manuscript will, first, examine the cornerstone elements, and limitations, of Du Bois's famed concept before delineating the philosophical underpinnings and theoretical usefulness of TCT.

NOTES

1. "American," throughout the entirety of this manuscript, refers specifically to the United States.
2. The acronym "TCT" specifically denotes my reimagined triple consciousness framework.
3. "Black women/female," throughout the entirety of this manuscript, refers specifically to "Black women in the United States."
4. In the realm of American studies, media scholar John Fiske played a significant role in vitalizing the study of popular culture with books like *Understanding Popular Culture* (1989) and *Reading the Popular* (1989).
5. My manuscript defines "authorship" as creators of works of art.
6. 2T denotes *The Second Treatise of Government*.
7. The show's date is not specified in the text but during a lecture prepared by Kimmel for the International Women's Day seminar in 2001 (Brussels, Belgium), he describes his appearance on the show as "recent."
8. #MuteRKelly is a petition started by Oronike Odeleye, an Atlanta arts administrator, to take R. Kelly's music off Atlanta's airwaves due to the persistent sexual abuse allegations.

Chapter One

Triple Consciousness

THE VEIL

W. E. B. Du Bois's concept of double consciousness, originally published in his seminal essay collection *The Souls of Black Folk* (1903), has been extensively researched and referenced since its inception. I must preface this chapter by underscoring that my primary focus is not to cover the breadth and depth of existing research on the concept. Rather, my goal is to carefully examine the conceptualization of double consciousness as articulated in Du Bois's essay "Of Our Spiritual Strivings" and, most importantly, problematize the globalist and gendered implications of its rhetoric. Du Bois's Black consciousness, often erroneously regarded as a collective Black consciousness, tends to skew toward patriarchal bourgeois epistemologies, epistemologies that propagate a problematic discourse on gender and cultural identity. There is an argument to be made that the more socialist and pan-Africanist influences in Du Bois's later works, particularly his critique of American imperialism during his tenure as editor of *The Crisis* (Hall 2001, 93) and his Marxist leanings in the 1950s (Lynn 2019), address and even rectify some of the rhetorical shortcomings of double consciousness. While this is a valid argument, it is important to point out that Du Bois's later works are not widely read and circulated. As philosophy and sociology scholar Paul Mocombe indicates, double consciousness remains Du Bois's most influential work because the concept continues to have a formidable impact on contemporary American scholarship (2010, 2). By returning to *The Souls of Black Folk* and conducting a close reading of "Of Our Spiritual Strivings," I invite a legitimate inquiry about the contemporary relevance of Du Bois's famed concept and, in the process, problematize the scholarly tendency to sideline the insights of his later publications.

The concept of double consciousness describes the phenomenon of two polarizing identities residing in one body. Black Americans, due to the physical and psychological anguish they have endured in America, often struggle to reconcile their Black identity with their American identity. They are thus fated to view themselves through two polarizing lenses, the Black experience and the perceptions of the white world. In "Of Our Spiritual Strivings," Du Bois ponders at length about the agony and unreconciled nature of this duality:

> Why did God make me an outcast and a stranger in mine own house? . . . The Negro is . . . born with a veil, and gifted with second-sight in this American world,—a world which yields him no true self-consciousness, but only lets him see himself though the revelation of the other world. It is a peculiar sensation, this double-consciousness, this sense of always looking at one's self through the eyes of others. . . . One ever feels his two-ness,—an American, a Negro; two souls, two thoughts, two unreconciled strivings; two warring ideals in one dark body. (1994, 2)

Du Bois argues that the antagonistic gaze of the white world, which causes a chasm between the white society and the Black race, debilitates the Black soul's humanity by characterizing Black selfhood as a pariah in the spatial memory of America's national identity, "a pitiable, contemptible figure, a creature less than human" (Grosholz 1996, 187). The chasm between soul and self therefore widens because the Black soul clinging to its innate humanity is now in direct conflict with its perceived subhuman self. Philosopher Emily Grosholz describes this chasm as "a ghostly *tertium quid* . . . that prevents the reconciliation of the soul with itself" (1996, 187). Why then does Du Bois refer to double consciousness as a "gift?" Although fashioned from strife, double consciousness can function as a "gift" because its cognizance of duality implies a self-consciousness capable of ascertaining the impact of external antagonism on perceptions of the self. In other words, this is a self-consciousness with the ability to realize when nefarious external forces are tampering with the authenticity of its selfhood. Without the awareness of this "gift," the soul is in jeopardy of being interminably divorced from its authentic sense of self. In brief, double consciousness can be described as both "a mythic blessing and a social burden" (Bell 1996, 95).

This phenomenon of a double consciousness shows up in other essays in *The Souls of Black Folk*. In "Of the Training of Black Men," for example, Du Bois discusses the racist ideology of the "older South" (1994, 55), which views the Black race as a "creature" (1994, 55) somewhere between man and animal, doomed to "walk within the Veil" (1994, 56). Like in "Of Our Spiritual Strivings," the Black race's humanity here is delegitimized by the antagonistic gaze of the white world, and the "Veil" functions as a "second-sight" capable of identifying the racial barrier, which relegates the Black race to the status of a semi-animal, keeping them away from the realm of men. Comparably stated, the veil sustains double consciousness because it underscores the racist antagonism of the white world that confines the Black race to the semi-animal category. Elevating the Black race above the semi-animal category and into the class of man requires crossing over the racial chasm, and Du Bois proposes proper education, the training of Black men, as the most qualified strategy to expedite this momentous leap over the barriers of prejudice (1994, 58–60). If the leap is successful, the Black race will no longer be characterized as a subhuman pariah in the spatial memory of American national identity, and they will finally become legitimate Americans, able to dwell harmoniously with the white world: "I sit with Shakespeare and he winces not. Across the color-line I move arm in arm with Balzac and Dumas . . . Aristotle and Aurelius . . . I dwell above the veil" (Du Bois 1994, 67).

Du Bois's conceptualization of the double consciousness concept can be traced back to six years before the publication of *The Souls of Black Folk*. On March 1897, in a speech titled "The Conversation of the Races" and delivered to the American Negro Academy, a newly created association of Black literati, he talks at length about the existential crisis of being both Black and American. The quote below from the speech is admittedly extensive, but it is necessary because it illustrates how, as early as the 1890s, Du Bois was already working through the intricacies and complexities of his double consciousness concept:

> Here, then, is the dilemma, and it is a puzzling one, I admit. No Negro who has given earnest thought to the situation of his people in America has failed, at some time in life, to find himself at these cross-roads; has failed to ask himself at some time: What, after all, am I? Am I an American or am I a Negro? Can I be both? Or is it my duty to cease to be a Negro as soon as possible and be an American? If I strive as a Negro, am I not perpetuating the very cleft that threatens and separates Black and White America? Is not my only possible practical aim the subduction of all that is Negro in me to the American? Does my black blood place upon me any more obligation to assert my nationality than German, or Irish or Italian blood would? It is such incessant self-questioning and the hesitation that arises from it, that is making the present period a time of vacillation and contradiction for the American Negro; combined race action is stifled, race responsibility is shirked, race enterprises languish, and the best blood, the best talent, the best energy of the Negro people cannot be marshalled to do the bidding of the race. They stand back to make room for every rascal and demagogue who chooses to cloak his selfish deviltry under the veil of race pride. Is this right? Is it rational? Is it good policy? Have we in America a distinct mission as a race—a distinct sphere of action and an opportunity for race

development, or is self-obliteration the highest end to which Negro blood dare aspire? (Du Bois 1897, 11)

This elaborate description of Black Americans possessing an acute self-awareness of the existential conflicts between their racial and national identities is the blueprint for double consciousness. How can a Black person be an American when the systemic fabrics of American society persistently subjugate the Black race and deters their best talent from marshaling "to do the bidding of the race" (Du Bois 1879, 11)? How can an American be a Black person if America possibly has a "distinct mission" (1879, 11) to devaluate and inevitably annihilate the Black race? Du Bois's response to this existential dilemma, delivered in the same speech, is twofold. First, the Black race must avert subsumption and subsequent annihilation by conserving its endowments: "We are that people whose subtle sense of song has given America its only American music, its only American fairy tales, its only touch of pathos and humor amid its mad money-getting plutocracy" (Du Bois 1879, 12). As a result, he continues, "it is our duty to conserve our physical powers, our intellectual endowments, our spiritual ideals" (Du Bois 1879, 12). Here, Du Bois is challenging essentialist methodologies of biological racialism and determinism by debunking the notion of the Black race as culturally inferior. He underscores the contributions Black people have made to American society and positions Black culture as a necessary counterbalance to destructive American pursuits like plutocracy. Second, Du Bois calls for a "broader humanity which freely recognizes differences in men, but sternly deprecates inequality in their opportunities for development" (1879, 12). Differences in men must be recognized in order to identify and address the unique challenges of the Black experience in America and measures must be institutionally implemented to prevent inequality by ensuring development opportunities for every American.

Differences here, I must stress, do not suggest differences in national culture because Black American culture is unequivocally American culture. Within the national borders of America, Black American culture, in all its iterations, cannot be labeled a cultural anomaly because despite its largely sub-Saharan African roots, it is a distinctly American sensibility, conceived entirely on American soil. As historian Thomas C. Holt states, "Blacks are not so much aliens as alienated. It is not cultural difference but cultural disfranchisement that shapes their struggle" (Holt in Bell 1996, 96). The conflict at the core of Du Bois's double consciousness is, hence, not sociocultural disparity. Rather, it is the bicultural state of existing in the spatial memory of America's national identity. The Black American is both intrinsically Black and American but because of an equally intrinsic American racial hegemony that historically venerates whiteness, Black and American identities cannot be, even in our contemporary time, seamlessly reconciled.

JAMESIAN INFLUENCES

Double consciousness, it is important to underline, was not originated by Du Bois. The phrase "double consciousness" appears in nineteenth-century psychological studies and was also used to embody the ideals of European Romanticism and American Transcendentalism (Bell 1996, 89). In Ralph Waldo Emerson's "The Transcendentalist" (1842), for example, the term describes an individual self-awareness in conflict with a larger sense of universality, and decades earlier, in 1816, the term was used in a psychological publication titled "A Double Consciousness, or a Duality of Person in the Same Individual." The publication partly discusses the fascinating case of Mary Reynolds, a young American woman who woke up from an overlong slumber and assumed a new personality (Schwarz 2013, 92–93).

Du Bois was most likely exposed to these prior conceptualizations of double consciousness during his time as a student at Harvard (1888–1890) and the University of Berlin (1892–1894) (Bell 1996, 90). At the University of Berlin, he was certainly exposed to German philosopher Wilhelm Friedrich Hegel, and some scholars like Shamoon Zamir believe Du Bois's racialized interpretation of double consciousness is directly appropriated from Hegelian thematics. Zamir argues that "Of Our Spiritual Strivings" borrows "heavily on the middle chapters of Hegel's *Phenomenology of Mind*" and views the former's sophisticated double consciousness dialectic as a Hegel-inspired departure from the sociological positivism in Du Bois's earlier works like the 1899 sociological study *The Philadelphia Negro* (Zamir 1995, 13–14). Visual and critical studies scholar Shawn Michelle Smith disagrees with this assessment. According to Smith, visual dynamics, the act of seeing and being seen from various vantage points, is crucial to Du Bois's racialized adaptation of double consciousness and, as a result, William James's *Principles of Psychology*, originally published in 1890, does a much better job at illuminating "the linking of self-consciousness to seeing and being seen" than Hegelian thematics (2004, 26). In other words, the ethics of visual observation, from within and beyond the veil, is the crux of double consciousness.

A prominent American philosopher and psychologist, William James taught America's first psychology course at Harvard between 1874 and 1875 (Croce 2018, xiv). In 1889, while Du Bois was his student at Harvard, he taught sections of *Principles of Psychology* (Smith 2004, 27), and both men went on to develop a profound friendship over the years, evidenced by Du

Bois calling James his "friend and guide to clear thinking" (Adell 1994, 13). James introduces the concept of the social self in *Principles of Psychology*:

> Properly speaking, *a man has as many social selves as there are individuals who recognize him* and carry an image of him in their mind. To wound any one of these his images is to wound him. But as the individuals who carry the images fall naturally into classes, we may practically say that he has as many different social selves as there are distinct *groups* of persons about whose opinion he cares. (2007, 294)

James's conceptualization of the social self stresses a consciousness that is affected by external perception, the act of being seen. The manner in which members of different social groups perceive an individual can influence the formation of the individual's sense of self. As psychology scholar Joseph Alkana points out, James suggests that the parameters of an individual's self-image are defined by internalizing the attitudes and judgments of others (1997, 122). Therefore, in the above quote about the social self, "him" signifies an innate humanity, an almost uncorrupted representation of the individual, while "image" is the externally conceptualized version of "him," a less intrinsic depiction forged by perceptions of different social groups. The visual dynamics of James's social self are effortlessly adopted and adapted in Du Bois's double consciousness. Notice the similarity between James's "a man has many social selves as there are individuals who recognize him and carry an image of him in their mind" (2007, 294) and Du Bois's afore quoted "It is a peculiar sensation, this double-consciousness, this sense of always looking at one's self through the eyes of others" (1994, 2) from "Of Our Spiritual Strivings." In the Du Boisian adaptation of the social self, "him" signifies the innate humanity of the Black soul, an uncorrupted representation of the Black individual, and "image" is the externally conceptualized version of "him," a distorted depiction of the self forged by the antagonistic gaze of the white world. Du Bois's racialized chasm between soul and self therefore epistemologically echoes the Jamesian chasm between "him" and "image."

With that said, Du Bois's racialized chasm should not be perceived as a mere replication of James's social self and earlier iterations of the double consciousness concept. Du Bois does engage with earlier influences not due to an inability to articulate the nuanced experiences of being a Black American in America. Rather, his engagement with these familiar concepts was an attempt "to refashion received models of inquiry" (Smith 2004, 27) and "develop new languages and methods for assessing and articulating African American life in all its geographic, economic, and gendered variety" (Smith 2004, 27). Received models of inquiry, at the time, relied on so-called universal theories to understand and articulate identity-related concepts. Because members of the dominant group often authored these universal theories, they tended to assume, normalize and, inevitably, standardize the dominant group's preferences and prejudices. Pre–Du Boisian discourse on identity in the enlightened Western world was, as a result, "clearly Eurocentric, white supremacist, and masculinist" (Smith 2004, 27). Du Bois's racialized adaptation of double consciousness is therefore an inspired scholarly product in its own right because it sought to challenge and widen the applicability of its era's canonized epistemologies on critical thought.

THE AGE OF DU BOIS?

Not surprisingly, the reaction to Du Bois's double consciousness was unparalleled. As African diaspora studies scholar Mar Gallego points out, its discourse on the almost schizophrenic dualism of Black ethnic identity challenged hegemonic knowledge systems and had a profound impact on racial discourse (2003, 153). Not only does Du Bois's work on the polarity of Black American consciousness continue to shape "contemporary understanding of African American life" (Mocombe 2010, 2), but some contemporary scholars like Bernard W. Bell also assert a more far-reaching impact: "Contemporary global ethnic conflicts . . . suggest that the correlative problem or sign of double consciousness will be central to identity formations in the twenty-first century" (1996, 88). In 2005, prominent British sociologist Michael Burawoy labeled Du Bois "perhaps the greatest public sociologist of the twentieth century" (2005, 417), and in 2006, the American Sociological Association's most prestigious prize, the Career of Distinguished Scholarship Award, was renamed after Du Bois (Meer 2019, 48). Aldon Morris, an award-winning sociologist and author of *A Scholar Denied*, must have been thinking about this rapturous acclaim when, in 2015, he boldly declared that we are now living "in the age of Du Bois" (2015, xix), an age where tensions around the globe are echoing the existential rift of double consciousness.

But are we really living "in the age of Du Bois?" I argue yes and no. Although sociologists generally recognize the richness and diversity of Du Bois's works, double consciousness, as I earlier pointed out, remains the lone Du Boisian concept with a tremendous influence on contemporary American scholarship. From scholarly publications to internet think pieces to newspaper articles, double consciousness is frequently referenced and debated in contemporary discourse on issues pertaining to race, identity and culture. Thus, when we talk about living in the age of Du Bois, we are really talking about the enduring popularity of double consciousness. According to Mocombe, Du Bois's double consciousness is a literary reiteration of his own dualist patriarchal sensibilities, sensibilities largely concerned with framing the identity of a liberal Black protestant heterosexual bourgeois male (2010, 2). The social identity of his double consciousness, Mocombe continues, strives to establish legitimate citizenship within the framework of an American imperial paradigm that marginalizes societies affected by Western protestant civilization but refuses to substantially engage with the array of fragmented identities created by this very marginalization (2010, 2). In brief, double consciousness reflects the imperialist dominance of white American patriarchy and can therefore not represent the interests of otherized groups who must remain marginalized for such a system to thrive.

I am only partially in agreement with Mocombe's assessment. Du Bois's fervent desire to reconcile his Black and American identities, a plea for the Black race to be treated with equality and respect in America's democratic constitution, is not entirely theorized by egalitarian principles. Another central motivation is "to be a co-worker in the kingdom of culture" (Du Bois 1994, 3). Du Bois conceptualizes the American "kingdom" as an institution of higher culture, and he desperately wants the Black race to be integral citizens in this cultured community because Black people possess special talents that can enhance the esteemed values of the American Republic (1994, 7). Americans and Black people, "two world-races" (Du Bois 1994, 7), must therefore work together to ensure the enhancement and durability of America's higher culture. Throughout *The Souls of Black Folks*, this notion of higher culture as an indispensable component of American life is repeatedly emphasized. In "Of the Wings of Atalanta," for example, Du Bois's solution to tumultuous race relations is the widespread creation of learning centers that will create white men and Black men of "broad culture" (1994, 53). Cultured Americans, he seems to argue, are the most effective antidote for even the gravest of race-related ailments.

Moreover, in "Of the Training of Black Men," he mentions the "Talented Tenth" theory, the possibility of one in ten Black men becoming an elite community leader, and talks at great length about using classical education to develop and enhance the special talents of these potential leaders, "the end of which is culture" (Du Bois 1994, 64). Black youth, Du Bois continues, are enthusiastic about using the cultured training of classical education to actualize their Talented Tenth potential. He states, "The demand for higher training steadily increases among Negro youth . . . by refusing to give this Talented Tenth the key of knowledge, can any sane man imagine that they will lightly lay aside their yearning . . . ?" (2014, 64–65).

Du Bois's push for education as a cultural development and enhancement tool for Black people is an appeal for legitimate citizenship and participation in the American kingdom of higher culture. The solemnity of this appeal, I argue, reflects a steadfast belief in America's potential, a sophisticated culture born out of amalgamating two "world races" (Du Bois 1994, 7).

Du Bois's fixation on higher culture is somewhat justified. As previously mentioned, prior to the proliferation of his double consciousness concept, received models of inquiry did not engage with any critical discourse on the sophisticated polarity of Black consciousness because Western civilization regarded the Black race as subhuman and lacking cultural refinement (Smith 2004, 27). Du Bois possibly anchored his theorization of double consciousness on higher culture in order to refute this widespread notion. By portraying Black Americans as cultured beings, he is making a case for the legitimacy of their citizenship in the "higher culture" of Western civilization, generally, and America, specifically. Regardless of his intentions, this fixation on higher culture has problematic consequences. For example, it ascribes a sense of superior morality to American imperialism. If America is indeed the kingdom of higher culture then the imperialistic ambitions of its transnational activities can be rationalized as a necessary mission to refine the outdated cultures of so-called primal societies. In other words, Du Bois's hierarchization of cultures propagates the historical trend of denying the legitimacy of cultures deemed "inferior" by dominant groups. In "Of Our Spiritual Strivings," what legitimizes the Black race's status as coworkers in the American kingdom of higher culture is not the innate legitimacy of their humanity. Rather, it is the exceptional "shadow of a mighty Negro past" (Du Bois 1994, 3) that "flits through the tale of Ethiopia the Shadowy and Egypt the Sphinx" (Du Bois 1994, 3). What if Black people were not architects of mighty civilizations? What if the Black race did not "flit through" tales of majestic Ethiopian and Egyptian kingdoms? Would they still be worthy coworkers in the American democratic project? Based on the previously referenced passages from *The Souls of Black Folk*, the answer is no. A worthy coworker in the kingdom of higher culture, these passages imply, must also possess "cultural refinement."

The American project, Du Bois stresses, can only remain the pinnacle of culture if its personnel are architects of culturally superior civilizations: "the American Negro . . . would not Africanize America, for America has too much to teach the world and Africa. He would not bleach his Negro soul in a flood of white Americanism, for he knows that Negro blood has a message for the world" (1994, 3). Notice the distinction between the "American Negro" and the African. The African cannot be a coworker in the American kingdom of higher culture because "America has too much to teach . . . Africa" (Du Bois 1994, 3), implying that the non-American African is culturally inferior. Black Americans, on the other hand, are exalted as a more cultured class because not only are they descendants of majestic African civilizations, but their strivings and successes in the spatial memory of America's national identity has also given them a uniquely important "message for the world" (Du Bois 1994, 3). In other words, the blend of Africa and America has endowed Black Americans with exceptional talents, making them an indispensable component of the American experiment. Characterizing America as a unique civilization of high culture reinforces the imaginary of American exceptionalism, the ethnocentric notion that Americans stand apart from the rest of the world because they are inherently exceptional (Morris 2020). As professor of international affairs Stephen M. Walt points out, the notion of American exceptionalism is strongly tied to foreign policy. "Most statements of 'American exceptionalism' presume that America's values . . . are unique and worthy of universal admiration," Walt states. "They also imply that the United States is both destined and entitled to play a distinct and positive role on the world stage" (Morris 2010).

The rich tradition of postcolonial perspectives like Frantz Fanon's *The Wretched of the Earth*, Aimé Césaire's *Discourse on Colonialism*, and Gayatri Chakravorty Spivak's "Can the Subaltern Speak?" have expansively illustrated how the Western rhetoric of cultural superiority (the culture versus nature dialectic) has historically been used to justify imperialism and annexation projects. In the Enlightenment age, when explorers from the West "discovered" new continents,

> their indigenous names were erased—America was named after the conquistador, Amerigo Vespucci; Aotearoa became New Zealand. White settler societies transported Western progress to the "darker," less "enlightened," parts of the world and white settler rule was premised on spatial and cultural segregation from the indigenous peoples. (Bush 2014, 85)

Du Bois's philosophical engagement with concepts of higher culture and American exceptionalism, thus, evokes similar justifications of colonialist expeditions and reveals a contradictory rationale: Protecting the imperial dominance of America's transnational ambitions entails the subjugation and consequent marginalization of non-American communities and cultures. As a legitimate coworker and patriotic participant in the imperial American kingdom of higher culture, Du Bois would have to partake in subjugation practices that deprive non-American communities and cultures of the same legitimacy he craves for Black Americans.

In 1904, a year after the publication of *The Souls of Black Folk*, Du Bois intellectually orbits this contradiction when, in his book *The Suppression of the African Slave Trade to the United States of America, 1638–1870*, he discusses the historical influence of the Haitian Revolution on anti-slavery efforts and legislation in Southern American states. Additionally, when the American occupation of Haiti began in 1915, Du Bois used his role as editor of *The Crisis*, the official magazine of the National Association for the Advancement of Colored People (NAACP), to rebuke America's foreign policy toward Haiti (Hall 2001, 93). Although both actions denounce the imperialist undertones in the higher culture rhetoric, they are not a part of the double consciousness discourse. Nowhere in *The Souls of Black Folk* does Du Bois address and problematize the inevitable contradiction of liberated Black Americans functioning within an imperial model with the ability to delegitimize the sovereign statehood of foreign nations and peoples.

The inevitability of this contradictory rationale is even more pronounced in our contemporary times. America's first Black/biracial president, Barack Obama, arguably embodied the tensions and contradictions of double consciousness. Obama was a Black/biracial man at the helm of a political institution responsible for upholding the values of American exceptionalism and imperialism (Mocombe 2010, 2). During America's "war on terror" in the Middle East, the Obama regime's excessive reliance on drone strikes, for example, continued to lead to the unjust killings of scores of marginalized non-American and non-Western civilians in countries like Pakistan and Yemen (Friedersdorf 2016). Moreover, American military involvement on the African continent intensified during the Obama presidency due to a heightened need to protect America's interests in politically unstable and resource-rich areas (Volman 2010). My argument, it is of the utmost importance to underscore, is not that President Obama purposefully and intentionally targeted marginalized groups. The US presidency is not an autocratic institution dictated solely by the wishes of a single individual. In addition to collaborating and negotiating with other contentious factions of government such as the House of Representatives, the Senate, and state legislatures, every American president is heavily influenced, and even controlled to some extent, by the wishes and aspirations of their party, voter base, political opposition, and foreign allies. In other words, certain decisions taken during a president's tenure often reveal the complex nature of the nation's political climate and not necessarily the president's personal beliefs. Regardless of intent, foreign policy decisions have tangible consequences, and Obama's administration unquestionably advocated for and implemented an imperialist agenda.

The Barack Obama example, an individual from a marginalized group at the helm of an imperialist project that marginalizes other communities and cultures, can be used to persuasively make a case for the contemporary relevance of double consciousness. The difficult reconciliation of layered identities is at the core of Du Bois's concept, and our contemporary time is rife with conundrums about belonging and individuality (Brexit, the rise of nationalism in Mainland Europe, widening racial tensions during and beyond Trump's presidency, Russia's geopolitical meddling in and eventual invasion of Ukraine etc.).[1] The same Barack Obama example ironically debunks the claim that we are living "in the age of Du Bois." The materialization of Obama, the uniquely exceptional Black coworker and patriotic participant in the American kingdom of higher culture, was Du Bois's end goal in "Of Our

Spiritual Strivings." But the materialization of Obama has revealed a profound quandary that the double consciousness concept either ignored or failed to anticipate: when the oppressed gains legitimate citizenship, they must still operate within the same systemic structures that facilitate regional and global oppression. The skin color of the president is ultimately inconsequential, because the operational components of America's institutional mechanism stay the same. We are therefore not living "in the age of Du Bois" because double consciousness does not accurately and fully represent the uncomfortable complications of contemporary American consciousness.

I am not suggesting that displays of patriotism by African Americans are unethical or unjustifiable. African American culture is American culture, and the contributions of African Americans to the ideological conception and materialization of American statehood are both plenty and unparalleled. African Americans are thus entitled to participate in the performance of patriotism. However, if this performance of patriotism is principally motivated by the imperialist rhetoric of higher culture, it ironically reinforces the same white supremacist rhetoric used to marginalize African Americans and deny them legitimate citizenship. I am also not attempting to characterize the entirety of America's political identity as an imperialist construct. To do this would be reductive because, as pointed out in the Introduction, the trailblazing founding fathers were pursuing democratic ideologies like liberty and the pursuit of happiness at a time when autocratic monarchs and colonial regimes governed Europe and most of the world. Moreover, America's democratic ideologies have often functioned as a positive and stabilizing force in the world arena of pernicious geopolitics. In World War II, for example, America played a significant role in the liberation of Europe from Nazism (Beevor 2009), and the organizational successes of the African American civil rights movement inspired similar democratic efforts in far-flung continents like the Aboriginal political organizations in Australia (Minestrelli 2017, 48). Other global democratic efforts include supporting decolonizing efforts on the African continent (Meriwether 2002, 243–44) and arguably being the Western world's strongest defender of sovereign democratic territories like Taiwan (Ward 2021).

With that said, ignoring centuries of political meddling by the American government in places such as the Caribbean, South America, the Middle East, and Africa would equally be reductive because I would be mischaracterizing the complex transnational framework of America's political machinations. Thus, I argue that it is problematic, in texts like Du Bois's *The Souls of Black Folk*, for the oppressed to aspire for legitimate American citizenship without, at least, addressing or problematizing the oppressive structures that sustain and promote America's imperialist ambitions. The emergence of contemporary progressive groups such as fourth-wave feminists, the Black Lives

Matter movement, and LGBTQ activism has inspired a concerted effort to amplify supplanted perspectives that are not properly represented in simplistic binary structures. Hence, double consciousness, in its traditional form, lacks sufficient contemporary applicability because its fundamental binary, the masculinely conceptualized Black soul/self versus the white world's antagonistic gaze, fails to account for the multiplicity of supplanted perspectives trapped in the intermediate space between both entities.

THE GENDERED PERSPECTIVE

A conspicuous example of supplanted perspectives trapped between the defined double consciousness binary is the varied experiences of Black women. Du Bois conceptualizes Black consciousness entirely in the masculine pronoun. In "Of Our Spiritual Strivings," he refers to Black consciousness as "him" (1994, 3), and the possessive pronoun used to describe the collective bearers of double consciousness is "his" (1994, 2). This practice continues throughout *The Souls of Black Folk*. In "Of the Dawn of Freedom," for example, he historicizes the struggles of his era as a color line division between darker- versus lighter-toned men: "The problem of the twentieth century is the problem of the color-line,—the relation of the darker to the lighter races of men in Asia and Africa, in America and the islands of the sea" (1994, 9). Moreover, in "Of the Training of Black Men," where Du Bois arguably makes his most persuasive case for using classical education as a cultural development and enhancement tool, Black American civilization is described as the process of civilizing Black men in America (1994, 58). As the title of the essay explicitly foreshadows, those capable of uplifting this civilization are Black men with access to classical education (1994, 61–65).

We should bear in mind, however, that in Du Bois's era, masculine pronouns were a universal referent. As linguistic scholars Gabriel Mejía González and Sally J. Delgado point out, in the nineteenth century and beyond, masculine pronouns in English prose (he, him, his) referred to both sexes and human beings in general:

> Grammarians of the 19th century insisted upon rigid adherence to the 'accuracy' of the universal male referent, which was further formalized by the 1850 Act of [British] Parliament that stipulated the use of the male pronoun to refer to female as well as male referents under the law. . . . The historical context of . . . the English male pronoun has come to be regarded as "natural" and "accurate." (2015, 224)

One can thus purport that Du Bois's masculinely gendered rhetoric was simply adhering to the grammar conventions of his times and was not a deliberate attempt to supplant the perspectives of Black women. This point notwithstanding, nineteenth-century grammar conventions were put in place to systematically maintain a gendered hierarchy: "That masculine forms are used to represent all human beings is in accord with the traditional gender hierarchy, which grants men more power and higher social status than women" (Sczesny, Formanowicz, and Moser 2016, 121). Maintaining this gendered hierarchy, with men at the top and women at the bottom, underlines how the masculine universal referent supplants female perspectives: "the English male pronoun . . . is an imposed grammatical device with the express function of asserting male superiority. This, in turn, implies female compliance" (González and Delgado 2015, 224). Hence, regardless of Du Bois's intent, using these conventions enforced the institutional assertion of male superiority over female-authored narratives. Emphasis, therefore, should be placed on consequences and not necessarily intent.

Nevertheless, I argue that Du Bois was not entirely shackled by conventions. The literary sophistication of how he uses pronouns reveals an acute awareness of the functionality of gendered language. In "Of the Wings of Atalanta," for example, Du Bois deviates from the "masculine as universal" literary trope and chooses the feminine pronouns "her" and "she" to describe the American South (1994, 53). The South, throughout *The Souls of Black Folk*, is depicted as an environment of backwardness, a hotbed for archaic practices, illiteracy, systemic racism, and an overabundance of prejudices (1994, 55–56). The pervasiveness of outdated customs in Southern culture must be stamped out, Du Bois argues, by the infiltration of higher culture (1994, 53). By moving away from the ubiquitous "masculine as universal" aesthetic in this specific instance and ascribing feminine qualities to the American South, a territory he conceptualizes as a mentally inferior milieu in dire need of civilization and sophistication, Du Bois demonstrates a literary awareness of his stylistic prejudices.

Granted, there is a long tradition of feminizing homelands and geographic locations. In the eighteenth century, for instance, Russian nationalism was represented by "the idea of Mother Russia" (Haarmann 2002, 69), and during the reign of the British Empire, colonial subjects regarded England as the "mother country" (Synge 2007, 231). Du Bois's feminization of the American South, some might argue, is a stylistic choice of little to no consequence because, once again, it is adhering to the conventions of its times. I also disagree with this viewpoint because the gender Du Bois ascribes to geographic locations is intentionally inconsistent: his alternation of gendered pronouns reveals a precise deliberateness to his method. When he talks about being a descendant of superior African civilizations in "Of Our Spiritual Strivings," the masculine pronoun is used: "The shadow of the mighty Negro past . . . the powers of single black men flash" (1994, 3). Juxtaposing the feminized American South, a culturally "inferior" wasteland in dire need of higher culture, with majestically masculine African civilizations worthy of worship and replication reveals that Du Bois's gendered rhetoric is a deliberate stylistic choice.

More juxtapositions are easily decipherable in "Of Our Spiritual Strivings." When Du Bois shifts his focus back to America, he conceptualizes the strength of Black Americans, often weakened by the white world's antagonistic gaze, as masculine: "Here in America, in the few days since Emancipation, the black man's turning hither and thither in hesitant and doubtful striving has often made his very strength to lose effectiveness" (1994, 3). Contrarily, when he discusses racist America's insistence on stifling the enormous potential of this strength, America assumes a feminine pronoun: "Will America be poorer if she replace her brutal dyspeptic blundering with light-hearted but determined Negro humility?" (1994, 7). Yet again, Du Bois emphasizes male superiority over female perspectives by ascribing positive attributes (enormous potential) to the masculine pronoun and negative attributes (American racism) to the feminine pronoun. The regularity of these variations, I argue, suggest some degree of intentionality in Du Bois's gendered language.

Moving beyond pronouns and into the realm of experiential discourse, the awakening of Black consciousness in "Of Our Spiritual Strivings," the first narrative in *The Souls of Black Folk*, is also masculinely conceptualized. The essay opens with a haunting question: "How does it feel to be a problem?" (1994 1), hinting at the ominous shadow of double consciousness. Du Bois proceeds to tell the tale of when he first realized his Blackness was a problem in America. He was a boy in the infancy of his childhood, in a New England schoolhouse exchanging beautiful visiting cards with other children (1994 1–2). All seems well until a white girl, a newcomer to the schoolhouse, rejects his card and bluntly yanks away his childhood innocence (1994 2). Her rejection shatters Du Bois's idealized self-image; he realizes that he is different from the dominant white group and because his Blackness is rejected as subhuman, he is not welcomed in the class of man.

Young Du Bois's realization is the only dawning of double consciousness described in *The Souls of Black Folk* and after this momentous epiphany, in essays like "Of the Black Belt" and "Of the Sons of Master and Man," double consciousness is repeatedly echoed in descriptions of the collective Black experience. The implication that young Du Bois's racial epiphany mirrors the racial awareness of a collective Black consciousness is somewhat misguided. One cannot ignore the possibility that gender relations might have played a role in young Du Bois's awakening. Would he have had the same response if his interaction was with a white boy? Most importantly, would a young Black girl have had the same response if a young white girl rejected her card? Are there differences in how young boys and girls react to rejection from their peers within and across color lines? How can we be certain that the specificity of young Du Bois's racial epiphany is substantially mirrored by the actions of a collective Black consciousness? As visual and critical studies scholar Shawn Michelle Smith points out, what is absent from Du Bois's double consciousness is "the African American woman, or the woman of African descent, independent of a man of color, negotiating her own double consciousness vis-à-vis the color line" (2004, 38).

Moreover, young Du Bois had the privilege of attending racially integrated schools. Thus, his more idealistic vision of the American democratic project varied dramatically from Black Americans in the segregated South. Because Black Southerners in segregated cities and counties were more accustomed to the rigidity of the color line, their response to rejection from a young white girl would have arguably not reflected the same kind of existential trauma young Du Bois endured. One can of course argue that regardless of gender, class, and geographic location, the ultimate consequence of racial rejection is alienation from the American imaginary of democratic inclusiveness and exceptionalism. While this is a valid assertion, the nature of alienation is not uniformly experienced. Because Black Southerners, at the time, never had the privilege of experiencing racial integration, they understood and coped with alienation in very different ways from Northern Black elites like Du Bois.[2] Thus, synthesizing the dawning of a collective double consciousness from the experiential standpoint of a comparatively privileged Black boy erroneously positions a singular Black male point of view as representative of the collective Black experience.

This practice of prioritizing a singular Black male perspective later became a defining trope in popular African American literature and culture. The Harlem Renaissance, for example, a Black cultural movement at the dawn of the twentieth century, often conceptualized the racial struggle from a Black male perspective, making it difficult for Black female artists to articulate their unique intersectional interests at the crossroads of race and gender (Wall 1995, 6–7). Furthermore, Richard Wright's groundbreaking *Native Son* (1940), popularly described as the first philosophical novel about the African American experience (Rowley 2008, 192), completely disregards the agency of Black women. Bigger Thomas, the male protagonist, is the only Black character with an accurate gauge of reality; he is the only one who has "taken fully upon himself the crime of being black" (Wright 2005, 296). Additionally, Bigger's brutal murder of his Black girlfriend, Bessie, underscores the ramifications of patriarchal violence and symbolizes the death of Black female voices in protest narratives. This tradition of prioritizing a singular Black male perspective will continue throughout the 1940s and 1950s in works like Chester Himes's *If He Hollers Let him Go* (1945) and Ralph Ellison's seminal novel *Invisible Man* (1952). Although the works of writers like Gwendolyn Brooks, Toni Morrison, and Alice Walker challenged the hegemony of this masculinist trope, its longevity remains undeterred.

Contemporary examples include the literary works of Ta-Nahisi Coates (debatably the most prominent voice in contemporary African American literature). His works often dissect aspects of institutional racism like police brutality through the contextual framework of the Black male experience. The title of his second book, *Between the World and Me* (2015), is borrowed from a Richard Wright poem about a Black man who discovers a lynching site and becomes philosophically divorced from the world. And the book's narrative on Dr. Mabel Jones, for example, a successful doctor who is a descendant of sharecroppers, ends up being a story about her slain son and the historical legacy of racial profiling he shares with Solomon Northup, a free Black man from the North who was abducted and sold into slavery in the South. Another example is *The Sellout* (2015), Paul Beatty's surreal and satirical fable about race in America. In this novel, Black identity is once again framed within the context of the Black male experience. While the duality used to satirize the contradictions and commoditization of Blackness are two Black men (the often-nameless protagonist and Hominy Jenkins), the Black female voice is frequently trivialized. The protagonist's absent mother is nonchalantly referred to as a beauty queen in her heyday, and lines like "Rapunzel, Rapunzel, let down your weave!" (2015, 101) are satire without sufficient purpose or context, I argue, because they fail to unpack how discourse surrounding hair length and texture has and continues to psychologically traumatize Black women.

These examples illustrate the historical pervasiveness of the Du Boisian trope of Black male authorship, the hegemonic Black voice, not sufficiently engaging with and/or unpacking the Black female experience. Male authors, it is important to clarify, are certainly entitled to tell stories from the experiential gaze of their masculine identities. Du Bois's dawning of double consciousness as a young boy in "Of Our Spiritual Strivings," for example, is autobiographical, so one can contend that he is merely describing on a pivotal moment in his maturation process. My argument here is not that Black men cannot write about their experiences as Black men in America. My point is simply this: if Black male authors are writing about how institutional practices have historically affected the physicality and psychology of Blackness, it is somewhat shortsighted to omit a meaningful conversation about how these same practices have uniquely affected the Black female experience in America. By consistently using the experiential gaze of Black men to understand and frame Black identity, intersectional perspectives between the masculinely conceptualized Black soul/self and the antagonistic white gaze, like the unique experiences of Black women, remain supplanted and even erased.

Beyond *The Souls of Black Folk*, African American studies and feminist scholars often hail Du Bois's entire body of work as progressive and feminist (Rabaka 2010, 176). Black feminist scholar Beverly Guy-Sheftall, for example, strongly argues that Du Bois was one of "the most passionate defenders of black women" and the "most outspoken [male] feminists in African American history and, more generally, American history" (1990, 13). African American Studies scholar Manning Marable reiterates Guy-Sheftall's declarations, stating, "like Douglass, Du Bois was probably the most advanced male leader of his era on the question of gender equality" (1986, 85). Du Bois's 1920 essay "The Damnation of Women," originally published in *Darkwater: Voices from Within the Veil*, is widely regarded as a momentous piece of Black feminist writing because it unapologetically advocated for better living conditions for Black women at a time when their interests where an afterthought, even within mainstream feminist movements.

With that said, "The Damnation of Women" is not without its complications. The essay uses the metaphor of a family unit to describe the role of different races. Asia is the venerated father, Europe is the precocious and innovative child, and the Black woman is the nurturing mother: "the father and his worship is Asia; Europe is the precocious, self-centered, forward-striving child; but the land of the mother is and was Africa. . . . No mother can love more tenderly and none is more tenderly loved than the Negro mother" (Du Bois 2000, 3). Two issues must be unpacked here. First, conceptualizing motherhood as the fundamental component of a Black woman's identity shackles her purpose to the practice of nurture; in other words, any existence beyond the parameters of the reproduction and nurture of the Black race is not legitimately recognized. Second, stripping Black women of attributes like "precocious" and "innovative," attributes Du Bois ascribes only to Europe, and (over)emphasizing the tenderly love of the Black mother encourages dependency and domesticity. If Black women are not precocious and innovative, attributes necessary for an independently managed life, they will remain dependent on the moral and financial guidance of patriarchal authority and, as a result, remain confined to domestic duties. "The Damnation of Women" is careful to prominently extol the values of the domesticated and doting Black mother because she is a woman very much under the gaze and control of the Black husband's authority. As Smith argues, "For Du Bois . . . the African American woman is the epitome of virtue—as long as she keeps her adoring gaze focused on an idealized African American authority" (2004, 40).

The strong Black mother myth is reinforced when Du Bois describes Black women, innate maternal beings, as "a vast group of women of Negro blood who for strength of character, cleanness of soul, and unselfish devotion of purpose, is today easily the peer of any group of women in the civilized world" (2000, 8). This myth is problematic because it denies Black women the permission to be vulnerable by normalizing the long-suffering Black mother stereotype, a beleaguered woman who must suffer in silence because she is not allowed to express weakness. As African American Studies scholar Reiland Rabaka points out, this image of Black women as nurturing and superstrong matriarchs

> praises black mothers' resilience in a white and male supremacist society that has historically labeled them as not only bad mothers, but matriarchs, "bitches," and whores. . . . In his subtle gender-blindness, Du Bois did not see that in order for them to remain on their pedestal, black mothers had to continue to be super-strong, self-sacrificing and long-suffering, and especially with regard to the men in their lives. (2010, 180)

I bring up these shortcomings not to discredit the scholarly vitality of Du Bois's work. Du Bois, to his credit, was contending with challenging intersectional components like race, class and gender, albeit superficially, at a time when most of his male contemporaries had little to no regard for anti-sexist discourse. He remained, however, informed by the prevailing gender conventions of his epoch, and, as a result, his conceptualization of Black consciousness, as articulated in the widely read *The Souls of Black Folk*, skews toward patriarchal and imperialist perspectives. When discussing the complicated consciousness of Black women in modern America, there is therefore an urgent need to amend the depth and scope of Du Bois's double consciousness. This book provides this amendment by proposing a new reading of the triple consciousness concept (TCT). Before I proceed with the delineation of TCT, I must emphasize that theoretical analysis on the in-between perspectives of Black women is not a novel phenomenon. Concepts like Frances M. Beal's "Double Jeopardy" (1969), Bonnie Thornton Hill's "The Dialectics of Black Womanhood" (1979) and Alice Walker's "the condition of twin 'afflictions'" (1979) have analyzed, in great depth, the uncomfortable intermediate space Black women inhabit between simplistic binaries.[3] However, Black feminist legal scholar Kimberlé Crenshaw's intersectionality concept is arguably the most famous discourse on the in-between identities of Black women.

In 1989, Crenshaw coined the term "intersectionality" in her groundbreaking essay "Demarginalizing the Intersection of Race and Sex: A Black Feminist Critique of Antidiscrimination Doctrine, Feminist Theory and Antiracist Politics." Crenshaw's intersectionality identifies and theorizes how multiple categories (class, gender, race etc.) congregate and establish new forms of oppressed identities. As feminist philosopher Ariane Poisson points out, the term intersectionality has, in recent times, become widely appropriated, watered down, and universalized. Simply belonging to multiple categories does not make one intersectional; intersectionality, as originally conceived by Crenshaw, only occurs when the convergence of these categories reveals an institutional practice of oppressing and supplanting identities not properly represented by hegemonic identity frameworks (Poisson 2018). In "Demarginalizing the Intersection of Race and Sex," Crenshaw uses a lawsuit five Black women filed against American car giant General Motors (GM) to illustrate how in the eyes of the law, Black women are viewed through the experiences of Black men and white women. This lawsuit, which accused GM of combined racist and sexist employment practices, was primarily dismissed by the courts because GM had previously hired white women; thus, their hiring practices could not be deemed discriminatory (Crenshaw 1989, 141).

This decision underscores the intersectional invisibility of Black women between race and gender. Because Black identity is often masculinely conceptualized, Black men are viewed as more legitimate targets of racial oppression than Black women. The courts' decision to diminish the racial angle and rest its decisive argument on the sexism claims reflects this tendency. In the realm of womanhood, as replicated in mainstream feminist movements, the interests and experiences of white women are prioritized. Thus, sexist oppression against Black women is also minimized because they are not white women. As Crenshaw points out "Black women are protected only to the extent that their experiences coincide with those of either of the two groups [Black men and white women]. Where their experiences are distinct, Black women can expect little protection" (1989, 143). If Black men and white women were part of this lawsuit, claims of racism and sexism would have arguably been legitimized. But because the lawsuit chronicled an experience that was distinct to Black women, they received no protection from the law.

This erasure of Black women, as conceptualized by Crenshaw's Intersectionality, remains relevant today. For example, as mentioned in the Introduction, Black women are still facing exclusion from mainstream feminist movements led by white women (Tolentino 2017), and although Black women such as Patrisse Khan-Cullors, Alicia Garza, and Opal Tometi founded the Black Lives Matter movement, followers of the movement exhibit visible gender bias (Alter 2015). While they marched passionately for Black male victims of police brutality like Trayvon Martin, their response to Black female victims of similar police misconduct incidences, like Sandra Bland, was relatively muted (Alter 2015).

By also highlighting the oppressed and supplanted identities of Black women trapped between reductive binary structures, my reimagined triple consciousness framework (TCT) is intersectionality's direct offspring. There is, however, a stark difference between both frameworks. Unlike intersectionality's identification and validation of established concurrent identities, TCT's foremost preoccupation is the aftermath of rupture. As previously stated, TCT is interested in exploring the rupture that happens in the third consciousness, an opening initiated by Black female artists in order to explore the uniquely complex dimensions of counternarratives, insights, and revelations with the capacity to dismantle binaries and challenge the dominant influence of conventional identity formation epistemologies. While these individualized counternarratives reflect the concurrence of intersectional identities, TCT's focus is largely on how they simultaneously reject and accept omnipresent claims of universality and community and contend with the aftermath of a rupture that is liberating but also messily unresolved. Thus, unlike intersectionality, TCT examines the discomforts of uniquely affirmative narratives, discomforts produced by the act of concurrently challenging and embracing the notion of collective identities.

I should also point out that contemporary discourse, both academic and journalistic, often uses the term "triple consciousness" to affirm the multiplicity of identities residing in one subject. For example, Juan Flores and Miriam Jiménez Román's "Triple-Consciousness? Approaches to Afro-Latino Culture in the United States" (2009) unpacks what it means to be Black, American, and Latino. Similarly, articles like "Triple Consciousness: To Be Black and an Immigrant in America" (2017) by Atima Omara explore the multifaceted identities of Black immigrants in America. In both instances, the focus is on broad ethnic/cultural identities and not on the unique perspective of the Black female experience, an experience that, due to its fundamental fixture in the American imaginary, is deserving of deepened philosophical analysis. Moreover, as stated in the introductory chapter, contemporary Black feminist writers like Danielle Moodie-Mills ("The Burden of Triple Consciousness") and Sara Lomax-Reese ("The triple weight of being Black, American, and a woman") often use the phrase "triple consciousness" to highlight Du Bois's omission of the Black female perspective.

To reiterate, TCT is a sharp departure from this interpretation because it does not characterize the third perspective as a distinct consciousness created and developed to correct the gendered limitations of the Du Boisian framework. TCT's emphasis on the aftermath of rupture engages with complex and chaotic counternarratives that simultaneously embrace and reject the hegemony of shared values. The philosophical framework I will use to characterize and understand the fragmentary nature of this contradiction is theoretically inspired by the ruminations of French philosopher Gilles Deleuze. Key Deleuzian concepts such as becoming and foldings illuminate TCT's theoretical substructure because they are anchored to a counter-actualizing mechanism that resists the stagnancy of collective knowledge systems and emphasizes the individual's right to difference. Thus, before elaborating on the TCT framework, I will discuss its philosophical origins and expose the theoretical gaps it aims to address.

INFINITELY BECOMING

Gilles Deleuze, a central figure in French philosophy, is widely known for reimagining and reorienting pervasive philosophical concepts like "becoming." Because his conceptual reimaginings often echo the destabilizing function of TCT's rupture, I will briefly describe the philosophical history of becoming. My goal here, I must emphasize, is not to deliver an exhaustive analysis on the conceptual transformations of philosophical terminology. Unpacking the breadth and depth of Deleuzian philosophy, I cannot stress enough, is not the focus of this section. However, it is important to provide a brief conceptual overview of becoming in order to better comprehend the foundational elements of TCT's theoretical infrastructure. According to philosophy scholar Samantha Bankston, Deleuze's works never explicitly theorize the concept of becoming, resulting in "inconsistent readings of the concept, from both critics and Deleuze scholars" (2017, 14). A prevalent misreading of Deleuzian becoming is identifying the concept "with change . . . change defined through mechanistic motion and individuated substance" (Bankston 2017, 13). Although change is a characteristic of the concept, an aesthetic object experiencing a transformative process is not necessarily engaging with the Deleuzian concept of becoming. For Deleuze, becoming is an inherent "counter-actualizing process which individuates actual states of being" (Bankston 2017, 14). This definition is supported by his descriptions of becoming, in texts like *A Thousand Plateaus*, as the continuous development and rupture of dimensions (Deleuze and Guattari 2004, 275). In other words, while change is preoccupied with the rejection of a former self and the actualization of a new self, the becoming concept is interested in a counter-actualizing process that rejects a former self but also rejects the notion of comfortably inhabiting an actualized self without tension. Unpacking becoming's rejection of the actualized self requires a brief examination of the concept's developmental trajectory, particularly as a response to Friedrich Nietzsche's eternal return and Henri Bergson's duration.

Bergson describes duration as "the unrolling of a spool, for there is no living being who does not feel himself coming little by little to the end of his span" (2007, 137). However, "it is just as much a continual winding, like that of a thread into a ball, for our past follows us, becoming larger and larger with the present it picks up on its way" (Bergson 2007, 137). This description of duration as an infinite multiplicity, the unrolling of the spool and the endless process of the past rolling into the present, is echoed in Deleuze's conceptualization of becoming as an equally continuous production of multiple dimensions. Deleuze describes multiplicity as "virtual and continuous" (1991, 38) and argues with fellow French philosopher Félix Guattari that multiplicity and becoming "are the same thing" because a "multiplicity is defined not by its elements, nor by the center of unification or comprehension. It is defined by the number of dimensions it has; it is not divisible, it cannot lose or gain a dimension without changing its nature" (Deleuze and Guattari 2004, 275). I must briefly note here that this process of continuous multiplicity echoes the nomadic subject, another Deleuzian concept. While discussing structuralism, Deleuze conceptualizes the individual, the subject of knowledge and action, an agent capable of knowing and doing, as an entity that is constantly being shattered and distributed by differential experiences and, as a result, remains in a constant state of metamorphosis. Structuralism, he states in *Desert Islands and Other Texts*,

> is not at all a form of thought that suppresses the subject, but one that breaks it up and distributes it systematically, that contests the identity of the subject, that dissipates it and makes it shift from place to place, an always nomad subject, made of individuations, but impersonal ones, or of singularities, but pre-individual ones. (2004, 190)

Returning to Bergson's duration, Deleuze broadens his analysis of the concept by describing it as "a becoming that endures, a change that is substance itself" (1991, 37). This emphasis on substance is what I want to underscore. Let us go back to the distinction between change and Deleuzian becoming. While change discards the former self and embraces the actualization of a new self, Deleuzian becoming discards a former self but also discards the notion of self-actualization. Deleuze's emphasis on counter-actualization is based on the Bergsonian idea that the subject is continuously unrolling and winding. Thus, if the changing process is infinite, the subject can never comfortably inhabit a new actualized self. Detractors of this interpretation might argue that the Deleuzian subject lacks meaning or substance because they are stuck in perpetual limbo. Meaning is often attached to the self-affirmation of actualization. Therefore, if the subject is infinitely becoming and never becomes, they can be described as lacking meaning or substance because they never self-actualize. Deleuzian philosophy discredits this perspective by emphasizing the significance of every change that occurs during the becoming process. The absence of a harmonious actualized self does not imply the absence of substance. The optimal harmony of self-actualization, Deleuze stresses, cannot be achieved because the subject is in an infinite tussle with all the elements of their past, present and future. However, as the subject endures the fragmentary experiences of the infinitely becoming process, substantial epiphanies and knowledge systems about the human condition are revealed and better understood (Deleuze 1991, 37). Consequently, every stage of the becoming process is a valid state of being with consequential implications for the subject and the world they inhabit.

While Deleuze uses Bergson's duration to broadly discuss the value of substance, he reorients Nietzsche's eternal return to specifically underscore how substance is produced by the eternal return of affirmations. Eternal return is admittedly a challenging concept to comprehend and theorize. Simply defined as "the idea that all events recur infinitely in an identical manner and order" (May 1999, 119), its obfuscating vagueness has been, over the years, problematic to "all commentators" and "interpreted as a cosmic cyclical vision, eternal return doesn't make much sense" (Strong 1988, 261). With that said, there seems to be a consensus among scholars that eternal return is preoccupied with recurrence and the ability of this repetition to perhaps enrich or transform the individual. Political theorist Tracy B. Strong nebulously describes eternal return as the process of going from "human to over-human" (1988, 263), and philosophy scholar Lawrence Hatab argues that "the 'eternal' in Nietzsche's eyes is more evaluative than a conceptual term" (2005, 63). I am not interested in developing or exploring a succinct definition of eternal return. My sole purpose of engaging with the concept, albeit briefly, is to illustrate how Deleuze reimagines Nietzschean doctrine as an affirmative experience in the becoming process. What returns, Deleuze claims in *Difference and Repetition*, is the notion of difference and not sameness. He states, "The Negative does not return. The Identical does not return. The Same and the Similar, the Analogous and the Opposed, do not return. Only affirmation returns—in other words, the Different, the Dissimilar" (Deleuze 2004, 372).

A few points must be addressed here. First, to return implies going back to a place of origin, so the difference returning to the individual originated from the individual. The difference can therefore be described as a mutated version of the individual, echoing the infinite multiplicity of the becoming process. Second, difference is associated with affirmation, a positive evaluation of the self. If difference creates a sense of affirmation, one can confidently argue that it possesses a knowledge system that intellectually enriches the individual. As Deleuze states in *Desert Islands and Other Texts*, when describing his nomadic subject concept, the individual breaks, dissipates and transforms every time it encounters the knowledge of differential experiences (2004, 190). The becoming process is therefore "an eternal returning of that which affirms life" (Bankston 2017, 34). In other words, the eternal returning of affirmations, positive evaluations of the self, at every stage of the becoming process guarantees the infinite production of substance.

But how exactly does a subject produce substance? What does the process concretely look and feel like? In another Deleuzian concept termed foldings, he provides the scaffolding of a mechanism with a three-stage process that attempts to demonstrate how the subject produces substantive affirmations without arriving at the optimal harmony of self-actualization. The process of a new autonomous self emerging from an oppressively conceived previous self is the overriding idea of Deleuze's foldings. In his book *Foucault*, Deleuze lays the theoretical groundwork of foldings by engaging with the philosophical historicity of power. He begins the chapter "Foldings, or the Inside of Thought (Subjectivation)" by directly addressing revered French philosopher Michel Foucault's conceptualization of power. Deleuze states:

> He [Foucault] himself put forward the following objection: "That's just like you, always with the *same incapacity to cross the line*, to pass over to the other side . . . it is always the same choice, for the side of power, for what power says or of what is causes to be said . . . the most intense point of lives, the one where their energy is concentrated, is precisely where they clash with power, struggle with it, endeavor to utilize its forces or to escape its traps." (1988, 94)

Power is, according to Foucault, oppressive, all-consuming, and all-determining. Even when we escape from power's trappings, it is still the central force orienting our experiences. Power is therefore the true architect of our destinies. Deleuze, on the other hand, is more interested in the changes in our lives created by resistance, the act of subverting oppressive power structures (1988, 95). If power is all-consuming and all-determining how then does resistance happen? Can resistance even happen? He states:

> If power is constitutive of truth, how can we conceive of a "power of truth" which would no longer be the truth of power, a truth that would release transversal lines of resistance not integral lines of power? How can we "cross the line'? And, if we must attain a life that is the power of the outside, what tells us that this outside is not a terrifying void and that this life, which seems to put up a resistance, is not just the simple distribution within the void of "slow, partial and progressive" deaths? (1988, 94–95)

If power is all-determining and the true architect of our destinies then we are nothing but powerless beings and the outside, our outwardly lived lives, infinitely remains oriented by the constitutive truth of power. Deleuze reexamines this insinuation by making resistance the central orientation of our outwardly lived lives. Resistance against the power of the outside can occur if "the outside were caught up in a movement that would snatch it away from the void and pull it back from death" (Deleuze 1988, 96). The outside being dead here refers to the death of its potential for resistance and not the cessation of biological life.

I am choosing to focus only on these passages because they hint at the makings of a mechanism capable of producing substance without self-actualization. This action of pulling our outwardly lived lives back from death is interpreted by women's and gender studies scholar Maria del Guadalupe Davidson as the ability of the subject to subvert hegemonic power in the outward or external realm by turning "inward . . . this inwardness is a place of resistance, self-constitution, self-renewal and self-knowledge" (2006, 129). Davidson's interpretation is supported by Deleuze's analysis of the historical awareness of an innate internal knowledge system, uncorrupted and ungoverned by external influences of the outside: "The classical age had already stated that there was an inside of thought. . . . And from the nineteenth century on it is more the dimensions of finitude which fold the outside and constitute a 'depth,' . . . an inside to life . . . in which man is embedded" (1988, 97). This process of subverting power, it is imperative to underscore, engages with both the internal self and the external realm. The inward space of self-constitution and self-renewal is only accessed when the internal self folds with the outside forces of the external realm (Deleuze 1988, 97). Although folding is an internal lived-in existence in relation to one's own self, it allows for engagement with the external realm in order to "unfold and merge, but not without new folding being created in the process" (Deleuze 1988, 105). Similarly put, the internal self of a subject cannot access the transformative powers of its self-renewing inward space without unfolding and merging with the external realm. The internal self and the inward space are therefore not synonymous.

This process can also be described as the folding of the outside in order to create a doubling that allows "a relation to oneself to emerge, and constitute an inside which is hollowed out and develops its own unique dimension" (Deleuze 1988, 100). New folding produces a new self with its own unique dimension that is not governed by the oppressive forces of the outside, what Davidson calls "external, marginalizing forces" (2010, 130). In other words, while the internal self is susceptible to the interference of malicious agents in the external realm, the alternate self, which is encountered by confronting these external marginalizing forces and folding their antagonism into the inward space of renewal, is a liberated selfhood consciously conceived by its own independent moral code (Deleuze 1988, 100). Folding, Davidson argues, is a relevant concept for Black feminists because their internal selves are self-aware of external marginalizing forces such as "the commodification and colonization of black women" (2010, 130). Thus, if they consciously unfold and merge with these malicious agents in the external realm, they can access alternate selves capable of promoting and preserving counternarratives such as "counterhistories and countermemories" (2010, 130).

Deleuze describes the affirmative process of unfolding and merging as "the right to difference, variation and metamorphosis" (1988, 106), interpreted by Davidson as "the struggle for subjectivity is just not a reaction to a prior situation; instead, it is a creative force and a source of change" (2010, 130). The subject's right to difference, the eternal return of the dissimilar, ensures an endless process of dissipation, distribution and transformation, and for Davidson, this emphasis on transformation means it is "critical . . . that black feminist subjectivity also unfold. It is in unfolding that she may encounter the world in a newly constructed identity that can resist external constitution" (2010, 130). The right to difference and the reminder to endlessly unfold are significant for two major reasons. First, like becoming, the fold is an infinite process; it is therefore counter-actualizing and attains affirmation without self-actualization. After accessing the alternate self, it is naïve to assume that the subject becomes infinitely free from external interference. As the subject continues to encounter differential experiences, new hegemonic structures will emerge. Additionally, there is also the possibility of the alternate self becoming an external marginalizing force. Because the alternate self can produce counternarratives such as counterhistories, it possesses the power of agency. As pointed out in the Introduction, Freire's *Pedagogy of the Oppressed* explains the psychology of the oppressed becoming the oppressor. If the oppressed subject developed an existential bond with its external oppressor, when the alternate self produces a counternarrative, the subject might crave the power of its former oppressor and seek to establish its counternarrative as an oppressively dominant master narrative. Thus, counternarratives avert becoming master narratives by allowing their subjectivity to constantly unfold.

In summation, the Deleuzian fold (as presented in the referenced passages from *Foucault*) produces substance by accessing an alternate self with a self-affirming moral code. The mechanism created to demonstrate this sojourn to self-affirmation can be condensed into three stages. The burgeoning maturity of the subject catalyzes the realization that external marginalizing forces are skewing and misrepresenting the subject's internal self: this is the first stage. In the second stage, the subject, now self-aware of external interference, confronts these external marginalizing forces in order to access the transformative powers of a self-renewing inward space. In the third and final stage, the inward space is accessed, as a result of merging the internal self and the external realm, and an alternate self is produced, a liberated self that is the governed by the subject's independent and self-affirming moral code.

Although this model attempts to describe the never-ending folding process of producing substantive affirmations without self-actualization, it remains a somewhat abstract methodology and offers no concrete clues on how to unpack the tangible concerns of contemporary popular culture narratives. There is still no strong sense of the emotional potency of affirmations, what they feel like and whether they differ from each other during varying phases of the becoming process. Gay, Beyoncé, and Rae are primarily preoccupied with confronting tensions that orient identity formation practices in the concrete settings of everyday life and while Deleuze develops a philosophical framework capable of identifying the counter-actualizing nature of these tensions, his discourse remains disengaged from the evident realities and complexities of the tactile world.

In both foldings and becoming, for example, there is no unambiguous acknowledgment that in many repressive societies, subverting the hegemony of external marginalizing forces has dire consequences for the subject such as social alienation, community ostracization and even death. Combating the effects of these tensions, beyond the conceptual realm, requires a sophisticated network of socioeconomic privileges, privileges that are usually inaccessible to marginalized subjects. Additionally, hegemonic forces in the external realm cannot always be characterized as marginalizing agents. While certain hegemonic forces oppress, others affirm. For example, the shared values of progressive societies such as gender equality and democratic principles reflect and celebrate infinitely affirmative traditions and habits. If certain shared values are, by nature, infinitely affirmative, why does Deleuzian philosophy expect all dimensions of a subject's value system to infinitely evolve? If difference (resisting shared values and hegemonic traditions) and sameness (embracing shared values and hegemonic traditions) can both function as affirmative experiences, how does the subject navigate the complicated tension between fluidity and permanency?

Deleuze does not satisfactorily unpack these questions because such tangible inquiries are admittedly not the focus of his more esoteric philosophical debates. However, Deleuzian philosophy remains a more appropriate theoretical framework for my book than other established "thirdness" concepts like Homi K. Bhabha's hybridity. In discussing relations between the colonized and the colonizer, postcolonial scholar Bhabha points out how colonial pursuits have led to the cultures of both parties overlapping, creating an interdependence that informs the nature of their subjectivities (1995, 206–8). This *hybridity* of cultures, Bhabha underlines, does not denote the absence of tension. Rather, the clash of cultures leads to a "third space . . . of enunciation" where new and emerging identities are produced from cultural contradictions, complexities and ambivalence (Bhabha 1995, 208). The "productive capacities" of this hybridized third space, Bhahba asserts, "may open the way to conceptualizing an *inter*-national culture, based not on the exoticism of multi-culturalism or the *diversity* of cultures, but on the inscription and articulation of culture's *hybridity*" (1995, 209). Although this *inter*-national culture is informed by the unresolved tensions of cultural differences, its characterization as a new kind of collective culture, for both the colonizer and the colonized, echoes an effort to establish a new entrenched belief system, which is the antithesis of Deleuze's counter-actualizing mechanism. For Deleuze, the individual can only infinitely become by resisting external knowledge systems that prioritize collective shared histories over the uniqueness of individualized affirmations (Deleuze 1998, 100–5). Because this emphasis on the individual, and their infinite right to difference, is the philosophical core of my reworked triple consciousness framework, Deleuzian philosophy is a better fit for the analysis of my primary materials than Bhabha's hybridity.

However, as I mentioned before, the abstract nature of Deleuze's musings is often unwilling to properly identify and unpack the tangible contradictions embedded in contemporary popular culture texts. Using an assemblage of complementary ideas and concepts, such as idioculture, aesthetic imaginaries and everyday aesthetics, TCT addresses this issue by working through a comprehensive framework that identifies but also builds upon the Deleuzian ideas embedded within the chaotic brilliance of popular culture narratives. In the works of Roxane Gay, Beyoncé, and Issa Rae, I argue, what produces substantive affirmations without arriving at the optimal harmony of orderly resolutions is the symbiotic tension between difference and sameness, a symbiosis that eschews the patriarchal exceptionalism of double consciousness by highlighting the intersectional complexities and anxieties of Black female artistry. Despite finding some sense of solace in the hegemonic value system of shared histories and cultural practices, Gay, Beyoncé, and Rae often pursue counternarratives that are uniquely affirmative but also contentious, contradictory and, most important, speak to a vastly understudied experiential dimension of the Black female experience, specifically, and the American imaginary, generally. TCT's theoretical framework ultimately attempts to understand the everyday manifestations and implications of a symbiosis that liberates but also complicates, a symbiosis that emerges from an existential rupture with an immediate and seismic impact on epistemologies about Black womanhood in contemporary American society.

In the following chapter, I examine Gay's *Bad Feminist* and *Difficult Women*. Compared to Beyoncé and Rae, Gay's works are more closely aligned with Deleuzian philosophy because they underline the oppressive tendencies of knowledge systems often controlled and weaponized by hegemonic power structures, and, as a result, gloriously celebrate the individual's right to difference. But unlike Deleuze, Gay acknowledges that the practice of deriving affirmations from difference is often necessitated by a key set of variables related to social privilege.

NOTES

1. In his book *The Road to Somewhere: The Populist Revolt and the Future of Politics*, David Goodhart conceptualizes this difficult reconciliation of layered identities as a division between Anywheres and Somewheres. The Somewheres represent the socially conservative less-educated small-town-dwelling working class who are weary of the recent social changes happening in society and the Anywheres represent the highly educated socially liberal urban-dwelling cosmopolitans who are more likely, at least in theory, to embrace social displacements that are changing the foundational fabric of contemporary society (2017, 1–8). The Somewheres versus Anywheres divide, Goodhart argues, is responsible for two of the biggest protest votes in modern political culture: Brexit and the election of Trump.

2. This perhaps explains the explosive ideological debate between Du Bois and acclaimed black Southern educator, author, and orator Booker T. Washington. While Du Bois demanded immediate socioeconomic and political equality for black Americans (Morrison and Shade 2010, 255), Washington, believing such demands were unfeasible due to his experiences in the South, proposed empowering segregated black communities through tertiary education while slowly building a legislative case for full equality at a later time (Healey 2011, 190).

3. Beal's "Double Jeopardy" was originally published in 1969, and Alice Walker's coinage of the phrase "the condition of twin 'afflictions'" in 1979. In the bibliography, I cite republications of both texts in the journal *Meredians* (Beal) and in the edited collection *Mother Reader: Essential Writings on Motherhood* (Walker).

Chapter Two

Popular Literary Culture

Roxane Gay's Bad Feminist and Difficult Women

WHO IS A "BAD" FEMINIST?

Writer, professor, commentator, and feminist Roxane Gay first burst into the literary scene with the publication of her 2014 novel *An Untamed State*. A few months later, she would gain widespread prominence with the *New York Times* (NYT) best-selling *Bad Feminist* (2014). Described as a vibrant collection of essays about the ambiguities of modern feminism, Gay's essay collection is anchored by anecdotes that "expertly weld her personal experiences with broader gender trends occurring politically and in popular culture" (Crum 2013). Because of her effortless ability to hybridize literary criticism and percipient popular culture commentary, *Slate* labeled Gay "the professor cum novelist cum voice-on-the-Internet" (Waldman 2014) who, in *Bad Feminist*, explores the power of imperfection and rejects the militancy and humorlessness of mainstream feminist ideology (Waldman 2014).

A huge part of Gay's appeal is her ability to "turn everything hard to deal with, hard to reckon with, hard to understand into a beautiful, recognizable moment" (OZY 2018). In an in-depth video interview titled "Breaking Big: How Roxane Gay Became the Voice of a Movement," editors of the online media platform *OZY* chronicled Gay's meteoric rise as a prominent writer and cultural commentator. The breakthrough moment in Gay's career was a 2011 essay she wrote for the online literary magazine *The Rumpus* called "The Careless Language of Sexual Violence" (OZY 2018). Her essay was a response to a *New York Times* article about the gang rape of an eleven-year-old girl in Cleveland, Texas. The article's focus on the "grieving" town's reputation and not the violation of the young girl left Gay in a state of fury, and in her essay response, she impeccably articulates the vile and ubiquitous brutality of gendered violence in a heartfelt and poignant manner. Gay's essay went viral: it was shared and discussed on multiple platforms all over the internet and went "well beyond the limits of the independent literature circle . . . that's when people in other spaces really started to take notice of her . . . who is she?" (OZY 2018).

Gay's relatable voice, usually quirky, often witty, sometimes self-deprecating, always astute, has now permeated most arenas of contemporary popular culture, from highbrow publications like *The Atlantic* to the social media sphere of Twitter to the superhero realm of Marvel Comics.[1] She is perhaps the only contemporary Black American female writer with such an impactful intellectual presence in all these spaces, and the raw honesty of her relatable persona, I argue in this chapter, redefines and reorients the dimensions of Black womanhood at and beyond the point of rupture.

The subject's burgeoning awareness of external marginalizing forces, the first stage of Deleuze's folding process, is echoed in the introductory chapter of *Bad Feminist*: "feminism is flawed because it is a movement powered by people and people are inherently flawed" (Gay 2014, x). As discussed in the Introduction, feminism has come under fire recently for ignoring the intersectional interests of non-white women (Tolentino 2017). The fact that the term "white feminism" is resolutely embedded in the lexicon of our zeitgeist reveals the profound level of distrust surrounding contemporary feminist activism. Moreover, the #MeToo movement's reverberations has led to many people, including women, accusing the anti–sexual harassment crusade of being too militant. In 2018, American news website *Vox* published the findings of their nationwide survey, carried out with media firm Morning Consult, about women's attitudes toward the #MeToo movement. The survey revealed that "significant numbers of women have concerns about the movement" (North 2018) and their top concerns were "men could be falsely accused of sexual harassment or assault. Women could lose out on opportunities at work because men will be afraid to work with them. The punishment for less severe forms of sexual misconduct could be the same as for more severe offenses" (North 2018). Of the women surveyed, 63 percent were anxious about false accusations, 60 percent were more preoccupied with the potential loss of professional opportunities and 56 percent were concerned about perpetrators of minor misdeeds being subjected to the same harsh punishments as perpetrators of more severe misdeeds (North 2018).

This widespread skepticism has unquestionably put a dent on the credibility of contemporary feminism but for Gay, such shortcomings are unavoidable because people lead movements, so movements will inevitably reflect our inherent human flaws (2014, x). With that said, skepticism and disappointment about certain beliefs or people associated with feminist activism should not be used to dismiss the morality of the movement (Gay 2014, x). Feminism's overarching goal, addressing "the inequalities and injustices women face, both great and small" (Gay 2014, x), is morally sound, so criticism should be directed at instances of human fallibility and not the feminist movement's egalitarian aspirations. This argument is the philosophical foundation of Gay's discourse in *Bad Feminist*. Although she is skeptical of hegemonic power structures and their tendency to act as external marginalizing forces, she acknowledges that some shared values such as feminist principles can have a positive impact on society. Thus, in order to prevent progressive ideologies from becoming marginalizing master narratives, the phenomenon Freire described as the oppressed becoming the oppressor, Gay argues that feminist subjectivities must infinitely unfold by remaining critical of institutional leaders and their mandates (2014, x). The failure to make this distinction between the egalitarian morality of the feminist movement and the human fallibility of the movement's gatekeepers reinforces, Gay points out, the simplistic and reductive "good feminism" versus "bad feminism" binary (2014, x–xiii). Good feminism epitomizes the irrational idea that feminism "must be everything we want and must always make the best choices" (Gay 2014, x), the unrealistic notion that institutions can exist without flaws or infiltration by corrupting outside forces. Bad feminism, on the other hand, epitomizes the moral shortcomings of the movement, women who are unfairly shunned and denigrated for failing to uphold or daring to criticize the hegemonic virtues of modern feminism (Gay 2014, x–xiii). Gay dismantles this reductive binary by proudly choosing to call herself a bad feminist: "I openly embrace the label of bad feminist. I do so because I am flawed. . . . I embrace the label of bad feminist because I am human. I am messy" (2014, x–xi).

By redefining "bad" as flawed, messy, well-meaning, nuanced, and disparate, the simplified good-versus-bad dichotomy ceases to exist. "Bad" moves away from denoting a universal notion of unacceptable behavior to representing behavioral patterns that are in a state of tension because they are difficult to define or categorize. In this moment, the moment when Gay embraces and redefines the "bad" label, her burgeoning awareness leads to an acknowledgment of tension. Tension here, I must point out, does not only refer to a general sense of friction between different entities; it also refers to skepticism regarding an expected mode of reconciliation. Going back to the paradigm of double consciousness, we see tension between the white gaze and the masculinely conceptualized Black self/soul. Du Bois hopes to reconcile Black and white by crossing the racial chasm, which drives an existential wedge between both parties. Thus, while there is tension between Black and white, there is no tension surrounding the expected mode of reconciliation because

Du Bois is certain that bridging the racial chasm is the remedy for America's racial problem. In *Bad Feminist*, on the other hand, generalized binaries (Black and white, good and bad etc.) do not exist because Gay's personal and affecting stories are chaotically intersectional. By setting up the "good" versus "bad" binary, Gay is hinting at the expected mode of reconciliation (bridging the racial chasm, which drives an existential wedge between both entities), but by portraying "good" as unpleasantly idealistic and redefining "bad" as an unresolved tension trapped somewhere between the fallacies and triumphs of human nature, Gay deconstructs the notion of binaries and seeks alternate modes of reconciliation.

Drawing inspiration from Deleuzian philosophy, TCT conceptualizes this acknowledgment of unresolved tension as the transformative moment of rupture that births a third consciousness, an alternate self with the ability to repudiate the hegemonic dichotomy of master narratives and begin the journey into the post-rupture realm where the possibilities of counternarratives reside. In the next sections, I aim to concretize Deleuzian concepts in popular culture by, first, identifying moments of rupture in Gay's texts and then working through her counter-actualizing exploration of counternarratives. As Gay's diverse personas and characters dissipate and evolve, shifting from place to place, changing shapes and shades and in some cases staying the same, they reveal and unpack the symbiotic tension between the pre- and post-rupture realms.

ME \ 'MĒ \: SINGULAR, PRONOUN, BLACK, FEMALE

The first section of *Bad Feminist* is called "ME," and its first's essay, titled "Feel Me. See Me. Hear Me. Reach Me," is a moving personal story about Gay, her insecurities, her triumphs, and her aspirations. The usage of a singular pronoun is an incredibly subversive aesthetic choice, I argue, because Gay is reframing and recentering the moral focal point of Black narratives. As mentioned in the Introduction, the rhetoric of masculine leadership and invincibility is integral to the African American community's social hierarchy. Black men are often viewed as the Black community's natural-born leaders and, as a result, their concerns are invariably prioritized (Eaton 2010, 1). Du Bois's double consciousness, extensively discussed in chapter 1, uses an imperialist patriarchal rhetoric to conceptualize collective Black identity, and this practice of framing Black identity from the contextual perspective of Black men later became a linchpin in Black American literary culture (as evidenced by the works of Harlem Renaissance writers, Richard Wright, Ralph Ellison and others). Consequently, although the first half of the twentieth century produced eclectic female writers like Dorothy West and Zora Neale

Hurston, they never received the same prominence and critical acclaim as their male counterparts (Beaulieu 2006, 325). Prior to 1970, very few Black female writers had considerable impact on scholarly discourse. This changed with the publication of Toni Cade Bambara's *The Black Woman*, the "first major feminist anthology" (Beaulieu 2006, 325) that showcased the work of Black female writers such as Paule Marshall and Alice Walker. Moreover, Toni Morrison began her acclaimed career in 1970 with the publication of her first novel *The Bluest Eye*. During this era, Morrison's judiciously nurtured "mentor relationships" (Beaulieu 2006, 325) with writers like Gayl Jones and Toni Cade Bambara contributed to the physical and intellectual expansion of Black feminist authorship (Beaulieu 2006, 325).

Although this expansion continues to grow, contemporary Black feminist writers, just like their twentieth-century predecessors, are still predisposed to backlash whenever they attempt to dismantle the male-centric hegemony of Black narratives. Richard Wright infamously condemned Zora Neale Hurston's 1937 novel *Their Eyes Were Watching God* because he found her work unacceptably sensual and ignorant of its era's racial prejudices: "'The sensory sweep of her novel carries no theme, no message, no thought. In the main, her novel is not addressed to the Negro'" (Hilfer 2014, 35–36). Moreover, his usage of the word "sensory" to dismiss Hurston's artistic merit is in keeping with a long sexist tradition of dismissing female-centric stories as senselessly sensual tales of romance (Loofbourow 2018). If Wright had looked beyond his apparent gender bias, he would have realized that Hurston's novel is a defiant work of protest art. Her protagonist, Janie Crawford, is a liberated woman seeking sexual and existential fulfillment on her own terms. In an era when mainstream depictions of Black women were mostly reduced to dehumanizing tropes like the tragic mulatto and the asexual mammy, Hurston challenged the status quo by reimagining Black women as autonomous and complex beings.

Decades later, renowned writer Alice Walker found herself in a similar situation. When *The Color Purple*, her Pulitzer Prize–winning novel, was adapted into a 1985 Steven Spielberg movie, its depiction of Black men sparked a nationwide debate (Crenshaw 1989, 163). *The Color Purple* is a coming-of-age story about how a young African American girl named Celie finds the strength to overcome the perils of abuse and abandonment. The movie's decision to depict the rape and abuse Celie is subjected to by the Black men in her life angered influential male voices in the Black community who accused the movie of dehumanizing Black men and propagating destructive narratives about the Black family unit (Crenshaw 1989, 163). Crenshaw argues in "Demarginalizing the Intersection of Race and Sex" that animating fear behind much of the publicized protest was that by portraying domestic abuse in a Black family, the movie confirmed the negative stereotypes of Black men. The debate over the propriety of presenting such an image on the screen overshadowed the issue of sexism and patriarchy in the Black community. . . . The struggle against racism seemed to compel the subordination of certain aspects of the Black female experience in order to ensure the security of the larger Black community. (1989, 163)

What is emphasized here, once again, is the notion that the unique perspectives of Black female-centric stories are of little consequence, and they must, as a result, remain subordinate to master narratives of Black masculinity.

Twenty-four years after *The Color Purple* debacle, Lee Daniels's Academy Award–winning movie *Precious* (2009) was released. Although directed by Daniels, a Black man, the movie is based on the novel *Push* (1996) by Black female writer Sapphire. Like Celie in *The Color Purple*, Precious, the titular character, is repeatedly raped by her father. She is also sadistically tortured by her tormented mother and shamed by society for being obese. Precious's coming-of-age story passionately polarized audiences. According to popular culture scholar Mark Anthony Neal, the 2009 controversy was *The Color Purple* "'all over again, with people writing and talking about what this film represents'" (Lee 2019). Controversial film critic Armond White, for example, professed that "'Not since 'The Birth of a Nation' has a mainstream movie demeaned the idea of Black American life as much as 'Precious.' . . . Full of brazenly racist clichés . . . it is a sociological horror show'" (Lee 2019). Lataya Peterson, founder of the now-defunct award-winning blog *Racialicious—the intersection of race and pop culture*, viewed White's criticism as dismissive of Black women's varied experiences. The story of Precious, Peterson argues, is necessary and relevant because it mirrors a plethora of issues affecting young Black girls in contemporary American society such as "'sexual abuse, poverty, violence and failing schools'" (Lee 2019). White's reluctance to acknowledge this reality, she continues, "'buys into the narrative that there can only be one acceptable presentation of black life . . . He's flattening the black experience, and in that way, he denies our humanity'" (Peterson in Lee 2019). Sapphire, the author of *Push*, also chimed in, stating that "'with Michelle, Sasha and Malia and Obama in the White House and in the post–'Cosby Show' era . . . people can't say these are the only images out there. . . . Black people are able to say 'Precious' represents some of our children, but some of our children go to Yale'" (Lee 2019). From an aesthetic and thematic point of view, *Precious* is admittedly excessive. Lee Daniels's signature cinematic flair for (over) amplifying the physical figurations of Black trauma can seem exploitative and even grotesque. This, however, does not negate the fact that the palpability of Precious's pain is an honest reflection of gendered violence in Black communities historically and systematically plagued by economic hopelessness.

As *The Color Purple* and *Precious* illustrate, artistry that destabilizes the status quo of Black narratives by unapologetically exploring the full spectrum of the Black female experience are predisposed to backlash. Gay's decision to begin her narrative with "ME," a bolded and bold focus on her unique female-centric experiences, is therefore the momentous moment of rupture because she is unshackling herself from the hegemonic grip of master narratives. In Deleuzian philosophy, fragmentation in the folding process occurs when the internal self unfolds and merges with the external realm in order to subvert external marginalizing forces and produce an alternate self with its own autonomous moral code. TCT's reading of *Bad Feminist* concretizes the formation of this process in popular culture by characterizing the alternate self as "ME," a pronoun shift in identification from the collective "WE" or the masculine "HE" to a singular "ME." The declaration of "ME" is thus the moment of rupture because it represents a fragmentation born out of tensions that seek to reorient the hegemonic status of master narratives.

As previously explained, the folding process, like becoming, is continuous. The alternate selves will continue to encounter other external marginalizing forces, and they will continue to unfold and merge with these forces in order to produce new affirmative alternate selves. While Deleuze does not emphasize a distinction between the varying magnitudes of these different folding processes, TCT does. Gay's "ME" echoes the third John Hancock moment, the most fragmentary of all three John Hancock moments because, unlike the previous two, it is rupture that audaciously and existentially shuns the pretense of harmonious hybridity between intersectional identities. Moreover, Gay's commanding presence in different popular culture genres (literary fiction, visual media, social media, academia, comic books, television, nonfiction etc.) has given her access to an unprecedented amount of agency, and her decision to use this agency to recenter the moral focal point of Black narratives by validating the legitimacy of her individualized point of view is profoundly consequential.

The aftermath of rupture is the exploration of counternarratives, and Gay begins her exploration in "Feel Me. See Me. Hear Me. Reach Me" with a solemn conversation about loneliness and the universal desire for belonging. Due to her pursuit of individual interests, she often feels a growing chasm between her identity and a collective sense of Black consciousness. A friend, for example, accuses her of only dating white men, an accusation that insinuates she abhors her own race (Gay 2014, 4). This accusation reinforces the aforementioned rhetoric that the principal function of Black femininity is to be a subordinate ally of Black men. A Black woman's worth, it seems, is only validated if she is shielded by the tutelage of Black male companionship.

Furthermore, this accusation automatically faults Gay without examining larger sociocultural issues affecting Black unions. Black men, for example, have a higher propensity to marry a non-Black spouse than Black women; data by the U.S. Census Bureau in 2005 revealed that in 73 percent of Black-white married couples, the husband is Black (Hattery and Smith 2007, 50). While self-hate, the result of systemic discrimination and prejudice, is certainly a contributing factor to this overwhelming desirability of whiteness, sociologists also argue that some Black men often view a white spouse as a status upgrade because such close proximity to whiteness, they believe, offers copious socioeconomic privileges (Judice 2008, 23). Looking at the statistical data, Black men are thus more likely to overlook Black women and actively seek white partners. Hence, faulting Gay for lacking a Black partner without entertaining the possibility of Black men overlooking her is unfair and, once again, conceptualizes the Black female point of view as a secondary orientation.

Gay rebels against her friend's accusation by saying, "If a brotha asked me out and I was into him, I'd go out with him, happily" (2014, 4). As echoed by the statistics, Gay is not actively avoiding Black men; it is more likely that Black men are actively avoiding her. Feeling wanted and desired is an innate human emotion, so it is sensible for Gay to entertain the men, regardless of their race, who find her desirable. By pursuing love on her own terms, Gay chooses individual preference over collective expectations. In other words, she refuses to spend her days waiting for validation from disinterested Black men and decides to satisfy her romantic urges by entertaining the men who find her desirable and worthy of companionship.

Despite this sense of freedom, tension lingers throughout the essay. When discussing the accusation that she is only attracted to white boys, she says, "I dated a Chinese boy in college. I told her I date the boys who ask me out" (Gay 2014, 4). Her clumsy defensiveness here reveals that she is still deeply irritated by the insinuated accusation of hating her own race. After vowing to love the men who love her, she ends this section of the essay with a somber statement about the desire to belong: "Wanting to belong to people or a person is not about finding a mirror image of myself" (Gay 2014, 4). This solemn declaration, like her defensive comment, reveals a sense of tension and uneasiness about her interracial relationships. She craves the freedom to find love across color lines, but she remains uneasy about the association between self-hate and interracial unions. Gay's exploration of the "ME" counternarrative can therefore be described as a counter-actualizing aesthetic because it does not achieve optimal harmony or conclusive resolution. However, it remains an affirmative experience because she asserts her innate human right to give and receive love.

There is a symbiotic relationship at work here. Rupture is born out of tension. Without the destabilizing forces of tension, the opening that paves the way for rupture, the third consciousness would never emerge. Tension is in the genetic makeup of rupture, and because counternarratives are the by-product of rupture, tension is inevitably intertwined in the chromosomal fabrics of counternarratives. In other words, the concept of symbiosis holds in it the entirety of the conglomerate of tension, rupture and affirmation that TCT rests on. Thus, in the tactile world of popular culture, TCT characterizes affirmations as a symbiotic relationship between rupture and tension, and in "Feel Me. See Me. Hear Me. Reach Me," symbiosis is represented by the expression of an inalienable right (Gay's right to love) that is both spurred and sustained by the negative perceptions of interracial unions.

Like symbiosis' affirmative relationship between rupture and tension, Bhabha's afore discussed hybridity concept is affirmed by the tension of cultures. There is, however, a major difference between both concepts. Bhabha's hybridity is primarily concerned with the clash of cultural systems in the postcolonial era and how the contradictions created by this existential collision can catalyze an "*inter*-national culture," which is affirmed by the third space of ambivalence (2015, 209). TCT's symbiosis, on the other hand, is primarily concerned with the clash between the individual and the collective and how the contradictions resulting from this existential collision affirms the individual's right to difference. Symbiosis does not attempt to forge an *inter*-national culture from the contradictory tensions of its third consciousness. Rather, its individualized narratives, like Deleuze's counter-actualizing mechanism, emphasize the affirmative right of an individual to exist beyond macro cultural systems, the affirmative right of the individual to think differently and *be* different. And while this difference might influence an emerging *inter*-national culture, this is not symbiosis' primary goal. As the subsequent paragraphs and chapters will reveal, symbiosis' overarching purpose is to unpack and amplify the individualized experiences of marginalized women, experiences that have historically been subsumed into and silenced by hegemonic, and usually male-dominated, cultural narratives.

Other examples of symbiosis can be identified in Gay's discourse on hip-hop and Lena Dunham's *Girls*. Gay often finds herself "singing along" (2014, Introduction) to the catchy music of rappers even though they use derogatory language like "bitch" to characterize women. Rap superstar Kanye West's album *Yeezus*, for example, is "compelling" (Gay 2014, 188) and "ambitious" (Gay 2014, 188), and Gay confesses to listening "to the album on repeat" (2014, 188). However, she cannot love the album "because of lyrics like 'You see it's leaders and it's followers/But I'd rather be a dick than a swallower,' from the song 'New Slaves'" (2014, 188). Kanye West's contempt for women, Gay argues, "overwhelms nearly every track" (2014,

188), but there are also songs like "Blood on the Leaves," songs that emanate so much poetic brilliance the listener struggles to "dismiss the album entirely" (2014, 188). Gay describes this feminist struggle to resist the allure of a brilliantly conceived piece of art that also harbors misogynistic characteristics as the "uncomfortable balance between brilliance and bad behavior" (2014, 188).

Black American artists pioneered hip-hop in the 1970s, and the genre has since played a significant role in the development and global visibility of American popular music. During hip-hop's inception, Black artists used rap lyricism to document and expose the economic hopelessness and violent realities of inner-city ghettos (Cosimini 2015, 252). As hip-hop grew in popularity and influence so did its economic prowess: "hip hop has provided one of the few significant employment and wealth-generating opportunities for African Americans, and has employed them in unprecedented numbers" (Watson A. 2016, 182). Despite its wealth-generating prospects and legacy of activism, feminists incessantly criticize hip-hop culture for its tendency to portray Black femininity as hyper-erotic (Gammage 2015, 8). As Snoop Dogg raps on Dr. Dre's *The Chronic*, "'Bitches ain't shit but hos and tricks'" (Gaunt 2006, 180). Hip-hop is hence an unresolved musical and cultural experience for Black women because despite its denigration of Black womanhood, the genre is also capable of uplifting Black communities both economically and sociopolitically.

Gay, I should point out, does not unpack the historical relevance of hip-hop in the African American community. However, the uncomfortable space she inhabits between appreciating artistic brilliance and pointing out bad behavior hints at, one can argue, the uncomfortable relationship between Black feminism and hip-hop: Black feminists must often acknowledge the aesthetic merit of Black art and the opportunities, tangible and aspirational, it affords to disenfranchised Black people while remaining cognizant of the fact that hip-hop culture regularly promotes a hypermasculine rhetoric, which devalues and degrades Black femininity. Gay confesses that it is difficult for a feminist not to feel humorless because they see misogyny in every facet of everyday life, manifested in various forms, both big and small (2014, 188–89). She concludes the essay "Blurred Lines, Indeed" with a poignant reflection: "Men want what they want. Sometimes they make their desires plain with music to which I can't help but sing along" (Gay 2014, 191). Even the affirming pleasure obtained from listening to good music is often spurred and sustained by tension.

Affirmation's symbiotic entanglement with tension is also evident in mainstream feminism. Gay has a complicated relationship with the institution of feminism because, as a Black woman with a unique set of intersectional interests, the white gatekeepers of feminist projects have historically shunned her. She states, "I decided feminism wasn't for me as a black woman, as a woman who has been queer identified at varying points in her life, because feminism has, historically, been far more invested in improving the lives of heterosexual white women to the detriment of others" (Gay 2014, xiii). This marginalizing experience of exclusion is what motivates Gay to ironically embrace the "bad feminist" label and deconstruct the notion of simplistic binaries. Racial discrimination within the feminist movement (tension) is responsible for Gay's reimagination of feminism as a nonbinary experience that allows women to be messy, flawed, and human (the aftermath of rupture). Thus, without tension, affirmative counternarratives in the post-rupture realm cannot exist.

This redefinition of messiness as a state of being that enables women to reject simplistic binaries is echoed by the works of feminist writer and scholar Sara Ahmed. In "Affect/Emotion: Orientation Matters," for example, Ahmed describes the world we inhabit as "messy" and argues that when we adhere to rigid categorizations, we lose connection to the rich insights of our chaotic lives: "Clear distinctions for a messy experience or a messy situation are neither helpful for a better understanding of reality nor interesting for the debate" (Schmitz and Ahmed 2014, 98–99). Moreover, in "Feminist Hurt/Feminism Hurts," she underlines the messy entanglements between feminism and violence. "How many of us became feminists because of experiences of violence? I cannot separate my feminist history from my experiences of violence," Ahmed states. "What a tangle. Messy" (2018, 59). Her characterization of messiness as a symbiotic relationship between marginalization and activism reflects the messiness of Gay's bad feminist manifesto, a manifesto that acknowledges, unpacks and even celebrates the feminist symbiosis of tension and affirmations.

This symbiotic performance of Gay's bad feminist persona also has a surprising consequence: empathy. If binaries do not exist then feminists are not all good or all bad. HBO's *Girls*, for example, is a critically acclaimed television series that acknowledges and affirms the complexities of modern feminist values. However, Lena Dunham, the creator and star of *Girls*, has been routinely criticized for the show's alleged erasure of Black women (Watson E. 2015, 148), and cultural critics have accused the show of "hipster racism," a television trope that uses awkward comedy and language to conceal dehumanizing commentary about people of color (Watson E. 2015, 150). Dodai Stewart's "Why We Need to Keep Talking About the White Girls on *Girls*," published on feminist website *Jezebel* in 2012 during the peak of *Girls* hysteria, highlights both issues. In the world of *Girls*, a story about four twenty-something girls coming of age in the idiosyncratic bubble of New York City, women of color are curiously absent. "I, too am a black woman who grew up in New York," Stewart asserts. "I went to both public and prep schools. I, too, have been a struggling twentysomething writer. And yet. The world in which Hannah and her friends inhabit seems familiar, except for its complete lack of diversity" (2012). Stewart also bemoans the problematic language of *Girls'* casting notices for secondary women of color characters. She protests,

> Actresses of color needed include a Jamaican nanny ("overweight, good sense of humor, MUST DO A JAMAICAN ACCENT") and a nanny from El Salvador ("sexy, MUST DO A SOUTH AMERICAN/CENTRAL AMERICAN ACCENT"). The fat sassy black woman and the sexy Latina have been two of the most pervasive TV stereotypes for years (Stewart 2012).

Without dismissing the justified anger of her fellow Black feminists, Gay offers a different take on the *Girls* debacle. While Gay is cognizant of *Girls'* problematic components (she calls the show narrow, limited, and myopic [2014, 56–57]), discourse about television representation cannot yield productive results if Dunham is held to unfeasible standards. Gay argues that it is unfair to expect Lena Dunham to solve television's representation problem while she, Dunham, attempts to craft a singular narrative about the existential awkwardness of sex and womanhood (2014, 58). Gay ponders, "Why is this show being held to the higher standard when there are so many television shows that have long ignored race and class or have flagrantly transgressed in these areas" (2014, 58).

This argument is threefold. First, expecting Dunham to create a multicultural world with multidimensional Black women, a world she is probably not familiar with, while telling her own singular coming-of-age story is impractical. Moreover, solely attacking Dunham without addressing the systemic problem of representation across all major television networks is an ineffective strategy because the network executives responsible for choosing the content displayed on their platforms are not held accountable. Hence, the principal target of representation advocates should be the executives of television networks, the ultimate gatekeepers deciding who gains access to their storytelling platforms. HBO would eventually hire Black actress and writer Issa Rae to create, write and star in *Insecure*, a comedy-drama television series about the trials and triumphs of a group of millennial Black women in contemporary Los Angeles, and in chapter 4, I will discuss the implications of shifting the representation discourse from in front of the camera to behind the camera. But back to *Girls*. Gay also acknowledges that Dunham is attempting to craft a meaningful narrative about the idiosyncratic misadventures of middle- to upper-class millennial women in modern New York City (2014, 58). While the execution of Dunham's intent is sometimes problematic, her effort at sincerely and intellectually exploring the angsts of contemporary feminism implies an attempt to unfold her subjectivity. Flawed young women, Gay seems to be arguing here, should be encouraged to evolve and not dismissed entirely.

Gay's defense of Dunham, I must emphasize, is not making excuses for whitewashed feminism. As earlier mentioned, Gay criticizes the problematic elements of Dunham's show. *Girls*, she points out, "represents a very privileged existence . . . one where young women's New York lifestyles can be subsidized by their parents, where these young women can think of art and unpaid internships and finding themselves and writing memoirs at twenty-four" (2014, 56). Depicting such a privileged world without sufficiently addressing the socioeconomic anxieties of contemporary millennial culture like increasing income equality and systemic injustices is, Gay argues, "a fine example of someone writing what she knows and the painful limitations of doing so" (2014, 56). With that said, Gay's take on *Girls* arguably possesses more empathy than her peers because she operates from the "all people are flawed" principle. And because all people are flawed, she encourages the younger generation of white feminists to learn from the past, unfold their subjectivities and arrive at their own moment of rupture. Once again, we see Gay diverging from collective opinions and emphasizing her intellectual right to difference. While she is not dismissive of popular viewpoints, her differing perspectives reveal that in the post-rupture realm, affirmative counternarratives are inherently skeptical of hegemonic voices and their tendency to rally behind a singular belief system. In the next section, I examine a diverse pool of counternarratives with similar tensions, paying particular attention this time to how they contend with issues of racial commodification and class privilege.

PROFITS AND PRIVILEGE

Black Entertainment Television (BET) is a television network that caters to a Black American audience. There is a general push in the Black community to support networks like BET because they "give African Americans a place on TV where they can see themselves consistently represented" (Leahey 2016). Black Enterprise, for example, a Black-owned multimedia company and fervent supporter of Black businesses, ran a piece about the representational power of BET programming like the BET awards and why it is imperative for Black people to support the network's content. They argue that "no matter how 'low-budget' and 'ghetto fabulous' some people might deem the BET Awards, it is still ours. Yes, ours. BET was doing it for the culture and giving black artists credit where it was due before others chose to honor them and allow them to be themselves on mainstream stages" (Blanco 2018).

Gay is not impressed with the quality of BET's content. She calls its programming mostly "shoddy" and bemoans its lack of diverse Black experiences. A TV show called *Toya*, for example, an attempt to glamorize the everyday life of a famous rapper's ex-wife, is emblematic, she argues, of BET's tendency to confine the definition of Black success: "If you watch BET, you get the sense that the only way Black people succeed is through professional sports, music, or marrying/fucking/being a baby mama of someone who is involved in professional sports or music" (Gay 2014, 6). Gay is not opposed to programming like *Toya* or the longevity of networks like BET that cater to the representational needs of Black Americans. She only wishes content like *Toya* is paralleled with programming that celebrates an array of other professions like school teachers, postal workers, jazz musicians, and writers (Gay 2014, 6).

This plea for the representation of diverse Black experiences demonstrates Gay's rejection of rigid categorizations about the collective Black consciousness. By emphasizing diversity beyond the point of rupture, she is making a persuasive case for affirmative counternarratives that can accommodate the dynamic nature of intersectional identities. Worthy of note here is the fact that although BET was founded by a Black entrepreneur and investor, Robert L. Johnson, the network is no longer a Black business (Wollenberg 2006). Viacom, a multinational mass media conglomerate corporation, bought BET in 2000 (Wollenberg 2006), and like most gargantuan corporations, profits are the paramount objective. The lasting endurance of BET programming, which tends to emphasize a limited view of the Black experience, speaks to the racial commodification of shared values. As Gay points out, stereotypical impressions of Black success in popular culture are generally limited to professional sports and hip-hop culture (2014, 6). Thus, across color lines, people are more inclined to watch shows about the Black experience if these stereotypes take center stage.

The implication here is racial commodification by corporate interests can function as an external marginalizing force because they suppress the full spectrum of the Black experience. The symbiotic relationship between tension and rupture is embedded in the intention and execution of BET programming. The network's moment of rupture, its decision to affirm

the representational needs of the Black American audience, is spurred by tension, the erasure of Black stories on mainstream networks. However, the execution of BET's representational intention remains motivated by the external hegemonic influence of corporate interests, revealing that even in the post-rupture realm, counternarratives are susceptible to the external interference of marginalizing agents. This explains why, for Gay, it is critical to always question and reassess shared values and perspectives, even if their intentions seem egalitarian and progressive.

In the "ME" section of *Bad Feminist*, essays like "Feel Me. See Me. Hear Me. Reach Me," "Peculiar Benefits" and "Typical First Year Professor" examine familiar symbiotic tensions through the lens of class privilege. "ME," for example, often feels overwhelmed by the burden of her students, students with behavioral issues and severe literacy shortcomings, students from inner-city households plagued by abuse, alcoholism, and addiction (Gay 2014, 8–10). And on some days, "ME" admits to being a "demanding bitch" (Gay 2014, 7) who is irritated by the apathetic attitude of these students and their lack of decorum (Gay 2014, 7). The entire teaching experience, "ME" admits, left her "completely burnt out. I had nothing left to give" (Gay 2014, 10) and when the semester ends, "ME" confesses to being "relieved . . . I . . . needed a break, a very, very long break" (Gay 2014, 11). Although she has immense sympathy for her institutionally disadvantaged students, she ultimately refuses to bear the full burden of a failed education system. This is not the clichéd inspirational story of an education activist "taking on the system" and successfully guiding their troubled students through the gilded path of professional success, a trope popularized by movies like *Dangerous Minds* (1995), *Take the Lead* (2006), and *Freedom Writers* (2007). Rather, this is an affirmatively realistic counternarrative about an educator who walks away because she is burnt out. Although there is no imminent resolution to the problem of America's broken education system, there is affirmation because she acquires a sobering education about the reality of learning disparities among students from different socioeconomic backgrounds. Her inner-city students are unable to thrive academically because they come from broken homes with no positive role models or established educational practices. Gay confesses: "Shame on me, certainly, for being so ignorant about the galling disparities in how children are educated" (2014, 8). Most important, Gay learns to prioritize her mental health. There is no point in serving a collective interest if she is mentally exhausted and has nothing left to give. In other words, to be of use to herself and her community, she needs to safeguard the buoyancy of her mental health. Tension and affirmations are once more tethered. Gay's decision to subvert the superhuman educator trope is both spurred and sustained by her unpleasant experiences as a young educator.

This episode invites a discourse on class privilege, which is not central to Deleuzian philosophy but relevant to my manuscript. Because my reimagined triple consciousness framework is engaging with the concrete settings of popular culture texts, it acknowledges the fact that physical and psychological maturations, central characteristics of the becoming process, often require a certain degree of socioeconomic privilege. Gay's resolution to protect her mental health by leaving a toxic workplace is an affirmative experience in her becoming process because after encountering different perspectives, experiences, and knowledge systems, she realizes that she can be a better advocate for her disadvantaged students in other arenas more conducive to her mental well-being such as the literary realm. And she accomplishes this goal with the publication with *Bad Feminist*, a widely read essay collection that partly addresses the impact of America's failed education system on marginalized communities. However, Gay's decision to prioritize her mental health and her ability to act on this decision is largely predicated by the privilege of human capital, a valuable combination of assets such as education, training, and intelligence, assets often inaccessible to historically disadvantaged Black communities. The implication here for the TCT framework is that the moment of rupture, and the subsequent exploration of affirmative counternarratives, is, in some cases, a manifestation of class privilege. But privilege does not denote the absence of suffering and stigmatization.

Gay's "ME" persona is also insecure: her confidence is profoundly bruised when she overhears a white colleague in graduate school calling her, the only student of color in the program, "the affirmative-action student" (Gay 2014, 13).[2] Years later, with multiple accomplishments to her name like a PhD and published books, "ME" still hears the voice of that white colleague in her head, questioning the validity of her credentials, "*Do I deserve to be here?* I worry, *Am I doing enough?*" (Gay 2014, 13). We see shades of double consciousness here because Gay must reconcile how she views herself (a competent writer and scholar) versus how the antagonistic white world views her (untalented and undeserving of success). Even Barack Obama, America's first Black/biracial president and arguably one of the most influential men in modern American politics, is not immune to the white world's antagonism. He was infamously called a chimpanzee by a Kentucky Republican state House candidate (Beam 2016), and Michelle Obama, his Harvard-educated Black wife, was described as "an ape in heels" by a public official in the state of West Virginia (BBC 2016). The implication here is that no amount of success can shield the Black subject from the demoralizing sting of racial prejudice.

But make no mistake, "ME" is not only a victim; as previously stated, she is a Black woman of tremendous privilege. "ME," the daughter of Haitian immigrants, "grew up middle class and then upper middle class" (Gay 2014, 16). "ME" comes from a stable two-parent household, went to elite schools, and has a flourishing career and "resources for frivolity" (Gay 2014, 16). This recognition of privilege, she argues, does not negate experiences of personal suffering and/or systemic marginalization. Rather, it is merely an understanding of the extent of her privilege and the consequences of her privilege and remaining "aware that people who are different from you move through and experience the world in ways you might never know anything about" (Gay 2014, 16). Unlike double consciousness, Gay recognizes that the affirmative dawning of her third consciousness is unique to the privileged specificity of her upbringing and, therefore, not representative of a collective Black consciousness. And her acknowledgment of being both privileged and marginalized is, according to the TCT framework, an acknowledgment of the unresolved tension infinitely embedded in the philosophical fabric of affirmative counternarratives. This acknowledgment, while extremely liberating, is also extraordinarily soul crushing, because it is an admission that all affirmative experiences beyond the point of rupture will never be rid of tensions and complications. In the next and final section on *Bad Feminist*, I will examine how Gay unpacks and concretely characterizes the existential nature of this weighted admission.

CATHARSIS

Bad Feminist can be characterized as an exploration of catharsis, an attempt to purify and reimagine a compromised self. Filtered through the TCT framework's analytical lens, the compromised self is a by-product of interference by external marginalizing forces, and the subject's resistance to this external interference leads to rupture and, consequently, the exploration of counternarratives in the post-rupture realm. As the examples in earlier sections illustrate, affirmative counternarratives are fundamentally oriented by unresolved tension. Because Deleuzian philosophy prioritizes abstractions, it does not articulate what unresolved tension feels like in a tactile setting. I use my reworked triple consciousness framework to address this issue by concretely defining and examining the *feeling* of symbiotic relationships between tension and affirmations in the post-rupture realm.

In her essay "Reaching for Catharsis: Getting Fat Right (or Wrong) and Diana Spechler's *Skinny*," Gay recounts her lifelong struggles with weight. Because this struggle is lifelong, weight symbolizes a continuous external marginalizing force, an infinite source of tension. While reading Diana Spechler's novel *Skinny*, a story about a troubled binge eater working as a fat camp counselor, Gay is reminded of her traumatic teenage experience in a fat camp (Gay 2014, 109). When the normally lanky Gay begins putting on weight during her teenage years, the reaction of the external world is immediate and abrasive. A vaguely described incident in the woods with a group of boys leaves her shaken, and she begins stuffing her face with pizza and Twinkies, trying, desperately, to fill the "ragged, ugly thing inside me that couldn't be filled or quieted" (Gay 2014, 110).[3] Her boyfriend and classmates ridicule her expanding waistline, and she begins to feel like an oddity (Gay 2014, 109). Her parents also disapprove of her new figure and urge her to practice dietary moderation. Young Gay does not heed their advice, and she ends up in a fat camp the summer after her sophomore year of high school (Gay 2014, 109). At fat camp, participants endure an avalanche of humiliating activities such as weigh-ins. If you lost weight during a weigh-in, you were congratulated and encouraged to improve; if the scale failed to register any progress, you were sternly lectured (Gay, 2014 112).

Such shaming practices by fat camps do not help obese children develop a healthy and nurturing relationship with food. Instead, due to an unethical emphasis on rapid weight loss through pressure and intimidation, fat-shamed victims are more likely to develop a toxic obsession with being skinny and, as a result, attempt to lose weight by indulging in unhealthy practices. Young Gay, for example, copes with the excruciating pressure to be skinny at fat camp by smoking cigarettes and making herself throw up (Gay 2014, 112–13). When she finally leaves fat camp, she had lost a significant amount of weight, and the compliments she receives for her much thinner frame make her feel good (Gay 2014, 120). She, however, soon succumbs to the complex cravings of her insatiable appetite: "But then I started eating again, worked even harder to make my body fill as much space as possible, tried to fill that ragged need inside of me" (Gay 2014, 120).

Adult Gay continues to battle with the trauma of obesity. She now religiously watches weight-loss reality TV shows like *The Biggest Loser* and *Extreme Makeover: Fat People Edition* as a form of "penance and motivation" (Gay 2014, 116), shows she calls "fat-shaming porn" (Gay, 2014 116). In these weight-loss shows, trainers and producers often coerce contestants into some dramatic form of catharsis by orchestrating a seemingly earnest conversation about "what went wrong" (Gay 116, 2014). This televised catharsis, Gay purports, is not earned because it is a contrived performance deliberately conceived to enthrall and entertain inquisitive spectators. Addressing the root causes of obesity requires a deeper psychological exploration of trauma and acquired habits, an exploration that cannot be properly executed by the levity of reality television.

Moreover, in 2018, Gay published a moving personal essay, titled "What Fullness Is: On Getting Weight Reduction Surgery," about her decision to undergo weight-loss surgery. She admits that her decision was not solely motivated by health concerns. There was also the desire to conform, the longing to find "a way to fit more peacefully into a world that is not at all interested in accommodating a body like mine" (Gay 2018). Despite the transformative promises of surgery, there is no guarantee, she admits, that the procedure will end her lifelong ordeal with obesity: "Some of these interventions have succeeded for people, and some have failed, because not even surgical intervention can overcome the reasons why many people gain and then struggle to lose weight. Some bodies and minds simply cannot be brought to heel" (Gay 2018). Weight loss for Gay has become more than just obesity.

The process carries with it the trauma of childhood, the vaguely described incident in the woods that made her to begin overeating, and the psychological impact of this trauma in her adult life. Hence, even if Gay lost the physical weight, like most victims of childhood trauma, it is impossible to completely lose the psychological weight.

In all the afore discussed examples, despite not arriving at the point of catharsis, there are affirmations. After fat camp, for example, young Gay is deceptively affirmed by positive comments about her temporary weight loss but, later in life, her obsessive experience with weight-loss TV shows enables her to realize that the physical fixation of dramatic weight loss seldom addresses the psychological trauma of dramatic weight gain. This uncomfortable bond between obesity and affirmations echoes the symbiotic relationship between tension and counternarratives in the post-rupture realm. Gay's persistent desire, from childhood to adulthood, to resolve this tension remains unsuccessful and undeterminable, so she ends the essay "Reaching for Catharsis" with a haunting declaration: "I started eating again. . . . I had not really found catharsis. Oh, how I hungered" (2014, 120).

This declaration, I argue, is her moment of catharsis. Although she is referencing a moment in her youth, the moment she returns from fat camp and regains all the weight she lost, her aesthetic decision to end an essay about her lifelong obesity struggle with a description of insatiable hunger affirms the infinite nature of her weight-loss battle. Catharsis for Gay is therefore not the purification of a compromised self. Rather, it is the realization that the arduous process to purify the compromised self will be infinite. Oriented by this realization, TCT does not conceptualize affirmations as wholly celebratory because there is a profound sense of sadness seeping through the ink of Gay's text. There is something existentially devastating about concluding a narrative on childhood trauma with the realization that this trauma will haunt one for the entirety of one's life. Affirmations without actualization or resolution can thus be *concretely* described as unfinished and despondent, a weighted existential predicament that burdens both the mind and body of the subject. This unresolved feeling is a solemn emotion, a terrifying reminder that the perils of life often have little to no consideration for our aspirations. Hence, unlike Deleuzian philosophy, TCT foregrounds the physical and psychological toll of affirmations in the post-rupture realm.

While some might view this reading as pessimistic, I argue otherwise. An honest acknowledgment of life's continuous obstacles can be both affirming and comforting to the subject. If the subject is aware that the hunger for catharsis is a lifelong craving, then they are better equipped to navigate and make sense of the process. Life is easier to manage, and perhaps even pleasurable, if the subject is aware of the challenges ahead. Gay's essay on catharsis is not the finale of *Bad Feminist*. She marches on after that, covering a plethora of trivial and profound topics, affirmed and empowered by her zeal to fight until the very end, whenever that end might be. The vitality of this zeal, according to the TCT framework, only exists at and beyond the moment of rupture because prior to the transcendental experience of the third consciousness, the subject's autonomous moral code was hijacked by marginalizing agents from the external realm. The exploration of counternarratives in *Bad Feminist* ultimately reveals that the affirmative feeling of liberation in the post-rupture realm does not exist in isolation and without contention. A subject can concurrently feel despondent about their inability to terminate tension and rejuvenated by the affirmative moments produced by this tension.

INTERLUDE

After the critical and commercial success of *Bad Feminist*, Gay redirected her focus to the fictional realm, where she tested similar ideas in a number of different scenarios. I too will attempt to test the TCT framework in this new realm, paying specific attention to how familiar concepts like rupture and symbiosis can also be relevant in the aesthetic expansion of Gay's literary universe. In her short story collection *Difficult Women*, published three years after *Bad Feminist*, Gay further nuances epistemologies about Black womanhood in contemporary American society by using literary approaches that complicate and transcend entrenched notions of race and identity. While *Bad Feminist* contends with the purification of a compromised self within the parameters of a historical and racial discourse on Black womanhood, *Difficult Women* focuses on the everyday manifestations of existential dilemmas that similarly compromise the self, sometimes irreversibly, but lack the experiential generality of racial markers because they are uniquely experienced. In other words, affirmative counternarratives at and beyond the moment of rupture are individualized experiences that cannot be comfortably categorized or replicated. I use Derek Attridge's concept of idioculture to strengthen this interpretation of TCT's realms of rupture. Idioculture argues that although we share similar experiences and points of view due to intersecting racial and social belief systems, our modes of behavior are ultimately dissimilar due to the unique circumstances of our specific realities (Attridge 2004, 21). Simply stated, no two individuals experience the world *exactly* the same.

As stated in the Introduction, contemporary creations and interpretations of the triple consciousness concept seek to amend the gender-based oversights of the double consciousness framework by introducing a third perspective, a philosophical emphasis on the Black female experience, to Du Bois's binary conceptualization of Black identity. This interlocking of the "third" consciousness with the "double" consciousness is often characterized as a correction and/or completion of the Du Boisian identity epistemology, an identity formation framework that still informs contemporary discourse on Black identity and authorship (Mocombe 2010, 2). The uniqueness of TCT's realms of rupture, as illustrated by the idioculture of *Difficult Women*, rejects the notion that interlocked experiences are the primary characteristics of identity formation practices in Black-authored narratives. Hegemonic identity epistemologies cannot fittingly contain or characterize the experimental exploration of Gay's authorship in *Difficult Women*. Although the text acknowledges the relevance of shared sociocultural and racial experiences, it chooses instead to emphasize moments of singularity, those moments in which we are disconnected from familiar strands of feelings and memories and, as a result, we affirmatively exist, even temporarily, beyond the trajectories of hegemonic narratives.

These moments of singularity, often sustained by unresolved tensions, are explorations of counternarratives that acknowledge a subject's right to difference. Accommodating the affirmative singularities of these counternarratives indicates that TCT's realms of rupture must be conceptually flexible. This flexibility allows the insights of Gay's atypical aesthetics, a literary framework not shackled by the omnipresent double consciousness rhetoric and its contemporary reimaginations, to inform my analysis and not the other way around. As illustrated in *Bad Feminist*, counternarratives are born out of a symbiotic relationship between rupture and tension. And although they often lack fixed meanings or tidy reconciliations, what makes them momentous are their efforts to explore new possibilities by forging unusual narrative paths. These efforts epitomize the right to difference, a right that is repeatedly challenged by hegemonic master narratives and can also be described as the problem of difference.

Gay's *Difficult Women* is a rousing litany of messy lives, a bravura spectacle of storytelling that reads as a manifesto about the affirmative triumphs and discomforts of difference. These women are uniquely wretched and sometimes sinister. They are labeled with collective titles such as *Mothers, Crazy Women* and *Loose Women* but just like in *Bad Feminist*, Gay subverts/mocks the inaccurate broadness of gendered labels by choosing instead to describe the idiosyncrasies of women who are distinctively affirmed and disturbed. In the section titled *Loose Women*, the narrator ponders: "Who a Loose woman looks Up To." The answer? "Never her mother. She is trying to kill . . . those parts of her mother lurking beneath her skin" (Gay 2017, 35). Moreover, the loose woman's apartment is "clean and bright . . . though her home doesn't look lived in" (Gay 2017, 35). The narrative's interrogator inquires about how the loose woman likes to be touched and receives a cryptic response: "There was a boy she once knew. . . . He was earnest and she didn't know what to make of that. . . . She didn't dare trust it. . . . She broke his heart"

(Gay 2017, 35). There are also *Frigid Women*. One of them "has a husband and a child and she loves them in her way though they both gang up on her, call her cold" (Gay 2017, 37). And then you have *Crazy Women* who cannot emotionally connect with their therapists (Gay 2017, 40) and decorate their kitchen shelves with cookbooks titled "*Light Eating Right, Getting Creative with Kale, Thin Eats*, and one very worn copy of *The Art of French Cooking*" (Gay 2017, 41). Let us not forget about *Mothers*, the ones who carry their babies, replicas of their fathers, stare at their infant faces and never find what they are looking for (Gay 2017, 41–42), the ones who murmur "'I cannot do it again'" when they find out they are pregnant again (Gay 2017, 43). And finally we have *Dead Girls*, made more "interesting" and "beautiful" by death (Gay 2017, 43). "Finally," the narrator ponders. "It might be said, they are at peace" (Gay 2017, 43).

Although the impact of tension and trauma in the lives of these women is evident, their backstories, the events that led to their present predicaments, are not always explicitly stated. The limited clues given about past incidents that may have shaped their present realities invite the reader to psychologize about their inner lives and speculatively put the pieces together. I argue that this aesthetic strategy to engage the reader psychologically in speculative world building foregrounds the uniquely experienced explorations in TCT's realms of rupture. Worthy of mention here is the existence of vibrant scholarship about Black American women and trauma. Valérie Croisille's *Black American Women's Voices and Transgenerational Trauma* (2021), for example, focuses on the gendered trauma of chattel slavery and its impact on the aesthetic formulations of neo–slave narratives and in Maria Rice Bellamy's *Bridges to Memory* (2016), she partly explores the nature and functionality of inherited trauma in the fiction of African American women. Because Gay is a Black American writer, there is an inclination to filter the traumatic experiences of her *difficult* women through the lens of established frameworks in African American trauma studies. Gay discourages this inclination by not revealing the racial identity of most of her protagonists. Readers, as a result, view these female characters as both messy and affirmative beings whose individual narratives are not rigidly tethered to the dogmatic tendencies of hegemonic epistemologies.

Although Gay's *difficult* women similarly endure patriarchal oppression, the process of psychologically unpacking their varied backgrounds and life choices underscores the uniqueness of their individual experiences. Thus, unlike the thematic conviction and political vitality of *Bad Feminist*, *Difficult Women* is a more psychological and sometimes abstract exploration of how tension and trauma infect and reorient the mind. I should clarify that trauma in this instance does not only refer to a defining traumatic event that continuously colors the trajectory of an individual's life. The day-to-day experiences of living through perilous situations like economic hopelessness and unrequited love can also trigger and/or catalyze traumatic feelings and memories. I should also clarify here that the centrality of trauma is not a recurrent characteristic in all realms of rupture. Although traumatic experiences fundamentally orient texts like *Difficult Women* and Beyoncé's *Lemonade*, Issa Rae's *Insecure* explores counternarratives in a post-rupture realm primarily informed by the aesthetics of ordinary life, transformative efforts by mundane objects and activities to subvert hegemonic perceptions of Black womanhood. In other words, the flexibility of TCT's theoretical apparatus accommodates a diversity of aesthetic approaches seeking to uniquely explore the possibility of new possibilities.

THE UNBEARABLE WEIGHT OF WATER AND WINE

In *Difficult Women*, Gay explores the weight women must bear for choosing to acknowledge and explore an existence at and beyond the point of rupture. Similarly stated, affirmations often come at an unbearable cost. "Water, All Its Weight," chronologically the second story in *Difficult Women*, opens with an eerie avouchment: "Water and its damage followed Bianca" (Gay 2017, 23). The protagonist Bianca is only a few days old when her mother notices a water stain above her crib (Gay 2017, 25). The inexplicable appearance of this water stain spells doom for baby Bianca and as she gets older, the stain grows and consumes "the entire ceiling in a mural of black mold" (Gay 2017, 25–26). Bianca's fate, it is implied, is tied to the mass of water spreading around her, growing as she grows, consuming everything and anything in its path. Her concerned parents alert a contractor and despite an exhaustive search, the source of the water stain is not found; they decide to replace the ceiling (Gay 2017, 26). To her parents' chagrin, replacing the ceiling does not solve or even curb the problem, and after the third replacement, "her parents gave up. It was their daughter or their sanity, their marriage" (Gay 2017, 26). Bianca's indeterminate abnormality, her difference, and its mysterious origin terrifies her family, so they decide to abandon her in an orphanage (Gay 2017, 26). Adult Bianca, now a career woman, remains hunted by the unbearable weight of water: "Everywhere she looked up . . . Fat droplets of water . . . on her forearm, her neck, her forehead, her lower lip" (Gay, 2017 23).

Bianca's allegorical origin story is laden with consequential connotations. Her unusual condition is distressingly undecipherable, and her parents reject her as a result. Ironically, what leads to her abandonment, an infinite spring of water trapped in the ceiling, is the most vital chemical substance necessary for all known life to function adequately. In other words, water, the source of life, nourishes Bianca while simultaneously alienating her from the people she loves, a contradiction that evokes the symbiosis between tension and affirmative counternarratives. Gay seems to be insinuating here that female-centric narratives are often inherently endowed with a sense of uniqueness and the potential to subvert the formulaic patterns of hegemonic expectations by affirmatively charting their own course. However, society's inability to accept and accommodate the divertive nature of uniqueness stifles these narratives and alienates them from a potentially engaged audience.

In addition to being abandoned by her parents, Bianca is also alienated from the orphanage community. The orphaned children are terrified of her (Gay 2017, 27), and the nuns "tried to love her as one of God's children but failed" (Gay 2017, 27). Priests are later summoned "to examine her, to anoint her with holy water" (Gay 2017, 27), but they too fail, and the religious community begins to suspect she is "the work of the devil" (Gat 2017, 27). In this instance, we see systemic institutions like the church refusing to accommodate or understand Bianca's right to difference and resorting to suppressing her uniqueness with draconian measures like sermons and holy water. Despite the unbearable weight of these challenges, Bianca somehow manages to "to grow up a happy child" (Gay 2017, 27). However, abandonment returns to plague her adult life when her husband Dean divorces her because he could not handle the overwhelming trail of water that followed Bianca everywhere (Gay 2017, 25). Like her parents and the church, Dean rejects her right to difference and once again, Gay underscores the notion that female-centric narratives, from their inception, are regularly deterred by societal forces from unique trajectories and forcibly incorporated into preordained histories. This is an example of the right to difference functioning as the problem of difference. Bianca's unusual condition (her right to difference) results in her alienation (problem of difference), society's inability to comfortably accommodate her singularities.

Water, as I mentioned earlier, is the source of life, an inorganic chemical substance that cannot decompose. Thus, the watery rot that follows Bianca everywhere is not caused by water itself, but by the infrastructures attempting to confine its sprawling spread: the ceilings, drywall, fiberglass panels etc. These infrastructures arguably metaphorize hegemonic paradigms responsible for restraining and subjugating the sprawling and boundary-less ideas and themes of atypical female-centric narratives. Thus, in order to evade the oversight of man-made edifices, narratives like Bianca's must find avenues beyond the restrictive parameters of ceilings and panels. Dean was, at the genesis of their relationship, such an avenue. After their first date, he asks her if they should retire to her home for a drink (Gay 2017, 26). She declines because her place is a "mess" (Gay 2017, 27) and suggests the park instead. Mess here obviously refers to her apartment being in a state of disarray, but it could also hint at the "messiness" of infrastructures, the constricting nature of their established dimensions. Perhaps Bianca's decision to go to the park instead of her apartment is an admission that compassionate relationships can only be fostered in environments not burdened by the fixed proportions of man-made structures.

There is a sense of liberation when they arrive at the park. Bianca slips out of her shoes and runs through a wide field of grass before stopping at a merry-go-round (Gay 2017, 27). Dean mounts the merry-go-round as well, and after kissing her forehead, eyelids, and lips, he marvels "at the dampness of her skin, and licked droplets of water from the hollow of her neck" (Gay 2017, 28). Beyond the judgmental glare of drywall and fiberglass panels, there is no rot in sight, and Dean is allowed to love Bianca and her oddities. He seems genuinely fascinated by the water oozing from her body, and his decision to lick droplets off her neck signals a form of acceptance. Bianca is pleased and as she looks "into his eyes, and her body opened to him completely, she hoped" (Gay 2017, 28). The reader is not explicitly told what Bianca hopes for, but it seems obvious that she is hoping for a companion who, unlike her parents and the church, chooses to understand and accommodate her uniqueness, a companion who endorses and encourages her exploration of an affirmative counternarrative instead of allowing her to be subsumed by master narratives.

Her hope never materializes because the relationship ends in a divorce, but this park episode remains significant because Dean is also portrayed as somewhat of a victim. He is not victimized as severely as Bianca is, but he is also a victim of hegemonic master narratives. When Dean is making love to Bianca in the park, he seems committed to understanding and supporting her. The sprawling green expanse of nature, unresponsive to the intransigent demands of man, appears to be a safe space for both parties. But as domesticated humans, they cannot spend the entirety of their relationship in nature. They must retreat to apartments and offices, churches and gyms, back to spaces under the exacting gaze of ceilings, drywall, and fiberglass panels, spaces that cannot confine the sprawling spread of water and ultimately succumb to rot. Now confined to the fixed parameters of towering infrastructures, Dean feels walled in (Gay 2017, 25). His commitment to Bianca begins to waver, and he is consequently socialized into rejecting her mysterious abnormality. The implication here is that men like Dean are also victims of systemic machinations. Patriarchal systems that rob female-centric narratives of the potential to chart their own course are only successful because they have subjugated and socialized all facets of society, including men, into upholding the value systems of master narratives.

In "The Mark of Cain," chronologically the third story in *Difficult Women*, Gay examines analogous ideas, but this time, she tones down the allegorical elements and shifts her focus to the tactile setting of a broken marriage. Like "Water, All Its Weight," "The Mark of Cain" opens with an eerie avouchment: "My husband is not a kind man and with him, I am not a good person" (Gay 2017, 29). The nameless protagonist is married to Caleb, an abusive alcoholic who owns an architecture firm with his identical twin brother Jacob (Gay 2017, 29–30). Both men were raised by an abusive father who was "shot in the head by a woman" he had assaulted too many times (Gay 2017, 30). However, "with each passing year, the brothers rewrote their past until they had beatified their father's memory," and Caleb's resentment toward his father's muddled legacy is now solely directed at women (Gay 2017, 30–33).

When Caleb overconsumes alcohol, usually wine, he berates his wife and the women in his father's life. In one instance, he returns home late at night "reeking of wine and cigarette smoke" and wakes up his "shivering" wife (Gay 2017, 32). He tells her a disturbing story about a woman who, at his father's request, performed oral sex on him, his father, and Jacob; he calls this woman a whore (Gay 2017, 32–33). "'Don't ever do something like that,'" he warns his wife, grabbing her waist and slapping her face. "'Don't be a fucking whore'" (Gay 2017, 33). Like water in "Water, All its Weight," wine in "The Mark of Cain" is an unbearable weight for the nameless protagonist because it triggers her husband's abusive behavior and symbolizes the toxicity of their marriage.

She is undoubtedly victimized by her toxic union with Caleb, but from the onset of the narrative, we are informed that she is not entirely powerless. As I earlier pointed out, "my husband is not a kind man and with him, I am not a good person" are her first words (Gay 2017, 29). She later confesses that she feels bound to Caleb because she first met him when she was impressionable and inexperienced, and they were both "drunk and numb . . . looking for trouble before it found us. . . . I worry about the day when he leaves me" (Gay 2017, 29). This confession reveals that her fate now feels tied to his, and the dissolution of her marriage would feel like the dissolution of her identity. In other words, she decides to stay with Caleb because she fears being completely alienated from him.

The symbiosis between rupture and tension is visible here. The protagonist is unquestionably at the point of rupture, the third consciousness, because she unambiguously acknowledges the state of tension in her marriage. Her opening declaration can be characterized as an affirmative feeling because it possesses no iota of pretense. She admits to being in an abusive relationship and admits that her fate is tied to the external marginalizing forces of abuse and trauma. Despite this affirmative acknowledgment of tension, she cannot end her tumultuous marriage because her identity is now entangled with Caleb's, and she fears complete alienation from him (Gay 2017, 29). While Bianca in

"Water, All its Weight" endures the unbearable weight of alienation, Caleb's wife endures the unbearable weight of fearing alienation.

Like Gay's essay "What Fullness Is: On Getting Weight Reduction Surgery," the role of trauma takes center stage in "The Mark of Cain." Our lived experiences are repeatedly shaped and sustained by traumas with the will and capacity to color the choices we make and the choices fate makes for us. The nameless protagonist came of age in an abusive relationship with Caleb, so her entire worldview is oriented by the dysfunctional morality of their unhealthy union. This explains why she is nameless; Caleb's world has completely subsumed her identity. Leaving him, in her present state, is not feasible, so she must explore the possibility of a counternarrative that does not require complete separation from Caleb.

Before proceeding, I must identity and clarify a potential misreading of my analysis. I am not implying that liberating a female protagonist from an abusive relationship is a reductive and/or an unrealistic literary trope. I am also not insinuating that severely traumatic experiences like abuse are the most appropriate literary approach to nuancing the female experience. As I will discuss in chapter 4's treatment of Issa Rae's *Insecure*, great writing, even about the most mundane activities like watching television and buying a couch, has the potential to identify and unpack composite perspectives about the female experience. "The Mark of Cain" in no way glamorizes abuse, either as a trope or as an experience. Rather, it explores the psyche of people trapped in toxic unions and how their sense of awareness remains in a bitter tussle with the aftermath of trauma.

Difficult women like Caleb's wife, women whose messy lives expose the complicated realities of human nature and the immense power trauma wields over our destinies, are sparsely represented in the American literary canon. From Ernest Hemingway's *The Old Man and the Sea* to John Updike's *Rabbit, Run* to Raymond Carver's eclectic short stories, literary classics have firmly established the trope of the *difficult* man, the man who is often repressed, volatile, and unlikable but remains profoundly moving because he speaks to the dark recesses of the human mind and confronts the unforgiving uncertainty of fate. Unlike the media realm of edgy filmmaking and subscription television where *difficult* women not only exist but also thrive, scholarship on the American literary canon tends to disregard female equivalents of *difficult* men.

In his seminal 1983 essay "Race and Gender in the Shaping of the American Literary Canon," literary scholar Paul Lauter argues that America's mostly white- and male-dominated literary canon was firmly established in the 1920s and credits recent "movements for change of people of color and of women" as the impetus behind efforts to resurvey entrenched knowledge systems about who belongs to the literary canon and why (435). Not a great deal has changed since Lauter's observations in 1983. Culture writer Doug Barry's bluntly titled 2012 article "The Literary Canon Is Still One Big Sausage Fest" discusses a *Commentary Magazine* list of "the top 25 American writers 'as determined by the amount of scholarship on each' over the past 25 years according to *the MLA International Bibliography*" (2012). Unsurprisingly, there is no woman in the top five and only five of the twenty-five names are women: Toni Morrison (8), Emily Dickinson (9), Willa Cather (13), Edith Wharton (16), and Flannery O'Connor (19) (Barry 2012). The writings of these five women, it is important to point out, are not necessarily centered on the lived experiences of messy and unlikable women.

Once again, I am not insinuating that the messiness of unlikable characters is the aesthetic cornerstone of great literature. I am simply pointing out the insufficient representation of *difficult* women in the American literary canon and, as Barry points out, these five canonized female writers were "already among the most academically investigated in 1987," revealing that the American literary canon's perception of great female writing has remained unchanged for over twenty years (2012). Thus, like the "ME" essays in *Bad Feminist*, Gay's decision to name her short story collection *Difficult Women* is a subversive aesthetic choice that reframes and recenters the moral focal point of female-led texts and, one can also argue, intentionally reimagines the nonthreatening and inoffensive titles of female-authored classics like Louisa May Alcott's *Little Women*.

In *Difficult Women*, we are introduced to women who are emotionally on par with the great male characters of the American literary canon, women who are messy, dynamic, flawed, and, most importantly, honest. Overlooking literature about the unpleasant and difficult dilemmas of the female experience restricts the full scope of the literary experience. Giving these stories avenues of expression, on the other hand, allows readers to have affirmative dialogues and debates about difficult but necessary themes and ideas. With that said, exploring the full depth of the human condition, an intellectual exercise with a propensity toward pretentiousness, is not the sole reason why Gay's litany of messy women deserves a place in the American literary canon. Going back to the most basic reason for literary consumption, Gay's *crazy* and *frigid* women are interesting and fun characters with the potential to thrill and shock readers. These stories will surely make for a more enjoyable read than predictable literary fare.

Returning to "The Mark of Cain," the nameless protagonist's acknowledgment of tension means she is in the moment of rupture, the third consciousness. However, she feels inseparably linked to Caleb's fate and, as a result, she cannot leave him. Thus, as she moves beyond the moment of rupture, she attempts to find and explore a counternarrative that does not require complete alienation from Caleb. In addition to being under Caleb's spell, the nameless protagonist's affinity for Jacob, Caleb's twin brother, is arguably the most important reason why she chooses to stay in the toxic union. Caleb and Jacob "sometimes . . . switch places for days at a time" (Gay 2017, 29). Jacob sometimes makes love to the nameless protagonist, pretending to be Caleb, and Caleb sometimes makes love to Jacob's girlfriend Cassie, pretending to be Jacob. Telling them apart is almost impossible because they have the same body type, mannerisms, and physical features (Gay 2017, 30). They think the nameless protagonist is unaware, but she confesses to indulging their deception (Gay 2017, 29). Once again, highlighted here is the third consciousness of the nameless protagonist. She is fully aware of the shenanigans going on in her marriage and her decision to indulge the deception demonstrates affirmative agency. She is not being forced to take part in these deceptive acts. Rather, she chooses to participate in the brother-swapping game because she has developed feelings for Jacob, the more tender version of Caleb who makes love to her with a "sorrowful kindness" (Gay 2017, 30).

The nameless protagonist's acceptance of this foursome entanglement is an exploration of a counternarrative with the potential to mitigate the impact of Caleb's abuse without completely alienating herself from him. She would actually prefer an increase in the frequency of the swap because that means she gets to spend more time with Jacob, the kinder version of Caleb. The arrangement also keeps Caleb satisfied because he is in love with Jacob's girlfriend Cassie, "who is really Caleb's girlfriend" (Gay 2017, 30).[4] Caleb is more agreeable when he gets what he wants, so spending time with "his girlfriend" Cassie would perhaps reduce the frequency of his abusive outbursts usually targeted at the nameless protagonist. The authorial objective with this foursome entanglement, I must reiterate, is not to moralize about or endorse the extramarital tomfooleries of toxic partnerships. Rather, what is revealed here are the desperate and disparate ways in which traumatized people try to prevent their lives from falling apart. The nameless protagonist is traumatized by abuse, and the twins are clearly traumatized by the deeds of their abusive father. They are all damaged people, and they try to conceal their hurt by resorting to perturbing tactics.

This interpretation is crucial to the theoretical substructure of TCT, particularly what it says about the nature and function of counternarratives. The post-rupture experience is not always "ethical" and by that I mean it does not always ascribe to the ethical characteristics usually associated with traditional narratives about gender liberation/emancipation. In other words, the subject in the post-rupture realm does not always do the "right" thing. I want to move away from the "right" and "wrong" binary because, like the "good" and "bad" binary in *Bad Feminist*, it is reductive and incapable to tracking and tracing the experiential trajectory of counternarratives. Being at the moment of rupture, the third consciousness that acknowledges tension and the meddling presence of external marginalizing forces, does not negate the lingering and lasting impact of trauma. As the subject takes the leap from the point of rupture into the post-rupture realm, trauma still looms large and can potentially contaminate and disorient the process of exploring counternarratives. Similarly put, counternarratives are not always exemplary tales of moral good because the human experience, even after a profound awakening like TCT's third consciousness, does not simply switch from "compromised" to "purified."

As I pointed out earlier, the journey to liberation is a lifelong commitment, but what is novel here is the revelation and emphasis that some women, like the nameless protagonist in "The Mark of Cain," make unethical decisions in the post-rupture realm. Due to a plethora of reasons, which can vary from racial background to mental health to education level to class privilege to geographic location, these women do not possess the buoyancy and assuredness of a persona like Gay's affirmative and learned *bad* feminist. They are still profoundly engulfed in the depths of their tensions and traumas and, as a result, they often struggle to see clearly through the haze. In the post-rupture realm, some individuals are intellectually further along than others but if the third consciousness remains alert and cognizant of the hegemonic meddling by external marginalizing forces, making "questionable" decisions does not send the subject back to a pre-rupture consciousness.

In "The Mark of Cain," the nameless protagonist's third consciousness remains alert throughout the entirety of the narrative. She first acknowledges the tension in her marriage, and, even though Jacob's tenderness comforts her during the brother swap episodes, she admits that the foursome entanglement is not a long-lasting solution because Jacob's first love will always be his brother, Caleb (Gay 2017, 32). Jacob and Caleb are bonded over their family trauma, and they will always be each other's number one priority. This explains why Jacob does not confront his brother about his abusive behavior even though he sympathizes with the nameless protagonist's suffering (Gay 2017, 33). His allegiance is ultimately to Caleb, not the nameless protagonist or Cassie.

The title of the story is a discernible allusion to the biblical story of Cain and Abel, a story about sibling jealousy and Cain's murder of his brother Abel. Once again, we have the "good" versus "bad" framework (good brother versus bad brother), and Gay subverts this dichotomy by making the good brother Abel (Jacob) complicit in the sins of the bad brother Cain (Caleb). The "mark" of Cain is, I argue, a metaphor for the imprint of trauma and how easily one traumatized individual can pass on their trauma to another individual in close proximity, just like a contagious disease. In other words, the people closest to traumatized individuals often suffer the most. The story ends with this grim acknowledgment and, like the counter-actualizing nature of previously discussed affirmations in the post-rupture realm, there is no resolution or optimal harmony. There is, however, a glimmer of hope.

In the final paragraph of the story, the nameless protagonist reveals that she is six months pregnant and at a doctor's appointment with a moody and somewhat indifferent Caleb (Gay 2017, 34). The doctor moves the sonogram across her belly, and "the room is silent but for the identical flutter of two heartbeats" (Gay 2017, 34). She is going to have twins, and the reader is left to speculate about her future. Considering the theme of generational trauma, one cannot help but wonder if the unsuspecting unborn twins will inherit the "mark" of Cain like Jacob and Caleb. Will they grow up consumed by the trauma of the "mark" and later pass it on to other unsuspecting individuals in close proximity? Perhaps the identical flutters of two heartbeats represent the nameless protagonist's most affirmative moment yet in the post-rupture realm. Perhaps she realizes her present predicament is unsuitable for raising children and opts for abortion or adoption. Perhaps she senses an opportunity to quarantine, stop the plague of Cain in its tracks, or at least slow it down, and salvage the future of her unborn children by leaving her toxic relationship with Caleb. Like TCT's realms of rupture where there is a symbiotic relationship between affirmations and tensions, the reader is affirmed by "the identical flutter of two heartbeats" (Gay 2017, 34) but remains unsettled by the unresolved tensions and traumas between the nameless protagonist and Caleb.

I cannot end this section without addressing the curious absence/ seeming minimization of race. At first glance, this might seem trivial, but there is a great deal to unpack here. In "Water, All its Weight," Bianca's whiteness is mentioned only once (Gay 2017, 24), the nameless protagonist in "The Mark of Cain" is not given a race, and the litany of messy women are defined by personality adjectives (*crazy, loose, frigid* etc.) and not by their racial backgrounds. Protagonists in Black-authored texts are seldom white or without a race. Writers generally write about what they know best, so it is logical to expect stories to mirror the racial backgrounds and experiences of their authors. In addition, the absence of adequate Black representation in the literary sphere means that Black authors are usually eager and motivated to tell stories about the lived experiences of their communities. As Black science fiction, horror, and fantasy writer Tananarive Due states, "I believe black characters in fiction are still revolutionary, given our long history of erasure" (Lewis-Giggetts 2015). There are however more sinister forces at work here. Black writers tend to feel pressured into writing about race because "it's commonly believed that 'good' writing by Black authors is birthed from oppression, and marginalization is viewed as a key marker for Black literature. This implies a direct link between the authenticity of literature and the sociological and political perspectives of African Americans" (Lewis-Giggetts 2015).

Simply stated, this perspective argues that the parameters of Black art cannot transcend racial marginalization.

White writers, on the other hand, are not defined by racial paradigms. As author and creative writing lecturer David Mura argues, there is a "literary rule that white writers seldom consciously consider: if the character is white, the race of the character does not need to be mentioned or indicated in any direct way. The absence of a racial marker means that the character is by default white. The exception to the rule is always the character of color" (2018, 24). Gay's decision to minimize race in *Difficult Women* is not an endorsement of this literary rule. Rather, she is subverting it. Coming off two critically acclaimed books about the intersectional and transnational layers of the Black female experience (*Bad Feminist* and *An Untamed State*), it is almost impossible to read *Difficult Women* without pondering about race, even when it is absent. When the character's race is not mentioned, one wonders if the character is white by default or if Gay, a revered Black feminist author, is forcing her audience to confront the hegemonic notion that the absence of race implies whiteness. Considering the subversive nature of *Difficult Women*, the latter is a more convincing scenario. Gay's audience does not encounter rigid racial markers in *Difficult Women* and because they are most likely acquainted with the racialized and Black feminist themes of her earlier works, they are predisposed to believing that these *crazy*, *frigid*, and *dead* women can be anybody and everybody, Black, white, and everything else in between. This notion destabilizes the "white is default" literary rule and demonstrates how Gay paradoxically subverts racial hierarchies in the literary arena by minimizing race.

With that said, the racial backgrounds of some characters are specified in the text. As previously stated, Bianca in "Water, All Its Weight" is a white woman. However, the social alienation she endures due to patriarchal hegemony echoes the experiences of characters of color in *Difficult Women* like Sarah in "La Negra Blanca." Gay therefore seems interested in pointing out a cross-racial cross-cultural institutional problem about how we conceive, comprehend, and consume the female experience. In other words, *difficult* women across racial and cultural lines are universally deprived of opportunities to acknowledge and affirm the state of tension in their messy lives, opportunities with the potential to understand the function and origins of their traumas. Universality in this instance does not denote sameness of experiences. Instead, it echoes what literary scholar Derek Attridge calls "idioculture."

An individual's understanding of the world, Attridge argues, is "mediated by a changing array of interlocking, overlapping, and often contradictory cultural systems absorbed in the course of his or her previous experiences" (2004, 21). These contradictory cultural systems can be described as "a complex matrix of habits, cognitive models . . . expectations, prejudices and preferences that operate intellectually, emotionally, and physically to produce a sense of at least continuity, coherence, and significance out of the manifold events of human living" (Attridge 2004, 21). Idioculture therefore refers to the embodiment of a wide array of "cultural norms and modes of behavior" in one individual (Attridge 2004, 21).

In Gay's short stories, *messy* women are universally marginalized by the hegemonic values of patriarchy. The manifestation of this marginalization, however, varies from character to character. As Attridge's conceptualization of idioculture stipulates, each individual embodies a complex maze of intersecting and contradictory values and preferences, and the cultural context of their specific realities affects the nature and impact of their lived experiences. This is not to say that the similarities of gender- and race-based group experiences do not exist. Attridge acknowledges shared group experiences when he describes idioculture as "interlocking" and "overlapping" (2004, 21). However, every individual's worldview is oriented by a uniquely circumstantial chain of events that can never be *exactly* experienced. Simply put, while hegemonic oppression is a universal experience, the manifestation of hegemonic oppression is an individualized experience that reflects the uniquely complex and contradictory cultural norms of the subject. Thus, the concept of idioculture supports and complements the TCT framework by emphasizing the distinctive dynamism of experiences at and beyond the point of rupture, experiences that broadly overlap but remain singularly experienced because the emotional entirety of a human life, from birth to death, is a unique orientation that can never be *exactly* replicated.

Gay illustrates this argument in *Difficult Women* by exploring the dynamic and different ways in which her messy characters use what Attridge calls a complex matrix of cognitive models and beliefs to establish a sense of coherence and continuity. In "The Mark of Cain," for example, trauma orients the nameless protagonist's worldview because she was groomed into adulthood by her abusive relationship with Caleb. This explains why even though she is acutely aware of the toxic state of her marriage, she remains committed to the union and uses her access to Jacob, a kinder version of her husband, as a coping mechanism. Her modes of behavior, the way she reacts to and copes with patriarchal abuse, are thus self-contradictory and fundamentally opposed to the behavioral practices of women operating with a different set of cognitive models. In the final section of this chapter, I will argue that the minimization of rigid racial markers in *Difficult Women* is not meant to negate the significance of race. Rather, the short story collection is an acknowledgment of difference, both within and beyond color lines, an affirmative reminder that the female experience is a contradictory symbiosis of intersections and singularities.

CONFIGURING CONTRADICTIONS

Unlike most stories in *Difficult Women*, the theme of race takes center stage in "La Negra Blanca." When the protagonist Sarah seeks employment at a strip club, she is given the name "Sierra" by the establishment's manager (Gay 2017, 61). Contrary to what this action implies, Sarah is not some lost girl who wandered into a strip club and was given a new identity by a male manager. Like the nameless protagonist in "The Mark of Cain," she is an active agent, acutely aware of her current predicament. Born and raised in Baltimore, Maryland, a predominantly Black city rife with systemic problems such as failed political leadership, violent crime, poor education, and dilapidated infrastructure (Shelden et al. 2016, 448), Sarah is looking for a way out, and the strip club presents her with a promising opportunity. To fulfill her dream of working for the CIA, she attends John Hopkins University. However, her financial aid only covers a small fraction of her tuition fees (Gay 2017, 62). Sarah must pay the rest out of pocket, in addition to her living expenses, and for an impoverished young woman from Baltimore with no social capital, stripping, unlike dead-end minimum wage jobs, offers her a viable opportunity to meet her financial obligations (Gay 2017, 62).

Sarah's ability in the strip club to attract crowds and cash is largely due to her racial ambiguity. Born to a white father and Black mother, she can pass for white with her blond hair and green-colored eyes (Gay 2017, 62). She has, however, what is colloquially referred to as a "juicy ass." On her first day at the job, Sarah's colleague instructs her to "dance to black girl booty-shaking music because guys love to see white girls with juicy asses" (Gay 2017, 64). What is implied here is that performing a stereotypical imaginary of Black femininity is more profitable in the strip club if the performer is white. The male consumers get the best of both worlds in one package: the "immaculate" desirability of whiteness and exotic "savagery" of Blackness.

The lasting fetishization of the Black female body in Western art and culture reveals an almost unholy appetite for the presumed sexual savagery of Black female femininity (Nelson 2010, 119–20). Thus, in spaces like strip clubs, where the male gaze mostly controls, commodifies and consumes female bodies, there is a preference for the more hypersexualized brand of femininity usually associated with Black women (Hobson 2012, 79). However, qualitative studies by scholars like African American feminist Siobhan Brooks insinuate that this preference is seemingly consumed with less guilt if packaged in a *whiter* body. Brooks's twelve interviews with Latina and Black women working in the exotic dance industry in New York City and Oakland, California, reveal that within the "racialized and hypersexualized" milieu of strip clubs, lighter-skinned dancers of color invariably receive more attention from men than their darker-skinned counterparts (2010, 74–75). Sarah accesses a similar color privilege in the strip club when she passes for white and performs as Black, an act with several consequential implications.

First, we have the apparent contradiction of Sarah's racial identity. She is a biracial woman who can pass for white but chooses to perform "blackness" in the strip club. As I previously hinted at, Sarah is past the moment of rupture. Her awareness of the "Sierra" persona is a third consciousness because she understands the functionality of the male gaze in the strip club and the potential to exploit the lustful preferences of this gaze for her own benefit. Before proceeding, it is important to underline that "La Negra Blanca" does not characterize Sarah as a more "respectable" stripper because unlike most in the profession, she is a gifted student with long-term goals of obtaining a college education and working for the CIA. What Gay emphasizes in this short story is the agency Sarah accrues by shrewdly manipulating the racial fantasies of the male gaze. Sarah's story is ultimately not a moral indictment of women who decide to earn a living by sliding down stripper poles. Rather, it is an honest human exploration of the difficult decisions we make when embroiled in desperate situations.

Sarah is not portrayed in "La Negra Blanca" as someone who is ashamed of her Black identity. She proudly displays a picture of her Black mother in her apartment and seems somewhat connected to her Black heritage (Gay 2017, 70). However, she yearns for a better future and as a young biracial woman on the crime-ridden streets of Baltimore with no money, no connections and very little prospects, opportunities to supplement her tuition costs and living expenses are few and far between. Thus, her decision to racially code-switch (passing for white, performing as Black) in the strip club and earn a significant sum of money (money used to finance her educational pursuits) is, within the context of her reality, an affirmative counternarrative.

The phenomenon of passing gained prominence in America during the era of chattel slavery when light-skinned slaves of African origin would "pass" for white in order to escape bondage and servitude in the South (Ginsberg 1996, 1–3). This visual ability to subvert the legitimacy of legal codes, which classified the enslaved Black population as property and, for the most part, recognized the rights and liberties of white Americans, was a terrifying act of so-called deceit because it destabilized the nation's imaginary of whiteness as a racially pure heritage, unpolluted and untouched by the stain of African blood (Ginsberg 1996, 3). But the concept of passing is a lot more complex than simply passing for white. There are instances in American history of women passing as men either due to a transgender identity (Ginsberg 1996, 2) or to gain access to career opportunities not available to women (Ginsberg 1996, 3). As race and gender studies scholar Elaine K. Ginsberg points out "both the process and discourse of passing interrogate the ontology of identity categories and their construction . . . passing challenges a number of problematic and even antithetical assumptions about identities" (1996, 4).

These challenges posed by the act of passing are imbued in Sarah's Sierra persona. She uses her white skin to access privileges unavailable to dark-skinned Black Americans, a decision that echoes the consumptive performativity of Blackness by white or *whiter* bodies, an enduringly problematic trend in American culture that goes as far back as the popularization of minstrelsy (white performers wearing "blackface") in the nineteenth century. Contemporary popular culture commentary is also rife with critiques about white celebrity personas like the Kardashians who are able to wear and commercialize traditionally Black hairstyles (cornrows, box braids etc.) while Black women face discrimination in schools and in the workplace for wearing the same hairstyles (Lawton 2018). The implication here is that society is generally more accepting of certain signifiers of Black culture if these signifiers are being performed by white bodies. While these critiques are unquestionably valid, Sarah's relationship with Blackness is more nuanced.

First, she has a Black mother, so she has an authentic connection to Black culture. Her visual whiteness exposes the arbitrariness of racial categories because from a genetic standpoint, she is just as Black as darker-skinned biracial Americans with Black and white parents. Second, the social and economic realities in Baltimore are dire and for a brilliant student like Sarah, a major in international studies and Romance languages (Gay 2017, 62), desperately seeking an exit strategy from economic hopelessness, she cannot often afford the luxury of a moral high ground. While an outsider spectator will rightly perceive racial code-switching for cash as unethical and even immoral, for a Baltimore resident, knee-deep in the systemic malaise of urbanized classism, racism, and sexism, the contradictions of Sarah's performativity might be construed as a valiant act of survival. Rather than toiling away at a dead-end minimum wage job incapable of covering her tuition and living expenses, she secures financial backing for her academic career by hoodwinking hegemonic racial hierarchies and sexist fantasies.

This comes at a cost as she later becomes a victim of sexual assault, but Gay smartly does not use her assault to sermonize about the stripping profession's shortcomings. When Alvarez, a burgeoning love interest, tries to persuade Sarah to report the incident to the police, her response is, "Occupational hazard . . . I'm too tired" (Gay 2017, 73). Highlighted here is the symbiosis of tension and affirmations. The strip club provides Sarah with the means to pay for her college education and evade institutional destitution. The same strip club, however, fosters a culture of sexual violence, and a wealthy client in due course assaults Sarah. The reader is thus left to ponder about Sarah's state of mind and what we would do in her situation. If the strip club is seemingly the most immediate and viable way out of economic hopelessness and the array of social problems that come with systemic poverty, can we truly berate Sarah for refusing to sever ties with her Sierra persona even after enduring the violence of sexual assault? If our lives were oriented by a similar idioculture, would we act similarly or differently? These are the psychologically challenging and unresolved questions Gay poses to her readers.

The concept of idioculture, I must restate here for clarification purposes, is not merely an acknowledgment of the contradictory and complex cognitive models and habits a single individual possesses. Rather, idioculture emphasizes how "an individual's grasp on the world is mediated" by these contradictory and complex cognitive models and habits (Attridge 2004, 21). Hence, "although one is likely to share much of one's idioculture with other groups (one's neighbors, one's family, one's age peers, those of the same gender, race, class, and so on), it is always a unique configuration" (Attridge 2004, 22). Sarah's race-bending counternarrative (passing for white, performing as Black) is therefore a contradictory cognitive model oriented by the unique configuration of her idioculture as an impoverished biracial stripper in Baltimore whose efficiency at passing for white offers her a uniquely rare financial opportunity. Her decisions are of course problematic, but they also speak to the socioeconomic possibilities and limitations of everyday life in Baltimore. Instead of moralizing about Sarah's actions, Gay unmasks the naked realities of her world, her idioculture, what Attridge describes as the "contradictory cultural systems absorbed in . . . her . . . experience" (2004, 21). There is no grand moral lesson here. Gay's intention is merely to show us how *difficult* women like Sarah live, the contradictory configurations of their counternarratives, the minuscule details of their everyday realities, and the impossible cards they have been dealt.

Similar contradictions are echoed in stories like "In the Event of My Father's Death" and "Open Marriage" where race is minimized or absent. "When I was a girl, my father once told me that women weren't good for much" reads the opening lines of "In the Event of my Father's Death" (Gay 2017, 125). Once again, we are reminded of the universal underestimation and marginalization of women but as idioculture posits, the individual experience of underestimation and marginalization is "always a unique configuration" (Attridge 2004, 21). The protagonist Stephanie recalls her father cautioning her as young girl not to become like her mother (Gay 2017, 125). "My father didn't love my mother. I don't even think he loved me," Stephanie continues. "But he did love making us miserable by refusing to leave" (Gay 2017, 125). This awareness of unrequited affection (between father and mother and father and daughter) reveals that in the context of family relations, the protagonist's moment of rupture, her third consciousness, developed at a very young age, and she has, ever since, struggled to develop and navigate a post-rupture relationship with her disinterested father.

The source of her father's discontent is never explicitly stated, but it is clear that he is damaged man. After an intense argument with his wife, for example, he drags a young Stephanie out of the house, drives to a mountain overlook, and gets drunk on Maker's Mark while Stephanie bites her fingernails in the back seat (Gay 2017, 125). He has also been cheating on his wife for years with a younger woman named Teresa. The relationship seemingly works because Teresa does not expect much from him; she is the type of woman who does not expect much from people (Gay 2017, 126). Although this character trait might imply passiveness, I argue that it is actually affirmative. Teresa has no delusions about the nature of their relationship. She knows he is destructive, and she knows he is never going to leave his wife; however, she is content with only having him for a few hours every week and sending him back to his damaged home (Gay 2017, 126–27). She genuinely loves Stephanie's father, but she seems to know that the version of him she gets every Saturday, the version of him smiling and stretching on the couch after long hours of passionate lovemaking, does not exist outside of that moment in time (Gay 2017, 126–27). In other words, Teresa's acute self-awareness is an alert third consciousness and her Saturday "arrangement" with Stephanie's father is the exploration of a romantic, albeit questionable, counternarrative.

As I previously stressed, counternarratives are not always bastions of decency and goodness. Teresa's affair with a married man is an unethical practice. With that said, she is also a broken woman, living in a trailer by herself, smoking shiny cigarettes and caking her face with too much makeup (Gay 2017, 126). We do not know her backstory but based on her somewhat pessimistic take on life (not expecting much from anyone) and the dehumanizing stereotypes associated with trailer dwellers (poverty, abuse, abandonment etc.), one can persuasively argue that Teresa has endured (and still endures) traumatic experiences. Thus, choosing to consensually indulge, once per week, in a romantic engagement that brings her great joy is, in the context of her idioculture, an affirmative experience and a counternarrative that offers her some semblance of autonomy beyond the point of rupture. In other words, affirmations are not an endorsement of unethical behavior. Rather, they are moments of, attempts at, engaging with the healing process in the post-rupture realm. This engagement is not always successful and depending on the idioculture of the subject, it is oriented by traumas and tensions of varying magnitudes. What is ultimately of utmost importance to the TCT framework is *the attempt* and what is revealed by this attempt about the complex dimensions of the subject's lived experience.

At first glance, Stephanie's relationship with Teresa seems testy. During her father's Saturday visits to Teresa's trailer, young Stephanie was always used as an alibi: "Every Saturday, my dad told my mom we were going fishing" (Gay 2017, 126). Once there, Stephanie is generally repulsed by Teresa's "shitty trailer" and the high-pitched laugh she lets out while engaging in "vulgar" sex with the philandering husband (Gay 2017, 126–27). But there are traces of tenderness between the two. "She called me Steph," Stephanie protests. "No matter how many times I corrected her and said, "'My name is Stephanie'" (Gay 2017, 126). Teresa tries to establish a friendly, and even affectionate, relationship with Stephanie, but she is always met with resistance. Stephanie is still not sure what to make of Teresa. The former finds the latter repulsive but also strangely alluring. When Stephanie and her father drive up to the trailer, for example, Teresa has a habit of standing in the doorway with a silky robe that falls open, revealing lacy panties (Gay 2017, 126). Stephanie would sneak in a look and then acknowledge Teresa's strange and enigmatic beauty, the kind of "hardened" beauty only women like Teresa possessed (Gay 2017, 126).

Years later, Stephanie's father dies after driving off a bridge, and Teresa is an emotional wreck at the funeral (Gay 2017, 128). "I guess she loved him," Stephanie admits to herself. "It was nice that someone did" (Gay 2017, 128). A week after the funeral, Stephanie, now an older teenager and almost ready for college, visits Teresa (Gay 2017, 128). "'He [Stephanie's father] loved spending Saturdays with you'" Teresa confides in Stephanie, and she is, at first, met with familiar resistance when Stephanie rejects this claim (Gay 2017, 128). Teresa tries again by moving her fingers over Stephanie's knuckles (Gay 2017, 128). Stephanie responds by squeezing Teresa's hand "gently" because, in that moment, she desired "something soft" (Gay 2017, 128). And then the shockingly unexpected happens. Teresa "stood, let her silk robe fall to the floor, and started walking into her bedroom" (Gay 2017, 128). She turns and looks at Stephanie "over her shoulder" and the story ends with the daughter of her dead lover standing up (Gay 2017, 128).

This utterly bizarre but strangely effective scene is fraught with contradictions. For most of the story, Teresa repulsed Stephanie. Why then does she decide to visit Teresa after the funeral? Why does she want Teresa to feel something soft? Most importantly, why is she possibly following a half-naked Teresa into the bedroom, just like her father did? "In the Event of My Father's Death" is a story about a young woman's inability to understand why her father does not love her. From a young age, Stephanie's third consciousness has struggled to make sense of her father's disdain for his family (Gay 2017, 125). This explains why she was repulsed by, and even envious of, Teresa, the trailer-dwelling woman who was somehow able to develop genuine feelings for her father and make him smile. Embodied in Teresa, Stephanie hopes, is a key that unlocks the mysteries of her dead father. Perhaps by following Teresa into the bedroom, she is intentionally tracing her father's footsteps, desperately hoping to discover the secret to loving him. Her decision to possibly engage in a sexual relationship with Teresa, as perverse as it sounds, is an exploratory counternarrative that, within the idioculture of a traumatized child craving a destructive parent's attention and approval, can be characterized as affirmative. The trauma of feeling rejected by her father orients Stephanie's entire life and in a grieving Teresa, the only woman who was able to exchange genuine affection with him, she sees the embodiment of whatever little goodness her father possessed. She wants a tangible experience with this goodness and by following Teresa into the bedroom, just like her father did, perhaps she is hoping to finally feel an iota, just a smidgen, of the love she always wanted from her father.

In "Open Marriage," a story completely devoid of race, the reader encounters another subversive contradiction. In a world where women are frequently robbed of agency, the wife in "Open Marriage" opts for a counternarrative that emotionally dominates, and even torments, her passive husband. Her husband was a virgin when they married, she states almost mockingly, revealing that he had little to no experience with women prior to their marriage (Gay 2017, 159). She also completely dominates him during sex, often leaving him tired and flummoxed: "I rock his world . . . we both know it . . . He just lies there, trying to catch his breath, muttering, *goddamn*" (Gay 2017, 160). When they argue, she is cordial but condescending, treating him like an infant incapable of functioning without adult supervision (Gay 2017, 159–60).

The wife is shrewdly aware of the unusual nature of the power dynamics in her marriage, and this explains why she constantly brags, albeit subtly, about her superior status in the union. As perverse as this also sounds, her domination of her husband is an affirmative experience because it subverts traditional power structures and empowers her sense of agency. As discussed in chapter 1, Freire's *Pedagogy of the Oppressed* articulates the psychology of the oppressed becoming the oppressor. After the awareness of external marginalizing forces and the acknowledgment of tension, the third consciousness birthed in the moment of rupture produces an alternate self capable of exploring the possibilities of counternarratives in the post-rupture realm. If the alternate self psychologically bonded with the morality of the pre-rupture realm, it could seek to reconfigure and reimagine its counternarratives as repressively dominant master narratives. The subversion of power roles in this relationship is a clear illustration of the pedagogy of the oppressed.

From an ethical perspective, equity is the ideal goal of human relationships. But human beings, both men and women, are seldom ethical due to our lingering traumas and the ambiguous morality of the world we inhabit. And from the vantage point of a lived experience steeped in patriarchal values, an experience in which women are deprived of active agency and classified as second-class citizens, one understands why the wife's position as the head of the household can feel affirmative and empowering. This feeling is of course a problematic coping mechanism in the post-rupture realm because it seeks empowerment at the detriment of others. But as I mentioned earlier, policing ethical behavior is not the primary orientation of the TCT framework. TCT's principal focus is to work through the complex and contradictory ways in which *difficult* women like Gay's litany of messy and mesmerizing characters attempt to heal and possibly thrive in the post-rupture realm.

Returning to "Open Marriage," the husband, aware of his inexperience and the power his wife wields over him, suggests that they "stay together but see other people" (Gay 2017, 159). He is not unhappy, he claims; he is just intrigued (Gay 2017, 159). His wife does not seem entirely convinced, and neither is the reader. His desire for an open marriage, I argue, is clearly an attempt to negotiate the balance of power in his marriage. Bringing other women into the marriage, he hopes, will loosen his wife's grip on him and perhaps expose him to intimate experiences with the opposite sex outside the realm of his wife's experienced gaze. There is also the implication here that he feels somewhat emasculated by the emotional maturity of his wife and her ability to dominate him during sex. In crude terms, he is being "fucked" by his wife and not the other way around. If this is the case then he ascribes to a patriarchal hierarchy that places the husband above the wife, a value system that is the antithesis of equity. And if the husband represents the antithesis of equity, the wife relinquishing her "male" role will only lead to her subjugation. In the idioculture of this marriage, you are either at the top or at the bottom, so the wife's ability to wrestle her way to the top can be described as affirmative victory over hegemonic patriarchy.

But how long will she stay at the top? It is unclear. Although she is not entirely persuaded by her husband's reason for desiring an open marriage, she is unfazed by his request, mostly because she believes he is incapable of successfully pursuing other women (Gay 2017, 160). Perhaps her nonchalance is a miscalculation. Perhaps he might surprise her and, after dominating a group of women, transform into a man with the will to knock her off the top position. The top-bottom binary (fuck or get fucked) echoes the rigid paradigmatic structures of master narratives. As I previously noted, the wife's ability to claim the dominant position in the marriage is a metaphorical representation of the pedagogy of the oppressed. As I also previously noted, the top-bottom binary in her marriage means if she relinquishes the top role, she automatically becomes the bottom, the "weaker" partner. Thus, there is a larger conversation to be had here about societal perceptions of gender and sex roles. Both the husband and the wife in "Open Marriage" are guilty of ascribing hegemonic power to the dominant sexual partner. The wife's overconfidence is rooted in her sexual prowess and her ability to "rock" her husband's world, leaving him gasping for air. The husband's lack of confidence, on the other hand, is rooted in his role as the passive partner during the sex. Passiveness in sex is typically associated with women, the "weaker" sex, so his inability to dominate his wife in the bedroom arguably leaves him feeling emasculated.

For fairness' sake, I should point out that the wife never comes across as purposely malicious. She does tease her husband and subtly taunt him, a natural practice in most human relationships, but we are never made to think that her intentions are malicious. Her third consciousness seems to be reveling in the fact that it has found a way to occupy the traditional male position in her marriage, reversing gender roles and subverting established power structures in the process. With that said, although malice does not seem to primarily motivate her intentions, her desire to stay at the top, without at least addressing or unpacking the problematic functionality of the top-bottom binary, reenacts the pre-rupture power structures of master narratives. I understand the hesitation of relinquishing power. Because her husband ascribes to the patriarchal hegemony of master narratives, relinquishing the top position would automatically make her the subjugated bottom, the receiver, the weaker partner "getting fucked." However, instead of reinforcing the prejudices of master narratives by, for example, smugly stating that she was the first woman to "fuck" her husband, she should perhaps allow her subjectivity to unfold by problematizing the patriarchal orientation of rigid sex roles.

This would be the ideal course of action but as I have repeatedly stressed, our traumas and tensions complicate and confuse our decisions and the decisions fate makes for us. This is the reality of the human experience and in *Difficult Women*, Gay does a phenomenal job at nuancing the contradictions of our decision-making processes even after grand episodes of epiphany like the third consciousness in the moment of rupture. There is no obvious rhyme or reason when it comes to configuring the contradictory counternarratives of *difficult* women like the nameless protagonist, Sarah, Teresa, and the wife. These counternarratives are affirmative but they are also unpredictable and messy, and the nature and magnitude of their functionality often depends on the unique idioculture of the subject, a singular worldview oriented by the enduring impact of tension and the ever-present threat of master narratives seeking to reestablish their hegemony in the post-rupture realm.

The diversity and depth of Gay's *difficult* women reveal that the exploration of counternarratives in the post-rupture realm is an exploration of new possibilities with the potential to access other new kinds of realms and realities. Thus, the post-rupture realm is a counter-actualizing opening to otherness, an experiential space with fluid subjectivities that infinitely echo and emphasize a subject's right to difference. If no two humans experience the world *exactly* the same then moments of singularity, moments not attached to structural paradigms of shared values and practices, deserve an affirmative space to mutate, evolve and explore the possibility of new meanings in new worlds. This reading echoes, almost verbatim, the counter-actualizing paradigms of Deleuzian philosophy. The Deleuzian fold is a never-ending process of achieving affirmation without self-actualization and like TCT, it is a philosophical modus operandi that celebrates "the right to difference, variation and metamorphosis" (Deleuze 1988, 106)

The Deleuzian fold is also an individualized activity that mostly engages with the collective sphere because it seeks to resist the marginalizing tendencies of external factors by alerting an inward resistance capable of sustaining the infinite process of self-renewal and self-knowledge (Deleuze 1988, 97). In other words, folding is inherently skeptical of the collective sphere because group identities tend to be static and naturally resist the notion of an infinite right to difference. Idioculture is also somewhat skeptical of collective identities. Although it acknowledges the legitimacy of interlocked human experiences, its philosophical priority is the existential affirmation of singularities (Attridge 2004, 22). This is where TCT problematizes the functionality of idioculture and makes a dramatic departure from Deleuzian philosophy. Unlike these concepts, TCT acknowledges and, in some cases, prioritizes the usefulness of collective identities over individualized experiences.

When discussing the lived experiences of minority and systemically subjugated groups, for example, the historical relevance of collective identities (in both the past and present) cannot be minimized or denied. Shared histories of oppression have a tendency to mandate certain codes of behavior, which function as a coping mechanism against external marginalizing forces. In other words, the shared values and camaraderie of a specific cultural group can function as a source of social support for its community members and consequently provide durable protection against systemic institutions of oppression. However, these same shared histories and values, reflected in the generality of racial and ethnic markers, also tend to resist the nonconforming and unresolved affirmations of individualized experiences within the cultural group. Thus, some explorations in the post-rupture must navigate the tricky balance of legitimizing an inherently affirmative right to difference while acknowledging the necessity of collective identities born out of shared histories. Gay nods to a similar navigation in *Bad Feminist* (acknowledging the necessity of a communal feminist fellowship while stressing the unique orientation of her feminist identity) but mainly chooses to unpack the ramifications of the right to difference and the problem of difference. As a second-generation immigrant, she is often culturally disconnected from certain ethnically specific nonimmigrant Black American experiences. This is evident when she confesses, as an adult, to lacking a profound awareness of the true extent of institutional discrimination in the American education system (Gay 2014, 8), and when she engages with hip-hop discourse without contextualizing the genre's historic significance and function within the nonimmigrant African American community (Gay 2014, 188). Gay's aesthetic process of asserting moments of singularity is therefore unrestrained, for the most part, by the hegemonic mandates and expectations of shared nonimmigrant African American values. In chapter 3's discussion of Beyoncé's *Lemonade*, the full weight of the shared nonimmigrant African American experience is addressed, and I use the TCT framework to nuance the tricky balance of legitimizing an affirmative right to difference while acknowledging the necessity of shared values.

NOTES

1. In 2016, Gay was one of the writers of *World of Wakanda*, a spin-off from Marvel Comics' *Black Panther*.

2. Affirmative action refers to American governmental policies that attempt to bridge systemic inequalities by providing socioeconomic opportunities to historically marginalized groups.

3. The most likely implication here is that she was sexually assaulted.

4. The story implies that Cassie is unaware of this deception. If she is unaware, Caleb is having sexual intercourse with her against her will. This is categorically rape.

Chapter Three

Popular Music Culture
Beyoncé's Lemonade

EVOLUTION

There has been a tremendous amount of research, from books to scholarly articles to think pieces, on the subversive triumphs and shortcomings of Beyoncé's visual album *Lemonade*. Works like Adrienne Trier-Bieniek's *The Beyoncé Effect: Essays on Sexuality, Race and Feminism* (2016) have unpacked, with great depth, the racial, political, and economic tensions embedded in *Lemonade*'s Black feminist identity. And in the spiritual essays of Kinitra D. Brooks's and Kameelah L. Martin's *The Lemonade Reader*, the relationship between *Lemonade*'s Christian orientation and indigenous African spiritual influences is largely presented as affirmatively noncontradictory. What is often missing from academic investigations of *Lemonade*, I argue, is an acknowledgment of its subversive entanglement with the aftermath of affirmative rupture, a sense of agency that nods to but resists a comfortable existence within the epistemological paradigms of ideologies and concepts like community, Christianity, feminism, and traditionalism. The most pivotal moments in *Lemonade* are oriented by unresolved discomforts that reside in the undetermined space between affirmative singularities and collective shared values. The discomfort of this space, a symbiosis that echoes the uneasy relationship between affirmation and actualization, is what I am arguing has been not sufficiently unpacked by existing scholarship. In other words, discourse in Beyoncé studies is usually about the tensions triggered by her adopted identities (feminist, Christian, indigenous African spiritualist etc.), but very little has been said about how Beyoncé, the artist, is intentionally creating a sense of aesthetic discomfort by simultaneously embracing and rejecting the categorizations of her adopted identities.

Lemonade largely focuses on the contradictory function of community as both the individual's ally and aggressor. By problematizing community's paradoxical role, TCT is a relevant framework for reading the visual album because it uniquely addresses how Beyoncé's unresolved religious and feminist identities attempt to find a compromise between individual affirmations and collective shared histories. Because *Lemonade*'s unfolding narrative is visually presented as a theatrical performance, my discussion of the visual album is divided into Acts. Act 1 focuses on how Beyoncé is concurrently marginalized and affirmed by community, act 2 on her efforts to challenge community's gatekeepers, and act 3 on how she attempts to negotiate a compromise between the individual's right to difference and community's preference for conformity. In all three acts, community is partly conceptualized as an affirmative life force, a conceptualization that inspires my TCT framework to rethink its earlier representation of hegemonic forces in the external world as mostly marginalizing agents. But before my analysis of *Lemonade*, a brief overview of Beyoncé's discography and artistic evolution is necessary for contextualization purposes.

Born in Texas, on September 4th 1981, Beyoncé Giselle Knowles-Carter rose to prominence as the lead singer of the successful all-girls group Destiny's Child. She later embarked on a solo career and cemented her status as a pop icon with a string of chart-topping songs that became part of the cultural zeitgeist, including "Crazy in Love," "Baby Boy," "Single Ladies," and "Halo." Beyoncé's triumph as an African American woman dominating mainstream American music is described in the music industry as "crossover success" (Cochrane 2019). Mainstream/crossover success in the context of the music industry refers to being a top-selling popular artist (top *Billboard* singles and albums, top-grossing tours, global brand endorsements and visibility etc.), an achievement that has historically eluded Black musicians. Because the American music industry, at its inception and beyond, was dominated by white artists and white-owned record companies, African American musicians often endure more obstacles in their musical journey to mainstream success. Despite these systemic hurdles, Black music has always influenced and been a part of American popular music. However, due to institutionalized racist practices in the music industry, Black artists have not always reaped the benefits of their contributions to the development and popularity of American music. In the late 1950s for example, a period literary critic Arnold Rampersad describes as the beginning of "the greatest revolution in the history of American popular music" (2001, 266), white performers such as Elvis Presley, Pat Boone, and Jerry Lee Lewis enthralled American audiences with their covers of songs by Black artists (Rampersad 2001, 266). While these white performers crossed over to mainstream success and "revolutionized" the American music scene, the Black artists whose songs made this crossover possible were poorly paid and promoted by their publishers and record companies. This led to Harlem Renaissance poet Langston Hughes bemoaning in a poem, "You've taken my blues and gone" (Rampersad 2001, 266).

The meteoric popularity of hip-hop in recent times has, to an extent, evened the playing field and arguably made the musical journey to mainstream success a less arduous process for Black artists in the hip-hop genre. However, within the genres of R&B and dance pop, the attainment of mainstream success remains a rare feat for African American women. Beyoncé is arguably the only African American R&B and dance pop female artist of her generation who has not only sold millions of records but has also dominated the cultural zeitgeist with both a string of critically acclaimed albums and top-grossing tours. In 2014, due to the $212 million gross of her "Mrs. Carter World Tour," she was named the "highest-earning black artist of all time" (Robinson 2014). According to *Pollstar*'s box-office data for the top twenty touring artists of the decade, Beyoncé is ranked #6 with an estimated gross of $857,405,819. She is the only African American woman on the list, and the only other Black artist in the box-office tally is her husband, hip-hop mogul Jay-Z (ranked #17) (Pollstar 2021).

A great deal has been written about the absence of Black women in mainstream R&B and dance pop. In 2017, for example, the *Los Angeles Times* ran a shocking article, revealing that in the past ten years, only three Black women (Beyoncé being one of them) were able "to land a No. 1 single on the *Billboard* Hot 100 and top album charts as a lead artist" (Kennedy 2017). While achieving mainstream success in the genres of R&B and dance pop is a challenging task for all Black women, darker-skinned Black women face greater obstacles because the skin tone is generally not considered marketable to mainstream audiences (Jones 2019). I will not engage with this discussion on colorism because it is not central to my analysis of Beyoncé's *Lemonade*. However, for the sake of a well-rounded discourse, I must point out that Beyoncé's ethnic background and heritage have given her a commercial advantage in the music industry.

Her father is an African American from Gaston, Alabama, and her mother's heritage is Louisiana Creole (Beyoncé 2016), the mixed-race descendants of African Americans and the mostly Francophone/Catholic white settlers of the Louisiana area (Graves Jr. 2013, 340). Due to her ethnic heritage, Beyoncé has a light skin tone, and when she first emerged on the musical scene as a solo artist, her physical aesthetic (long blonde hair and fair skin) echoed the commercial sensibilities of popular white and Latina female artists at the time like Britney Spears, Christina Aguilera, Jennifer Lopez, Shakira, and Lady Gaga. This arguably made Beyoncé a more marketable artist, and top beauty brands like L'Oréal tapped into the potential of her marketability by promoting her heritage in global beauty ads as "African American, Native American and French" (Stodghill 2012).

I do not bring this up to discredit Beyoncé's achievements and accolades. She is unquestionably an artist of immense talents. Her octave vocal range is arguably around four, "which is one of the strongest in the music industry" and places her just one octave shy of iconic vocalists like Mariah Carey (School of Popular Music [SOPM] Editorial Team 2018). Although Beyoncé does not possess Carey's whistle register, "her incredible vocal flexibility and dexterity more than make up for it . . . [her] exceptional breath . . . means she can hold notes long and dance with little decline in vocal quality, which is a rare but great quality for live performances" (SOPM 2018). What makes Beyoncé a "rarity" in today's pop music, culture and entertainment reporter Alex Abad-Santos argues, is that although contemporary pop artists are either great singers *or* great dancers, Beyoncé excels at both (2015). These observations demonstrate that Beyoncé's talents, not her skin color, make her worthy of her achievements and accolades. However, due to the difficulties and discrimination darker-skinned Black women face in the mainstream music industry, the commercial viability of Beyoncé's light skin functions as a form of privilege.

After the commercial success of Beyoncé's first three solo albums, her artistic direction dramatically changed course with her next musical project, the album titled *4* (2011). This was the first album she composed after severing working ties with her father (he had served as her manager from the beginning of her career) and taking full creative control of her career (Nilles 2020). *4* is edgy, experimental, and a fusion of "warm old-school R&B, soul and funk with touches of Afrobeat influence" (Nilles 2020). What makes her new artistic direction even more audacious is that during this period, electro pop dominated the airwaves and all mainstream artists flocked to this genre (Nilles 2020). Beyoncé's decision to march to a different beat came at a commercial cost. *4* was the first album "in her career that failed to yield a No. 1 single. In fact, none of the singles released even cracked the top ten on the Billboard Hot 100" (Nilles 2020).

Music critic William Nilles's "Why Beyoncé's *4* Deserved Better" makes a case for the artistic excellence of *4*. He views the album as a career-defining transitional period between the commercially inclined Beyoncé of the past and the more subversive Beyoncé of today. "One listen to the album," Nilles points out. "And it's clear that there were opposing forces at work" (2020). *4* represents, he continues, "an artist emerging from the chrysalis of commercialism, striving to make things more intimate, more experimental, but still not entirely sure of the vision" (2020). You can also sense the intrusive interference of label executives "who wanted to keep the cash coming in. It's there in the 'Run the World (Girls),' the album's Major Lazer–sampling lead single that acts not as a representative of the full body of work, but an outlier and a naked bid for airplay" (Nilles 2020). I am in agreement with Nilles's assessment of *4*. The album represents a musical reawakening for Beyoncé and an attempt to break free from commercial trends and expectations. This is not to say that pre-*4* Beyoncé is not an authentic representation of her artistry. Artists, like everyone else, grow and evolve, and their musical tastes should be allowed to reflect this evolution. However, this is not always the case due to a plethora of reasons I will not get into for fear of derailing my discussion. What is important to remember here is that *4* represents the transformative genesis of the subversive Beyoncé we will encounter in *Lemonade*.

Although *4* commercially underperformed, it was not a flop (Nilles 2020), and while some artists might have reverted to their tested and true formulas for commercial success, *Beyoncé* chose to amplify the experimentation factor for her fifth musical project, the self-titled album *Beyoncé*. On the evening of December 13, 2013, without any prior notice or obvious hints, Beyoncé unexpectedly released the self-titled album, with a music video accompanying each song, on iTunes and set the internet ablaze. In the hours following the visual album's release, "social media was talking about Beyoncé and nothing but Beyoncé" (Watercutter 2013). Mentions of *Beyoncé* "on Twitter hit somewhere between 500,000 and 1.2 million in the hours after *Beyoncé* landed. iTunes reportedly crashed as people rushed to download the album in a . . . frenzy. It sold 80,000 copies in three hours" (Watercutter 2013). This was an unprecedented music release strategy for a mainstream artist in the modern era because Beyoncé completely boycotted the promotional gatekeepers of the music industry (radio, interviews, talk shows, etc.). Remember that 2013 was an era before the uncontested dominance of streaming platforms like Spotify and Apple Music, and mainstream artists still relied on traditional channels and strategies when promoting their music. Beyoncé's surprise "drop" is thus significant because for the first time in her career, we see Beyoncé trying to take full creative control of her artistry, from conception to execution to distribution.

In addition to its bold release strategy, the self-titled album *Beyoncé* is likewise thematically and musically bold. The Beyoncé in *Beyoncé* embraces both her insecurities and her strengths. In "Pretty Hurts," she rebukes society's obsession with the "perfect" female body and how this drive for perfection negatively affects women's mental health and in "Flawless," she brags about waking up looking flawless and encourages other women to own their beauty. In "Jealous," she sings about the toxic lows of being in a relationship and in "Drunk in Love," she sings about the intoxicating highs of being in a relationship. In "Haunted," she reveals her skepticism of music industry gatekeepers, and in "Partition," she is both artistically and sexually liberated. Worthy of note here is that in the song "Flawless," she proudly labels herself as feminist at a time when her fellow pop stars like Taylor Swift and Katy Perry shied away from the label (McDonough 2013). Once again, we see Beyoncé forging her own path and rejecting the commercial expectations of pop stardom. The last thing I will mention about *Beyoncé* here is that it is more musically cohesive than *4*. Although *Beyoncé* has influences from other genres and visual art forms (in "Partition," for example, she samples a conversation about feminists and sex from the French-dubbed version of the Coen Brothers movie *The Big Lebowski*), there are no songs that feel jarringly out of place or like an obvious bid for airplay.

The afore discussed overview of *4* and *Beyoncé* is necessary contextualization for my analysis on *Lemonade*. *4* represents the awakening of Beyoncé's artistic independence, *Beyoncé* sees her engaging with the discomfort of contradictions, and in *Lemonade*, her sixth solo studio album, she fully embraces the subversive implications of discomfort. Subscription television service HBO premiered Beyoncé's visual album *Lemonade* on April 23, 2016, and it was met with near universal critical acclaim. *Rolling Stone*, for example, awarded *Lemonade* its rare five-star review, declaring it "a major personal statement from the most respected and creative artist" in popular music (Sheffield 2016). "All over these songs," Sheffield continues. "She rolls through heartbreak and betrayal and infidelity . . . she makes it all seem affirming, just another chapter in the gospel according to Beyoncé" (2016). *Billboard* echoed similar sentiments, hailing *Lemonade* as "a revolutionary work of black feminism" that uses "American Southern . . . and Afrofuturist utopian imagery" to tell a both historical and personal story about the vulnerabilities and strengths of African American womanhood (Bale 2016). The album currently holds a "92%" rating on Metacritic, making it one of the highest-rated albums of all time, a rare feat for a female mainstream artist (Metacritic 2021).

By subverting the artistic expectations of a female pop star, Beyoncé is continuing a rich legacy of Black female artists who reimagine popular music as an aesthetic form of counterculture. In political activist, philosopher, and Black feminist writer Angela Davis' *Blues Legacies and Black Feminism*, she discusses the subversive careers of blues artists Gertrude "Ma" Rainey, Bessie Smith, and Billie Holiday, paying careful attention to how they used blues music to rethink and sustain an "emergent feminist consciousness" (1999, xv). Black women were the first artists to record the blues in the 1920s (Davis 1999, xii). Mamie Smith's rendition of Perry Bradford's "Crazy Blues," for example, "was so popular that 75,000 copies of the record were sold within the first month of its release" (Davis 1999, xii). This popularity paved the way for a wave of Black female blues singers who were later eclipsed in the 1930s by the male intrusion and eventual takeover of the genre (Davis 1999, xii–xiii). Despite their short-lived dominance, Davis argues that artists like Gertrude "Ma" Rainey and Bessie Smith instrumentalized blues music in subversive and unexpected ways. Because their music often embodied a raw sensuality typically associated with "working-class black life," this placed them at odds with the Harlem Renaissance cultural movement (Davis 1999, xiii). The Black artists who pioneered the Harlem Renaissance sought to elevate the status of Black art by emphasizing aspects of high culture such as classical music, painting, literature and sculpture (Davis 1999, xiii). They thus regarded the sexually raw and honest music of 1920s blues female artists as regressive forms of low culture with the potential to derail the cultural movement's objectives (Davis 1999, xiii).

Notwithstanding the criticism from Black elites, Davis argues that artists like Smith and Rainey had a profound impact on Black art and popular culture because they, first, audaciously voiced the anxieties and triumphs of the Black working class and, second, developed a unique feminist consciousness, which construed the tension of simultaneously succumbing to and rebelling against male desire as "noncontradictory oppositions" (Davis 1999, xv). In other words, "oppositions" are so profoundly inherent to their culturally specific American experience that they cannot be labeled as "contradictions." This artistic tension, both with cultural gatekeepers of the Harlem Renaissance and between the "oppositions" in their musical content, is arguably the genesis of African American female artistry using popular music as an aesthetic form of counterculture. This trend will continue into the postwar years and beyond, with artists like Nina Simone personifying "militant black cultural politics" during the civil rights era of the 1960s and setting "a benchmark for black music of protest and affirmation" (Martin 2005, 68). Beyoncé's artistic evolution from the musically experimental *4* to the thematically subversive *Lemonade* is thus a continuation of the counterculture traditions embedded in Black female artistry.

It is of the utmost importance to stress here that Beyoncé is not the only contemporary Black female R&B and dance pop artist to explore subversive Black feminist themes with nuance and depth.[1] The works of African American female singers like *Heavn* by Jamila Woods and *A Seat at the Table* by Solange (who also happens to be Beyoncé's younger sister) have explored similar Black feminist themes with arguably more depth in certain instances. Jamila and Solange, however, cannot be characterized as crossover/mainstream artists. While they are popular acts in certain circles, they are not consistently profiled in mainstream press, they do not top the *Billboard* charts, they do not sell millions of records, they do not embark on top-grossing tours, and they are not international ambassadors for global brands. For this reason, the challenging nature of their musical themes and aesthetics do not often permeate popular culture discourse.

What makes *Lemonade* unique is not always its Black feminist subject matter (although I will argue later that *Lemonade*'s subject matter does possess subversively unique elements) but the fact that a mainstream artist is tackling this specific subject matter and, as a result, forcing the usually inoffensive mainstream press to engage with difficult discussions about African American womanhood. As I mentioned in the Introduction, the study of popular culture is the study of shared values (Hall 1997, 2). Thus, by engaging with Black feminist themes in the popular culture sphere, Beyoncé is making, or at least attempting to make, discourse on the tensions and triumphs of African American womanhood an integral component of contemporary American culture.

Beyoncé is often criticized by the more radical wing of feminist scholarship for operating in the commercial space of capitalism. bell hooks, for example, dismisses *Lemonade* as "capitalist money-making at its best" and argues that "Beyoncé's audience is the world, and that world of business and money-making has no color" (2016). Narratives about African American womanhood, hooks claims, are culturally specific experiences that become aesthetically diluted, and thus lose their authenticity, when marketed to a global audience (2016). She views *Lemonade* as a "commodity" and "commodities, irrespective of their subject matter, are made, produced and marketed to entice any and all consumers" (hooks 2016). This capitalist critique of commercialism in the music industry echoes a widespread notion that the creative outputs of mainstream performers lack artistic truth and dynamism because they are diluted to reach the widest audience possible and maximize profits. Broadly labeling an artist as inauthentic because they operate in the corporate space of popular music is misguided because one cannot accurately measure or determine how much money a musician should accrue from the sales of their products in order to be characterized as artistically inauthentic and a "money-making capitalist." In other words, there is no precise barometer to measure the financial threshold that determines the status of authenticity regarding an artist's creative output. Moreover, hooks's argument implies that the authenticity of a culturally specific experience can never be widely consumed and appreciated. While there are certainly a significant number of mainstream artists whose works are diluted to reach a large audience and maximize profits, to reduce all mainstream art to nothing but "capitalist money-making at its best" is, I believe, a preposterous accusation.

Lauryn Hill's critically acclaimed and award-winning album *The Miseducation of Lauryn Hill* (1998), for example, has been consistently lauded by both music critics and Black female scholars as an authentic representation of Black feminist artistry (McDonald 2018), and it also contains an anti-capitalist rhetoric that parallels some of hooks's feminist ideologies (Hill 1998). *The Miseducation of Lauryn Hill* is, however, a mainstream album. It sold millions of records, spawned top *Billboard* hits, and won top honors at the Grammy Awards, arguably the world's most mainstream music awards show (Ahlgrim 2020).[2] Every now and then, we do encounter mainstream artists like Lauryn Hill who challenge the status quo, and Beyoncé is one of these artists. As music critic Naima Cochrane points out, "crossover success can be precarious for a black artist: For most of modern music history, hitting pop stardom meant diluting black sound and imaging, and moving away from black centered spaces to choose platforms with maximum exposure" (2019). Beyoncé, on the other hand, "is one of the handful of black megastars utilizing their platforms to put our [black] cultural heritage on full display, without apology" (Cochrane 2019). Before delving into how *Lemonade* explores the richness of Black cultural heritage, it is important to describe (or at least attempt to describe) what kind of album *Lemonade* is.

Defining and/or describing *Lemonade* is a challenging and sometimes confusing exercise. Like the self-titled album *Beyoncé*, *Lemonade* is a visual album (a studio album accompanied with music videos) but unlike the self-titled album *Beyoncé*, *Lemonade* premiered on HBO, a venue for movies and prestige TV shows. Because *Lemonade* premiered on HBO and has a clear narrative arc, a chronological plot with titled chapters such as "Intuition," "Denial," "Anger," "Reformation," and "Redemption," some music critics argue that it is feature film (Bale 2016). Moreover, because the visual album incorporates historical elements from indigenous African culture and the antebellum South to explore the rich history of Black women in America, it can also be characterized as part historical documentary. Furthermore, while *4* and *Beyoncé* draw influences from different genres and art forms, both albums are musically grounded in the genre of alternative R&B. *Lemonade*, on the other hand, completely rejects the notion that a studio album/artist can be comfortably categorized in a single genre.

The album has traditional pop ballads like "Pray You Catch Me" and "All Night," a fusion of R&B and hip-hop tracks like "Sorry" and "Formation," rock ("Don't Hurt Yourself" featuring Jack White), reggae influences ("Hold Up") and country ("Daddy Lessons"). This impressive blend of musical styles is a nod to the rich tradition of multi-genre Black female performers like Tracy Chapman, Tina Turner, Sister Rosetta Tharpe, Merry Clayton, and Linda Martell. And although this genre-defying approach might seem chaotic, there is a method to the madness. The different genres are strategically placed at specific points along the narrative arc for reasons that I will elaborate on later. Adding to the cross-genre madness is the inclusion of poetic monologues written by Somali-British poet Warsan Shire and recited by Beyoncé. Thus, the album can also be described as both spoken word and visual poetry.

Assembling all of these disparate parts together in a single intermedial project required a highly collaborative team. Although Beyoncé shares a songwriting credit on every song, she is supported by a group of diverse songwriting collaborators like James Blake, Diana Gordon, Jack White, Kevin Cossom, Diplo, Carla Williams, Boots, Malik Yusef, and MNEK. These writers come from different genders, genres, cultures and races and reflect *Lemonade*'s musical diversity and versatility. She also has a producer credit on all the songs, and she shares director credit with Kahlil Joseph, Melina Matsoukas, and Mark Romanek. *Lemonade* sees Beyoncé undertaking an exercise in imaginative and genre-defying world building and while she never loses the authenticity of her voice and purpose throughout the visual album's narrative arc, she does require an army of collaborators to assist her with constructing this almost borderless world from the ground up.

Lemonade's disparate intermedial and multi-genre components echo the African diaspora tradition of syncretism, a tradition Beyoncé uses in the visual album to explore the affirmatively varied dimensions of her transatlantic identity. In divinity studies, syncretism can be broadly defined as the amalgamation of different religious practices in order to bridge ethnic divides, mediate cultural tensions, and develop new identities capable of accommodating spiritual diversity (Stump 2008, 184). When enslaved Africans were forcibly shipped to the New World, for example, some of their indigenous spiritual beliefs endured and syncretized with the dominant Christian denominations of the Americas (Stump 2008, 184). Zora Neale Hurston's autoethnographical text *Mules and Men* (1935) describes some of these syncretic practices in the American South. Hurston, a former student of revered German-born American anthropologist Franz Boas, traveled to New Orleans in 1928 and conducted extensive fieldwork on syncretic practices like hoodoo, a set of spiritual traditions developed by enslaved Africans (Turner 2002, 113–16). The data collected during this anthropological expedition materialized into *Mules and Men*, an incisive folkloric study that identifies the intricate ways in which syncretic practices adapt and adjust to the hegemonic dogmas of Christianity. "Hoodoo . . . is burning with all the intensity of a suppressed religion," Hurston writes. "It has thousands of secret adherents. It adapts itself . . . to its local environment, reclaiming some of its borrowed characteristics to itself" (1990, 185). Despite these flashes of intensity, syncretic practices like hoodoo remain subordinate to the uncontested dominance of Christianity, so their believers must "conceal their faith" (Hurston 1990, 185). South of the United States border, however, in countries like Haiti, Cuba, and Brazil, similar syncretic practices, although still marginalized, enjoy greater support. In Brazil, for example, "the majority of . . . Roman Catholics, over 60 million," incorporate syncretic beliefs of African origins like Candomblé and Umbanda "into their faith" (Johnson and Zurlo 2015, 77).

Because the fusion of different belief systems is the core practice of syncretism, a practice that authentically reflects the transatlantic engagements between Africa and the Americas, syncretic believers do not necessarily view the tension between Indigenous African spiritualism and Christianity as contradictory. Put differently, in this spiritual milieu, oppositional forces are the norm and not a contradiction because African diasporic identities are inherently rooted in the physically and philosophically chaotic act of displacement. This argument reverberates Davis's description of the emergent feminist consciousness of 1920s blues music as "noncontradictory oppositions" (Davis 1999, xv) and in *Lemonade*, Beyoncé continues this tradition by celebrating, and even normalizing, the oppositional tensions of her transatlantic expeditions.

Worthy of note here is the fact that, like the normalization of syncretic tensions, the phrase "noncontradictory oppositions" insinuates that these oppositions do coexist. Filtered through the theoretical lens of Bhabha's hybridity, "noncontradictory oppositions" can thus be characterized as the emergence of an *inter*-national culture born out of syncretic tensions and ambivalence. Although Beyoncé's *Lemonade* also attempts to normalize oppositions, unresolved contradictions overwhelm the narrative and ultimately reject the notion of hybridity by exposing and problematizing the incompatible nature and power imbalances in some syncretic unions. In other words, *Lemonade* engages with knowledge systems that advocate for cultural separation and reject the notion of cultural interdependence. Notwithstanding the foregoing, *Lemonade* remains a syncretic text because, despite its thematic focus on the incompatibility of certain syncretic unions, it is affirmed by shared transatlantic histories and values.

As I approach the conclusion of this section, I should point out that even though *Lemonade* is celebrated by contemporary critics as a landmark intermedial project, the album does have musical precedents. The concept of the visual album, for example, is not new. As far back as the 1960s to 1980s, artists like The Beatles, Pink Floyd, Prince, and Michael Jackson explored the concept of a cinematic experience that is accompanied by a set of songs (two or more complete songs is a fair criterion. A single song couched in a cinematic experience is simply a well-shot and directed music video). However, music writer Kat Sommers argues that *Lemonade* revolutionized and strengthened the concept of a visual album by effectively combining music and visuals with an extended and musically sustained narrative (2016).

In the next sections of this chapter, my analysis of *Lemonade* will unfold, paying particular attention to how the visual album's three acts expand TCT's elasticity by emphasizing the uncomfortable existential rift between individual affirmations and collective shared histories. Unlike Deleuze's fold and Attridge's idioculture, concepts that are critical of community's tendency to enforce conformist practices, practices labeled by feminist scholar Davidson as "external, marginalizing forces" (2010, 130), *Lemonade* partly characterizes hegemonic communal customs as an affirmative life force. This interpretation of community is at odds with TCT's analysis of Gay's efforts to unburden her narratives from the patronizing shackles of community policing and prioritize the affirmative legitimacy of singularities. Although *Lemonade* begins by establishing community as an oppressive fellowship, it also derives affirmative strength from the collective reservoir of shared histories and values. The discomfort of this duality dismantles the notion of the external space as a marginalizing force and ultimately pushes the TCT framework to rethink the relationship between the pre- and post-rupture realms. In other words, the discomfort of this duality is an aesthetic imaginary that blurs the borders of earlier demarcated sections of the three-part TCT process by engaging with the fluid "callings and constraints of cross-border epistemic and cultural circulations" (Ghosh 2017, 450).

As I afore discussed, *Lemonade* was met with near-universal critical acclaim. The visual album also created buzz for addressing the persistent rumors of infidelity in Beyoncé's marriage to hip-hop mogul Jay-Z (Hess 2016). Before proceeding, I must unequivocally state that my analysis is not interested in elements of celebrity gossip. Although there are obvious autobiographical references in *Lemonade*, Beyoncé has never explicitly stated that the visual album, in its entirety, is a work of nonfiction. She is clearly drawing inspiration from her personal life to weave a broader historical narrative about African American womanhood that is radical and Afrofuturistic. By navigating different emotional layers of pain, betrayal, triumph, and uncertainty, she is able to syncretize conflicting cultural modes and develop an aesthetic that is shaded by community influences but also uniquely hers. Similarly put, the Beyoncé in *Lemonade* is Beyoncé the *artist* and not Beyoncé the *person(a)*. I thus conceptualize *Lemonade* as a multimodal *text* and afford it the same analytical gravitas I would give to an acclaimed literary work or movie.

Act 1's thesis sets up the discomfort of community's fluid functionality in *Lemonade*, and in acts 2 and 3, I will use the concept of aesthetic imaginaries to examine the implications of this fluidity, both in *Lemonade* and on the TCT framework. Worthy of emphasis here is that TCT's acknowledgment of duality (community's dual function as the individual's ally and aggressor) does not retread the binary paradigm of Du Bois's double consciousness. While Du Bois is interested in aligning the two parts by bridging the racial chasm, TCT is interested in the rupture created by the collision of the two parts and the affirming but uncomfortable aftermath of this rupture.

ACT 1: DEATH BY COMMUNITY, RESURRECTION BY ANCESTRY

Lemonade opens with Beyoncé on a stage, mournfully dressed in all black and crouching in front of a closed curtain. The stage setting (performer, curtain, and theatrical light bulbs) signals to the viewer that they are about to witness a performance. As I previously stated, there are possibly autobiographical elements in *Lemonade*. However, this emphasis on performativity hints that Beyoncé is mostly interested in the inventive powers of storytelling. In other words, the theatrical setup of this opening shot is our first clue that *Lemonade* is about imaginative possibilities. The curtain behind Beyoncé is closed but instead of jubilant actor bowing to applause, Beyoncé is mournfully crouching, seemingly dejected and unpleased with the role she plays in this performance. The song playing is "Pray You Catch Me," and she sings, "You can taste the dishonesty/It's all over your breath/As you pass it off so cavalier. . . . My lonely ear/ Pressed against the walls of your world" (Beyoncé 2016). Distraught and alone, she prays to catch her partner "whispering" about his extramarital exploits, and she prays he catches her "listening" (Beyoncé 2016).

"Pray You Catch Me" is a mournful and atmospheric pop ballad, evocative of songs like Mariah Carey's "We Belong Together" and Sinéad O'Connor's "Nothing Compares 2 U." This mournful mood is directly tied to the central theme of betrayal. Beyoncé is steeped in sorrow because she feels betrayed by the cavalier dishonesty of her romantic partner, and she presses her lonely ear against the wall, eavesdropping, praying to catch him whispering and praying he catches her listening. This scene sets up the power dynamics in the relationship. She is in an unhappy romantic union, but she lacks the agency to confront her dishonest partner. For this reason, she hopes to avoid the trouble of confronting him by praying he catches her eavesdropping on his dishonest conversations. This explains why she is mournfully crouched on a stage, dissatisfied with her subservient role in the performance of their romantic union. Performativity has a dual function here. It refers to both the unfolding performance of *Lemonade*'s narrative and her performance as a subordinate partner. I call the latter a performance because she is clearly unhappy in this role but lacks the agency to rewrite the trajectory of her character. Suffering through the predetermined performance leads to her having a mental breakdown on stage. The only way to end her character's torment is to be killed off the play. She thus decides to end her ordeal by leaving the stage and jumping off a building.

This section of *Lemonade* is titled "Intuition," and it reveals the subject's awareness of the state of tension in the performance of her romantic union.

Using the TCT framework, awareness represents the third consciousness, the moment of rupture. To reiterate, unlike comparable triple consciousness frameworks, TCT's third consciousness is not a definite identity or concept. Rather, it represents a rapturous opening that rejects the autonomy of hegemonic narratives and seeks out counternarratives in the post-rupture realm, which are affirming but also destabilizing. Beyoncé acknowledgment of her powerlessness at the genesis of *Lemonade* thus represents the moment of rupture in her marriage, and her decision to kill off her character in a narrative mandated by external marginalizing forces is her first plunge into the post-rupture realm.

Up to this point, betrayal has mostly been associated with one man, the dominant male partner in Beyoncé's relationship. As Beyoncé prepares to jump off the precipice of the building, she recites a poetic monologue. "I tried to make a home out of you," she begins. "But doors lead to trapdoors. A stairway leads to nothing. Unknown women wander the hallways at night" (Beyoncé 2016). This is the first mention of a community, a community of women. The implication here is that the brokenness of Beyoncé's romantic relationship, and her doomed attempts at making a home, is an affliction that plagues other women in her community. This explains why they are "unknown," a nod here to lacking agency, and wandering through hallways at night, seemingly without purpose.

Beyoncé's usage of poetry here is consequential. Compared to music lyrics, nonmusical poetry is arguably a more meditative and metaphorical art form because it engages the reader emotionally and intellectually without the assistance or intrusion of instruments and sounds. When Beyoncé is reciting the poetic monologue, there are no pronounced rhythms or dramatic visuals, so the viewer mostly focuses on her meditative voice and the gothic metaphor of Black women wandering hallways at night, trapdoors leading to more trapdoors. This haunting image of the trauma of Black women in Beyoncé's community, visually represented by simple yet unnerving black-and-white images of a deserted piece of land, is highly effective, I argue, because it is delivered through the meditative and metaphorical intensity of nonmusical poetry.

"You remind me of my father, a magician . . . able to exist in two places at once. In the tradition of men in my blood, you come home at 3 a.m. and lie to me," the poetic monologue continues. The speaker then ponders, "What are you hiding? The past and the future merge to meet us here. What luck, what a fucking curse" (Beyoncé 2016). These words are consequential to the philosophical core of *Lemonade*. First, they connect Beyoncé's personal tragedy to a larger community problem of unfaithful husbands and broken homes. Her partner lies like her father, a magician existing in two places, and upholds the community tradition of philandering husbands who creep back into their homes at 3 a.m. after debasing the sanctity of their unions. Community here is conceptualized as a curse. The trauma of patriarchal traditions moves from one generation to the next and because the women in this community are "unknown" and have little to no agency, they, like Beyoncé, are stifled by the hegemonic mandate of external marginalizing forces.

This opening monologue, it is imperative to point out, is interspersed with cinematic shots of a sisterhood, a community of Black women posing stoically in what looks like an abandoned Southern plantation. They are surrounded by the imposing branches of live oak trees and disturbing images of what appears to be the dilapidated shacks of a slave quarter. They are also mostly dressed in white garments with what *Lemonade*'s stylist Marni Senofonte describes as a "Victorian aesthetic" (Gonzales 2016). The visual elements of these scenes are a clear cinematic reference to Julie Dash's masterpiece *Daughters of the Dust* (1991), a movie about African American Gullah women who are mostly dressed in pristine white Victorian-era garments. The Gullah people are descendants of enslaved Africans who lived on both the coastal plain and islands of the Lowcountry region of South Carolina, Georgia, and Florida (Joyner 2003, 40). Because the ancestors of the Gullah people mostly worked on isolated plantations, they were able to preserve some of their African customs and developed a unique language known as Gullah creole (Conlin 2014, 418). *Daughters of the Dust* is, at its core, a movie about African American women torn between remaining attached to the cultural ties of their Gullah community on Dataw Island or pursuing individual freedoms on the industrialized mainland of modern America. Thus, *Lemonade*'s cinematic nod to *Daughters of the Dust* reveals the visual album's intention to weave a narrative about the existential rift in African American culture between the individual and the community.

Like the women in *Daughters of the Dust*, Beyoncé is at a crossroads. As she stands on the edge of the building, trying to muster up the courage to jump, she is torn between her individual freedom and loyalty to the shared values of her community. Behind her is the performance of a community narrative authored by external marginalizing forces and burdened by generational trauma and in front of her is the possibility of an escape, the pursuit of individual freedom. She takes the plunge and right before her body hits the concrete pavement, a mass of water of appears. A submerged Beyoncé sheds her old skin by taking off her mournful black garments; the implication here is she has killed off the externally mandated character, and she is now mutating into a new being, an alternate self. Beyoncé's journey so far is aligned with the three-step counter-actualizing TCT process. The first phase is the subject's awareness external marginalizing forces (community), and the second phase is the subject's momentous moment of rupture, the moment her third consciousness emerges by rejecting external interference and creating opening into the third stage: the post-rupture realm of possible counternarratives.

As she mutates into a new being in the post-rupture realm, she revisits her ordeal above the water surface in another poetic monologue and describes how she tried to suppress her true self in order to appease the patriarchal gatekeepers of her community. "I tried to change," she says. "Closed my mouth more/Tried to be soft, prettier/Less . . . awake" (Beyoncé 2016). As she utters these words, the viewer is introduced to two identical Beyoncés. The first Beyoncé, the assumed narrator, is awake and observant, and she swims toward the second Beyoncé, who is lying dormant on a bed. Dormant Beyoncé represents the Beyoncé above the water who tried to be prettier, softer, calmer and less awake. Trying to be less awake implies that she is trying to conform to the patriarchal standards of her community by consciously suppressing her individuality and performing the role of the idealized wife. Alert Beyoncé, on the other hand, represents the Beyoncé who, after the development of her third consciousness in the moment of rupture, decides to stop conforming to hegemonic narratives by jumping off a building and into the post-rupture realm. With the two Beyoncés now facing each other, alert Beyoncé curiously observes the lifeless body of her dormant counterpart and after a few seconds, she transfers her consciousness into the lifeless Beyoncé. The two Beyoncés now embody the amalgamated alert Beyoncé in the post-rupture realm.

The theme of the submissive and obliging Black wife must be examined in the context of hypermasculinity in African American culture. As we saw in earlier chapters, Black hypermasculinity in the American context is an offshoot of white patriarchal institutions and heteronormative cultural practices (Benson 2014, 13). The origins of hypermasculinity in the African American community have been traced to the slavery-era myth of the Black rapist. This was a myth created and propagated by the white South to justify "the brutal killing of African American men" (Benson 2014, 13). Reimagining Black male bodies as untamable and hypermasculine savages with insatiate sexual appetites dehumanized African American men and justified, legally and physically, efforts by white patriarchal institutions to enslave and brutalize them. Eventually, scholars argue, "scores of black men . . . embraced the myth of the black rapist, as well as the baser patriarchal aspects of white south southern male power, such as violence, sexism" (Benson 2014, 13). This historical development of patriarchy in African American culture is often downplayed by the indispensable role of community in the lives of Black Americans.

The pursuit of individual freedom and happiness is a fundamental American value. The value of community, I argue, is just as important to African Americans because the act of fellowship has historically functioned as the most significant source of social support for their community. Thus, walking away from the community is tantamount to abandoning an indispensable source of social support, which cannot be easily substituted. During the slavery era, "The Negro church was virtually the only place where slaves were allowed to congregate" (Schmidt 2001, 285). The community of the Black church thus functioned as a source of social support because it offered slaves both a physical and spiritual escape from the hardships of everyday plantation life. After the abolition of slavery and the end of Civil War, the Black church became a strategic location for both worship and community organizing. Black preachers, usually men, were at the time the most educated group in the community because they had learned how to read the Bible. Freed slaves therefore looked to Black preachers "for leadership, not only in religious matters, but in all other areas of life as well" (McKinney 1971, 458–59).

This influence of the Black church in both secular and non-secular dimensions of African American life continued into the 1950s and played a central role in the civil rights movement. An example of their influence is the bus boycott in Montgomery, Alabama (1955–1956). The arrest of civil rights icon Rosa Parks for refusing to sit at the back of a segregated bus in Montgomery angered the local Black church, and meetings were held to galvanize the community and plan a response. Minister Martin Luther King Jr. emerged from these talks as the chosen community organizer, and the Montgomery bus boycott, an effort staged by the protest movement he invigorated, led to the desegregation of public transportation by the Supreme Court (McKinney 1971, 466–467).

Despite these community-led civil rights successes, and their ability to function as a source of social support for community members, the civil rights movement was still an oppressive space for African American women. As I mentioned in both the Introduction and chapter 2, civil rights activism in the African American community usually adheres to the rhetoric of organizational masculine leadership (Eaton 2010, 1). Although African American women activists such as Ella Baker, Septima Poinsette Clark, and Fannie Lou Hamer were the organizational foundation of the civil rights movement, their voices and intersectional concerns were often sidelined (Associated Press 2005) in favor of an almost cultlike obsession with charismatic male leadership (Delinder 2009, 987).

The reverberations of this sidelining still ripple through our contemporary society. For example, the 2020 death of George Floyd (an unarmed Black man murdered on video by white police officers in Minneapolis, Minnesota) galvanized African American community organizing efforts and propelled the Black Lives Matter movement to the global stage. On the other hand, the 2020 death of Breonna Taylor (an unarmed Black woman murdered in her apartment by white office policers in Louisville, Kentucky) failed to inspire a similar reaction both nationally and globally. *Time* ran a story called "Why Are Black Women and Girls Still an Afterthought in Our Outrage Over Police Violence," bemoaning the fact that "Breonna Taylor's death does not fit the spectacular forms of police killing that we have come to associate with America's nefarious lynching past" (Cooper 2020).

This comparison echoes the Trayvon Martin/Sandra Bland comparison I mentioned in chapter 1. African American women are often expected by their community to be central participants in civil rights protests, organizing in meeting rooms and chanting on the streets. They must always support the cause, because their efforts are crucial to the fate of their race. However, they must never destabilize the hegemonic rhetoric of organizational masculine leadership because African American men are considered the natural-born community leaders (Eaton 2010, 1). This explains why the dormant Beyoncé feels pressured by her partner and community into being softer, less confrontational, less awake. The dual function of community is highlighted here. Community is both an ally and an aggressor.

Filtering *Lemonade* through this historical perspective, Beyoncé's decision to abandon her community by jumping off a building is a rebuke of the legacy of Black hypermasculinity and, because community is the foundational pillar of African American culture, a gutsy act of rebellion. Her future is uncertain, but she has had enough, so she takes the plunge anyways. Arguably more rebellious is *Lemonade*'s indictment of Christianity in the post-rupture realm. As previously stated, the post-rupture realm repudiates the hegemony of external marginalizing forces and facilitates the exploration of possible counternarratives. Beyoncé's first attempted counternarrative in the post-rupture realm is the possibility of an existence that is not fundamentally oriented by the salvation of the church.

Beyoncé's new alert consciousness uses poetry to remember and catalog the dramatic ways in which she tried to adhere to the role of the submissive wife. "I . . . confessed my sins," she says. "And was baptized in a river . . . I whipped my own back" (Beyoncé 2016). These are obvious Biblical references (confession of sins, baptism in the river and self-flagellation), so Beyoncé here is unrepentantly equating patriarchal oppression with Christianity. Because she was struggling to play the role of the subservient wife, she had to confess her "sins" to the church and her penance was purification through baptism and self-flagellation. Christianity is thus characterized an accomplice in the patriarchal act of community oppression. As I previously explained, Beyoncé uses the meditative and metaphorical intensity of poetry when she wants to draw attention to a specific issue and create a heightened sense of severity. This is a clue that her rebuke of Christianity's patriarchal tendencies is central to *Lemonade*'s philosophical orientation. To fully appreciate the audacity of this moment, more historical contextualization is necessary.

African Americans are arguably America's most loyal ethnic group to the Christian faith. A 2018 Pew Research Center study revealed that "Nearly eight-in-ten black Americans (79%) identify as Christian. . . . By comparison, seven-in-ten Americans overall (71%) say they are Christian, including 70% of whites, 77% of Latinos and just 34% of Asian Americans" (Masci, Mohamed, and Smith 2018). Christianity is fundamental to African American life, and there are justified reasons why. As I previously discussed, during the era of slavery, the church was the only place enslaved Africans could congregate. They thus became deeply religious because the church offered them a spiritual escape from the dehumanizing experience of chattel slavery. Moreover, the Black church, from the period of emancipation into the civil rights era and beyond, was and still is the cornerstone of activism, political leadership, and community organizing efforts. The influence of this role positions the Black church at the very center of both secular and non-secular African American life. Therefore, if a member of the Black community repudiates the Black church, they risk alienation and ostracization.

There is, however, a darker side to the role of Christianity in African American history and culture. Scholars claim that the Black church has always embraced and promoted patriarchal values. As African American studies scholar TeResa Green points out, "Although Black churches have throughout history been involved in seeking justice and equality for African Americans, the inequality of Black women within Black churches remains an unresolved issue . . . the role of Black women has often been marginalized" (2003, 115). Additionally, the Black church upholds the values of Christianity, a Western doctrine with a well-documented history of dehumanizing Black people. According to Africana studies scholar Wunyabari O. Maloba, European colonialism in Africa was chiefly motivated by "the racist principle that barbarism pervaded Africa and therefore there was no culture to be salvaged" (1995, 11). European states thus supported and financed Christian missions in Africa, which sought to Christianize the "dark" continent by likening indigenous African spiritual practices to demonic forces of the Christian devil, the apex of evil in the Western world (Garraway 2005, 146–47). These efforts were largely successful, and today, Africa is projected to have "640,460,000 professing Christians" by 2025, potentially making "the Christian Church in Africa the largest of the six continents" (Gehman 2005, 4).

Similar efforts to systematically eradicate indigenous religions were also successful in America. There was a strong evangelical push to Christianize "barbaric" African slaves and for this reason, the New World was deprived of durable structures capable of sustaining the longevity of indigenous African spiritual practices on a large scale (Scherer 1997, 627–28). Also, Christian doctrine only guarantees salvation (eternal life in heaven after death and/ or judgement by God) through the unchallenged supremacy of Jesus Christ. Without the grace of salvation, acquired by accepting Jesus Christ as one's only lord and savior, Christians cannot be "saved from the guilt of sin" (Wesley 1833, 236). Thus, in a traditional church, there is ultimately no room for indigenous African spirituality because Jesus's anointed role as the sole dispenser of salvation cannot be challenged.

The dormant Beyoncé was driven to death by the patriarchal institutions of her community (Black hypermasculinity and the church), and the alert Beyoncé was brought to life by her moment of rupture, her awareness of the state of tension in her community. However, she is still trapped beneath the water, unable to breathe. She needs a life force to propel her to the surface and, because she has been betrayed by the men in her community and her church, she must find a new source of rejuvenation. She ironically returns to the same concept of community, digging past its current state and going as far back as her precolonial African ancestry. She finds what she is looking for, and she swims to the surface, emerging triumphantly as a reincarnation of Oshun, a river goddess who belongs to a sacred pantheon of indigenous West African deities. This physical manifestation of Oshun is *Lemonade*'s first counternarrative in the post-rupture realm and represents Beyoncé's attempt at exploring a spiritual identity that is not fundamentally oriented by the dominant dogmas of Christianity.

According to African theology scholars Joseph M. Murphy and Mei-Mei Sanford, Oshun (also spelled Osun) is a multidimensional deity. The adjectives often used to describe her powers are "political, economic, divinatory, maternal, natural, therapeutic" (2001, 1). Pay attention to these adjectives, particularly to therapeutic, because as *Lemonade*'s narrative unfolds, you will notice that they also describe Beyoncé's affirmative experiences in the post-rupture realm. Oshun's origins can be traced back to Osun state in the Yoruba territory of Nigeria (Murphy and Sanford 2001, 4). The name "Oshun" means a life source that "runs, seeps, flows, moves as water does" (Murphy and Sanford 2001, 2). Her elemental manifestation is fresh water (Murphy and Sanford 2001, 2) and because water is the most important resource for human survival, she represents the very essence of life. This explains why Beyoncé finds Oshun while she, Beyoncé, is submerged in a mass of water, despondent and looking for a new life source. When Oshun takes a physical form, she is usually represented by the color yellow. Legend has it that Oshun "was very tidy and would go to the river constantly to wash her white garment. Eventually, the dress turned yellow from washing in the water, and this is how yellow became one of her colors" (Alarcón 2008, 733).

Two other important qualities to note about Oshun are her feminist orientation and her compassion. In the Yoruba story of creation, Oshun is one of the seventeen orishas (deities) who breathed life to the world at the beginning of time (Abiodun 2001, 18). She is also the only female orisha in this sacred group of gods, meaning she is accustomed to the dominance of male leadership and the battles women and outcasts on the fringes of society must endure to prevent their voices and interests from being sidelined. For this reason, she is regarded as the most compassionate orisha, with extraordinary powers capable of healing and influencing both man and gods.[3] Oshun "is believed to have the power to influence the destinies of men, women, and the orisa" (Abiodun 2001, 11) and when "she is invoked her presence is felt to bring lightness and effervescence to illness, want, and gloom. Osun's ability to heal is based on her sovereignty and her compassion. She is a warrior who can fight for her children and vanquish enemies visible and invisible" (Murphy and Sanford 2001, 8).

The first clue that the Beyoncé who returns to the surface as a reincarnation of Oshun is the color of her garment. She emerges from a building in a yellow gown, water gushing at her feet. The costume styling and cinematography are crucial devices here. First, her dress is billowy and regal and echoes physical representations of the goddess Oshun. The first few stills of her reappearance on the surface are wide shots, and this is important to note because wide shots are used by directors and cinematographers to emphasize the importance of scenery and physicality to the narrative. Beyoncé is centrally placed in the wide shots as she emerges from a building that evokes the Greek and Roman architecture of classical antiquity. These architectural styles and models are generally regarded as one of the crowning achievements of Western civilization (Jones 2014, xi). Thus, by positioning the reincarnation of Oshun at the center of a majestic classical building, *Lemonade* makes Oshun an aesthetic and spiritual equivalent to the artistic triumphs of Western civilization. The wide shots also allow the viewer to appreciate Beyoncé's physicality in her new form as a vessel for Oshun. The gown is cinched at her waist and billows at the bottom, giving her the shapely appearance of a classical painting. Once again, the emphasis here is that Oshun, and the indigenous culture she represents, is just as aesthetically refined as sophisticated European art.

This moment is also one of the first, and most glaring, examples of *Lemonade*'s Afrofuturistic aesthetic. Due to the late twentieth-century popularity of Black science fiction writers like Octavia E. Butler and Steven Barnes, author Mark Dery coined the term Afrofuturism, describing it as "speculative fiction that treats African-American concerns in the context of . . . technoculture and, more generally, African-American signification that appropriates images of technology and a prosthetically enhanced future" (1994, 180). Oshun's reincarnation scene echoes Dery's words by appropriating and amalgamating iconography from both Western and indigenous African cultures to prosthetically construct an affirmed persona who rejects the traumas of the past and embraces the speculative possibilities of a more liberated future. The act of imagining new worlds that subvert the epistemological structures of current or past societal paradigms echoes the trajectory of counternarratives in TCT's post-rupture realm. Thus, when filtered through the TCT framework, Afrofuturism in *Lemonade* can also be described as a counternarrative because it is interested in the possibility of futures that look radically different from the present and the past.

Worthy of note here is that *Lemonade*'s emphasis on the spiritual vitality of Oshun and indigenous culture is a stark contrast to double consciousness' emphasis on "high culture." As I discussed in chapter 1, Du Bois's *The Souls of Black Folk* views the American democratic project as the pinnacle of world culture and considers African Americans legitimate participants in this project due to their cultural contributions to the American experience and the unique insights produced by their double consciousness (1994, 3). In contrast, Beyoncé dismantles the high-culture rhetoric by elevating the indigenous healing powers of Yoruba orishas to the same status as Western cultural practices. Also worthy of note is that Oshun does not subsume Beyoncé's consciousness. Beyoncé remains acutely aware of her former life, and Oshun mostly functions as an empowering energy force motivating her to finally confront the patriarchal perpetrators of community discord. And she does just that in "Hold Up," the emotively vengeful song that plays after the reincarnation sequence.

The newly acquired confidence of resurrected Beyoncé is palpable as she struts down the sidewalk in her billowy yellow gown, wearing a cheeky smile and smashing windows and cars with a baseball bat. "Hold up, they don't love you like I love you," she sings. "Slow down, they don't love you like I love you" (Beyoncé 2016). Although "Hold Up" plays like a traditional dance pop song, it has a subdued but noticeable reggae beat and features Beyoncé's signature rap singing technique with additional influences from genres like neo soul and R&B. The musical diversity of the track reflects the fusion of diverse personalities in resurrected Beyoncé (alert Beyoncé, dormant Beyoncé, and the spiritual vitality of Oshun) and echoes the Afrofuturistic process of appropriating and amalgamating iconography from different cultures and knowledge systems in order to create a future that is uniquely new.

Beyoncé in the post-rupture realm is finally embracing her self-worth and as evidenced by the quoted lyrics above, she bluntly tells her dishonest partner that the accomplices of his philandering escapades will never love him like she did. "What's worst, lookin' jealous or crazy /Jealous or crazy?" she continues while smashing the window of a car with her baseball bat. "Or like being walked all over lately, walked all over lately/I'd rather be crazy" (Beyoncé 2016). This is another clue that the resurrected Beyoncé is a reincarnated Oshun. In Yoruba folklore, Oshun is known for having a "malevolent temper and sinister smile when she has been wronged. In 'Hold Up,' a smiling, laughing and dancing Beyoncé smashes store windows, cars and cameras with a baseball bat nicknamed 'Hot Sauce'" (Roberts and Downs 2016). This correlation between anger and divinity is tremendously significant.

The angry Black woman stereotype is arguably one of America's most enduring tropes. Scholars of women and race studies like Kimberly C. Harper argue that due to the persistence of sexist practices, both within and beyond the African American community, Black women have historically been branded as "loud, angry, and aggressive" whenever they attempt to publicly address their unique intersectional concerns (2020, 59). The angry Black woman is a recurrent trope across multiple literary and media platforms such as novels, tv shows, movies, theatre etc. Classic manifestations of this trope in American popular culture include the sassy best friend, the sapphire, the tragic mulatto, and the hypersexualized hip-hop video vixen. There even exist medical studies on the psychological impact of the angry Black woman pejorative on Black women's mental health. Public health scholarship argues that an "awareness of the angry Black woman mythology, including its genesis, manifestations, and the unique experiences of Black women, may raise the standards of cultural competence for clinicians and provide more successful treatment outcomes in working with this population" (Ashley 2014, 27).

Sieving "Hold Up" through this historical perspective, the image of a vengeful Beyoncé smashing windows and cars with unapologetic glee is an audacious moment of rebellion. Old Beyoncé was frightened of being associated with the angry Black woman trope. This explains why she tried to be softer, prettier, and less awake. In other words, she embraced silence and internalized the oppressiveness of patriarchal policing. The impact of embracing silence was dire. We find her at the genesis of *Lemonade* in a severe state of depression, draped in melancholy on an empty stage. Resurrected Beyoncé, on the other hand, is not frightened of being associated with the angry Black woman trope. She realizes that to move forward, she must allow herself to grieve by angrily exorcizing the pain of betrayal. "Hold Up" thus functions as a kind of exorcism, which allows Beyoncé to unburden internalized trauma by embracing the affirmative emotions of anger.

In the earlier chapters, I point out that Deleuzian philosophy is often trapped in the theoretical ruminations of the conceptual realm and does not adequately describe what affirmations would feel like in the tactile world of the contemporary. The lyrical and visual vitality of "Hold Up" addresses this issue. Post-rupture affirmations can look and feel like pure rage. Vengeful Beyoncé in "Hold Up" holds nothing back. She mocks her husband for undervaluing her, "the baddest woman in the game," and fantasizes about beating up his lovers when she sings, "Scrolling through your call list/I don't wanna lose my pride but I'ma fuck me up a bitch" (Beyoncé 2016). In another scene, while chastising him, she adopts traditionally masculine poses, swaying from side to side, the baseball bat resting on her shoulders. These poses are typically associated with African American men in hip-hop culture and evoke the legacy of Black hypermasculinity in the African American community.

Her display of these poses implies that Beyoncé has now assumed the authority position of a man, giving her the "legitimacy" to berate and ridicule her philandering husband. The function of role reversal here echoes my discussion of Gay's "Open Marriage" in chapter 2. In both narratives, the formerly inferior female protagonist becomes the dominant "masculine" partner, and I problematize this representation of power in chapter 2 because it echoes Freire's pedagogy of the oppressed, the tendency of the oppressed becoming an oppressor when they acquire traditional signifiers of authority. As I also mentioned in chapter 2, the TCT framework does not regard the post-rupture realm as an arbiter of morality. Rather, it simply aims to identify and understand the varying forms and dimensions of affirmative experiences. Although fantasizing about beating up the lovers of her cheating partner and displaying her acquisition of power by performing masculine mannerisms are not necessarily morally sound practices, they allow resurrected Beyoncé to publicly unleash, for the first time, her repressed feelings of betrayal and anger. Unleashing these feelings is an almost ritualistic act of liberation because it unburdens her, both physically and psychologically, from the generational trauma of repressed emotions.

"Hold Up" is also an artistic reframing of the angry Black woman trope. The images of Beyoncé strutting down the sidewalk and smashing windows with a baseball bat is a direct reference to the artwork "Ever Is Over All," a 1997 video installation by critically acclaimed Swiss visual artist Pipilotti Rist. "Ever is Over All" features a white woman in a billowy blue dress, jubilantly and vengefully smashing car windows with a rod that resembles a cleaning mop. A female police officer (also a white woman) walks past the woman in the blue dress and applauds her "destructive" behavior with a salute. In this video installation, "Rist positively describes the negative aspects of femininity, which have been rejected by women themselves" (Medien Kunst Netz 2021). In other words, she is aestheticizing female traits often deemed destructive by patriarchal standards, standards upheld by both men and women, and reimagining these "destructive" female traits as a beautiful art form capable of celebrating the complexity of the female experience.

Although white women are also victims of patriarchal institutions, they are not psychologically burdened by a comparable racialized angry woman trope. Thus, art that aestheticizes a "destructive" white woman as beautiful is more palatable to the artistic inclinations of a mainstream consumer. By using the template of Rist's video installation to document resurrected Beyoncé's therapeutic discharge of repressed emotions, *Lemonade* reimagines the angry

Black woman trope as a legitimately ritualistic art form. Beyoncé's anger is an artistic performance of generational trauma and speaks to the uniquely specific history of African American womanhood. Thus, like Rist's "Ever is Over All," the angry Black woman deserves the "privilege" of artistic nuance.

Resurrected Beyoncé, emboldened by Oshun's agency, grows in confidence throughout the narrative sequence of "Hold Up" and when the song nears its conclusion, she smashes the camera screen, the viewer's gaze, and we see her walking away from a distorted perspective and with the camera images now in black and white. This cinematic technique unsettles the viewer, and it is a testament to Beyoncé's newfound narrative authority. The implication here is she now has the power to redirect our gaze and doctor images. In other words, she is no longer a passive actor in someone else' script; she is now the author of her narrative in this new realm of affirmative possibilities.

"Hold Up" ends on what should feel like a high note, but when filtered through TCT's characterization of community as both a positive life force and a marginalizing agent, there are obvious ironies and contradictions that unnerve the viewer and cause a grave sense of discomfort. First, as I pointed out above, the shared values of community fellowship are both capable of marginalization (the legacy of patriarchy in the African American community) and emancipation (the civil rights successes of community organizing efforts and the spiritual practices of precolonial Yoruba societies). In other words, community is ironically responsible for Beyoncé's death and resurrection, and this poses a series of uncomfortable questions. If the post-rupture realm affirms an individual's right to difference, why is Beyoncé's first post-rupture expedition existentially motivated by an indigenous Yoruba religion, a communal practice of spiritual sameness? Unpacking this observation unavoidably confronts Deleuze's counter-actualizing concept of infinitely becoming and initiates the process of rethinking and expanding the elasticity of the TCT framework.

If Beyoncé can tap into her ancestry and access an unchanged community life force capable both of affirming singularities in the present and imagining uniquely new worlds for the future then the Deleuzian concept of producing affirmative moments by constantly unfolding one's subjectivity is, in some instances, flawed. Based on *Lemonade*'s reincarnation sequence, one can argue that the static nature of certain knowledge systems resists mutation and evolution because they are inherently and infinitely affirmative. This interpretation reorients TCT's conceptual understanding of the pre- and post-rupture realms by contending that external forces in the pre-rupture realm (such as the precolonial hegemony of Yoruba orishas) are also capable of producing affirmative singularities in the contemporary, a cornerstone characteristic of the post-rupture realm. Moreover, *Lemonade* upends the TCT framework's chronological understanding of time. The three-part TCT process has defined demarcations between the past (the hegemony of external marginalizing forces in the pre-rupture realm), the present (the third consciousness/post-rupture realm) and the future (the possibilities of counternarratives). Because the past in *Lemonade* can be fully or partially reincarnated in the present (Beyoncé summoning the spiritual life force of a dated indigenous culture to inform and affirm the contemporary) and also used to shape the future (imagining the possibility of radically new Afrofuturistic futures by fusing dated and modern transatlantic cultures), all three concepts of time (past, present, and future) lack clear distinctions because they overlap with each other.

Another moment of grave discomfort in "Hold Up" is resurrected Beyoncé's almost schizophrenic personality (echoed in the song's hodgepodge of musical influences: reggae, dance pop, rap, R&B, and hints of neo soul). Although "Hold Up" is a vengeful and jubilant anthem about liberation in the post-rupture realm, it is punctuated with profound moments of sadness. At one point, Beyoncé acknowledges that her partner is still her true love, "Can't you see there's no other man above you?" and in the lyric that follows, "What a wicked way to treat the girl that loves you," she confesses to still being saddened by how he treated her (Beyoncé 2016). Resurrected Beyoncé is emboldened by the agency of Oshun, but she still longs to return to her loved ones. As powerful as she now is, she still wants to find a way back to her husband, back to familiar social support, back to her community roots, back to the sisterhood she left behind, back to the church, back to the men who tried to make her less awake. But why must she go back? The answer lies in the culturally specific historical function of the African American community.

As I explicated earlier, the African American community, from the slavery era through the civil rights movement to our present times, has historically functioned as a source of social support for its members. Thus, if one has deep ancestral roots in the African American community, like Beyoncé has, one is more likely to feel a sense of an existential debt to the shared values of this community, a sense that one has benefited from the civil rights activism of previous generations, and one must therefore do one's part to ensure that the future generations inhabit a more equitable world—a "pay it forward" kind of mentality. This compelling sense of existential debt is arguably not present in Gay's afore discussed works because as a second-generation immigrant, she has no deeply rooted ancestral ties to the African American community.

Her "ME" persona in *Bad Feminist*, for example, is constructed with an awareness of the historical challenges, and triumphs, of African American womanhood, and in the "Feel Me. See Me. Hear Me. Reach Me" section of *Bad Feminist*, she addresses, albeit briefly, the institutional inequalities and challenges plaguing inner-city students, a nod here to the generational marginalization of nonimmigrant Black Americans, the American descendants of chattel slavery (2014, 8–9). With that said, there is an ease with which Gay unpacks these issues. And for clarity's sake, my usage of the word "ease" here bears no negative connotations. I am simply pointing out the almost clinical practicability Gay adopts when discussing issues plaguing the African American community, a practicability that requires a certain level of community detachment.

When Gay addresses the generational marginalization of inner-city communities, she acknowledges that the institutional failure to meet the needs of these communities has spawned toxic cycles of poverty, alcoholism, drug abuse, and addiction (2014, 10). Her analysis, however, is not in depth. She simply provides an overview of these issues and returns to prioritizing her "ME" persona. Working with troubled inner-city students in institutions that do not provide robust support for both the students and educators left Gay "completely burnt out" (2014, 10). She does feel guilty for leaving the students and pursuing another career opportunity, but she realizes that she alone cannot fix a profoundly broken system and, most importantly, she must protect her mental health. "I . . . needed a break," Gay says. "A very, very long break" (Gay 2014, 10). I am in no way implying that Gay's decision to prioritize her mental health is a selfish act. I argue in chapter 2 that she makes the right decision because she can better advocate for the rights of disenfranchised students if she is well rested, energized, and inspired. And she does just that in *Bad Feminist*, a *The New York Times* best-selling essay collection, by using her large literary platform to underline the treatment of inner-city students in the American education system.

However, there is a quickness, what I referred to earlier as a sense of ease, to how she practically identifies and reacts to these problems. As the upper-middle-class daughter of educated immigrants from Haiti (Gay 2014, 16), she does not have a tangible connection to the traumas and dysfunctions these inner-city communities have inherited from previous generations. Thus, she does her job to the best of her ability and "moves on" with a quickness that is somewhat inaccessible to someone with deep ancestral ties in disenfranchised nonimmigrant African American communities. Gay's works do not reflect the feeling of an existential debt to "the community," a feeling a lot of nonimmigrant American descendants of chattel slavery possess due to how the African American community has historically functioned as a source of identity formation and collective social support. As a result, she discusses the tribulations of inner-city students from an almost observational outsider perspective.

I must underscore here that my brief engagement with these distinctions is not a performative attempt at some kind of oppression Olympics. I am in no way insinuating that nonimmigrant African Americans have endured greater suffering than Black Americans of Haitian descent (and vice versa).

Because the nation of Haiti was equally victimized by chattel slavery, Haitian Americans are certainly burdened by similar traumas and dysfunctions. Moreover, Haitian Americans are largely racially Black, so they too are victims of anti-Black racism in the United States. With that said, the Haitian American and nonimmigrant African American experiences have dramatic distinctions because they are each informed by a different set of variables such as language, colonial influence, political systems, geographic location, culture, ethnicity etc. A refusal to acknowledge these differences dismisses the diversity of Black ethnic identities and ignorantly characterizes the Black race as a monoculture. Thus, when I discuss Gay's distance from the culturally specific nonimmigrant Black American experience, I am not negating the historical marginalization of the Haitian American experience. Rather, I am simply pointing out that the Black experience is not ethnically universal, so as a second-generation immigrant of Haitian parents, the discourse in Gay's *Bad Feminist* about the nonimmigrant African American experience often reads like a clinical observational analysis from a well-meaning but aloof outsider.

The last few years have seen the emergence of a controversial social movement called American Descendants of Slavery (ADOS). The movement, created and promoted by authors and culture commentators Yvette Carnell and Antonio Moore, promotes the uniqueness of ADOS ethnic heritage and has dramatically shifted the focus of online discourse about race and identity in contemporary America (Staples 2020). ADOS ethnic heritage is indeed unique. Not only did Black descendants of chattel slavery have to endure and internalize the culturally specific racial terror and trauma of institutionalized slavery in the United States, but they also lived through the devastating failures of Reconstruction, Jim Crow segregation, postwar redlining, the crack epidemic, the prison-industrial complex, etc. Their American experience is thus very different from that of Black citizens with immigrant backgrounds. The overarching objectives of the ADOS movement is to, first, highlight the fundamental differences between American descendants of chattel slavery and other Black American citizens who do not share this ethnic heritage and, second, to expose the fact that reparation efforts like affirmative action that were "put in place to right the wrongs of slavery and Jim Crow" have shifted from "racial-justice remedies" and are now "using diversity as a goal instead" (Russ 2018).

This shift toward diversity initiatives and not ADOS-specific remedies, they argue, reveals that communities not directly affected by slavery and Jim Crow are benefiting from reparation efforts meant for the ADOS community (Russ 2018). Arguments like these have led to critics labeling them as a hateful anti-immigration group. In 2020, for example, journalist Samara Lynn of *ABC News* ran a story titled "Controversial group ADOS divides black Americans in fight for economic equality." Lynn points out the movement's alleged tendency to spew "hateful, xenophobic rhetoric" and their attacks on "high-profile black politicians, influencers and journalists, including Kamala Harris, Joy Reid, Jonathan Capehart and others" who are not descendants of American chattel slavery (Lynn 2020). I must clarify that this discussion of the ADOS movement is neither an endorsement nor a repudiation. Regardless of where one stands on the issue, it is hard to deny that the movement has brought to light important distinctions within America's diverse Black populations, distinctions that are rethinking contemporary discourse on the Black experience in America.

Herein lies the fundamental difference between Beyoncé's *Lemonade* and Gay's *Bad Feminist* and *Difficult Women*. Although both artists acknowledge the benefits of communal social support, they confront the oppressiveness of community conformism and seek to reimagine a new world based on the principles of individual freedom and equity. In Gay's case, the trajectory of individual freedom and equity is an outward movement from community's clustered sphere. While she remains cognizant of the ways in which community can positively affirm the present, she is somewhat skeptical of the idea that systemic and long-lasting change can occur from the epicenter of a clustered culture of uniformity. Gay's works do not have a profound sense of existential debt to the African American community, so in their effort to reimagine a more equitable world, they have no qualms about abandoning old cultural structures and (re)constructing new affirmative knowledge systems. With Beyoncé, the trajectory of individual freedom and equity is an inward movement into community's clustered sphere. Her post-rupture expedition beyond the borders of the African American community is ironically affirmed by the ancestral bonds of the same African American community. She thus believes that the tools for systemic and long-lasting change are rooted in the ancestral DNA of community's clustered epicenter and because she has a profound sense of existential debt to the African American community, she must return and attempt to inspire change by working with and within the parameters of old structures.

The aim of this juxtaposition is not to label one camp right and the other wrong. Both approaches are radically engaging and critically valid. Gay's efforts in both *Bad Feminist* and *Difficult Women* to demolish all old structures of power and (re)create a new equitable world order is audaciously liberating because it unshackles marginalized peoples from generations of trauma and offers the possibility of starting anew. With that said, such a world-building exercise is capable of operating without the social support of existing communal structures because it is buoyed by a plethora of socioeconomic privileges. As Gay points out in *Bad Feminist*, the success of her intellectual and professional explorations is a direct result of her upper-middle-class second-generation immigrant upbringing, an upbringing that exists beyond the unique traumas of disenfranchised Black American communities (2014, 16). On the other hand, in *Lemonade*, Beyoncé's Southern/Creole ancestry places her at the very epicenter of the ethnically unique nonimmigrant African American experience. Although she is a glamorous and wealthy pop star with a tremendous amount of privilege and influence, she remains existentially haunted by and anchored to the shared values and traditions of the nonimmigrant African American community.

By placing Gay's and Beyoncé's ideologies side by side, their differences and similarities are enhanced, and a strong case is made for the relevant vitality of TCT because its critical apparatus uniquely identifies and problematizes these thematic contradictions and discomforts. While *Bad Feminist* and *Difficult Women* mostly celebrate the affirmative singularities of the post-rupture realm, *Lemonade* boldly asserts that post-rupture affirmations are tied to pre-rupture practices. I will use the concept of aesthetic imaginaries to interrogate the implications of this radical rethinking of TCT. The aesthetic imaginary's preoccupation with entangled figurations and its philosophical practice of (re)constructing worlds that are both real and unreal, elements already teased in *Lemonade*'s opening sequence, illuminates the visual album's aesthetic dynamism and, I argue, exposes understudied revelations with consequential consequences for contemporary scholarship on race, gender and culture.

ACT 2: THE RETURN

Beyoncé's return to her community is a momentous spectacle. She is loud but meditative, humble but egocentric, unforgiving but patient, an individualist but also a collectivist, a schizophrenic blend of personalities that echo an even more heightened commitment to the exploration of multiple musical genres in this section of *Lemonade*. She begins with the guitar-clobbering "Don't Hurt Yourself," an empowering rock anthem featuring Jack White of the White Stripes fame, and then flows into "Sorry" and "6 Inch" (featuring pop star The Weeknd), visually and lyrically mesmerizing songs that amalgamate elements of rap, R&B, and dance pop. She concludes this section of the narrative with the soothingly nostalgic "Daddy Lessons," a country tune with wide-reaching implications for *Lemonade*'s world-building exercise. As I stated earlier, while these cross-genre adventures might seem messy, there is an aesthetic strategy to the madness. With each genre, Beyoncé confronts instances of inequity in the contemporary by tapping into her community's ancestral DNA and journeying to the past, revealing snapshots of affirmative moments in the lives they used to live and the lives they could live. Looking to the past for affirmative inspiration subverts the omnipresent trend of contemporary progressivism, the belief that the past is archaic, repressive, and traditional and the idea of the present and its possible futures as bold, egalitarian, and imaginative. *Lemonade* does not see the present and the future as an outward movement from the past. Rather, the visual album collapses the past into the present and future, creating what the concept of aesthetic imaginaries describes as the disaggregation and reconstruction of traditions and cultures (Ghosh 2017, 450). In act 2, I will examine how the songs in this section of *Lemonade* confront fixed notions of space and time, paying particular attention to the implications of this momentous confrontation on Black patriarchy, cultural identity, and religious dogmas. Before beginning my analysis, an overview of the aesthetic imaginaries concept is required.

The term "aesthetic imaginary," coined by literary and cultural studies scholar Ranjan Ghosh, is an extension and rethinking of already established "imaginaries" such as Marguerite La Caze's *analytical imaginary*, Cornelius Castoriadis's *social imaginary* and Michèle Le Dœuff's *philosophical imaginary* (Ghosh 2017, 449). I will not delve into the philosophical background of this field Ghosh calls "imaginary studies" (2017, 449) because the findings of such an exercise are not directly relevant to my theses. With that said, it is important to mention that the concept of aesthetic imaginaries is an offshoot of an already rich scholarly discourse about imaginative world-building across multiple genres. But "do we really need another concept that ends with 'imaginary?'" American literature and culture scholar Lene Johannessen ponders. "Already there is the postcolonial imaginary, transatlantic...American...digital, visual, urban" (2018, xi). These diverse "imaginary" variants, Johannessen continues, "aspire to demarcate areas, be they geographical, social, cultural, disciplinary, and they come bounded and mediated by a set of coordinates that more or less define their reach" (2018, xi). Broadly speaking, they are "traceable to certain key confluences of cultural and political deep currents" (Johannessen 2018, xi). The aesthetic imaginary, on the other hand, resists identifiable categories and recurrent tropes. Unlike its precedents, Johannessen argues that it circulates in and out of various "imaginary" variants, exchanging ideas and taking on different shapes and forms, refusing to be confined to "one category, one area, discipline, or period" (2018, xi). The concept is admittedly vague and sometimes confounding, so I will not attempt to articulate a succinct definition. I do, however, want to focus on specific key elements that are relevant to my theses such as the implications of "opposition."

The aesthetic imaginary, Ghosh states, "begins in negativity" and does not avoid "the recurrent problematic of the 'opposite'" (2017, 449). Ghosh's usage of opposites here is not merely the existence of oppositional forces. These opposites are active agents with an innate attraction to each other, which causes constant frictions, inflections, amalgamations, and reconfigurations.

As a result of this incessant activity, opposites, like the contradictions in Bhabha's postcolonial third space, are endowed with imaginative abilities to construct an almost indefinable "life of their own, inflected and emplotted" (Ghosh 2017, 449). The complexities that arise from the oppositional nature of these new inflected lives challenge us, Ghosh argues, to reconsider our generic framing of "the cultural politics of learning and reception" by bearing out "the promise of 'shared realities'" (2017, 450). Unlike hybridity, Ghosh is not primarily interested in the cultural interrelations between the colonizer and the colonized. The broader and more imaginatively abstract focus of his cultural circulations allow for theoretical engagements with more individualized perspectives, which are not necessarily tethered to hegemonic postcolonial narratives about cultural hybridity. In other words, because the African American experience is fundamentally different from the experiences of non-American communities subjected to European colonial rule on their Native lands, the aesthetic imaginary's artistically broader perspective is a better fit for my manuscript than hybridity's (post)colonial focus.

In *Lemonade*'s opening sequence, resurrected Beyoncé's attempts to reconstruct a new personhood by pulling influences from different cultures, time periods, and genres can be characterized as an aesthetic imaginary. The Beyoncé in "Hold Up" is a cultural confluence of African American history and culture, Yoruba mythology, contemporary music genres and art, classical antiquity, Christian precepts, etc. Although the audience is not always sure how these disparate elements complement each other, their wildly imaginative nature forces us to rethink preconceived ideas about the creation and development of cultural identities. The aesthetic imaginary's end goal is ultimately not about conclusive statements or fixed meanings but, as Ghosh states, it is the process of rethinking the generic frameworks of our cultural practices.

Ghosh's assertions echo a central moment in the TCT framework, the moment of rupture when the subject rejects a generic understanding of the pre-rupture realm and develops a third consciousness as a result. As repeatedly stated in previous chapters and sections, the third consciousness is not a definite identity. Rather, it is a portal into the post-rupture realm where the subject is affirmed by the possibilities of counternarratives. Although these counternarratives, inherently liberating in nature, offer the subject a sense of self-autonomy, they are ultimately unpredictable and messy because they inhabit a contradictory world whose disparate parts do not always align or make sense. Within this chaos, however, we get to see the full spectrum of their humanity, from outlandish performances of subversive declarations to quiet moments of vulnerability and everything else in between. In "Don't Hurt Yourself," the first song in the narrative arc I have labeled "The Return,"

Beyoncé fully embraces the confrontational chaos of the post-rupture realm as she attempts to boldly remap the orientation of her community.

Emboldened by the restorative agency of Oshun, Beyoncé returns to her community with the blaring sound of drumsticks and guitar strings. "Who the fuck do you think I am?" she screams. "You ain't married to no average bitch, boy . . . /And keep your money, I got my own." (Beyoncé 2016). This moment is significant because she finally confronts her philandering partner and asserts her emotional and financial independence from his controlling grip. She is also able to connect this personal triumph to the larger problem of Black patriarchy in the African American community. This claim is supported by the group of Black women who surround Beyoncé in what looks like an abandoned garage, watching her angrily sing to the camera as she condemns the gatekeepers of patriarchy in their community. The garage scenes are interspersed with black-and-white shots of a carefully choreographed ritual. The surrounding Black women are eerily wrapped in white garments, and as Beyoncé belts out emotionally intense lyrics, they contort their bodies in unison. There are also several close-up black-and-white shots of Beyoncé's expressive face, and she literally looks possessed. The aim of this ritual, it seems, is to orchestrate a community exorcism. Unlike Beyoncé, the less-awake women in her community have not had the opportunity to exorcize the pain of betrayal and unburden themselves of the trauma of generational repression. This explains why they are fixated by the visual spectacle of Beyoncé's return and seem to draw energy from the emotional intensity of her declaration of independence.

The connection between individual affirmations and collective redemption is evident here. The lyrics of "Don't Hurt Yourself" represent moments of individualized affirmations because they solely address Beyoncé's husband, rebuking his attempts to stifle the autonomy of her self-expression. The visuals, on the other hand, underscore a group of Black women who are inspired by Beyoncé's individualized affirmations and decide to support each other by communally exorcizing the generational traumas of anger and betrayal. There is an almost circular movement here that echoes the cultural circulations in the aesthetic imaginary. The communal practice of an indigenous religion (Oshun and Yoruba mythology) catalyzes Beyoncé's individualized affirmations, which in turn catalyzes the collective affirmations of Black women in her community. These cultural circulations between the past, present and possible futures are reinforced by a reference to an iconic ally from the past. The liberation efforts of Beyoncé and her sisterhood are endorsed by a recording of Malcolm X's famous 1962 quote, which plays around the halfway mark of the song. "The most disrespected person in America is the black woman," Malcolm X authoritatively states. "The most unprotected person in America . . . is the black woman" (Beyoncé 2016). These iconic words, culture writer Christine Emba argues, represented then and represents now "a rallying cry for black women who felt sidelined in the fight for civil rights" and "ignored during the feminist awakening" (2019).

There is a great deal to unload here. As I stated earlier, Beyoncé subverts standard expectations by looking to the past for a progressive rhetoric with the potential to affirm the present and positively inform possible futures. She first did this by tapping into the agency of an indigenous African spiritual life force, and she is repeating the pattern here by resurrecting the seemingly progressive words of Malcolm X at the dawn of the civil rights movement. The argument here is not that these periods in the past where she draws affirmative inspiration from were broadly more egalitarian and tolerant than our present society. In 1962, for example, when Malcolm X sent out his alleged rallying cry for Black women, the Civil Rights Act of 1964, which outlawed discrimination on the basis race, color, sex, religion, and national origin, had not been passed. Moreover, Malcolm X was a member of the Nation of Islam, a Black-led political and religious organization notorious for its sexist values. Founded in the United States in 1930 by a mysterious figure called Wallace Fard Muhammad, The Nation of Islam (NOI) "appropriated and repackaged" (Gibson 2012, 13) Islamist teachings for the "African American proletariat in Detroit" (Gibson 2012, 14). NOI can thus be characterized as a syncretic religion because it is an amalgamation of African American culture and Islamist teachings. As NOI's influence grew throughout the 1930s and beyond, it became a formidable Black nationalist movement with tremendous influence on Black Power activists (Austin 2006, 51). Despite claiming to alleviate the plight of all Black people, NOI held profoundly conservative views about gender and "relegated women largely to the domestic sphere. Women's duties were to serve men and care for children. Men were responsible for protecting women" (Austin 2006, 51). Hence, when Malcolm X calls Black women the most unprotected people in America, he is arguably stating that Black men have been "emasculated" and depowered by institutional racism to the point that they are incapable of "protecting" their domesticated women. This argument is endorsed by Malcolm X's own sexist views. He used, for example, "gender ideals to distinguish the Nation of Islam from its rivals in the civil rights movement" (Austin 2006, 53). He condemned the movement for "pursuing what appeared to him to be a docile, subservient, and emasculating mode of political engagement" (Austin 2006, 53), reinforcing the notion that Black nationalism must be led by aggressively masculine leadership. Highlighted here is the nature of power imbalances within syncretic unions, power imbalances that echo Zora Neale Hurston's documentation of suppressed African spiritual practices in inequitable relationships with hegemonic dogmas of Christianity (1990, 185).

Some Black feminist scholars like Sheila Radford-Hill, however, have refused to broadly characterize Malcolm X as a misogynist. Although he was a product of the masculine sensibilities of his time, he did make efforts to engage with and learn from Black feminist writers and political thinkers. For example, after severing ties with NOI, he sought the political counsel of women like Maya Angelou, Coretta Scott King, Shirley Graham DuBois, and Fannie Lou Hamer (Radford-Hill 2010, 65). Additionally, he "was also recruiting women such as Lynne Shifflett, Muriel Feelings, and Alice Mitchell to play key roles in the early development of the Organization of Afro-American Unity" (Radford-Hill 2010, 65) Thus, although Malcolm X was deeply engulfed in the misogynistic values of NOI when he delivered his famous "the most disrespected person in America is the black woman" speech, his later decision to engage with Black feminist thought nuances his legacy.

By replaying Malcolm X's words, Beyoncé is possibly pointing to the progressive evolution of a Black political icon whose journey was cut short by his assassination in 1965. Beyoncé sees herself as continuation of this culturally specific journey that charts Malcolm X's feminist evolution and culminates into her plea for gender equity as she returns to her embattled community, hell bent on confronting the gatekeepers of Black patriarchy. By looking to the past for progressive ideals capable of neutralizing persecution in the present and beyond, Beyoncé is pointing out that even in periods of history we might label as the pre-rupture realm due to the widespread normalization of bigoted policies and practices, there existed defiant enclaves with divergent ideologies. She also draws attention to the fact that her post-rupture existence is physically present in a culturally specific contemporary community dominated by the external marginalizing forces of Black patriarchy. Therefore, her newfound agency, and the women who are inspired by her antiestablishment rhetoric, also represents a defiant enclave with progressive and divergent ideologies. The argument extrapolated from this comparison between past and present is that the third consciousness is not some novel progressive contemporary concept. Human history, from its inception, is peppered with disruptive moments of reformism and even during periods of "enlightenment," tensons still loom and linger at every corner.

In my analysis of Gay's *Bad Feminist* and *Difficult Women*, tension from the pre-rupture realm still lingers in the post-rupture search for counternarratives, a phenomenon I described as a symbiotic relationship between tension and the affirmative aftermath of rupture. Affirmations in both texts are stimulated and even sustained by hegemonic tension. Thus, they do carry genetic traces of the pre-rupture realm in their post-rupture expeditions. With that said, there is a sense of distance between Gay's affirmative singularities and the oppressiveness of communal spaces. I talk about this distance in the first section of this chapter when I discuss the ease at which she moves through and away from spatial dimensions of institutionalized oppression. Simply put, Gay's texts look to the future for an affirmative transformation and not to the past. In *Lemonade*, oppositional forces are not separated by distance. Rather, like aesthetic imaginaries, they are cultural circulations in the same spatial dimension, and their innate attraction to each other guarantees constant frictions, inflections and reconfigurations. Beyoncé wrestles with her community's gatekeepers at the epicenter of tension, looking for strands and enclaves of progressivism in her ancestral DNA with the potential to reevaluate the past, inform the present and reimagine the future. Also worthy of note is that these enclaves can be both real and unreal. To an active member of a defiant enclave, their divergent ideologies feel concrete, immediate and affecting. On the other hand, to citizens of the dominant society that overwhelms and eclipses the defiant enclave, these divergent ideologies might seem like abstract ideas because they lack macro institutional support and thus have no tangible impact on their everyday life.

The aesthetic imaginary is fundamentally oriented by the real versus unreal dialectic. The word "imaginary" naturally evokes the imaginative process of simulating new ideas, thoughts, images and sensations. Because this process, at its current stage, is intangible, it often represents the realm of the unreal. What is therefore "real or actual in the aesthetic imaginary?" (Ghosh 2017, 457). Johannessen's response is the classic paradox: "Imaginaries are *always* imaginary; imaginaries are *never* imaginary" (2018, xi). In other words, the aesthetic imaginary is both real and unreal. There is a danger here of derailing my discussion by going down the rabbit hole of logic philosophy and its extensive reflections on what is real and what is not. I will stay with a traditional understanding of reality as tangible manifestations as I broadly summarize my take on Ghosh's response to the real versus unreal dialectic in the aesthetic imaginary discourse. Ghosh argues that "reality, at times, ceases to be real and becomes the dynamic actual" (2017, 457). The phrase "dynamism actual" is a reference to the constant and dynamic movement of cultural circulations. Culture is always in a state of mutation and these changes, both big and small, are enabled and propelled by imaginative forces, intangible agents capable of disaggregating and reconstructing the concrete nature of our reality. The aesthetic imaginary is therefore a constitution that encompasses both tangible and intangible manifestations of cultural practices, a constitution principled in what Ghosh calls "embeddedness," the notion that "thoughts, images, ideas, and figures are in a state of permanence and . . . motion, belongings of culture and simultaneously trans-belongings" (2017, 462).

This aesthetic focus on the imagination, and how it fluidly navigates the real versus unreal dialectic, is a relevant theoretical model for my manuscript because it echoes the imaginative nature of Beyoncé's Afrofuturistic world-building expedition in *Lemonade*. The aforesaid negotiation between tangible and intangible elements to produce circulating thoughts and ideas that simultaneously belong to culture and exist beyond culture (trans-belongings) is, I argue, strongly represented in "Don't Hurt Yourself." Beyoncé's attempt to build a new order of gender equity is met with resistance from gatekeepers of her community. According to these guardians of tradition, the practice of prioritizing the intersectional concerns of Black women is alien to their culture because it undercuts the historical hegemony of Black patriarchy. This resistance to gender equity is illustrated by the absence of men in the visuals of "Don't Hurt Yourself" and the ritualistic revelation that only Black women are enthralled by Beyoncé's feminist sermons. One can therefore argue that while Beyoncé presents her affirmed feminist agency, and its potential to alleviate the generational plight of her belabored sisterhood, as a real belonging of the culture, the patriarchal gatekeepers of her community believe that it is an unreal belonging of the culture.

Lemonade's engagement with the real versus unreal dichotomy is also discernable in the afore discussed Malcolm X discourse. Malcolm X remains one of the most significant figures in African American history and culture. Like Martin Luther King Jr., he epitomizes the rhetoric of organizational masculine leadership in the Black community and the almost cultlike support surrounding charismatic Black male leadership. Malcom X's perceived feminist evolution, albeit incomplete, challenges the patriarchal practices of the 1960s civil rights era. His evolving feminist inclinations, a result of severing ties with NOI, can thus be described as a defiant enclave surrounded by the hegemony of external marginalizing forces. At the same time, he was a significant cog in the wheel of NOI and the civil rights movement. Hence, his evolving feminist perspectives did not exist apart from this era. Instead, they were in circulation with civil rights discourse of the 1960s and can be persuasively described as being a "real" belonging of the era. I argue that in "Don't Hurt Yourself," Malcolm X represents a cultural moment in the past when arguably the most influential civil rights leader in the Black community was intellectually gravitating toward an acknowledgment, and even prioritization, of Black women's intersectional concerns. Although this acknowledgment did not fully materialize during the civil rights era of the 1960s, it remained part of the epoch's cultural conversation and can thus be characterized as a "real" belonging of the culture. The implication here is that culture is both fixed and in a constant state of metamorphosis. Certain cultural traits society considers "unreal" today were possibly "real" in bygone eras and vice versa. And "real" cultural traits from past periods can return to the present and influence the future, reinforcing the hegemony of cultural constancy across generations. The tendency of community values to disappear and later reappear is reinforced by Beyoncé's decision to record "Don't Hurt Yourself," a quintessential rock song featuring, coproduced and cowritten by Jack White, an acclaimed rock artist.

The rock genre is generally associated with white artists. Although Black artists pioneered the genre and remain active in it, the mainstream image of rock music is systematically embodied by white artistry. A Google search for the most famous rock artists yields results that are dominated by white musicians and bands like the Beatles, Pink Floyd, Led Zeppelin, the Rolling Stones, Queen, Davie Bowie, Elvis Presley, and Aerosmith. In 2016, music writer and historian Jack Hamilton wrote a piece for *Slate* titled "How Rock and Roll Became White: And how the Rolling Stones, a band in love with Black music, helped lead the way to rock's segregated future." The technical elements of rock music have their origins in the artistry of African American artists like Fats Domino and Little Richard, but even as early as the 1960s, there was an ingrained persistence by popular culture discourse to make a distinction between "Black" and "white" music (Hamilton 2016). Having both entities in one category, I speculate, might have elevated Black art to the same standard as white creativity. This was before and during the civil rights movement, so views about race in American society had not yet evolved to what they are today. Due to this need for racial distinction, rock music was classified as "white" and soul music as "Black" (Hamilton 2016). Black singers making rock music during this era were thus often stripped of their rock credentials by the mainstream music industry and erroneously labeled as "soul" artists. This led to the Black community becoming so alienated from the genre that in the mid 1970s, anthropologist Maureen Mahon claims, Black artists who wanted to sing rock music endured ridicule and backlash from both their white and Black peers (Hamilton 2016).

Hamilton goes on to argue that the "whiteness" of rock music was solidified by the commercial and cultural ascendancy of The Rolling Stones, a white British band. "Crucial to the ascendant mythology of the Rolling Stones throughout the 1960s," he points out, "was the band's purported connection to blackness and racial transgression, both in a musical sense and a more vague, imaginative one" (2016). The band borrowed heavily from African American artists like Chuck Berry, Bo Diddley, Little Walter, and Jimmy Reed, in ways Hamilton describes as both "complex" and "controversial," and became disruptive outliers in a genre already actively distancing itself from Black artistry (2016). This arguably made the Rolling Stones the only white-led rock act that presented rock music as an artform "obsessively rooted in tradition, and a black musical traditional specifically" (Hamilton 2016). They reveled in their new role as "conservators of a musical past that they had borrowed from by their own admission and doggedly tried to make their own" (Hamilton 2016), and as the times changed and their popularity soared to stratospheric heights in the post-1960s era, they became an "authentic" representation of the creation and development of rock music (Hamilton 2016). As Hamilton succinctly puts it, "the band that wanted to be Muddy Waters now surrounded by a world of rock musicians who wanted to be them" (2016).

From pioneers like Little Richard and Chuck Berry to celebrated icons like Prince and Tina Turner to contemporary musicians like Gary Clark Jr. and Brittany Howard, Black artists have always been a part of rock music culture. However, because the mainstream imaginary of rock music is strongly tied to white acts like the Rolling Stones and Pink Floyd, the Black origins of the genre are often whitewashed, and Black rock artists seldom achieve mainstream success. "Don't Hurt Yourself" sees Beyoncé reclaiming the Black musical roots of rock music in the mainstream arena and enduring the backlash that comes with challenging the status quo. When the song received a Grammy nomination for Best Rock Performance, there was an uproar on social media with rock fans dismissing Beyoncé's recognition as fraudulent and miscategorized (Joseph 2016). Moreover, since the introduction of the Grammy Award for Best Rock Song in 1992, only two Black artists (Tracy Chapman in 1997 and Gary Clark Jr. in 2020) have won the award (Grammy Awards 2022). This reluctance to associate rock music with Black artistry reinforces Hamilton's argument that mainstream gatekeepers have systematically alienated Black artists from the rock genre.

But resurrected Beyoncé, affirmed by the agency of Oshun, has a strong aversion to hegemonic suppression, so she returns to her community with the thrashing sounds of an electrifying guitar, reclaiming the rich musical diversity of her African American heritage. Having an acclaimed artist like Jack White as a feature, a cowriter, and a coproducer gives her legitimacy in the contemporary rock arena. Recalling the creative process during an interview with NPR, White recalls Beyoncé telling him that "I wanna be in a band with you" (NPR Staff 2016). He was shocked but flattered, so he sent her a "sketch of a lyrical outline," and she transformed it "into the most bodacious, vicious, incredible song. . . . I'm so amazed at what she did with it" (NPR Staff 2016). Beyoncé is thus using "Don't Hurt Yourself" to channel the energy of Black female rock pioneers like Sister Rosetta Tharpe and Big Mama Thornton and (re)educate mainstream gatekeepers about the Black origins and development of the rock genre. Rock music is a real part of Black culture.

This action mirrors Beyoncé's address to Black patriarchy about prioritizing the intersectional interests and demands of Black women. Like some gatekeepers in the mainstream music industry who believe rock music is not an authentic part of Beyoncé's culture, the gatekeepers of Beyoncé's community do not consider gender equity as a real belonging of their culture. She is therefore using rock music to make a point, specifically, to her community gatekeepers and, generally, to the mainstream music industry. Certain cultural traits of a specific community can be silenced over time due to a multitude of reasons. However, the cultural heritage and legacy of these traits should not be dismissed or labeled as "unreal" simply because they lack adequate representation in the contemporary. If these traits still possess the ability to confront external marginalizing forces by affirming both the individual and the community, they can be summoned and used to remap the present and reimagine the future. Using the TCT framework, "Don't Hurt Yourself" can consequently be conceptualized as a counternarrative that sees Beyoncé taking on the role of an educator and innovator because throughout the song, she educates her community, and the mainstream music industry, about a forgotten past with consequential implications for the present and possible futures.

In "Don't Hurt Yourself," as I pointed out earlier, Beyoncé is surrounded by a group of Black women who ritualistically distort their bodies as she angrily rebukes her partner. She is visually depicted as a high priestess because her vocal energy and mannerisms are in complete control of the pace and feeling of the ritual. Because she had already experienced her moment of rupture, she now has the ability to design and execute a similar experience for the women in her community seeking out a third consciousness. In "Sorry," the song that follows "Don't Hurt Yourself," the ritualistic somberness of education and indoctrination is traded for the lightheartedness of sarcasm and laughter.

"Sorry" finds Beyoncé returning to her R&B and hip-hop roots, and the song opens with a poetic monologue titled "Apathy." This particular monologue is not as somber and meditative as the previous ones. There is a sarcastic sadness in Beyoncé's voice as she asks her philandering partner, "So what are you going to say at my funeral now that you have killed me?/Here lies the body of the love of my life, whose heart I broke" (Beyoncé 2016). Another ritual takes place as Beyoncé continues to narrate the monologue. We see Black women seated on a bus, covered in intricately painted body art, elegantly swaying back and forth, and playing from a musical jewelry box is Pyotr Ilyich Tchaikovsky's ballet *Swan Lake*. In *Swan Lake*'s final act, the heroine Odette, a beautiful but cursed maiden, consoles and is consoled by a supportive sisterhood (Green 2018), an act that echoes the nurturing congregation of Black women in Beyoncé's post-rupture realm. In addition to this Afrofuturistic melding of cultural influences, an effort to conceptualize African American womanhood as a cultural experience of aesthetic value, the *Swan Lake* jewelry box music plays like a nursery rhyme and adds a sense of lightheartedness to the serious themes of betrayal and death. As I previously explained, Beyoncé uses nonmusical poetry in *Lemonade* to emphasize tone and subject matter. In "Apathy," she is signaling a change in mood. The blend of lightheartedness and seriousness represents a ritualistic transition from exuberant angst to joyous lightness. In other words, Beyoncé is gesturing that she has exorcized the generational traumas of betrayal and repression, and she is now ready to have some fun with her sisterhood. She ends the monologue by stating that during the torturous period prior to her moment of rupture, "Her god was listening/Her heaven will be a love without betrayal/Ashes to ashes/Dust to sidechicks" (Beyoncé 2016). The colloquial slur for a woman who sleeps with married men is "sidechick," so by saying "ashes to ashes, dust to sidechicks," Beyoncé confirms that she is no longer tormented by the sting of her partner's betrayal. She is ready to have some fun.

"Sorry" revisits the abandoned slave plantation we first encountered in *Lemonade*'s opening monologue. During the first encounter, the mood on the plantation was somber and meditative and the mossy branches of the Southern live oak trees eerily draped the black-and-white cinematography. In "Sorry," this sense of Gothic dread is replaced with a mischievous playfulness as we watch Beyoncé and her sisterhood inside the plantation mansion, singing, dancing, and having a good time. "I ain't sorry," she sings, refusing to apologize for reclaiming an oppressive space that once represented the death of their humanity (Beyoncé 2016). Once again, we see Beyoncé remapping the present into a new aesthetic imaginary. She is attempting here to redraw the borders of the American slave narrative by folding those inhumane centuries of American history into contemporary affirmations designed and experienced by the Black descendants of chattel slavery. She is a manifestation and continuation of the past, so her radical moments of triumph must be folded into the narratives of her ancestors who were abused and dehumanized on this plantation.

This practice of finding affirmative strength from moments of profound sadness is echoed in the song's narrative arc. Beyoncé was inspired to rebel against external marginalizing forces by the prolonged period of despondency in her marriage, and in "Sorry," she refuses to apologize for jumping off the cliff and into her third consciousness. Her husband, it is revealed, has been trying to get in touch with her to no avail. "He trying to roll me up (I ain't sorry)," she sings. "I ain't picking up (I ain't sorry)/Headed to the club (I ain't sorry)/I ain't thinking 'bout you" (Beyoncé 2016). The remarkable weight of her emotional intensity in "Don't Hurt Yourself" must have made an impression on him, so he attempts to reach out, possibly seeking reconciliation. But affirmed Beyoncé does not seem interested. She is going to the club with her sisterhood instead and cheekily tells him to "Suck on my balls, pause, I had enough (Sorry, I ain't sorry)" (Beyoncé 2016). The emphasis on sisterhood here is probably one of *Lemonade*'s strongest arguments for the indispensable value of community. The visual album's historical narrative of African American womanhood is painstakingly detailed and culturally specific. The audience is given tools and cues to learn how to accurately understand and consume this narrative because it is an experience that can only be visually and lyrically re-created with such depth by the women who have chromosomally and culturally lived these lives. Thus, there is an overwhelming sense throughout *Lemonade* that because African American women are the only ones capable of understanding and documenting the full extent of their traumas, they must rely on each other in times when they feel misunderstood and unsupported by the rest of the world.

This argument is strengthened by the appearance of Serena Williams, arguably the greatest female tennis athlete of all time who currently holds the Open era record with twenty-three grand slam singles titles. Tennis is a historically white-dominated sport, so Williams' four decades of accumulating trophies and breaking records have caused a great deal of discomfort in the upper echelon of tennis institutions. In a 2021 article for *The Guardian*, tennis journalist Tumaini Carayol extensively documents how tennis authorities and gatekeepers have consistently undermined Williams over the years. From calling her a man, to making fun of her weight, to even ridiculing the skin color of her biracial baby, "the examples are legion," Carayol stresses. "And tennis is scarred by the failure of the sport's authorities to tackle a culture that enables people with abhorrent views to hold positions of power" (Carayol 2021). Williams herself has acknowledged feeling "'underpaid and undervalued' for her entire career" (Sherry 2020) despite her unparalleled accomplishments. Thus, when she has a "meltdown" on the tennis court, it is important to contextualize these episodes with the decades of aggressions, both micro and macro, she has had to endure and internalize. The Serena Williams we see in "Sorry," however, bears no trace of her fierce intensity on the tennis court. She playfully dances next to Beyoncé in the plantation mansion, flipping her hair, making silly faces and pointing at the camera. In this sisterhood of Black women, she feels understood and appreciated, so she lets her guard down.

Right up to this point, every watershed moment in *Lemonade* is motivated, at least partly, by the social support of sisterhood. In the opening sequence, Beyoncé's personal decision to find a new affirming life force beyond the borders of her community is partly motivated by the historical mistreatment of her sisterhood. This is revealed when she connects the "curse" of philandering fathers in her family to a larger community problem of unfaithful husbands and broken homes. Her decision to seek a different path is strongly influenced by that haunting image of her victimized and neglected sisterhood, wandering hallways at night, trapdoors leading to more trapdoors. Moreover, when she returns to her community with her feminist sermons, she encounters resistance and no male converts. What keeps the intensity of her emotional outbursts consistent is the ritualistic congregation of her sisterhood. They willingly participate in her ritual, giving her, the high priestess, the autonomy to wield unprecedented power in a male-dominated society. Like the symbiosis between affirmations and tension, Beyoncé, the individual, has a symbiotic relationship with her sisterhood, the community.

"Sorry" concludes with Beyoncé providing specific details about the day she left her philandering husband. "I left a note in the hallway/By the time you read it, I'll be far away," she sings. "Let's have a toast to the good life/Suicide before you see this tear fall down my eyes" (Beyoncé 2016). Although these lyrics celebrate her emotional independence from his controlling grip, the tear falling down her eye is a hint that she still loves him. But she cannot stay because he is unreformed, and he will mistake her tear for weakness. After her departure and subsequent return to the community as a "dragon breathing fire" rockstar, he makes several attempts to reconnect with her, but Beyoncé remains unimpressed (Beyoncé 2016). "Big homie better grow up," she sings, insinuating that he still does not fully understand the depth and breadth of her transformative journey (Beyoncé 2016). "He only want me when I'm not here/He better call Becky with the good hair," she continues, quickly sneaking in a cheeky smile before the camera fades to black (Beyoncé 2016).

Becky is colloquial term in African American culture for a basic or unimportant white woman, so the implication here is that Beyoncé's partner cheated on her with a Becky or several Beckies. Before I address the Becky saga, it is important to point out that when Beyoncé sings about Becky with the good hair, she embodies the persona of Egyptian Queen Nefertiti with her caramel skin, elongated neck, sculpted jawline, and Afro textured hair braided into a crown. She sits regally on an empty floor like an art display, her body contorted to resemble an ancient Egyptian monument from the era of the pharaohs. Nefertiti has always represented an almost fairytale longing for "a time of Black female reign and majesty . . . she has been a malleable symbol for many who insist on constructing a notion of black regality" (McDonald J. 2018). The reasons for this association are plenty and complex. This is another rabbit hole I will avoid for fear of derailing my discussion. However, I must briefly mention that due to the degradation of Black womanhood throughout America's contentious history (from the violent objectification and defilement of enslaved black women to the recurring descriptions of Black female bodies as "manly"), African American women have historically lacked compelling symbols of Black femininity and regality. Placed within this context, the enduring potency of the Nefertiti imaginary, especially in Black and Afrofuturistic beauty traditions, makes sense. Beyoncé's partner leaving her, a physical manifestation of the African Queen Nefertiti, the regal apex of Black beauty, for a generic white woman is a crushing reminder of the generational undesirability of Black women. As I discussed in chapter 2, some Black men intentionally seek out white spouses because they view them as a status upgrade (Judice 2008, 23). This explains why even Beyoncé, a walking and breathing representation of Queen Nefertiti, is seemingly no match for a generic white woman and her straight flowy "good" hair, less "difficult" to manage than the kinky texture of Afro hair.

The goal here, I must emphasize, is not to objectify women and reduce their worth to physical beauty. However, it is consequential to point out that despite the historic regality of Beyoncé's beauty and accomplishments, her husband still chose to cheat on her with Becky. This demonstrates the extent of how some Black men have been socially indoctrinated to discredit and diminish the value of Black women in their own communities. But resurrected Beyoncé now knows her worth as an African American woman and refuses to be undervalued. This newfound self-assurance is illustrated when, surrounded by her supporting sisterhood, she sneaks in a cheeky smile after singing, "He only want me when I'm not here/He better call Becky with the good hair" (Beyoncé 2016).

Like "Hold Up," "Sorry" ends on what should be a triumphant note. But when filtered through TCT's characterization of counternarratives as a symbiotic relationship between tension and affirmations, unresolved inconsistences persist. As I briefly mentioned earlier, "Sorry" hints that Beyoncé might still be in love with her husband. Thus, one cannot help but wonder if this feminist spectacle is, to some extent, a staged performance, a ploy to get his attention by acting like he is now an afterthought. Moreover, in the poetic monologue at the genesis of "Sorry," she refers to her "god" watching over her during her pre-rupture tribulations: "Her [Beyoncé's] god was listening/Her heaven will be a love without betrayal" (Beyoncé 2016). But which "god" is she referencing here, the Christian God or Oshun? Although she chastises the patriarchal practices of the church at the beginning of *Lemonade*, she never disavows the Christian God, and in "Sorry," she insinuates that her prayers to him played a role in revealing her partner's philandering exploits. "He always got them fucking excuses," she sings. "I pray to the Lord you reveal what his truth is" (Beyoncé 2016). On the other hand, Beyoncé's post-rupture agency is affirmed and bolstered by the Yoruba Goddess Oshun. Her presence is visible in the body art of Beyoncé and her sisterhood. In specific scenes interspersed throughout the song, their bodies are intricately painted in the sacred Yoruba art of Ori, geometric and twirling patterns of white ink that represent a divine intuition guiding the soul to its destiny (Klein 2015). The implication here is that during the ritual in "Don't Hurt Yourself," Beyoncé educated her sisterhood about the healing powers of Oshun and in "Sorry," they are all affirmed by the Yoruba Goddess who is guiding them to their destiny. This messy discomfort between the Christian God and Oshun echoes the unresolved affirmations of TCT's counternarratives and the aesthetic imaginary's entangled figurations. And in the final stage of act 2's narrative arc, both sanctified entities have a tête-à-tête in the country song "Daddy Lessons," a confrontation with consequential implications for religious scholarship and the efficacy of the aesthetic imaginary.

In the video for "Daddy Lessons," there are recurrent shots of a New Orleans–style funeral procession, exuberantly marching out of a Black church. The decorated coffin swings from side to side and, amid the sorrow of death, the jubilant crowd celebrates the vitality of life. As I extensively discussed previously, the Black church has been routinely accused of propagating patriarchal practices, and the institution has its roots in a Western Christian philosophy that discredits the indigenous humanity of Africans. The same Black church, however, from offering a sense of spiritual solace during plantation slavery to community organizing efforts during the civil rights movement, has often functioned as a positive force for good in everyday African American life. This conflicting role as ally and aggressor is reflected in the funeral procession's ability to simultaneously mourn death and celebrate life. Beyoncé is thus paying homage to the rich legacy of the Black church by specifically highlighting the festive jazz funerals mostly associated with Louisiana, the home state of her maternal ancestry. While she acknowledges the Black church's problematic elements, she cannot, in good faith, discredit the work they have done over the centuries to champion for the spiritual and civil rights interests of her community. This argument is reinforced later in *Lemonade*, during a conversation with an ordinary and unidentified Black woman, a symbol of the dignity of everyday Black life. "So how are we supposed to lead our children to the future? What do we do? How do we lead them?" the woman is asked (Beyoncé 2016). Her response is, "Love. L-O-V-E, love. Mm-mmm-mmm. Hallelujah. Thank you, Jesus. I just love the Lord, I'm sorry, brother. I love the Lord. That's all I got" (Beyoncé 2016). For many African Americans, the benevolence of Jesus's divine love continues to be the only way forward.

Where then does this leave Oshun? She is still the fundamental spiritual force guiding resurrected Beyoncé and her newly affirmed sisterhood, but she is also competing for spiritual influence with the Christian God. Religious scholars will argue that there is not necessarily a divine conflict of interest here. During the colonial era, the Roman Catholic Church was able to rapidly infiltrate and convert the indigenous people of Latin America by integrating their Catholic religious practices with local indigenous customs (Stump 2008, 184). Pursuing religious integration was an effective strategy because the indigenous people saw some aspects of their cultures positively reflected in the practices of the Catholic Church. They were therefore less resistant toward conversion efforts and ultimately embraced, in overwhelmingly large numbers, Catholicism. As I stated prior, religious integration of this nature is described in divinity scholarship as syncretism, and in the Caribbean nation of Cuba, we can find another recognizable syncretic practice known as Santeria (Stump 2008, 184). Santeria's origins can be traced back to the arrival of African slaves in the Spanish-occupied Caribbean Island. Santeria "fashioned a Roman Catholic framework around the traditions of the Yoruba people regarding the worship of orishas, animistic deities associated with forces of nature and human concerns" (Stump 2008, 184). The syncretic practice "retained African elements . . . but linked these practices to the veneration of particular Roman Catholic saints. Specific associations included . . . Our Lady of Charity, the patron saint of Cuba, with Oshun, the goddess of love" (Stump 2008, 184). Oshun thus has a long tradition in the New World of functioning as a mediator between Yoruba mythology and Christianity. We see her performing a similar role in *Lemonade*. She spiritually empowers and affirms her descendants without completely dismantling their faith in the Christian God.

Although these syncretic cultural circulations broadly echo the "shared realities" of cross-border navigations into the aesthetic imaginary (Ghosh 2017, 450) and the hybridized *inter*-national culture emerging from the cultural contradictions of Bhabha's ambivalent third space, they are more philosophically aligned with the womanist ethics of divinity scholars Katie Geneva Cannon, Emilie M. Townes and Angela D. Sims. Woman theologians "critique sacred writings, philosophical formulas, and theological reflections" from a Black feminist point of view (Cannon et al. 2011, xv). They focus mostly on Black Christianity, paying particular attention to how the gender and racial dimensions of cross-cultural tensions expose inequities within the social ecosystem of religious practices (Cannon et al. 2011, xv). Although they engage with the diverse religious heritage of African American culture, they unequivocally describe their primary goal as translating "womanist scholarship into the service of the church and community" (Cannon et al. 2011, xvi). In other words, despite their attempts at challenging institutionalized hierarchies in the Church, they remain fundamentally Christian. This is where the cracks of cultural circulations begin to show because there is an unaddressed resistance here that embraces the hegemony of constancy and ultimately rejects the compromise of integration. The significance of this rejection is the emergence of a knowledge system, which expresses its skepticism of cultural circulations by underscoring the necessity of cultural separation. Below, I will begin with a critique of womanist theology before circling back to the aesthetic imaginary. Addressing this critical omission (the aforementioned unaddressed resistance) will provide a fuller understanding of Beyoncé's unresolved discomforts in *Lemonade* and emphasize the need for a theoretical expansion of the TCT framework.

As I pointed out earlier in this chapter, the concept of salvation is the fundamental doctrine of Christianity. Christians acquire the gift of God's grace by accepting Jesus Christ as their lone lord and savior. Without the salvation of this divine grace, Christians are "insensible of God and the things of God" and cannot be "saved from the guilt of sin" (Wesley 1833, 236). In other words, believers who contest Jesus's role as the sole dispenser of salvation are destined for eternal damnation. If religious integration, the practice of syncretism, is about equity, then believers should be able to allocate the same level of spiritual importance to both Oshun and Jesus. This is not the case, I argue, in womanist theology. Despite their attempts to unveil and unpack the history and cultural tensions within the African American religious space, they remain, by their own admission, fundamentally in service to the church and cannot, as a result, challenge Jesus's uncontested role as the sole pathway to divine grace.

A similar resistance occurs in Santeria. Although Santeria incorporates elements of Christianity into its iconography and practices, Jesus Christ is not the sole pathway to spiritual redemption. According to Santeria scholar Miguel A. De La Torre, divine grace, the concept of acquiring the largesse of God's favor through salvation, "does not exist in Santeria. . . . Rather than being offered grace, the sinner must supplicate for mercy, making offerings to placate the offended orisha" (2004, 18). Earning forgiveness entirely "depends on the whim of the orisha, which may grant or withhold grace irrelevant to the sincerity of the sinner's remorse" (De La Torre 2004, 18). The religious supremacy of orishas is therefore unchallenged, and they will not tolerate seeking penance elsewhere. Before proceeding, it is important to acknowledge the more sinister aspects of Yoruba mythology. Unlike the Christian God who does not withhold grace from sinners seeking penance, orishas prefer to toy with their transgressed devotees, offering or denying grace based on how they feel at any given moment. Hence, Yoruba mythology, depending on the scenario, has unjust religious practices, which can equally function as an external marginalizing force. However, as I stated earlier, Oshun is known as the orisha of compassion, and her feminist agency as the only female orisha in the sacred pantheon of seventeen orishas who came to Earth at the dawn of time makes her more sympathetic toward the struggles of marginalized groups.

While there is a degree of integration happening in both Yoruba mythology and Christianity, they each retain certain nonnegotiable tenets that problematize the act of cultural circulations in the aesthetic imaginary. Ghosh describes "the recurrent problematic" (2017, 449) of oppositional forces as a negativity that exposes callings and constraints and causes frictions, inflections and reconfigurations (2017, 449–50). While frictions and constraints certainly exist between Yoruba mythology and Christianity, inflections and reconfigurations imply a mixing and molding that does not happen with the concept of salvation. Like oil and water, the mercy of orishas and the salvation of Jesus refuse to mix. Compromise is impossible because a Christian who welcomes the mercy of orishas inadvertently challenges the supremacy of Jesus and thus ceases to be a Christian. The same outcome happens in Santeria. A devotee who embraces God's divine grace invalidates the practice of supplicating for mercy from the offended orisha and thus ceases to be a Santeria believer. The cultural circulations of the aesthetic imaginary imply movement, a flow, a sense of spreading and distribution, with or without resolution. In this specific example of salvation, however, both institutions are stationary.

Lemonade, one can argue, is an attempt to equitably integrate Yoruba mythology and Christianity. Although Beyoncé is affirmed by the positive role of the Black church in the African American community, her ritualistic performances supplicate for mercy from Oshun. When filtered through the afore discussed concept of salvation, this divine double act falls apart. The versions of salvation offered by the two deities directly contradict each other, so she cannot be both a Santeria devotee and a Christian. This emphasis on separation and stagnation illustrates a weakness of using the template of the aesthetic imaginary to read the full spectrum of *Lemonade*'s unresolved discomforts. While the circulations of entangled figurations deepen an understanding of Beyoncé's post-rupture attempt to construct a novel universe by pulling together various cultural influences and references, the end result of her spiritual expedition, I argue, is ultimately an acknowledgment of oppositional forces that refuse to circulate. While describing the applicability of the aesthetic imaginary in the visual realm of filmmaking, visual culture scholar Asbjørn Grønstad points out that "undecidability" is one of the emerging concept's epistemological underpinnings (2018, 13). In the context of *Lemonade*, undecidability can be conceptualized as Beyoncé's inability to choose between Yoruba mythology and Christianity. She is affirmed by both religions and thus chooses to exist somewhere in between. Undecidability can also be conceptualized as the antithesis of both religious practices. While they are willing to mutate and compromise in certain areas, they have decided and fixed precepts about the theological doctrine of salvation, a fixedness that problematizes Beyoncé's attempt at trying to be both a Christian and a Santeria devotee.

The refusal of these oppositional forces to circulate or overlap also points to a central difference between TCT's symbiosis and the concept of hybridity. Unlike the interrelations and interdependence of cultures in hybridity's third space, *Lemonade*'s symbiotic tensions, affirmative feelings produced by the tension between the individual and the collective and the tension between community's conflicting role as both ally and aggressor, are, in certain instances, oriented by fixed knowledge systems that resist the notion of hybridizing with other cultural practices to produce a new *inter*-national culture. Thus, to accommodate this theoretical complexity, the TCT framework has to reengage with the notion of the right to difference, the idea that affirmative experiences occur when the subject rejects the fixed knowledge systems of external marginalizing forces and seeks the liberation of difference in the post-rupture realm.

My reading of *Lemonade*'s religious identity reveals that the dogmas of fixed knowledge systems (like Yoruba mythology and the Black church) can also affirm the individual in the post-rupture realm. To a Santeria devotee, Oshun represents the resilience of their indigenous African culture despite centuries of institutionalized attempts to discredit its integrity. And to the Black Christian, the Black church represents the resilience of the African American spirit despite centuries of institutionalized attempts to discredit its humanity. Hence, filtered through the TCT framework, a push to inflect and reconfigure foundational elements of salvation in both religions can also be conceptualized as an external marginalizing force. This brings us back, almost full circle, to the unresolved discomfort between community's fight for constancy and the individual's right to difference. Both approaches, TCT argues, are affirmative and destructive in equal part.

Amid the backdrop of act 2's divine showdown between Christianity and Santeria is another central dilemma: Beyoncé begins to contemplate reconciliation with her husband or moving forward alone. "Daddy Lessons" begins with Beyoncé conversing with a mother figure. "Mother dearest let me inherit the Earth," she begins. "Teach me how to make him beg . . . / Did he bend your reflection . . . /Are you a slave to the back of his hand?" (Beyoncé 2016). These harrowing words, draped with dread and sadness, revisits the theme of generational trauma. Beyoncé, first, ponders if the more experienced mother figure has any remedies to make the men in Beyoncé's life "bend," a metaphor here for reformation—another hint that despite her elaborate spectacles of feminist emancipation in "Hold Up" and "Don't Hurt Yourself," she is still in love with her partner. More troubling is when Beyoncé confesses that she cannot make a behavioral distinction between the mother figure's husband and father: "Am I talking about your husband or your father?" (Beyoncé 2016). This revelation, once again, emphasizes how African American women are tormented by the generational trauma of Black hypermasculinity. Their fathers become their husbands, and their husbands inevitably become their sons.

"Daddy Lessons" is a country song, and, as with "Don't Hurt Yourself," Beyoncé is reclaiming a genre that is white dominated but has its roots in Black artistry. In a 2016 article for *Vox*, culture writer Victoria M. Massie documents the Black and West African roots of country music, arguing that "Daddy Lessons" pushes against the myth that the genre has no Black influences. "Before Nashville was the home of the Country Music Hall of Fame and Museum, country music was a genre borne of African slaves," Massie argues. "Indeed, musicologists have traced country music's iconic banjo back to the ngoni and xalam, plucked stringed instruments rooted in West Africa" (Massie 2016). She also mentions DeFord Bailey, a Black pioneer of 1920s country music who "drew from the black folk music tradition he grew up with," and Ray Charles's 1962 album *Modern Sounds in Country and Western Music*, "the first country record to sell 1 million copies, ushering in the possibility" of mainstream success for country music acts (Massie 2016). In both "Don't Hurt Yourself" and "Daddy Lessons," Beyoncé uses cross-genre experimentation as an educational tool that uses the past to rethink the present and its possible futures. While she uses rock music in "Don't Hurt Yourself" to partly educate her community's patriarchal gatekeepers about their ancestral commitment to gender parity, she uses country music in "Daddy Lessons" to educate herself about how her father's upbringing impacted the decisions he made as an adult. Beyoncé's conversation with the mother figure has left her haunted by the contagious curse of Black hypermasculinity, and she begins to wonder if she should empathize with the contaminated men in her family. To find out, she journeys to her Southern roots, the area of America most identified with country music. Effortlessly riding a horse through the fields of her childhood, she uses country music to explore the rugged terrain of her father's decisions.

"Texas, Texas . . . Texas," Beyoncé sings affectionately in the intro of "Daddy Lessons," letting us know that she in her beloved home state (Beyoncé 2016). "Came into this world, daddy's little girl," she continues. "And Daddy made soldier out of me" (Beyoncé 2016). Her relationship with her father is established in this verse. He is deeply in love with his daughter, so he tries to protect her from the traumas of adulthood by making a soldier out of her. His fondness for whiskey in his tea ("And Daddy liked his whiskey with his tea" [Beyoncé 2016]) suggests he is trying to numb his own traumas. He is perhaps arming his daughter for the perils of adulthood because he does not want her to be plagued by the same traumas haunting him. As he tries to make his daughter a "tough girl" by teaching her how to ride motorcycles, appreciate the art form of classic vinyl, and play blackjack, he begs her to "'Take care of your mother'" (Beyoncé 2016). This simple but devastating request is an acknowledgment of his own failure to protect his wife. He, like his father before him, inherited the generational trauma of Black hypermasculinity, and his inability to break the cycle damaged his relationship with his wife. Plagued by guilt, he dedicates the rest of his life to teaching Beyoncé how to protect herself and her family by "shooting" men who look like him: "'When trouble comes in town and men like me come around'/Oh, my daddy said shoot/Oh, my daddy said shoot" (Beyoncé 2016).

The contradictory role of community is, once again, highlighted. The visual Southern aesthetic embodies community's function as the source of social support. We see Black men affectionately carrying their daughters, horse rides on dirt roads, ranches, lush greenery and scenes of camaraderie among friends. There is a sense that Beyoncé's South is profoundly nourished not only by their proximity and attachment to nature, but also by the emotional connections within the community. Buried on this same land, however, are the seeds of Black hypermasculinity, a toxic ideology born out of Southern white patriarchy and plantation slavery. This contradiction is echoed in the actions of Beyoncé's father, a family man who embodies but detests the culturally inherited traits of Black hypermasculinity. My objective here is to contextualize his behavior and not to excuse it. While "Daddy Lessons" does not portray him as an innocent victim, his backstory is given the dignity of nuance. He is the product of a deeply patriarchal environment and without institutional interruption and the influence of positive role models, he was destined to repeat the same mistakes his forefathers made.

As Beyoncé contemplates forgiveness in "Daddy Lessons," one cannot help but wonder if she sees parallels between her father and her husband. With the knowledge she has acquired from going down memory lane, Beyoncé is perhaps wondering if like her father, her husband is drinking whiskey with his tea, plagued by the guilt of failing to end the cycle of generational trauma. But given her earlier feminist declarations, reconciling with a philandering husband might appear to some as an act of hypocrisy. There is a plethora of published research on feminism and infidelity. While there are differing takes on this issue, the consensus is that most societies are more forgiving of philandering husbands. When men cheat, it is considered as "expected" and "okay" (Sacco and Laino 2011, 91). Conversely, when women engage in similar extramarital affairs, they are perceived as "used/damaged goods" and unworthy of forgiveness (Sacco and Laino 2011, 91). Thus, when women take back their unfaithful husbands, they are arguably propagating the double standard of this power imbalance. Grand ideologies about empowerment and liberation tend to seem uncomplicated and rational in a public intellectual sphere. But when these ideologies retreat into the emotional entanglements of a smaller individualized space, they must contend with the complicated feelings of interpersonal relationships and cultural baggage. In the uniqueness of Beyoncé's lived experience as a Black woman in a culturally specific African American community, she has to make a decision that complements the vision of the world she is trying to build, and "Daddy Lessons" serves as a witness to this process.

Where then does Beyoncé go from here? By the end of "Daddy Lessons," she is in a state of limbo, unsure of her religious identity and undecided on forgiving her philandering husband. In the next and final Act, she is visibly exhausted and somewhat confused by the challenging spectacle of imaginative world building, so she retreats inward to recuperate and realign her priorities. The outcome of this meditative retreat is, at first, shocking but, upon further reflection, foreseeable. What Beyoncé has been fighting for all along is her radical right to traditionalism. In act 3, I will conclude chapter 3 by using the remodified TCT framework to understand how in the cultural specificity of Beyoncé's lived experience, the assumed backwardness of traditionalism's constancy is inverted to represent the most subversive act in the performative spectacle of *Lemonade*.

ACT 3: RADICAL TRADITIONALISM

The final act begins with Beyoncé crouching mournfully on a football field.[4] As tears roll down her cheek, two members of her sisterhood watch over her from the seating area in a stadium devoid of spectators. We are almost back to where we began in the opening of *Lemonade* when we were introduced to a mournful Beyoncé crouching on an empty stage. A football field is typically associated with the rowdiness of live games and cheering spectators. Here, it is eerily quiet. Only two members of her sisterhood are present, but they watch in silence from a distance, suggesting that Beyoncé is retreating from the spectacle of public performativity and withdrawing into herself. A poetic monologue titled "Reformation" sees her revisiting life with her philandering husband. "I ask him to look me in the eye when I come home," she recounts. "Why do you deny yourself heaven? . . . / Why are you afraid of love?" (Beyoncé 2016). And then she declares, "But you are the love of my life" (Beyoncé 2016). The impact of revisiting her father's past and the generational curse of Black hypermasculinity is evident in these words. She begins to understand that perhaps her husband cannot genuinely receive love because he lacks the emotional tools to navigate and express his feelings. This would explain why Beyoncé's husband feels undeserving of love and inevitably hurts the woman who tries to love him. Throughout the "Reformation" poem, we see brief flashbacks to moments like the ritualistic scenes in "Don't Hurt Yourself" and the eerie branches of Southern live oak trees. The arduous efforts of *Lemonade*'s world-building exercise have culminated in this moment: The grand stage of community redemption has ironically cornered her into a private space where she must confront the difficult and conflicted emotions attached to her personal relationship with her husband, a relationship she cannot seem to terminate.

As Beyoncé prepares to have a frank conversation with her spouse, I argue that she anticipates the backlash that usually comes with empowered feminists extending grace to their cheating husbands. This argument is supported by the visuals of the somber ballad "Love Drought," the first song in *Lemonade*'s "Reformation" chapter. "Ten times out of nine, I know you're lying/But nine times out of ten, I know you're trying/So I'm trying to be fair," she sings, echoing the compassion of Oshun, and acknowledging for the first time that her husband did make attempts in the pre-rupture realm, albeit insufficient, to break the toxic cycle of philandering husbands and broken homes (Beyoncé 2016). As Beyoncé revisits the ordeal of trying to love a man who struggles to receive love, her sisterhood returns and together, they march solemnly in a single file into the ocean, a scene photographer and visual artist Mikael Owunna compares to folkloric descriptions of the 1803 Igbo Landing on St. Simons Island, Georgia.

The Igbo Landing, arguably one of the most iconic images of resistance in American history, occurred when "a group of Igbo slaves revolted and took control of their slave ship, grounded it on an island, and rather than submit to slavery, proceeded to march into water while singing in Igbo, drowning themselves in turn" (Owunna 2017).[5] This formidable act of "mass resistance against the horrors of slavery . . . became a legend, particularly amongst the Gullah people living near the site of Igbo Landing" (Owunna 2017). If you recall, Beyoncé references Julie Dash's *Daughters of the Dust* earlier in *Lemonade*, a movie about Gullah women torn between their individual freedom and commitment to culture. In this full circle moment, Beyoncé uses the collective resistance of the Igbo Landing to validate the unique orientation of her personal resistance. Let me elaborate. In the context of a philandering spouse seemingly incapable of receiving love, an expected reading of feminist resistance would be terminating the relationship by denying him a grace society refuses to extend to unfaithful wives in similar scenarios. In the culturally specific reality of Beyoncé's lived experience as an African American woman, however, feminist resistance can take other forms. What the Igbo Landing illustrates is that the African American experience, from its inception, has been plagued by institutional efforts to discredit its humanity, efforts that in addition to historically devaluing Black womanhood, have also propagated destructive patriarchal values in the African American community. Thus, feminist resistance to Beyoncé can also mean breaking the generational curse of Black hypermasculinity by building a stable traditional family, a two-parent household sustained by the values of gender equity and capable of safeguarding the next generation of Black children from the traumas of long-suffering mothers and emotionally absent fathers.

What the average modern American considers traditional might be interpreted as progressive to an African American community directly affected by systematic efforts to dismantle the Black family unit. There is an almost infinite amount of research about the generational effects of institutional poverty and oppression on Black families. During the crack epidemic of the 1980s, for example, African American users of the substance, mostly poor and residing in inner cities, were overpoliced and over punished. Richard Nixon's "war on drugs" in 1971 inspired and facilitated the passing of laws like the 1986 bipartisan Anti-Drug Abuse Act, which normalized the excessive criminalization of Black Americans (Equal Justice Initiative 2019). First, there was the scapegoating. Exaggerating narratives about the violence of "crackheads" and their doomed "crack babies" repeatedly "portrayed crack users as Black, even though most crack users were and still are white" (Equal Justice Initiative 2019). Darryl Strawberry, a former Major League baseball player who had a publicly known addiction to crack and other drugs, argues that "the stigma was so wrong for African Americans. They couldn't get the help they needed because everybody looked at them as 'less than.'" (Equal Justice Initiative 2019). As a result of this widespread racial stigma, humane rehabilitation efforts were shunned, and Black drug users suffered harsher penalties than their white counterparts. Between 1991 to 2001, for example, "nine times as many Black people as white people went to federal prison for crack offenses. . . . Black people's sentences for crack were double that for white crack offenders in federal court during that period: 148 months compared to 84 months" (Equal Justice Initiative 2019).

Because Black users were systemically stigmatized and denied adequate rehabilitative assistance, the qualitative findings of sociologists including Eloise Dunlap, Andrew Golub, and Bruce D. Johnson reveal how the crack epidemic violently consumed and fundamentally destabilized inner-city Black households. Their studies reveal stories of absent fathers, patriarchal violence, resentful mothers, child abuse, and generational dysfunction (Dunlap et al. 2006, 7–12). The children "born to members of the Crack Generation are avoiding use of crack but face major deficits from their difficult childhoods" (Dunlap et al. 2006, 1). Thus, to members of the African American community still impacted by systemic stigmatization and oppression, traditional families, two-parent households with emotionally supportive fathers and mothers, represent a subversively progressive illustration of everyday family life. This is the claim Beyoncé tries to make, I argue, by using the Igbo Landing imagery, a symbol of African American suffering in the institutional reconstruction of the New World, to validate her subversive interpretation of traditionalism as reconciliation with her reformed husband, an act capable of breaking generational curses and reimagining bolder futures. "If we're gonna heal, let it be glorious," Beyoncé says in the subsequent poem. "There is a curse that will be broken" (Beyoncé 2016).

This is admittedly a controversial argument to make because the burden of fixing broken men and transforming communities should not be disproportionately placed on women. For this version of resistance to work, broken men must be genuinely reformed and just as willing to remap a bolder and better future for their progeny. In the soulful redemptive ballad "Sandcastles," Beyoncé's husband is ready for the task. "We built sandcastles that washed away," she sings as he walks into her home, pleading for forgiveness. "I made you cry when I walked away" (Beyoncé 2016). This is the first admission that her departure left him emotionally distraught and the act of crying here emphasizes that he was forced to confront and understand his emotions, possibly for the first time in his life. The most aesthetically jarring element of "Sandcastles" is the visual performance of forgiveness. We finally see her philandering partner, a role played by hip-hop mogul Jay-Z, and he submits completely to her interrogation. "Your heart is broken 'cause I walked away" she tells him but remains somewhat skeptical of his plea for reconciliation (Beyoncé 2016). She needs more evidence that he is at last emotionally attuned to the generational role Black men have played in the devaluation of Black womanhood and is now ready to begin the gargantuan task of reimaging their community's future. "Show me your scars," she demands and promises not to "walk away" if they are real (Beyoncé 2016). He complies without hesitation, submitting to her will and cuddling her bare feet. This vulnerable image of Jay-Z, the hypermasculine rapper who once bragged about "big pimpin,' spendin' G's" (2000) and having "ninety-nine problems but a bitch ain't one" (2004), now cradling Beyoncé's bare feet unsettles the viewer because unfettered vulnerability is not a trait one associates with the patriarchal boastfulness of hip-hop culture. The unveiling of his emotional scars is a transformative deconstruction of Black hypermasculinity that broadens the spectrum of who Black men are and what they can become. It is also arguably the most significant moment in *Lemonade*, because it represents the possibility of breaking a generational curse, which has haunted and tormented African American women for centuries. *Lemonade* is therefore an odyssean journey about one woman's determination to save her family. Desperate to accomplish her goal, Beyoncé constructs a new Afrofuturistic world from the ground up, finding sources of strength from various transatlantic influences in order to rethink and remap her community's institutional understanding and implementation of cultural knowledge systems.

Before proceeding, I must underscore that Beyoncé's conceptualization of heterosexual traditionalism as a progressive institution does not negate or discredit other affirmative experiences such as same sex couples, single parent households, unmarried women and childless mothers. The cultural specificity of *Lemonade* is a celebration of the unique experiences of heterosexual African American women, experiences that are classified as "heteronormative" but, like other marginalized groups and alternative ways of life, still endure hegemonic humiliation and devaluation. *Lemonade* thus makes a persuasive case for an understanding of identity that is not rigidly bound to fixed categorizations. While some modern feminists and LGBTQ activists label the traditional family as patriarchal and backward, the social support afforded to children by the nurturing union of loving wives and their committed husbands is viewed in other marginalized communities as a progressive institution of stability. Both ideas represent two truths, and they are not mutually exclusive. *Lemonade*'s emphasis on the constancy of traditional family values takes us back to Beyoncé's moment of rupture, the moment she leapt off the edge and journeyed through her ancestral past to find an affirmative life force in the constancy of Yoruba spiritual practices. TCT's identification of the thematic and aesthetic recurrence of constancy once again demonstrates that unlike the aesthetic imaginary and the presumed hybridity of syncretic unions, certain concepts like religious salvation and heterosexual unions reject circulations and inflections. Their power to inform, inspire, and potentially reconstruct new worlds is rooted in the fixedness of their meanings across generations. Community is thus simultaneously fixed and fluid.

The song that follows the momentous act of reconciliation is "Forward," a one-minute ethereal ballad featuring British singer and songwriter James Blake. "Forward/Best foot first just in case/When we made our way 'til now/ It's time to listen, it's time to fight/Forward," the evocative softness of Blake's voice sings (Beyoncé 2016). "Forward" prepares the reunited lovers for the journey that lies ahead and functions as a brief transition into the post-reconciliation experience. Worthy of emphasis here is the fact that Beyoncé's vocals are mostly in the background and the rawness of Blake's soft voice takes center stage. The implication of this technical arrangement is that the masculine voice has at last emotionally matured by embracing the tenderness of vulnerable feelings. "Forward" also features the mothers of Trayvon Martin and Eric Garner, Sybrina Fulton and Gwen Carr respectively, holding photos of their slain sons. Martin and Garner are arguably two of the most recognizable examples of unarmed Black men killed by the police, and they have become the martyred figures fueling grassroot movements aimed at critiquing and reforming racialized police brutality in law enforcement institutions.

The intertwined nature of the individual and the community resurfaces. After confronting a deeply personal family issue and choosing the transformative agency of reconciliation, Beyoncé feels reenergized and reaffirmed and ready to take on larger institutional problems affecting her community. While there is no indication that her community has been systematically rid of patriarchal values, her husband's presumed reformation is proof that her counternarrative as an educator and innovator is yielding dividends. Beyoncé's return to larger institutional problems affecting all members of her community is magnified in "Freedom," an R&B- and hip-hop-influenced song featuring socially conscious rapper Kendrick Lamar. When both Beyoncé and Lamar sing about freedom's ability to "break chains" and cut them loose from the constraints of bondage, they are not only singing about Beyoncé's feminist emancipation from the patriarchal grip of Black hypermasculinity but also about their community's institutional emancipation from systemic oppression. The message here is that Black women should no longer be expected to champion the interests of a community that refuses to acknowledge and support their intersectional interests. Beyoncé only returns to the public sphere of civil rights activism after her husband acknowledges the legitimacy of her pain and decides to move forward as an equal contributor to the spectacle of imaginative world building in *Lemonade*. Simply put, she will only champion the interests of Black men if more Black men like her reformed husband are willing to champion the intersectional interests of Black women. Beyoncé, it seems, has finally made sweet lemonade out of sour lemons, but as experience dictates, the messiness of unresolved discomforts is always lurking nearby.

"All Night," *Lemonade*'s final ballad, is heralded by a poem titled "Redemption." The poem begins with a lemonade recipe by her grandmother, "the alchemist" who "spun gold out of this hard life" (Beyoncé 2016). "Take one pint of water," her grandmother instructs. "Add half a pound of sugar, the juice of eight lemons, the zest of half a lemon/Pour the water from one jug." (Beyoncé 2016). This lemonade recipe, passed to her daughter, Beyoncé's mother, who then passed it down to Beyoncé, is a generational message about making something sweet out of something sour, a motivational appeal to find inner strength in moments of despondency and darkness by tapping into the collective reservoir of African American traditions (Beyoncé 2016).

From the era of chattel slavery to the civil rights movement, African Americans have always used recipes and cookbooks to preserve their cultural traditions and resist total assimilation into dominant white culture (Zafar 1999, 451–53). By preserving the secrets of her inner strength in a lemonade recipe and passing it on to her daughter, Beyoncé's grandmother is continuing the legacy of an established African American culinary tradition. And this is the inner strength Beyoncé taps into when she journeys to her ancestral past and supplicates for mercy from Oshun, a compassionate orisha who embodies the feminist agency of her indigenous African heritage. This strength is responsible for her bodacious counternarrative as the community educator and innovator, the role that encourages other Black women to exorcize the generational trauma of betrayal and inspires her husband to seek redemption.

The interconnected nature of the individual and the community is again underscored. Even when Beyoncé is burdened by the public spectacle of performativity and retreats inward, some of the cogitations informing her personal family decisions are rooted in a collective reservoir of African American history and folklore. The individual and the community become indistinguishable as they move in and out of each other, a symbiotic existence that blurs epistemological demarcations. Despite its shortcomings, the aesthetic imaginary's real versus unreal dialectic reemerges here and remains a central component of my analysis. In *Lemonade*, conceptual differences between the individual and the community feel tactile and self-evident in key moments like the visual album's opening scene when a melancholic Beyoncé feels like the only self-aware individual within a predestined and externally mandated community performance. Her loneliness and disconnect from the master narratives of the pre-rupture realm are both visually and aesthetically palpable, and as she moves from scene to scene, re-creating and reimagining her identity, the affirmative liberation of individualism arguably becomes the visual album's epistemological cornerstone. However, in other parts of *Lemonade* like the afore discussed poem "Redemption," the concept of individualism is culturally inapplicable to the specificity of Beyoncé's lived experiences as an African American woman. Every epiphany she has ever had or any decision she has ever made is informed in some shape or form by the wellspring of community wisdom. There is no resolution to this discomfort between individual and community but like the aesthetic imaginary, the intermingling of both concepts, ideological circulations in spatial dimensions, provides insight on the cultural complexities of identity formation. To reecho the classic paradox, "Imaginaries are *always* imaginary; imaginaries are *never* imaginary" (Johannessen 2018, xi)

"All Night" celebrates the reunification of true love and the wisdom Beyoncé and her husband have acquired from working through their tumultuous breakup and coming out on the other side, reformed, refreshed and reimagined. "I found the truth beneath your lies/ And true love never has to hide," she soothingly sings. "I'll trade your broken wings for mine" (Beyoncé 2016). The implication here is that her husband no longer conceals his vulnerabilities. Their true love never has to hide, so he is learning to give and receive love in equal part. As Beyoncé croons about making "Sweet love all night long," we see endearing snapshots of a variety of couples, lesbian, old, gay, interracial etc., in candid moments of tenderness and affection, an ode to the enduring power of true love in all its forms (Beyoncé 2016). But amid this joyous multiracial, multigenerational, and multidimensional celebration of love is a tinge of melancholy and apprehension. Although the lyrics affectionately serenade the listener, there is a haunting sense of hurt and exhaustion in Beyoncé's voice. To get to this point, she has had to jump off a cliff, build a time machine for a journey back to an almost mythological past, traverse the high tide waves of the Atlantic and, brick by brick, rethink, remap, and reconstruct an entirely new universe with an assortment of cultural influences and references. As she slowly moves alone through a picturesque field in an antebellum gown made with African wax print, an Afrofuturistic fusion echoing the depth of *Lemonade*'s cultural references, one cannot help but notice that she looks somewhat fatigued, weighed down by the sting of battle scars. While singing about the healing power of transformative love, she is possibly also wondering if it was all worth it. We sense this apprehension when she sings, "Give you some time to prove that I can trust you again," admitting that she still fears the imminent collapse of this world she has meticulously reconstructed with every morsel of strength in her being (Beyoncé 2016). But the show must go on; she must move forward. There is no turning back now. "All Night" ends with a scene on the empty football field where she crouched in isolation earlier, tears streaming down her cheeks. This time, we see Jay-Z and Blue Ivy Carter, her husband and daughter, playfully running around and affectionately falling on the lush green pitch. Her daughter is growing up with an emotionally present father who is attentive to the needs of all the women in his life. The curse, it seems, has been broken.

Lemonade concludes its odyssean journey with "Formation" a disruptive Black power anthem that fittingly lays bare and celebrates the unresolved discomforts of Beyoncé's narrative arc. The R&B and rap-influenced track, a celebration of her Southern cultural heritage, uses musical horns to create a harmonical heaviness by mimicking New Orleans marching bands and distorted 808 beats. Affirmed by Oshun's agency and the transformative power of true love, Beyoncé returns to the South to present her true self in all its shades, forms, affirmations and contradictions. "Formation" begins with images of a post-Katrina New Orleans, its infrastructure and economic vitality still grieving from the effects of the natural disaster. These scenes reference the institutional failures to protect the low-income Black families of New Orleans in the wake of Hurricane Katrina (Belkhir and Charlemaine 2007, 126), and Beyoncé connects these failures to another institutional problem of police brutality. "Formation" was released on February 6, 2016, "the day after what should have been Trayvon Martin's 21st Birthday. One day before what should have been Sandra Bland's 29th" (Cross 2016), an intersectional reference that highlights both the intersectional interests of Black women and the institutional police persecution of unarmed Black men. There is a shot of Beyoncé a in Gucci shirtdress (Ward 2016), sitting on a drowning cop car in a flooded neighborhood. She is pointing out the tendency of natural disasters to disproportionately harm marginalized people with little to no institutional protection. And by placing a drowning cop car in the center of Hurricane Katrina, she makes a direct correlation between institutional failures and desecrated African American communities.

There is an obvious sense of irony when Beyoncé sings about "rocking" haute couture Givenchy clothes while wearing Gucci and sitting atop a cop car in a low-income neighborhood completely decimated by Hurricane Katrina. As I mentioned earlier, Beyoncé often draws the ire of radical feminists and activists who accuse her of promoting capitalist values in her music and business ventures. While I do not sufficiently engage with the capitalism discourse because it is not central to my research, it is important to underline that the accumulation of wealth has a different function in the traditions of

African American music and culture. African Americans, despite their plentiful contributions to American society since the 1600s, did not have a consequential seat at the American democratic table until civil rights movement in the 1960s. Because they have historically been denied their equitable share of America's abundant resources, the allure of wealth and power is naturally more intense in the African American community. Thus, the obsession with wealth in Black and hip-hop music is "a natural response to poverty, violence, and oppression" (Kornhaber 2016). My goal here is to contextualize, not justify, the lust for wealth in certain parts of *Lemonade*. There is certainly a problematic insensitivity demonstrated by the action of flaunting overpriced designer clothes in a destitute neighborhood completely ravaged by natural and human disasters.

For Beyoncé, however, there is seemingly nothing ironic or problematic about wearing Gucci in a low-income neighborhood. She is the daughter of the slave plantations on this land, but she now wields an immense amount of influence that was unfathomable to her enslaved ancestors. She thus returns home to pay her respects to her Southern heritage by unapologetically celebrating her socioeconomic accomplishments. She sees her wealth and her power as an extension of her ancestors' legacy, and she uses this influence to reimagine the South not only as land of suffering and slavery, but also as a fertile ground for undying hope and transformative triumphs. This argument is corroborated by her emphasis on lineage. "My daddy Alabama/momma Louisiana," she raps in a custom bodysuit and Chanel necklace (Ward 2016), flanked by her supportive sisterhood in the hallway of the reclaimed plantation mansion. "You mix that negro with that Creole, make a Texas bama" (Beyoncé 2016). She brings both the physical and emotional weight of her wealth and influence to reclaim the plantation mansion and replace hanging portraits of its white slaveholders, some of them in her DNA due to her mixed Creole heritage, with regal paintings of her Black ancestors. "Earned all this money, but they never take the country out me," she sings, implying that her wealth and influence is always going to be used for the betterment of her community (Beyoncé 2016). All shades of Southern history, from the slaves to the slaveholders, reside uncomfortably in Beyoncé's DNA. And while they do not harmoniously coexist, they circulate within her like the entangled figurations of the aesthetic imaginary and fuel her belief that transformative triumphs are birthed from generational suffering.

Another unresolved discomfort that lingers is her religious identity. One of the opening shots in "Formation" is an image of a dignified Black preacher leaning over his pulpit, staring powerfully into the camera like he is trying save the viewer's soul from eternal damnation. This brief but intense moment is in stark reminder that Beyoncé remains torn between two versions of salvation. Her undecidability, one can persuasively argues, exposes the tensions of existing between different cultural and religious identities. Beyoncé is not obliged to make a choice between both deities. By residing in the spatial dimension between Christianity and Yoruba mythology, she echoes the unresolved complexities of identity formation in our modern world, a historic age of globalization that is rethinking and remapping our entrenched perceptions of borders, space and time. This is certainly a valid reading of religious identity in *Lemonade*. However, when examined through the prism of the remodeled TCT framework, I find a glaring loophole in this syncretic hypothesis. As I pointed out earlier, although both religious systems allow for some nuance and flexibility in certain areas, their understanding of the nature and dispersion of salvation remains fundamentally unchanged. In Christianity, Jesus is the only and nonnegotiable pathway to divine grace and in Santeria, supplicating mercy from orishas is the only and nonnegotiable pathway to spiritual redemption. These ideologies, unlike the mobile negotiations of the aesthetic imaginary, the syncretic principles of Angela Davis's noncontradictory oppositions and the intermingling of postcolonial cultures in Bhabha's hybridized third space, remain in a perpetual state of constancy, and they derive their affirmative powers from the fixedness of their meanings. In other words, the concept of religious salvation is inherently a rejection of syncretism.

One can argue that Beyoncé's subversive decision to remain affirmed by the grace of both deities challenges power structures in both institutions and reimagines an interfaith framework that allows the African American experience, an experience rooted in both Christianity and indigenous African mythology, to celebrate the full diversity of its religious heritage. While this is a fair counterargument, it comes at an existential cost. To a devout Christian, labeling the healing powers of the orishas as a legitimate substitute for Jesus' divine grace is a sacrilegious act that defiles the sacredness of biblical scriptures by engaging in the "heathen" practice of polytheism. Beyoncé's syncretic religious identity can thus be viewed as an external marginalizing force seeking to invade and corrupt the belief system of well-meaning Christians who too might be advocates of gender and racial equity but prefer to operate within the philosophical dimensions of their religious epistemology. And to the Santeria devotee, labeling Jesus's divine grace as a legitimate substitute for the healing powers of the orishas is an equally sacrilegious act that arguably undermines the humanity of indigenous Africans by viewing their spiritual practices as remnants of a lost barbaric polytheist era. There is a colonial subtext in saying that the gods of indigenous peoples have an omnipotent, omnipresent, and omniscient monotheistic Western substitute, a subtext that functions as an external marginalizing force seeking to invalidate the richness and sophistication of precolonial cultures.

The TCT framework thus argues that in our contemporary age of forward-looking movements and progressivism, we tend to overstate the affirmative triumphs of cultural circulations, syncretic negotiations and integration. What my reading of *Lemonade* reveals is that the fixedness of certain practices across centuries and generations also possess transformative powers capable of affirming the present and remapping the future. This argument is paralleled by *Lemonade*'s radical rethinking of traditionalism. As aforementioned, Beyoncé rethinks traditionalism as a stable two-parent household capable of breaking the generational curse of Black hypermasculinity and reshaping the futures of her progeny. An even more radical reading of traditionalism in *Lemonade* is the concept of salvation but not in the context of prior discussions. During the visual album's rousing finale, it becomes clear that the divine dispenser of Beyoncé's salvation is neither Jesus's divine grace nor Oshun's healing powers. Although she remains existentially empowered by both sacred philosophies, what ultimately resuscitates her from the depths of melancholy and brings her back to life is the old and traditional concept of true love. As unbelievably cliché as it sounds, true love is her salvation. In the "Redemption" poem, she remembers her grandmother telling her that "Nothing real can be threatened" (Beyoncé 2016), so when her husband returns, reformed and bowing at her bare feet, the prophecy is fulfilled. The solid foundation of true love, she realizes, can conquer any and every obstacle. "True love brought salvation back into me," she confesses. "With every tear came redemption and my torturer became my remedy" (Beyoncé 2016). In this epiphanic moment, she finally understands that all along, true love has been the driving force behind her post-rupture motivations.

This emphasis on love echoes James Baldwin's philosophical ruminations in the 1960s. Baldwin had spent most of his career discussing race relations, arguing "succinctly and powerfully" that white Americans must contend with the "the kinds of power they held just because they were white" and "what kinds of things they could take for granted that nonwhite folks could not" (Schultz 2018, 49). After gaining an awareness of this power, Baldwin urged them to cross racial lines and fight with all Americans "like lovers . . . to end the racial nightmare, and achieve our country, and change the history of the world" (1963, 105). In other words, true love is America's only salvation because it confronts the destabilizing nature of tension by taking "off the masks that we fear we cannot live without and know we cannot live within" (Baldwin 1963, 95). Love, Baldwin clarifies, is not "merely in the personal sense but as a state of being, or a state of grace—not in the infantile American sense of being happy but in the tough and universal sense of quest and daring and growth" (1963, 95). In this context, true love is a personal and collective commitment "premised on complete honesty and forgiveness of sins and abuses" (Schultz 2018, 49)

While Baldwin focuses on a collective performance of true love capable of alleviating the existential weight of racial trauma on both the individual and the community, *Lemonade* concludes by drawing attention to an individual expression of true love capable of alleviating the existential tensions and traumas of community leadership. Although Beyoncé had broader motivations like reuniting with her sisterhood, civil rights activism, and promoting gender equity values, her undying love for her husband was the wind in the sails of her odyssean sojourn. Her soul mate's misgivings plunged her into the depths of melancholy and set her on the arduous path to saving her marriage. It was this personal sense of true love that sent her over the edge and into her third consciousness and inspired her to find an affirming ancestral life force capable of reframing and remapping her community, an act that inspires her husband to find his way back to her by beginning the process of deconstructing the inherited trauma of Black hypermasculinity. "So we're gonna heal/We're gonna start again . . . " Beyoncé declares (2016). "Pull me back together again, the way you cut me in half," she tells her reformed husband. "Make the woman in doubt disappear . . . /The audience applauds . . . but we can't hear them" (Beyoncé 2016).

These romantic but haunting words platform the central role of true love in Beyoncé's narrative arc. The whole point of the lavish spectacle of *Lemonade* was to arrive at this moment of a redemptive reunion: her reformed husband proving his worth by stitching her back together after cutting her in half. The fading sound of the audience's applause is Beyoncé's acknowledgment that as a ubiquitous popular artist, every moment of her life will be infinitely observed, scrutinized, praised and critiqued. She is aware of the polarizing performance of her persona in the public sphere (greedy capitalist versus community advocate, empowered modern feminist versus traditional wife, Christian versus Oshun devotee, etc.), but in this tender moment of her redemptive reunion with her true love, they both drown out the noise of the ever-present audience and retreat into themselves. While she embraces her role as an educator and innovator, a role rooted in the rich history of civil rights leadership, she is human, so she often feels the crushing burden of her communal responsibilities. Community needs leaders to change the present and inspire the future but for leaders to be emotionally effective, they deserve periods of individual respite, periods not burdened by the crushing weight of communal discomforts. In the poem "Redemption," individualism momentarily triumphs when true love offers Beyoncé sanctuary from the unresolved tensions and discomforts of public life.

This yearning for an ordinary life away from the overwhelming discomforts of hegemonic concepts and categories transitions to the fourth and final chapter of my manuscript, a discussion of the HBO television series *Insecure* (2016–2021), and further deepens the dynamism of counternarratives by Black female authorship in contemporary American culture. *Insecure*'s focus on the everyday objects and activities in the ordinary lives of millennial Black women in modern day Los Angeles inspires the TCT framework, once again, to rethink the use and applicability of recurrent concepts like rupture, affirmations, and external marginalizing forces. Using the aesthetics of the everyday life as my theoretical substructure, I work through a revised framework that conceptualizes ordinary life as a disruptive aesthetic, which is different from but remains in conversation with Gay's subversive singularities and Beyoncé's feminist spectacle.

NOTES

1. Contemporary here refers to post-1999.
2. Hill's win for Album of the Year made her, Natalie Cole, and Whitney Houston the only black women to ever win Album of the Year in the Grammys' sixty-something-year history (Ahlgrim 2020), an award that has been won by the likes of Taylor Swift, Beck, Billie Eilish, Daft Punk, and Kacey Musgraves. This speaks to a much larger issue, the systemic disrespect of African American female artistry despite its unparalleled contributions to the development and evolution of popular American music.
3. Although Oshun is still revered and worshipped in some parts of modern Nigeria (Alarcón 2008, 733), her influence pales in comparison to the modern influence of imported religions like Islam and Christianity. As aforementioned, the intensification of Europe's colonialization of Africa in the eighteenth century led to the delegitimization and near eradication of indigenous African religions on the continent and similar eradication efforts were carried out in the New World. Many people of Yoruba descent were captured and enslaved during the transatlantic slave, and although their indigenous spiritual practices failed to prosper in America, a small but active group of Oshun devotees thrived in Caribbean and Latin American countries like Cuba (Murphy and Sanford 2001, 4–5).
4. American football.
5. The Igbo people are from a territory in what is now known as Nigeria.

Chapter Four

Popular Television Culture

Issa Rae's Insecure

EXTRAORDINARILY ORDINARY

Insecure's origins can be traced back to African American writer, actress and producer Issa Rae's first foray into writing and acting, her 2011 comedy web series *The Misadventures of Awkward Black Girl* (Jung 2016).[1] Rae's web series premiered on YouTube in 2011 with Rae playing the lead character J, an ordinary young Black woman who has the hilariously profound capacity to navigate "race, dating, and office politics" with "quick, observational humor" (Jung 2016). *Awkward Black Girl*, movie and film critic Alex Jung points out, "capitalized on the promise of the internet, where a funny, original Black woman could make a hit series that you wouldn't likely see on TV at the time" (2016). In an era dominated by mainstream television hits like *Game of Thrones*, *Black Mirror*, and *Homeland* and Black-led sitcoms like *For Better or Worse* and *Let's Stay Together*, the everyday "plainness" and raw relatability of Rae's quirky characters offered audiences a refreshingly different take on the Black experience. The novel uniqueness of *Awkward Black Girl* caught the attention of industry powerhouses, and after over three years of writing *Insecure*, Rae's script made the transition from internet to television (Davis 2016).

Created by Issa Rae and African American actor, writer, and producer Larry Wilmore, HBO premiered *Insecure* on September 23, 2016, to near universal critical acclaim. While David Sims of *The Atlantic* hails *Insecure* as an exploration of the "regular lives of people of color" (2016), Bethonie Butler of the *Washington Post* praises the show for spinning "the mundane into hilarity, while defying stereotypes" (2016). Additionally, Amber Dowling of The Wrap describes the first season as "an honest, unflinching look at dating, relationships and life, told from a refreshing and hilarious perspective" (Rotten Tomatoes 2021), and Jade Budowski of Decider argues that the show "has a way of making even the most mundane activities interesting, and there's a relatable sincerity present that should not be missed" (Rotten Tomatoes 2021). This refreshing emphasis on mundanity is central to my analysis, because it has the aesthetic ability to rethink and reimagine previously conceptualized and argued tenets of the TCT framework. While the aforementioned critics have applauded *Insecure* for its celebration of a Black female experience that is refreshingly awkward and nonconformist, not enough has been said about the aesthetic function of ordinariness. *Insecure*'s aesthetic form, I argue in this chapter, beckons for a temporary space of reprieve, a space rebelling against the hegemonic mandates of the external world by nurturing what I term an enclosed enclave, which allows its subjects to relish in the transformative power of ordinary life. By moving away from grand epiphanies and moments of spectacle in the external world and retreating into enclosed enclaves that celebrate the value of everydayness, *Insecure*'s affirmative experiences are prompted and sustained by traditions of ordinary life. Traditions in the enclosed enclave, it is imperative to point out, are not always reflective of the shared practices within the African American community. Rather, they are mostly simple and, in some cases, seemingly irreverent acts like eating at a restaurant and buying a couch. Imbued in these acts, however, are everyday activities with the transformative potential to subvert hegemonic notions of race and gender and, as a result, complexify the experiences of Black womanhood. Thus, unlike *Bad Feminist*, *Difficult Women* and *Lemonade*, *Insecure*'s subversive affirmations reside in the quietude of ordinary pursuits. Traditions, it is also important to point out, are often an effort to preserve a fixed set of values and practices. The enclosed enclave's attempt to seek solace in the affirmative constancy of mundane practices consequently puts it at odds with the Deleuzian concept of infinitely becoming and idioculture's emphasis on a unique orientation divested from broader value systems. These tensions compel the TCT framework to reorient its analytical apparatus and work through a theoretical scaffolding that recognizes ordinary life as an audacious representation of rupture.

Before elaborating on my argument, it is imperative to mention that *Insecure* is not the first Black-led television show to celebrate ordinary Black life. According to media and television scholar Adrien Sebro, the first Black television show was a sitcom that "'originated from a radio program, *Amos 'n' Andy*, in which two white men portrayed the characters'" (Chen 2021). When the radio show was adapted to television in the 1950s, Sebro continues, "'it was the first show to have an all-Black cast, to talk about the Black community, but it was obviously still othered'" (Chen 2021). Othered here refers to the fact that some viewers found the setting and themes of the show dehumanizingly unrealistic. *Amos 'n' Andy* mostly ignored "real-life problems" facing the Black community, and the "get rich schemes" of its animated and occasionally dishonest characters were accused of perpetuating "demeaning stereotypes" of Black people (Buck 2018). With that said, the diversity of the show's everyday Black characters has been praised for "normalizing" Black life and providing employment for Black actors during a period of minimal Black representation on American television (Buck 2018). *Amos 'n' Andy* premiered on Columbia Broadcasting System (CBS), a mainstream broadcast television and radio network, in 1951 (Buck 2018). Shortly after the show aired, it was ranked number thirteen by Nielsen ratings and remained in syndication for thirteen years after it was taken off the network's schedule (Buck 2018). Thus, despite its archetypal and offensive sensibilities, *Amos 'n' Andy* is indisputably the first television show to expose mainstream America to an imaginary of ordinary Black life.

The next milestone for Black representation on mainstream television was arguably the premiere of *Julia* (1968–1971) on the National Broadcasting Company (NBC). Starring the regal Diahann Carroll as *Julia*'s titular character, the sitcom lightheartedly explores the idiosyncrasies of Julia's everyday life as she juggles the responsibilities of mother, nurse, and friend. Created by Jewish American writer, director and producer Hal Kanter, the idea for *Julia* was conceived during a National Association for the Advanced of Colored People (NAACP) meeting with Kanter in attendance. According to Diahann Carroll, the meeting alerted Kanter to the absence of positive portrayals of Black Americans in media, which in turn inspired him to create an uplifting show with a middle-class Black female lead (Bush 2016). *Julia* thus made Diahann Carroll the first African American actress to star in a non-stereotypical role on a weekly broadcast television series[2]. Like *Amos n' Andy*, *Julia*'s critical reception was mixed. *Variety*, for example, dismissively decried, "In matters as sensitive as race relations, even sitcom characters will have to have a little substance" (Bogle 2015, 144), and the *Saturday Review* described Julia's suburban lifestyle as "a far, far cry from the bitter realities of Negro life in the urban ghetto, the pit of America's explosion potential" (Haywood 2017). Supporters of *Julia* dismissed the criticism as an unfair, and even sexist, double standard. Sitcoms, the New York *Daily News* pointed out, have always functioned as "'escapism television . . . so why, when a Negro actress is starred in the same kind of series does she suddenly have to carry the weight of the whole racial question on her delicate shoulders?'" (Bogle 2015, 144). *Ebony* magazine also chimed in, arguing that although Julia's everyday experiences as a middle-class nurse do not necessarily mirror the experiences of most Black Americans, the show should be applauded for exposing its audiences to a different side of the Black experience (Bogle 2015, 145).

Other milestones include, but are not limited to, *I Spy* (1965–1968) starring Robert Culp and Black comedian Bill Cosby. Set in the heightened reality of the spy world, the show can be described as the antithesis of ordinary life. However, Cosby's role as a competent intelligence agent normalized Black men in non-stereotypical roles and promoted an imaginary of the Black co-lead as "acceptable" in mainstream media narratives (Buck 2018). Then came the epic television miniseries *Roots* in 1977. The drama's unflinching look at systemic racial oppression, from the transatlantic slave trade to lynchings, was "the first of its kind," and its widespread popularity (about 85 percent of households in America watched the miniseries) helped to normalize discussions about Black history in everyday life (Buck 2018). Also worthy of note here is *The Jeffersons* (1975–1985), widely considered to be one of the greatest sitcoms of all time (Buck 2018). Its comedic focus on a Black American family achieving their American dream of economic prosperity is peppered with profound insights about the challenges of cultural assimilation, generational disconnect, classist prejudices, gender roles, and interracial relationships. *The Jeffersons* depicts ordinary Black family life in all its complicated shades and ushered in an explosive new era (beginning in the 1980s and fully blossoming in the 1990s) of the Black family sitcom.

The Cosby Show (1984–1992) is arguably America's most famous Black family sitcom. Created by Bill Cosby, Ed Weinberger, and Michael J. Leeson, it was "the first of its kind to have a primarily Black cast" and "proved to naysayers that you can have an all-Black cast and become successful without leaning on the shoulders of white actors to bring in the ratings" (Buck 2018). Known for its polished and respectable depiction of Black family life, the show used its humor to deliver "moral messages" such as "getting your children to eat vegetables" and the strategies to employ when your daughter is "dating someone undesirable" (Griffith 2014). The enduring success and legacy of *The Cosby Show* facilitated the explosion of Black television in the 1980s and 1990s and "networks fought to create positive programming for an engaged demographic" (Griffith 2014) with sitcoms of everyday Black life such as *The Cosby show* spin-off *A Different World* (1987–1993), *The Fresh Prince of Bel-Air* starring Will Smith (1990–1996), and *Living Single* starring Queen Latifah (1993–1998).

I would be remiss if I did not briefly discuss the recent dent on the legacy of *The Cosby Show*. The goal of this slight detour is to acknowledge Bill Cosby's cultural impact on Black representation in mainstream television without disregarding the current discourse about how his alleged predatory behavior problematizes Black women's relationship with his art. This detour will also demonstrate the central theme of my manuscript: the uncomfortable intermediate existence Black women often inhabit between racial and gendered identities. During the apex of the #MeToo movement, sexual misconduct allegations against Bill Cosby came to light. Despite denying the claims, he was eventually sentenced in 2018 "to 3 to 10 years in prison" for the 2004 assault of then Temple University employee Andrea Constand (Lockhart 2018). The day after his sentencing, the *Los Angeles Times* chronicled a fifty-year time line of approximately two dozen accusations, from the 1960s to the 2000s, levied against Cosby (*Los Angeles Times* 2018). Like my discussion in the Introduction about sexual misconduct allegations involving R. Kelly (a R&B legend greatly beloved by the Black community), Cosby's Black supporters were conflicted about these revelations (F. Jones 2015). Here is a Black man who normalized Black family life in the American media imaginary and promoted a positive portrayal of the Black family unit as stable, educated, cultured, ambitious, and resilient. His impact is deeply felt in African American culture, and this explains why many Black women, impressed by his respectable depictions of Black femininity, decided to stand by him. For example, celebrated Black actress Phylicia Rashad, who played his wife on *The Cosby Show*, described the allegations in 2015 as an "orchestrated" demolition of his legacy, a sentiment supported at the time by other Black female celebrities like Jill Scott and Whoopi Goldberg (F. Jones 2015).

As I also discussed in the Introduction and elsewhere, the Black community tends to succumb to a masculine rhetoric of organizational leadership (Eaton 2010, 1). Because Black men are often viewed as the true leaders and gatekeepers of African American culture and legacy, there is usually a rallying cry from within the Black community to defend their honor when they are under attack or scrutiny. The fact that an overwhelming majority of Cosby's accusers are white women also adds another layer of complexity to the controversy. As Black writer and mental health social worker Feminista Jones puts it, "one reason some have defended Cosby is because many of the women coming forward are white and there is a well-documented history of white women making allegations against Black boys and men that have destroyed towns and sparked resistance movements" (F. Jones 2015). With that said, Jones does not see the institutional mistreatment of Black men as a persuasive enough reason to defend the alleged actions of Cosby. Not only is Cosby also accused of sexually assaulting Black women, the credible testimonies of most of his accusers, regardless of race, suggest he "was methodical and intentional in his approach to allegedly drugging women and patterns of physical assault" (F. Jones 2015). Black women, Jones continues, "are too often charged with prioritizing race over gender under the cloak of a racial 'unity' that doesn't always benefit us because of sexism and misogyny within our communities" (2015). Thus, for Black feminists like Jones, the legacy of Cosby is forever compromised. There is a case here for separating the art from the artist. One can simultaneously reprimand Cosby the person while acknowledging that his artistic legacy engineered a creative boom on television, a creative boom primarily responsible for reimagining popular perceptions of what everyday Black family life looked like or could look like. Such an acknowledgment, I must clarify, is not an incentive to fund the Cosby estate by supporting and/or purchasing his art. Rather, it is merely an admission of the cornerstone role his art has played in popular television culture and beyond.

Controversies aside, the impact of pioneering sitcoms like *The Cosby Show*, *Living Single*, and *The Fresh Prince of Bel-Air* is still visible in a wide range of Black-led shows in today's television landscape. From *Girlfriends* (2000–2008) to *Black-ish* (2014–2022), these contemporary shows follow a similar pattern of demystifying the Black experience by attempting to depict Black life as ordinary and universally relatable. However, like their predecessors, the full spectrum of their narrative depth is often stifled by the sitcom/comedy genre. The sitcom genre is usually frivolous and inoffensive. Because its primary goal is to comfort and entertain, it relies on a carefully curated comedic template that strives to make audiences feel better about themselves and the world. Thus, despite the social commentary in shows like *The Jeffersons* and *A Different World*, the comfort of convenient resolutions awaits the audience at the narrative's conclusion. Moreover, the situational nature of humor in sitcoms follows a formulaic structure that requires characters to function within unrealistic scenarios, lessening, in the process, the authenticity of their ordinariness. This is where *Awkward Black Girl* comes in. Operating in the expansive digital realm of the internet, far removed from the heavy regulations of mainstream network television, Rae was able to craft and star in a web series that is both funny and gritty. Unlike the brightly lit Banks family in *The Fresh Prince of Bel-Air* or the statuesque femininity of *Girlfriends*, the characters of *Awkward Black Girl* are plain and almost unremarkable. But this is precisely the charm of Rae's web series. Despite the punchlines and sitcom tropes (the best friend/sidekick, the love interest, the archnemesis, etc.), the characters are not "polished" and reformatted for television. They look, sound, and act like the ordinary people in our schools, jobs, social circles, etc. and although, in keeping in the sitcom/comedy tradition, they do not have moments of portentous spectacles and explosive epiphanies, they unsettle their audience, in ways traditional comedies are incapable of, by exposing, mocking, and ultimately succumbing to the all-consuming drudgery of everyday life.

HBO's *Insecure* finds Rae re-creating the winning formula of her web series for the television format. Worthy of mention is the fact that HBO's creative output, often dubbed "prestige television," is vastly different from standard television fare. Although it is a mainstream network (due to its massive commercial reach), HBO is subscription-based. Unlike broadcast television that generates revenue by transmitting its typically innocuous programs to any television set in America within range of a broadcast transmitter, HBO's audience pay a subscription fee to watch a specific kind of niche and gritty programming. Examples of HBO shows that challenged and reimagined the creative boundaries of television include *The Sopranos*, *The Wire*, *Sex and the City*, *Curb Your Enthusiasm*, *Veep*, *Girls*, the earlier seasons of *Game of Thrones*, the first season of *True Detective*, and even the afore discussed multimodal visual album *Lemonade*. Lena Dunham's *Girls*, mostly applauded for its "honest" take on millennial girlhood, was briefly mentioned in chapter 1's analysis of Gay's essay collection *Bad Feminist*. Dunham's show, although critically acclaimed, was widely panned by feminists of color for its "whitewashed" depiction of millennial life in New York City (Stewart 2012). Although cognizant of the show's problematic elements, Gay points out that burden of representation in media should rest on the shoulders of television executives making decisions about what kinds of stories they choose to amplify on their platforms and not young creatives like Dunham who can only write about what they know (2014, 58). HBO was perhaps listening. Their decision to collaborate with Rae, giving her the creative license to craft a funny, nuanced, and ordinary narrative about millennial Black women in modern-day Los Angeles, makes a case for the argument that true representation requires allowing a diverse pool of creatives telling authentic stories about their worldview and not shoehorning token characters of color into unfamiliar narrative scenarios in a desperate bid to appease representation advocates.

There is no obvious shoehorning in *Insecure*. Like *Awkward Black Girl*, Rae plays the lead role (Issa Dee), and the characters feel like people you recognize in your everyday life. The comedic finesse and narrative templates of Rae's writing borrows from the rich legacy of Black television shows and sitcoms about ordinary Black people and families. However, a few important characteristics make *Insecure* extraordinarily unique. *Insecure* is HBO's first foray into gritty and realistic narratives about African American womanhood. Although complex stories about the female experience have long thrived on the network (*Sex and the City*, *Girls*, etc.), the Black female perspective as the driving narrative force was absent until *Insecure*. Also worthy of note is the fact that an examination of everydayness is an intrinsic component of television shows belonging to the comedy-drama genre (FX's *Better Things*, BBC Three/Amazon Studios' *Fleabag*, Netflix's *The Kominsky Method*, etc.). However, the Black female narrative voice is often missing from these mainstream depictions of everydayness. Rae's presence on HBO is therefore a cultural milestone because for the first time in popular television culture, a young Black female creative in the comedy-drama genre is being elevated, as a creator, writer, and actress, to the upper echelons of scripted prestige television.

Moreover, unlike Black-led sitcoms, *Insecure*'s dramatic discourse is unafraid to tackle serious themes, which refuse to comfort audiences or offer them a satisfying resolution at the conclusion of the narrative. The show generally does not rely on situational comedy for the mere sake of eliciting laughter. Instead, comedy is used to humanize its characters and prevent them from becoming remarkable beings and stereotypical figures. In addition to revealing her relatable insecurities, the comedic clumsiness of Issa Dee, the lead character played by Rae, is mostly used as a segue to profound explorations about the micro and macro aggressions deeply embedded in the fabric of ordinary life. Issa Dee is not a larger-than-life pop star engaging in the gargantuan task of imaginative world building. She also has very little in common with the transgressive characters of *Difficult Women* and lacks the tonal assuredness of *Bad Feminist*. What makes her extraordinary, however, is the ordinariness of her aesthetic style. In *Insecure*, Black women are not transgressive feminists with almost superhuman world building abilities. They are simply human, mostly flawed, sometimes funny, always ordinary.

This reimagination of African American womanhood has consequential implications for the TCT framework because there are no grand moments of rupture comparable to those found in Gay's and Beyoncé's texts. In *Bad Feminist*, *Difficult Women*, and *Lemonade*, the quintessential moment of rupture occurs during an explosive confrontation with external marginalizing forces and what follows this contentious encounter is the exploration of possible counternarratives usually sustained by the affirmative grandeur of transgressive and transatlantic knowledge systems. Although similar external marginalizing forces lurk beyond the borders of *Insecure*'s enclosed enclaves, affirmations in this universe are mostly derived from the simplicity of ordinary people, activities, and objects. Because *Insecure* begins with a strong affirmation of the unique value of ordinariness, it *begins* as an exploration of a possible counternarrative, a counternarrative seeking to reimagine Black womanhood as extraordinarily ordinary. Its most momentous rupture thus resides in its aesthetic construction of ordinariness as an affirmative live force and not in its narrative arc. My analysis will therefore emphasize the aesthetic style (mise-en-scène and cinematography) of *Insecure*'s enclosed enclaves over a chronological discussion of narrative threads from season 1 through 5, the final season.

In the next section, I will use concepts about the aesthetics of ordinary life by writer Njabulo Ndebele and philosopher Yuriko Saito to illustrate why and how *Insecure* aestheticizes ordinariness, paying particular attention to the implications of this aestheticization on television tropes, rap music, female agency, and the pervasive allure of Black hypermasculinity. My analysis in this section argues that characters, activities and objects within *Insecure*'s mise-en-scène, its locations and set designs, affirmatively celebrate the ordinary nature of everyday traditions and emotions, traditions and emotions that must coexist with outbursts of tension in new and familiar places. And in the final section, I will shift my attention to the photographic distortion of Black skin, a result of cinematography's inherent color bias. Although *Insecure* attempts to address this cinematic shortcoming by properly lighting its Black cast, its camera techniques tend to over glisten Black bodies, creating a sense of cinematic spectacle and wonderment that undercuts a prior emphasis on everyday relatability. This symbiotic tension between the loudness of spectacle and the quietude of ordinariness is at the core of TCT's remodeled framework because it unearths and amplifies a pivotal philosophical dimension in my discourse on the affirmative discomforts of Black female authorship in contemporary American culture.

TROPES, LOOPS, AND SPECTACLE

Insecure chronicles the everyday happenings of Issa Dee and Molly Carter, two Black women in their late twenties from Los Angeles, California. Best friends since their college days at Stanford University, both women are on different paths in life. Molly dominates the corporate world. She settles seemingly impossible cases and has an effortless rapport with her coworkers. With her long straight hair, petite frame, and confident swagger, she echoes a more familiar representation of Black womanhood in Black-led shows and sitcoms. Issa, on the other hand, is physically and aesthetically a novelty.[3] The pilot episode, written by Rae and Wilmore and directed by Melina Matsoukas, begins with Issa standing in front of classroom, representing We Got Y'all, the nonprofit she works for, an after-school program for underserved and marginalized middle-school and high-school students. Passionate and eager, Issa outlines their services (after school tutoring, mentoring programs, community service etc.) to uniformed students of color and cheekily assures them, "whatever it is you need to succeed, We Got Y'all" (Rae and Wilmore 2016–2021). The students are disinterested and unimpressed. They mock her appearance (mom jeans and a thrifty oversized shirt), her hair (short coiffed and tightly coiled natural hair) and career choice. And they also wonder, out loud, if she is single and why she talks "like a white girl" (Rae and Wilmore 2016–2021).

This opening sequence is emblematic of *Insecure*'s aesthetic audacity. By having disinterested students posing rude and invasive comments about Issa's appearance and mannerisms, Rae, the creator, is acknowledging and confronting the visual novelty of Issa in the mainstream media space of prestige television. Issa, in my opinion, is not a homely woman. She has an infectious smile, smooth skin, and an angular face. However, she does not look like any of the leading ladies, regardless of race, we are familiar with seeing on critically acclaimed mainstream television shows. She is dark-skinned, has visible Sub-Saharan African features, wears her 4C natural hair (the kinkiest texture of Black hair) and is not shaped like a supermodel. She looks healthy and fit but in an ordinary kind of way, the vision of fitness one would normally associate with an everyday healthy-looking individual and not the toned and polished image of a leading lady on a hit television show. Issa's visual presentation is a deliberate aesthetic choice that challenges audiences at the very genesis of *Insecure*'s narrative to rethink and reorient their hegemonic perceptions of what a lead actress on prestige television should look like.

Moreover, Issa's response to the discourteous students demonstrates an awkwardly passionate defense for her right to difference, her right to be unburdened by societal expectations and her right to be ordinary. "I came from a great family. I have a college degree," she tells the young teenagers. "I work in a nonprofit world because I like to give back. I've been with my boyfriend for five years, and I did this to my hair on purpose" (Rae and Wilmore 2016–2021). There is an attempt at defiance here, but her delivery is mostly clumsy. She tries to sound upbeat and confident, owning her appearance and life choices, but there is a tinge of sadness and anger in her tone. The truth is she is not entirely satisfied with her job (as We Got Y'all's only Black employee, she endures microaggressions from her white coworkers), feels emotionally disconnected from her boyfriend, and is trammeled by the pressure society puts on Black women to adhere to Eurocentric beauty standards. Although she puts on a brave face to perform her job responsibilities, she is visibly insecure about her ability to cope with these daunting pressures of everyday life.

By emphasizing the relatable nature of Issa's insecurities and the ordinariness of her appearance, Rae reimagines Black womanhood as the girl next door, one of television's most recognizable tropes. Entertainment writer Dustin Bowles describes the archetypal girl next door as "sweet . . . wholesome . . . and unassuming" (2014). "She's not interested in social status," he continues. "And in the end, she becomes the favored choice over the likes of the flashy, provocative, or overly sexualized love interest" (Bowles 2014). Popular examples of girls next door include Pam Beasley from *The Office* (US), Winnie Cooper from *The Wonder Years*, Julie Taylor from *Friday Night Lights*, and Rory Gilmore from *Gilmore Girls*. As you might have noticed, the girl next door in mainstream television is usually white, and her "all-American" persona (Bowles 2014) reveals a collective understanding of white femininity as a refreshingly likable and morally unspoiled component of everyday American life. While Black-led shows do tend to have girl-next-door characters, very few of them gain crossover success and become a staple in the American imaginary, possibly because their shows are often viewed as "niche" programming for Black audiences (hence the ubiquitous label "Black shows"). One can of course problematize the functionality of this trope. For example, it is typically used to chastise forms of femininity deemed by patriarchal standards as subversive and destructive. I will not unpack the layers of this criticism because it is not central to my analysis. What I do want to focus on is how the trope is used to normalize the relatability of a specific kind of womanhood. As I have stressed repeatedly, Black women are seldom portrayed in popular media as relatable and nonthreatening. I discussed the strong Black mother myth in chapter 1 and the angry Black woman stereotype in chapter 3, enduring tropes, deeply embedded in the fabric of American history and culture, that rob Black women of their everyday relatability by theorizing Black womanhood as indestructibly tough and interminably hostile.

Recent discourse on Black femininity continues to extend the longevity of these tropes by popularizing slogans like the #BlackGirlMagic hashtag, a phrase coined by teacher and early childcare development expert CaShawn Thompson to "promote the positive aspects of Black girlhood" (Toliver 2019, 2). The phrase has now ballooned into a thunderous movement, "affirmed by major figures like Michelle Obama and Misty Copeland" (Toliver 2019, 2) and used to celebrate "the beauty, influence, and strength of Black women and girls" (Toliver 2019, 1). The hashtag clearly serves as a counterpoint to the pervasiveness of dehumanized depictions of Black women in the American imaginary. However, some critics have pointed out that labeling Black women as "magic" once again perpetuates the dehumanizing myth of Black womanhood as invulnerable and superhuman (Toliver 2019, 2). In October 2016, a few days after the premiere of *Insecure*, Rae spoke candidly about the depictions of Black women in popular media. "I don't want to invalidate anybody's black experience," she begins. "But it seems to me [on television], we're either extremely magical, or we're extremely flawless. But we don't get to just be boring . . . it's a privilege to be able to be boring" (Mohdin 2017). Her "magical" comment is a reference to both the #BlackGirlMagic hashtag and enduring tropes of Black women as flawless and strong. By describing "boring" as a privilege, she is pointing to the historical absence of ordinary Black female characters, relatable girls next door, in popular media culture. Self-identified "magical" Black women certainly do exist. However, Rae argues that their values should not be upheld as cornerstone characteristics of African American womanhood because they negate, and even erase, the unique diversity of the Black female experience. Boring and ordinary Black women also exist, and they too deserve representation in popular media.

Although this argument echoes Attridge's idioculture, the affirmed singularities of an individual's "unique configuration" (2004, 21), there is a familiar distinction here. As I explained in chapter 2, idioculture, like Deleuzian philosophy, is somewhat skeptical of the autonomy of collective identities, which in turn makes the concept skeptical of the uncontested hegemony of certain race- and gender-based identities. *Insecure*, on the other hand, is a narrative that unmistakably champions and celebrates the sisterhood of African American womanhood. When Issa and her group of girlfriends (Molly, Kelli, and Tiffany) endure microaggressions from the external world, they always retreat to their enclosed enclaves where they can vent, heal, and feel normal again. Their sisterhood is therapeutic and thus celebrates the function of community.

Nevertheless, chapter 3's much debated and inconclusive tussle between the individual's right to difference and the community's right to sameness resurfaces when discourse on race and gender is used in *Insecure* to admonish a world in which Black women like Issa are incapable of transcending restrictive markers and hegemonic tropes. An example of this argument is the pilot's opening sequence, where we find Issa being interrogated for not adhering to a hegemonic image of Black womanhood. This probably explains why Rae does not allow marginalizing forces like racism and sexism to overwhelmingly color the narrative and aesthetic texture of *Insecure*. Although these external marginalizing forces are central to *Insecure*, Rae affords her characters plenty of opportunities to exist beyond race, gender and other broad categories. They are unmistakably Black millennials experiencing modern Los Angeles through the philosophical prism of their gendered Blackness. However, when they retreat into their enclosed enclaves and are afforded the "privilege" of ordinariness, they become unshackled from the crushing burden of tropes, markers and stereotypes. Moreover, as I previously stated, traditions in *Insecure* do not always denote the shared practices of a monoracial community. In many instances, traditions are simply individualized practices such as wearing a particular hairstyle or a daily practice of watching television on a couch. Similarly put, the emphasis on regular traditions in everyday life is often a celebration of an individual's right to difference, the right to derive affirmative strength from a unique set of practices and routines. In the subsequent paragraphs, I will use three everyday activities (eating at a restaurant, talking to a therapist, and buying a couch) to examine the nature and implications of *Insecure*'s mise-en-scène. Using a remodeled TCT framework, I argue that these activities are sustained by ordinary objects and locations, which reveal the affirmative ability of mundane traditions to combat the hegemony of master narratives.

An enclosed enclave in *Insecure* takes many shapes and form, its role shifting slightly depending on the situation and figuration. As you will see in the following paragraphs and sections, the enclosed enclave can take the form of a physical location, an object, music, and even cinematography. The breadth and depth of these different forms are central to the TCT framework's analytical apparatus because they reveal the multidimensional richness of affirmative enclaves and explorations in the post-rupture realm. Staying with the pilot, one of the enclave's iterations is an Ethiopian restaurant. After a stressful day at work, Issa and Molly meet at Merkato, an Ethiopian restaurant, to celebrate the former's birthday. Far away from the competitively stressful corporate environment and intrusive questions from disrespectful students, Merkato is shot to evoke a calming sensibility. With shelves of neatly stacked spices in plastic jars and exotic art hanging on its walls, the dimly lit restaurant is soothingly quiet and destresses the heaviness of earlier emotional scenes like a massage. The center of Issa and Molly's table has a comparatively higher intensity of fluorescent light, illuminating the relaxed emotions on their brown faces. This longing for the comfort of Ethiopian food, a recurrent motif throughout *Insecure*'s narrative, is never adequately explained.

There is of course the obvious correlation between Ethiopia and the legacy of Afrocentric discourses in Black American scholarship. In the early twentieth century, while most of Africa was under European occupation, uncolonized Ethiopia asserted its sovereignty under the leadership of "the much revered and reviled" Emperor Haile Selassie I (Scott 2004, 41). For African Americans at the time, a marginalized Black race within a dominant white culture, Ethiopia thus became "a mythical space, an idealized place of singular Black power and special promise . . . a sacred land, the center of Black power and prestige second only perhaps to dynastic Egypt" (Scott 2004, 41). This idealized imaginary of Ethiopia profoundly permeated Black American thought and influenced the Afrocentric scholarship of political activists like Jamaican-born Marcus Garvey (Scott 2004, 41–43). The image of Ethiopia in African American culture is therefore weighted with political subtext.

Insecure, however, does not directly, or even indirectly, engage with the Afrocentric and Pan-Africanism discourses associated with the Americanized imaginary of Ethiopia. As my analysis reveals, the most affirmative moments in *Insecure* are triggered by seemingly trivial aspects of everyday life, not grand political symbols and gestures. Because *Insecure* is often striving to unburden its Black protagonists from the full weight of racialized tropes and ideologies, I do not characterize Merkato as a loaded political metaphor with consequential implications. While the restaurant might be a nod to Ethiopia's role in shaping Black American thought, no obvious political motivations are thematically presented to justify Molly's and Issa's preference for Ethiopian food. One gets the sense that they just seem to like Merkato's ambiance and the flavor of its food. I find this interpretation affirmatively refreshing because like Gay's *Bad Feminist* and *Difficult Women*, it enables Molly and Issa to exist beyond the restrictive boundaries of racialized epistemologies. Many aspects of our daily routines and practices are not always motivated by grand ideologies or performed to dramatize a politicized point of view. Rather, they are often arbitrary and stemming from inexplicable habits and predilections. *Insecure* simply presents Merkato as a place of solace for Issa and Molly, an enclosed enclave where they are allowed to eat, laugh, and be their true selves.

As both women browse Merkato's menu, Molly complains about the perils of dating as a highly successful career-oriented Black woman. "It's like it doesn't matter what I do, Issa," she vents. "If I'm into them then I'm too smothering. If I take my time and try to give them space 'oh! I didn't think you were into me.' Fine! Sex right away. Lose interest. Wait to have sex. Lose interest" (Rae and Wilmore 2016–2021). This complaint echoes the barrage of recent research and media stories about the perils of dating as an educated Black woman. According to the *Journal of Blacks in Higher Education*, "over the past few decades, black women in America have made historic strides . . . at least 60 percent of black students who get awarded college degrees are women. Black women make up 71 percent of black students" (Johnson 2010). These promising numbers "point to another issue: Many of them are single. According to a recent Yale study, 42 percent of African American women have yet to be married, compared to only 23 percent of white women" (Johnson 2010). The Yale study also revealed "a gap in numbers. The 2000 U.S. Census counted 1.8 million more African-American women than black men" (Johnson 2010). The last few years have also seen the extensive production of research on the discriminatory practices of online dating. In 2014, for example, "user data on OkCupid showed that most men on the site rated black women as less attractive than women of other races and ethnicities" (Brown Ashley 2018). Although some Black female culture commentators argue that the impact of these numbers is often exaggerated to promote dehumanizing stereotypes of Black women as bitter and lonely (Johnson 2010), there is no denying that educated Black women disproportionately endure obstacles such as finding Black male partners with an equivalent socioeconomic status and encountering prejudiced attitudes in the interracial dating scene. Molly's dating woes are thus emblematic of a systemic malaise afflicting many professional Black women. However, in this instance, for the enclosed enclave to function as a reprieve from the burden of the external world, these problems must be kept at bay. Issa decides to use deflective humor to cheer her dejected friend up. "I think your pussy is broken," she blurts. "I read about it. It's like pussies breaking everywhere. I think your pussy is sad. It's had enough. If it could talk, it would make that sad Marge Simpson groan" (Rae and Wilmore 2016–2021). Molly reacts by playfully spreading lips and making Marge Simpson's iconic long low sound, "mmmmm." Both ladies laugh infectiously, hunching over their illuminated table and reinforcing the escapist sacredness of their enclosed enclave. In the tenderness of this beautiful moment, they become just two ordinary girls having a laugh and ordering dinner, unbothered by the problematic politics of the external world.

The potency of the Merkato scene, I argue, strongly echoes South African writer Njabulo Ndebele's seminal essay "The Rediscovery of the Ordinary." Ndebele is a fiction writer and academic whose award-winning 1983 short story collection *Fools and Other Stories* examines the complicated lives of ordinary Black South Africans during the closing days of the apartheid regime. The South Africa context takes us away, albeit briefly, from American popular culture. However, there are relevant parallels here that speak to the epistemology of using ordinariness as an aesthetic in Black-authored narratives. The *Journal of Southern African Studies* published Ndebele's essay "The Rediscovery of the Ordinary: Some New Writings in South Africa" in 1986, three years after the publication of *Fools and Other Stories*. "The history of Black South African literature has largely been the history of the representation of spectacle," Ndebele begins. "The visible symbols of the overwhelmingly oppressive South African social formation appear to have prompted over the years the development of a highly dramatic, highly demonstrative form of literary representation" (1986, 143). The spectacle of demonstrative drama Ndebele is describing here is a reference to the rise and development of South African protest literature, a genre that developed "at the end of the fifties," following the apartheid regime's ban on the Black liberation party the African National Congress (ANC) (1986, 145).

Similarly, the rise and development of American protest literature was also a response to systemic injustices. Harriet Beecher Stowe's *Uncle Tom's Cabin* (1852) and Richard Wright's *Native Son* (1940) are widely considered as canonical American protest novels because they subversively captured and reacted to institutionalized racial oppression in ways that shocked and stimulated readers. While Stowe's text champions the abolitionist cause by highlighting the barbarism of slavery and martyrizing the nobility of enslaved Black people, Wright's novel depicts the shockingly violent repercussions of racial discrimination and economic hopelessness. Both works reflect the "highly dramatic" and "highly demonstrative" forms of literary representation in South African protest literature and reveal a transatlantic tendency to seek out the exuberant defiance of politically charged language and symbols during moments of systematic marginalization.

To understand how Ndebele's discourse on demonstrative drama relates to *Insecure*, I will briefly examine his analysis on the tropes and techniques of spectacular writing. He looks at the stories of South African historian, journalist and writer R. R. R. Dhlomo, for example, and argues that they are "characterized by tightness of plot, emphasis on the most essential items of plot, the predominance of dialogue, and sudden, almost unexpected shocking endings, all of which are the ingredients of dramatic writing" (Ndebele 1986, 144). He labels such writings "mind-bogglingly spectacular" and argues that they are primarily focused on depicting politically explosive moments in South African history such as war raids, mass killings, civil injustices, Black poverty in the townships, the luxurious lifestyles of the white minority population, etc. (Ndebele 1986, 143). Ndebele, it is of the utmost importance to stress here, is not against the use of politically charged symbols and language. These are certainly relevant and highly effective tools in civil rights movements across the globe. What he is pointing out is that the "protest" in "protest literature" is a misnomer. The word "protest," he argues "carries the implications of political *and* specifically *expository* declaration of dissent" (Ndebele 1986, 149). Literature, he continues, "while definitely labouring under the pressure of the expository intention, deliberately sets out to use conventions of fiction not of exposition" (Ndebele 1986, 149). Thus, "To call it 'protest literature' is to deny it any literary and artistic value" (Ndebele 1986, 149). There are obviously counterpoints to this school of thought, but I am intellectually intrigued by Ndebele's distinction between fiction and exposition. The goal of exposition is often to clarify in a linear and matter-of-fact fashion. Because fiction, on the other hand, explores the human condition's complex shades and dimensions, literary narratives must employ a diverse pool of devices (metaphors, dramatic irony, symbolism, motif, foreshadowing, anachronism, etc.) capable of depicting and possibly understanding the intricate layers of everyday life. Ndebele therefore argues that the emphasis on concise and agenda-driven exposition in protest literature robs literary texts of sophisticated narratives about ordinary people.

This argument echoes James Baldwin's seminal critique of American protest literature in his controversial 1955 essay "Everybody's Protest Novel." Because Stowe's *Uncle Tom's Cabin* is a straightforward exposition about the ills of slavery, Baldwin argues that the novel lacks the aesthetic dynamism and complexity of a true literary text. He dismisses Stowe as "not so much a novelist as an impassioned pamphleteer; her book [*Uncle Tom's Cabin*] was not intended to do anything more than prove that slavery was wrong; was, in fact, perfectly horrible. This makes material for a pamphlet but it is hardly enough for a novel" (Baldwin 1985, 28). Baldwin also went after his former mentor Richard Wright. In its expository attempt to condemn the functionality of institutional racism in America, Baldwin argues that Wright's *Native Son* relies on extremely violent language and symbols and, in consequence, reduces the Black experience to an infinite "thrust and counter-thrust" tussle with whiteness, a tussle devoid of complex human emotions and completely drenched in lust, fear, and death (1985, 33). If the expository emphasis of protest literature oversimplifies the human experience, how then can Black-authored narratives mirror and understand the nuance of social conditions? Ndebele believes this can be achieved by "rediscovering the ordinary," moving away from spectacle and reengaging with ordinary life. The mundane activities of everyday people, he points out, are more adept at capturing and problematizing the fluid and transformative functionality of oppression in a society (Ndebele 1986, 154). Mundanity also allows literary characters to transcend restrictive racial categorizations and tropes by philosophically engaging with different and unpredictable layers of their humanity (Ndebele 1986, 153).

Ndebele examines the short story "Man Against Himself" by Joel Matou, an example, he claims, of new writing from the South African townships "that is the very antithesis of spectacle" (1986, 152). "Man Against Himself" is a story about the labor exploitation of Black South Africans in mines. The story chronicles the young protagonist's long and tedious odyssey to a mine in search of work and when he gets there, "he undergoes further suffering, and humiliation" (Ndebele 1986, 152). Despite the politically charged nature of the plot, Ndebele points out that the narrative avoids the "inherent simplifications of spectacle" (1986, 153). When the protagonist receives his pay, for example, the raw texture of money in his pocket inspires him to ponder about a time when "'life was not endless but everlasting,'" and he later confesses that "'suffering taught me many things. . . . Suffering takes a man from known places to unknown places. . . . You will never suffer a second time because you have learned to suffer'" (Ndebele 1986, 153). On his way home, he remarks on the beauty of township girls, a beauty that reminds him of his "'own beautiful sweetheart'" with "'green-coloured eyes like a snake, high wooden shoes like a cripple . . . with black boots for winter like a soldier, and a beautiful figure like she does not eat, sleep, speak or become hungry'" (Ndebele 1986, 153). He concludes his introspections by underscoring his zeal for life despite his present circumstances. "'I learned to forget yesterdays and to think of tomorrows,'" he states. "'Each morning in the township, I said to myself: 'today is a new life.' I overcame my fear of loneliness and my fear of want. I . . . have a lot of enthusiasm and love for life'" (Ndebele 1986, 153).

These complex emotions and thoughts, triggered by ordinary objects and activities, resist a simplistic characterization of the young protagonist as just a long-suffering Black miner trapped in the abyss of Apartheid-era South Africa. The depth of his philosophical ruminations acknowledges the hopelessness of his surroundings but also finds a sense of normality and hope in the traditions and happenings of ordinary life. By emphasizing ordinary objects and activities, and the emotions they evoke, literature about ordinary life is capable of portraying and celebrating the full spectrum of the human condition. As Ndebele eloquently states

> We must contend with the fact that even under the most oppressive conditions, people are always trying and struggling to maintain a semblance of normal social order. They will attempt to apply tradition and custom to manage their day to day family problems: they will resort to socially acquired behavior patterns to eke out a means of subsistence. They apply systems of values that they know. Often those values will undergo changes under certain pressing conditions. The transformation of those values constitutes the essential drama in the lives of ordinary people. (1986, 154)

While the present chapter's analysis is focused on the media realm of television in American popular culture, Ndebele's manifesto on rediscovering the ordinary echoes the aestheticization of ordinariness in Rae's *Insecure*. Like in protest literature, there is a scarcity of complex narratives about ordinary Black characters in mainstream television, and *Insecure*, like Ndebele's essay, seeks to understand the ways in which ordinary people struggle to maintain some semblance of normality under oppressive social conditions. As seen in the afore discussed scenes from the pilot, when Issa and Molly are burdened by the crushing weight of social expectations, racial prejudices, and sexist tropes, they retreat into an enclosed enclave, the Ethiopian restaurant Merkato, where they can just exist as two goofy and awkward girls next door having dinner. The de-stressing tone and lighting in the Merkato scene are therefore a televisual aestheticization of ordinariness that allows the viewer to engage with a different version of Issa and Molly, a different version with the imaginative abilities to transcend dehumanizing tropes and stereotypes.

Before proceeding, I should acknowledge that I often use the word "spectacle" to describe Gay and Beyoncé's texts. Although *Lemonade*, *Difficult Women*, and, to a lesser extent, *Bad Feminist* do have "highly dramatic" and "highly demonstrative" episodes, which are evocative of the lavish performativity of spectacular actions, I would argue that they cannot be entirely classified as expository protest narratives. While all three texts do have specific agendas delivered through some form of exposition, they are unafraid to engage with contradictory and confounding aspects of the human condition. Their narrative arcs are not matter-of-fact or linear, and they employ a wide range of literary and visual aesthetics to rethink entrenched knowledge systems and reimagine new worlds in ways that are mostly liberating but also unsettling and unresolved. Nevertheless, the grand scale of their thematic ambitions and the transgressive tools they use to concretize these ambitions set them apart from the quiet subversion and everyday mundanity of *Insecure*.

Despite the affirmative aestheticization of ordinariness in Merkato, tensions, as always, lurk nearby. The second Issa and Molly step out of Merkato, the enclosed enclave, they are immediately confronted by the challenges of the external world. Molly remembers that she is still "crying tears of singleness," a reference to her dating woes as a professional Black woman, and Issa is reminded of her emotional disconnection from Lawrence, her unemployed boyfriend whose big dreams have not panned out, so he spends his days sleeping, moping and lounging on the couch (Rae and Wilmore 2016–2021). During the confrontation scene at the start of the pilot, one of the kids wonders why Issa is not yet married, and she nervously responds, "I am just not right now" (Rae and Wilmore 2016–2021). The student presses on, inciting laughter from her peers by remarking that "my dad said ain't nobody checking for bitter ass black women anymore" (Rae and Wilmore 2016–2021). Issa attempts a candid and heartfelt response: "Tell your dad that black women aren't bitter. They are just tired of being expected to settle for less" (Rae and Wilmore 2016–2021). But her strategy flops. Another student yells, "her outfit settled for less," inciting an even more hysterical response from the classroom (Rae and Wilmore 2016–2021).

This scene, although expository and maybe on the nose, is layered with subtext. What Issa's back-and-forth with the students reveals is the pervasive normalization of the bitter Black woman trope. Even the Black students are laughing, implying that they too have internalized these destructive stereotypes. When Issa tells Molly in front of Merkato that she is thinking about ending her emotionally stagnated relationship with Lawrence, Molly is shocked and cautions her about the perils of single life as a Black woman. Issa begins to contemplate why she is indecisive about terminating the relationship: is she still in love with Lawrence and believes they can mend the fissures in their romantic bond or is she worried that due to the widespread stereotypes of Black women and the dating woes they endure when they seek out new partners, she might never find a man better than her couch-ridden boyfriend? Lawrence is educated and still has ambitions, so at this stage of the narrative, it is unclear to the viewer if he is completely hopeless. However, due to the societal perception of African American women and the tensions they must navigate in the dating scene, some of them inevitably settle for less because they worry about their perceived limited options. When Issa attempts to reason with the recalcitrant student by stressing that "black women aren't bitter. They are just tired of being expected to settle for less," she is in a way trying to convince herself that she has not settled for less. But for the entirety of the episode, and most of the season, doubt casts a gloomy shadow over her, and she remains insecurely uncertain about the true nature of her motivations.

Like in Gay and Beyoncé's texts, there is a symbiosis here between affirmation and tension. What drives Issa and Molly into their enclosed enclave are the racial and gender-based pressures of the external world. These pressures motivate them to carve out an autonomous sphere of influence where they can exist as regular girls, an affirmative spatial dimension divested from the historical hegemony of visual storytelling tropes and techniques. But unlike the lotus-eaters of Greek mythology, they cannot stay in this enclosed enclave for an extended period of time because the pressures of the external world are constantly nibbling at and finding a path into the sanctity of their protected enclave. Thus, to protect its rehabilitative function, Issa and Molly must venture back into the external world and attempt to keep the intruders at bay. And when they once again feel overwhelmed, they retreat into their enclave to reemphasize the restorative humanity of an ordinary life beyond the encroaching borders of external marginalizing forces. As Ndebele argues, the traditions, habits, and routines of an ordinary life give people a sense of purpose, dignity, and optimism. Thus, even under the most oppressive circumstances, people find inventive ways to carve out safe spaces where they can perform ordinary practices, a reminder of their humanity. *Insecure*'s narrative begins in a post-rupture realm where affirmations and external marginalizing forces are contesting for agency and influence and the continual entry into and exit out of the enclosed space creates a loop, which echoes the counter-actualizing movement of Deleuzian concepts. I will use two settings from different episodes (the therapist's office in episode 9 of season 4 and the mustard-colored couch in episode 3 of season 1) to illustrate how *Insecure*'s mise-en-scène is an aestheticization of ordinariness, which nods to but also digresses from Deleuzian philosophy. Moreover, like Merkato, these settings reemphasize the aptitude of ordinary locations and objects to widen the depth of individual emotions and experiences.

In "Lowkey Trying," episode 9 of season 4, Molly visits her therapist Dr. Rhonda to discuss her flailing relationships. Some might argue that therapy, the treatment of mental or psychological disorders, cannot be characterized as an everyday activity. The specificity of its processes is debatably the antithesis of ordinariness because they require complex existential explorations and medical methods. The normalization of mental health discourse in contemporary American society is an effective counterpoint to this argument. Recent studies have described American millennials as the therapy generation. "People in their 20s and 30s seek mental-health help more often," psychology scholar Peggy Drexler points out. "The stigma traditionally attached to psychotherapy has largely dissolved in the new generation of patients seeking treatment" (2019). Drexler alludes to a 2018 report by Blue Cross Blue Shield Association, a Chicago-based federation of health insurance companies, which attributes a rise in depression diagnoses among young adults (a 47 percent upsurge between 2013 and 2016) to their willingness to seek mental help (2019). This normalization of therapy is echoed in *Insecure*. No one shames or ridicules Molly for having a therapist, and her visits to Dr. Rhonda are treated as a regular, and sometimes refreshingly comedic, activity in her everyday life. Moreover, although therapy often unearths and unpacks explosive episodes of life-altering traumas, this is not the case in Molly's situation. Her conversations with Dr. Rhonda are mostly centered on somewhat serious but mostly regular topics such as jealousy in friendships and the pressures of romantic relationships. Therapy in *Insecure* is thus an ordinary activity, which emphasizes the transformative value of everyday life.

As I previously mentioned, Molly's confident swagger and luminous personality are more in keeping with traditional portrayals of Black women in popular media. In her therapist's office, however, the façade dissolves and her vulnerabilities are laid bare. These raw moments of tenderness and hurt are significant, because *Insecure* is exposing viewers to a different side of the strong Black woman trope. Molly might strut through life like a superwoman, but when she sits across from Dr. Rhonda in the enclosed enclave of her therapist's office, she must confront that the fact she is an emotional mess. Molly's dating woes as a professional Black woman, I stressed earlier, are tied to larger systemic issues. But this is just half of the story. Molly's idea of a thriving romantic relationship is modeled after her parents' marriage, a union she unhealthily venerates because she believes it is infallible. Season 2, for example, sees Molly running the gamut of emotions as her experiences with different men fail to live up to the standard she aspires. "Is no one married like my parents anymore?" she exasperatedly asks (Rae and Wilmore 2016–2021). In season 4, episode 9's therapy scene, we find Molly reeling from a dreadful vacation with Andrew, her current boyfriend. Andrew is incredibly laid back, the opposite of hyperactive Molly's need for control, and he is also Asian American. The interracial nature of her relationship causes frictions in their daily interactions and also with Andrew's family, further frustrating Molly's tendency to control her environment. She is also drifting apart from her best friend Issa because she believes Issa does not respect her boundaries. "I can see how much this has affected you, this stress with Issa and Andrew . . . so what is all of this bringing up for you?" Dr. Rhonda asks, and Molly confesses that she has "just been feeling so tense all the time." (Rae and Wilmore 2016–2021). Dr. Rhonda notes that when someone angers Molly, she has a tendency "to put up the walls and then . . . shut down" (Rae and Wilmore 2016–2021). In other words, when she is unable to control people's reactions, she becomes defensive and closes all channels of productive conversation. A similar situation occurs in season 2 when she finds out her father once cheated on her mother, a revelation that shatters the idealized union she had exuberantly venerated as a model to replicate. Despite her mother's insistence that her father pertinently worked through the betrayal and restored trust in their union, Molly is repulsed and chooses to ostracize him. The implication here is that Molly also plays a central part in the chaos of her dating life. Andrew, for example, embodies the noble values of the kind of man she was dreaming about in the pilot episode. Her incorrigible character, however, erodes the stability of their romantic relationship and at the end of season 4, he breaks up with her. While racial and gender bias play a significant role in the chaos of her dating life, in the enclosed enclave of Dr. Rhonda's office, Molly must confront the fact that her character traits are equally culpable.

By using an ordinary visit to a therapist's office, a habit, custom, or tradition of everyday life, to unfold Molly's complicated layers, *Insecure* imbues her with agency. Molly is not simply a doomed Black woman who, due to racist and sexist tropes and stereotypes, cannot find a romantic partner. There are other autonomous factors at play such as her personality, so by working through her issues with Dr. Rhonda, she is exercising a form of agency and acknowledging that she has a say in the nature and outcome of her relationships. The role of therapy here echoes the afore discussed counter-actualizing Deleuzian concept of infinitely becoming. As I discussed in chapter 1, Deleuze sees the subject as an entity in an infinite tussle with different perspectives and knowledge systems (1991, 37). While the optimal point of self-actualization is never achieved, the subject remains enlightened by these philosophical encounters, which trigger an infinite loop of learning and unlearning (1991, 37). In other words, the subject is infinitely becoming and never becomes. Unlike sitcoms, Molly's issues are never conveniently resolved, but she presses on with the therapy sessions because after every experience in the enclosed enclave of Dr. Rhonda's office, she gains new insights that allow her to better navigate her complicated emotions and flailing relationships. The continuous entry and exit loop (exit from the external world and entry into the enclosed enclave) mirrors the Deleuze's counter-actualizing loop. However, just like *Lemonade*, there is a constancy to the tactile world of *Insecure* that rejects the fluid notion of infinitely becoming. As I will explicate in the subsequent paragraphs, the ability of ordinary objects to preserve fixed emotions and traditions enables them to function as a dispenser of affirmations.

In the third episode of season 1, we are treated to a couch montage, a sped-up sequence of events chronicling the demise of Issa's relationship with Lawrence. As they move in and around their apartment, the one thing that remains constant is their mustard-colored couch. Deceptively simple and ordinary, it becomes the viewer's cinematic reference point to the changing and dynamic shades of the deteriorating relationship. Perfectly placed at the center of the screen, the montage begins with Issa and Lawrence ripping off the plastic wrapping around the newly purchased couch. As they celebrate the purchase by hugging and flirting, the couch becomes a representation of a safe space away from the brutalities of the external world, a space where they can just be lovers and bask in the nurturing glow of their burgeoning union.

Philosopher Yuriko Saito's *Everyday Aesthetics* arguably deepens Ndebele's discourse by homing in on the complex emotions stored in and triggered by specific objects and figures like the mustard couch in *Insecure*.[4] Her text poses more questions than answers, but the conversational and probing nature of her analysis invites the reader to consider the uniquely diverse ways in which our everyday aesthetic choices reveal our habits and inform our actions and attitudes (2008, 55). Saito argues that "our everyday aesthetic choices are neither uncomplicated nor insignificant" (2008, 55). The design of a commercial product, for example, its style and visual aspects, says a great deal not only about the consumer but also about the society producing and consuming this product. The prevailing "aesthetic aspirations and expectations" of a society typically dictates "the particular appearance of various consumer goods, determining the kinds of resources and manufacturing processes needed for the desired results" (Saito 2008, 65). Thus, the preference for a specific color or shape reveals consumers' preferences and can have a long-lasting environmental impact. As Saito points out, "the unfortunate outcome of the popular penchant for vivid colors, smooth texture, and slick appearance in consumer goods is that it discourages designers . . . from producing green objects made with sustainable resources" (2008, 68).

But who engineers these preferences? Are they externally mandated by corporations and other systemic bodies through subtle and unsubtle forms of indoctrination such as advertisements or are they often nurtured in autonomous private spaces protected from the overbearing mandates of the corporate world? The answer is not always clear. Based on the vast diversity of examples and scenarios Saito lists, she insinuates that corporate and private spaces inform each other's preferences, another loop-like structure echoing *Insecure*'s entry/exit loop and Deleuzian philosophy. She, for example, uses the example of Disney's animated classic *Bambi*, a heartwarming story about a young deer whose mother is shot dead by a hunter. The popularity of *Bambi*, a product created by the Disney corporation, has generated an overwhelming sense of sympathy for and attraction to deer (Saito 2008, 59). Thus, people tend to project sentimental thoughts and tender emotions onto all deer because the creatures remind them of a specific set of externally curated emotions. With that said, these same individuals can also influence systemic institutions and government policies on issues pertaining to conservation and the environment. Paraphrasing philosophy scholar Marcia Eaton, Saito states that "our tender emotion stirred by the sentimental image of all deer as Bambi, makes it difficult for forest managers 'to convince the public that their numbers should be severely decreased in some areas'" (2008, 60). These same individuals, now hyperaware of issues related to land and animal conservation, can also end up being at odds with the large-scale consumerist practices of Disney, the same corporation responsible for awakening their conservationist sensibilities.

I use this philosophical perspective in the TCT framework to understand and unpack how ordinary objects like the mustard couch in *Insecure* function as an affirmative enclosed enclave that absorbs, holds, and protects the emotions and traditions certain characters deem sacred and worthy of conservation and preservation. As aforesaid, the newly purchased mustard couch represents the romantic excitement of Issa and Lawrence's burgeoning relationship. As the montage continues, the couch becomes a meeting place to demonstrate the range of emotions they feel toward each other. First, they happily watch television, Issa's head on Lawrence's lap. There are also tender scenes of lovemaking, cuddling, and camaraderie, but as they start to drift away, a pivotal scene captures Issa sitting on the couch alone with a plate full of food, rebuffing Lawrence's request to eat together at the dining table. When she accidentally spills food on the couch, he rushes to the stained spot with a piece of cloth, aggressively and annoyingly wiping off the contamination, almost as if he is worried of tainting the love they have projected onto and preserved in the couch. The stain foreshadows the demise of their relationship as everything goes downhill after this point. Their arguments on the couch reveal upsetting emotions of annoyance and hatred and when they now sit together, there is visible distance between them, a space that metaphorizes their emotional disconnection.

At some point in their worsening relationship, they swap the mustard couch for a blue one. On a literal level, they simply wanted a newer couch of better quality but because the mustard couch is the viewer's point of reference when examining the time line of their relationship, its abandonment signals an attempt to suppress and discard the one object that vividly reminds them of happier times. In season 1's finale, when Lawrence dumps Issa due to a betrayal, a betrayal I will address in the subsequent section, she returns, heartbroken, to the mustard couch, now disheveled and sitting outside, waiting for the trash collector. Molly later joins Issa on the couch, and Issa collapses into her best friend's lap, sobbing uncontrollably. Issa, it is evident, still wants to protect the emotions she and Lawrence projected onto the couch at the genesis of their relationship. This yearning for a return to the past is a yearning for constancy, an unchanged emotional state capable of preserving the profound love they shared with each other. While the concept of infinitely becoming might see the demise of their relationship as a natural order of things, both parties encountering different perspectives and knowledge systems during their maturation process and growing apart as a result, in the tactile world of ordinary life, people derive affirmations and hope from the constancy of relationships and practices. Like the young protagonist in Matou's "Man

Against Himself," seeking solace from the black boots and beautiful figure of his sweetheart, in a moment of utter hopelessness and indescribable grief, Issa seeks solace from the unchanged emotions preserved in the deteriorating mustard couch, an ordinary object imbued with longing for the past.

This reading evokes nostalgia scholarship by the likes of Svetlana Boym and Edward Casey. Boym describes restorative nostalgia as a transhistorical attempt at reconstructing a "lost home" (2001) and Casey ponders about objects of nostalgia, both definite and indefinite, and whether they trigger memories of past events that cannot return to the present or represent feelings of the past lingering "into the present" (1987, 361). When Issa is curled up on the mustard couch, an indefinite object imbued with affirmative memories of her now-doomed relationship, she is longing to reconstruct and restore the lost home she once shared with Lawrence. Whether these nostalgic feelings are firmly trapped in the past or are returning to the present and influencing the future remains unclear at this point in the narrative. And to avoid derailing my discussion, I will not delve into nostalgia scholarship because there is a great deal of discourse about the philosophical complexities of nostalgic feelings: are they authentic, imaginative, a blend of both, some form of amnesia or something else? Although nostalgia plays a critical role in the couch montage, my analysis in this chapter chooses to focus on how indefinite locations and objects like the mustard couch can reveal and amplify the affirmative nature of fixed traditions and emotions in ordinary African American life. While some of these traditions and emotions can be associated with nostalgia, others, like Merkato, are mostly preoccupied with the ongoing performance of affirmative routines in fixed spaces.

To recapitulate, the function of ordinariness in the couch montage is twofold. First, like *Lemonade*'s steadfast adherence to the constancy of affirming knowledge systems, ordinary objects are embedded with the affirmative potency of fixed emotions and practices, a fixedness in conflict with the notion that affirmations are a result of counter-actualizing negotiations. Second, using the mustard couch as a motif, *Insecure* depicts a nuanced portrayal of millennial Black love. We seldom see such tender and raw depictions of Black relationships on popular television. The ensuing section of this chapter will thoroughly unpack the subversive nature of Issa and Lawrence's relationship, but for now, I will briefly mention that the couch is a quiet stage that allows both to display a wide range of complex emotions, a complexity that subverts expectations and transcends tropes. Unlike the grandness of spectacle, the simplicity of the couch and the emotions it absorbs and retains adds a relatable charm to the narratology of the love story. Anyone who has ever been in a long-term relationship, regardless of race, gender, and class, will recognize and react to the small but profound moments on the couch: the tender cuddles, the laughter, the silence, the bored look, the side-eyes, the distance, and everything else in between. Simply put, like Merkato and the therapist's office, the mustard couch provides affirmative layers of nuance to specific kinds of characters often robbed of aesthetic and narrative complexity in popular television culture.

I should also point out that *Insecure*'s emphasis on constancy is also at odds with the aesthetic imaginaries process of cultural circulations, the notion that ideas, thoughts, figures and images are capable of reimagining affirmative worlds and perspectives by melding, disaggregating and rebuilding (Ghosh 2017, 462). Although the external world and the enclosed enclave remain in conversation with each other, Rae's persistent effort to keep both worlds separate reveals her skepticism of cultural circulations in certain situations. We see this skepticism strongly represented in season 2 and 3's discourse on gentrification. The historically Black and brown areas of Inglewood, where Issa resides, are undergoing a face-lift. As white corporations and residents move in, soaring housing prices accompany a new whitewashed moniker "I-wood," further pushing away local businesses and natives into the fringes of society. The implication here is that cultural circulations mostly lack equity. In the main, there is usually a dominant cultural force that envelopes, misrepresents, and even erases its inferior counterpart. Thus, like *Lemonade*'s critique of the subjugation of indigenous African spirituality in the new world and Gay's attempts to distance her affirmative singularities from the marginalizing forces of the pre-rupture realm, *Insecure* challenges the historical normalization of syncretic unions in American culture by pointing out the power imbalance between the hegemonic external world and the enclosed enclave. But as Rae struggles to keep both worlds apart, she must also contend with tensions from within the enclosed enclave. Despite the enclave's restorative powers, it harbors forces seeking to reestablish power structures similar to the marginalizing forces of the external world. In next section of this chapter, I will pay attention to these internal destabilizing forces, using the hypermasculine overtones in Issa's relationships with rap music and Lawrence as the analytical backdrop.

RAP, RAGE, AND RESTITUTION

As I mentioned in chapter 2, the hip-hop musical genre has its roots in Black lyrical and linguistic self-expression. Pioneered in the 1970s, hip-hop's ability to address issues of systemic oppression and economic hopelessness in everyday life positively inspired and impacted communities of color (Cosimini 2015, 252). The music of socially conscious rappers like Kendrick Lamar, J. Cole, Tierra Whack, Rapsody, Common, and Chika have continued this tradition by engaging with social justice issues affecting both the African

American community and the world at large. However, as I have stated on numerous occasions, the genre's tendency to glorify hypermasculinity often silences the agency of Black women by emboldening, and even normalizing, patriarchal power structures (Gammage 2015, 8). Worthy of mention here is the fact that in addition to its global popularity, American hip-hop is widely consumed by white America and "much of the infrastructure for American rap is owned by mainstream, predominantly white companies" (Austin 2006, 48).[5] In other words, because hip-hop's hypermasculine charisma is marketable, nationally and internationally, rap artists have little or no incentive to disengage from the genre's patriarchal rhetoric.

This contradictory function of hip-hop culture as both a progressive and regressive force in the African American community is represented in *Insecure*'s enclosed enclaves. When Issa retreats from the microaggressions of the external world, she uses the rich lyrical history of rap music as a form of therapy. Through her often-awkward rhymes and comedic lyrics, she is able to embrace the individuality of her quirks and legitimize her right to difference, her right to resist the suffocating grip of hegemonic tropes and narratives. But hip-hop's affirmations are unbreakably intertwined with its repudiations. Although the genre imbues Black womanhood with affirmative agency by tapping into its cultural reservoir of civil rights activism, it also tends to repudiate affirmative counternarratives of Black womanhood by prioritizing and promoting hypermasculine values. Thus, when Issa invites hip-hop's affirmations into an enclosed enclave, she is also summoning the genre's repudiations, agents of Black hypermasculinity seeking to compromise the enclave's function as a temporary space of reprieve. As I will examine below, the marginalizing agents infiltrating an enclosed enclave are not always foreign entities. The vast and almost inescapable influence of hip-hop culture on everyday African American life means that even a nonconformist and affirmative subject like Issa can subconsciously internalize the agenda of marginalizing agents and jeopardize the restorative sanctity of her own enclave. In the subsequent paragraph, I will revisit the pilot, paying careful attention to how the everyday happenings of Issa and Lawrence's relationship problematize and ultimately rethink master narratives of hip-hop culture.

After relishing a meal with Molly within the soothing confines of Merkato, Issa dreads returning to the apartment she shares with Lawrence. As beforementioned, Lawrence's enduring joblessness prompts her to question the longevity of their relationship. She tries to be supportive, but his lack of motivation makes her wonder if, like many other professional Black women, she has settled for less. When Issa returns home from Merkato, Lawrence is reclining on the couch in loungewear. They are scheduled to see "a show" at 10 p.m. to celebrate Issa's birthday, so she asks him, "why aren't you dressed?" (Rae and Wilmore 2016–2021). "I bombed the interview," he answers, referencing his failure to make a great impression at a job interview earlier in the day (Rae and Wilmore 2016–2021). He develops feelings of dejection as a result of this failure and is now unable to motivate himself to dress up and go out. Issa tries to be encouraging by saying "I'm sure it wasn't that bad," but he responds with a decisive "No! I literally spit on him. Then I spilled hot coffee all over his desk" (Rae and Wilmore 2016–2021). "Never mind then," she replies with a mixture of sadness, exhaustion, and exasperation (Rae and Wilmore 2016–2021). There is a great deal to unpack here. First, Lawrence is clearly in a depressive state. His dream of becoming a successful software developer continuously encounters professional obstacles, and this career setback has left his self-esteem bruised. When you factor in his current state of mind, his inability to dress up and celebrate his girlfriend's birthday is somewhat understandable. Similarly said, his lack of enthusiasm for Issa's big day is mostly due to depressive feelings and not selfishness. However, Issa's frustration is also justified. For any romantic relationship to thrive, emotional support must be a two-way street. Because Lawrence is mentally consumed by his perceived failures, he is often unable to emotionally support Issa through her trials and tribulations as a professional Black woman attempting to negotiate the pressures of both her career and personal relationships. The afore discussed couch scene where she rejects his offer to eat together might seem inconsiderate and even cruel. But when you take into consideration that her emotional investment in the relationship is usually not reciprocated, her exasperation and thoughts of ending the relationship are justified.

Insecure's portrayal of Lawrence's deteriorating mental health in the everyday setting of an apartment is significant for a multitude of reasons. First, the usage of ordinary objects like the mustard couch and loungewear allows the viewer to witness in real time the deceptive and demoralizing depth of depression. Although Lawrence does not outwardly exhibit depressive symptoms such as excessive crying, volatile behavior, and lack of appetite, we repeatedly encounter him on the couch or in bed, shabbily dressed, unbothered about his appearance, and somewhat disengaged from the world around him. His sluggish and unmotivated movements in shabby loungewear on the couch and the bed and through the apartment highlight his deteriorating state of mind and uncovers how depressive feelings can be cunningly interwoven into every fabric of ordinary life. The implication here is that in our everyday interactions and environments, mental health disorders are not always overtly detectable. Rather, they are camouflaged by our ordinary habits and traditions, projecting some semblance of outward normality while inwardly compromising our mental fortitude.

Most importantly, Lawrence's portrayal as sensitive and insecure is the antithesis of how Black masculinity is generally portrayed and celebrated in hip-hop culture (Gammage 2015, 8) (Gaunt 2006, 180). I have already pointed out on numerous occasions that the legacy of Black hypermasculinity, an ideology engineered by Southern white patriarchy and plantation slavery, is heavily endorsed and promoted by the male-dominated rap music industry. A plethora of anecdotal and qualitative studies have investigated the nature and implications of how Black men are depicted in hip-hop culture. Qualitative research by social scientist Andrea A. Hunt, for example, demonstrates how contemporary rap music repeatedly portrays Black men as "macho" and "tough" (2019, 75). The emphasis on macho toughness reinforces the cultural conceptualization of Black men as the legitimate leaders and custodians of the African American community. According to Hunt's study, Black men who do not ascribe to this hegemonic rhetoric are derogatively labeled as "punks" (Hunt 2019, 75). Although there is an emerging group of talented young rappers like Kendrick Lamar and J. Cole who are combating these toxic narratives in rap music with positive and nuanced depictions of Black masculinity, mainstream hip-hop culture, as Hunt's data reveals, remains dominated by hypermasculine tropes and themes. The Black male participants in the qualitative study also reported that foremost themes in today's hip-hop include "'selling drugs... gang relations... shooting... jail'" (Hunt 2019, 75). The pervasiveness and glamorization of these themes, they continued, "appeals to not only African American men in inner-city areas but even to 'a normal dude from the suburbs'" (Hunt 2019, 76). These representations, Hunt argues, have "larger implications for the identity development of African American young men" (2019, 76).

The larger implications of these representations do not only impact the psyche of Black men. Hunt also interviews Black women who admit that they too internalize the hypermasculine and sexist tropes of hip-hop culture (2019, 76). We see a similar internalization process throughout *Insecure*'s first season. As I stated above, Issa has legitimate reasons to be exasperated with Lawrence. However, the idea of breaking up with him in the pilot is spurred by a happy birthday message from her ex-boyfriend Daniel, a handsome rapper with the kind of charismatic swagger and confidence one would typically associate with mainstream rap artists. There is no indication that unlike Lawrence, Daniel has a thriving career and is attuned to Issa's emotional needs. There is also no indication that he is willing to commit to a long-term monogamous relationship. Just the mere sight of his message, "Happy birthday I miss you," sends Issa fantasizing about breaking up with Lawrence and reuniting with him, a fantasy that emphasizes the allure of hip-hop masculinity (Rae and Wilmore 2016–2021). Later that day, Molly calls Issa to vent about feeling jealous of a recently engaged colleague. This is the day after the broken pussy moment in Merkato, and now that Molly is back in the external world, her Asian colleague's engagement announcement reawakens her frustrations about the dating challenges for professional Black women. Issa seemingly decides to cheer her best friend up by taking her back into an enclosed enclave. This time, the enclave takes the form of an open mic night, a showcase for burgeoning rap talent.

In addition to hip-hop's history of civil rights activism, the central role Black female artists played in the creation and development of rap music reinforces the function of hip-hop culture as an affirmative performance for Black women. For example, musician and rapper Roxanne Shanté is generally considered by hip-hop scholars and historians as one of the most innovative pioneers of the genre (Brown August 2018). Hailing from Queensbridge, New York City, Shanté, in 1984, at the age of just fourteen, released one of the most iconic songs in hip-hop culture. Titled "Roxanne's Revenge," the song is an audacious response to "Roxanne, Roxanne," a wildly popular single by acclaimed male rap group UTFO. In "Roxanne, Roxanne," the male rappers encapsulate hip-hop culture's hypermasculinity by ridiculing and chastising a "stuck-up" girl called Roxanne who rejects their advances (UTFO 1984). Although UTFO's Roxanne is not related to Roxanne Shanté, the musician and rapper, the latter saw the song as a prime opportunity to assert her feminist agency on the hip-hop scene.

In "Roxanne's Revenge," fourteen-year-old Shanté assumes the persona of UTFO's Roxanne and cheekily derides the male hip-hop trio by mocking their talent and inflated arrogance (Shanté 1984). The song feels like a watershed moment of restitution in hip-hop culture because you have this young girl inserting herself into a notoriously hypermasculine space and demanding an end to the proliferation of sexist tropes, which denigrate Black womanhood. This audacious act harkened back to the advocacy origins of hip-hop culture and paved the way for the next generation of female rap artists such as Queen Latifah, Da Brat, Foxy Brown, and Eve. Shanté ultimately forced rap music to confront its sexist prejudices and broaden the scope of what a rap artist should look and sound like. Thus, in addition to civil rights activism, hip-hop culture also has a rich feminist heritage.

This explains why Issa often turns to hip-hop lyricism in moments of discomfort and insecurity. In the pilot, she describes writing raps as a form of therapeutic journaling that allows her to cope with the microaggressions of everyday life in the external world. On the morning of her birthday, for example, she raps about her feelings in the mirror. "Go shawty, it's my birthday," she begins. "But no one cares because I'm not having a party. 'Cause I'm feeling sorry for my—self" (Rae and Wilmore 2016–2021). By saying these words out loud, she is able to not only acknowledge her insecurities, but she also realizes that she is being somewhat dramatic by feeling overly sorry for herself. This therapeutic act of rapping through her feelings allows Issa to identify and unpack relatable insecurities of ordinary life such as feeling unloved or underappreciated. Her emotional attachment to the language and rhythm of hip-hop justifies the genre's function as an enclosed enclave.

Now that I have provided some context on how rap music can affirmatively function as an enclosed enclave, Issa's decision to console Molly by taking her to the open mic rap event might seem genuine. However, hypermasculinity remains an integral and undetachable component of hip-hop culture. Thus, when Issa retreats into the enclosed enclave of hip-hop lyricism, the external marginalizing forces of hypermasculinity also journey into her temporary space of reprieve and attempt to corrupt the restorative purpose of the enclosed enclave by replicating the external world's hegemonic power structures. This first trace of this corruption is Issa's overwhelming attraction to Daniel. Because she is constantly writing raps, she has subconsciously internalized the preferences of hip-hop's hypermasculine culture. Daniel's reappearance in her life exacerbates her annoyance with the more sensitive Lawrence, and she begins to fantasize about a new life with her rapper ex-boyfriend. When Molly called Issa to vent about her colleague's engagement, Issa had just found out that Daniel might be at an open mic event. Eager for a reunion, she invites Molly to the event under the pretense of cheering her up. Her primary intention is to see Daniel, but she needs a plus-one (Molly) in case her mission is unsuccessful. This is the second and most consequential sign of internal corruption within the enclosed enclave. Retreating into the enclave is supposed to be a restorative tradition oriented by trust, an honest escape from the intrusion of external mandates. In this scenario, however, Issa uses the enclave's existence to advance the preferences of the external world. She is hopelessly enamored by rapper Daniel's confident demeanor and charm and fails to realize that this infatuation is desecrating the enclave's regenerative sanctity.

When Issa and Molly arrive at the open mic event, Molly is suspicious. Something does not feel right. They are in an unfamiliar part of town, and the venue's energy lacks Merkato's soothingly comforting vibe. "Will you stop being all judgmental?" Issa tells Molly, assuring her that they are in a safe space (Rae and Wilmore 2016–2021). While inside, a guy approaches Molly and they begin a conversation, giving Issa an opportunity to wander off and attempt to reconnect with Daniel. He finds her at the bar, and after a few drinks and flirtatious conversations, he challenges Issa to get onstage and perform. Desperate to impress him, she agrees and to Molly's chagrin, Issa raps about a broken pussy. "Maybe it's dry as hell, maybe it really smells, broken pussy" Issa sings, gaining more confidence as the crowd starts reacting positively to her decent "flow" and comedic lyrics (Rae and Wilmore 2016–2021).

The event ends and Issa and Daniel go their separate ways. On the car ride back home, Molly is visibly upset. When she saw Issa and Daniel sitting together at the open mic event, it finally dawned on her that the outing was simply a selfish ploy by Issa to reunite with her ex-boyfriend. Moreover, Issa's decision to sing the broken pussy song is a grave breach of trust that compromises the sanctity of the enclosed enclave. The broken pussy gag, an intimate and private joke between both friends, functions as affirmative escapism in Merkato because it offers Molly a comedic reprieve from the overwhelming pressures of the external world. In the open mic event, however, Issa simulates a fake enclosed enclave and uses the broken comment joke at Molly's expense. Although Issa never publicly reveals that the song stems from a joke about Molly, Issa is guilty of luring Molly into a false sense of security and then exploiting the affirmative comedy of a private joke to impress Daniel. "This was always about you. . . . Is my life a joke to you?" Molly asks Issa, her rage revealing the sting of betrayal (Rae and Wilmore 2016–2021).

We see shades of Freire's pedagogy of the oppressed returning to the discourse. When a marginalized subject dwells and operates within spaces dominated by oppressive narratives, they inevitably internalize and replicate similar oppressive narratives within their own spheres of influence. In Issa's case, her internalization of hip-hop's oppressive tropes sees her enacting similar oppressive structures within the enclosed enclave. In order to align her romantic interests with a more macho version of hip-hop masculinity, she uses her knowledge of the enclosed enclave's functionality, a bubble of agency shielded from outside interference, to lure Molly into a deceitful plot that, like the burdens of professional Black women in the external world, leaves Molly feeling worthless and unappreciated. Worthy of emphasis here is the fact that Issa does not assume the role of a hegemonic marginalizing entity from the external world. External marginalizing forces possess vast systemic tools of oppression, which are usually embedded in society's foundational pillars. Issa does not wield such macro power and influence. However, because she uses the oppressive tactics of the external world to inflict harm on Molly, she can thus be characterized as an agent of external marginalizing forces, a co-conspirator of sorts. In other words, although she does not become the literal oppressor in Freire's pedagogy, she is a cog in one of the many wheels of systemic structures facilitating the marginalization of the oppressed. Issa's attraction to Daniel reinforces a general stereotype of some women's attraction to the seductive charisma of "bad boys" over the boring ordinariness of nice guys. In a more culturally specific context, her attraction to Daniel is also an indictment of the oppressive implications of hypermasculine tropes on African American men. Sensitive Black men like Lawrence whose range of emotions represent a more realistic depiction of the challenges of everyday life are often sidelined by hip-hop culture in favor of a masculine rhetoric of invulnerable patriarchy. One can thus argue that the ordinariness of Lawrence, a regular guy next door, is just as subversive as the normalization of Issa's everyday relatability. Like Issa, Lawrence is a flawed character but by documenting his everyday routines and traditions, his love for his girlfriend, his career ambitions, his depressive feelings triggered by rejection, etc., *Insecure* rebels against the hegemonic mandates of hip-hop's hypermasculine tropes and celebrates Black masculinity's right to difference.

As analysis of the TCT framework in preceding chapters points out, external marginalizing forces have the capacity to infiltrate the post-rupture realm. Even after momentous episodes of rupture, marginalizing agents from the external world still linger, actively attempting to reestablish their hegemony. Thus, although Issa does not become a hegemonic oppressor, her betrayal of Molly at the open mic event reveals that the ordinary comforts of her enclosed enclaves are vulnerable to the hegemonic influence of oppressive narratives. This takes us back to chapter 1 in which I discuss how women's and gender studies scholar Davidson uses Deleuzian philosophy to argue that feminist subjectivities should constantly unfold and adapt to new knowledge systems in order to recognize and resist the infinite attempts by external marginalizing forces to infiltrate, corrupt, and occupy their autonomous constitutions (2010, 130).

Issa's subjectivity begins to unfold after she cheats on Lawrence with Daniel. The scene of betrayal occurs in Daniel's recording studio, another false enclosed enclave that epitomizes the creation and dissemination of hip-hop music. Blinded by her obsession with Daniel, Issa convinces herself that, due to their shared passion for rap rhymes and lyrics, accepting an invitation to meet him in his recording studio can function as a regenerative escape from the pressures of the external world. They both predictably succumb to their lustful desires and after having sex, Issa is consumed with guilt. She realizes that her longing to pursue Daniel is a corruptive influence violating the authentic bond of love and trust she shares with both Lawrence and Molly. To make matters worse, her unfaithfulness coincides with Lawrence putting more effort into making their relationship work. In episode 4 of season 1, for example, we see Lawrence taking the initiative to improve his mental health by exercising more. He also takes a job at Best Buy while continuing to pursue his dreams of software developing by working on his app "Woot-Woot." Moreover, in episode 6 of season 1, he takes Issa to a jewelry store to try on engagement rings, an act that reveals his long-term commitment to their relationship. Guilt-ridden, Issa has flashbacks to her indiscretion with Daniel and abruptly requests, "can we go?" When Lawrence asks why, she says "I just don't feel good" (Rae and Wilmore 2016–2021). Her suspicious behavior continues and when Lawrence confronts her in season 1's penultimate episode, she sorrowfully confesses, sobbing and begging him for forgiveness.

An enraged Lawrence rejects her plea and storms out, leaving Issa to face the consequences of succumbing to the allure of external marginalizing forces.

The reverberations of this breakup scene encapsulate the central arguments of my analysis in this section of chapter 4. The demise of Issa and Lawrence's relationship foregrounds hip-hop as an everyday aesthetic with consequential implications on the ordinary lives of African Americans. Issa's ability to validate the relatable ordinariness of her humanity through raps and rhymes functions, I argue, as a form of restitution because it is a return to the egalitarian promise of the genre's advocacy origins. With that said, mainstream hip-hop is often dominated by a hypermasculine culture, which dictates and polices the performance of masculinity within the African American community. By operating within this cultural space, Issa inevitably internalizes some of these hegemonic mandates of masculinity and, as a result, jeopardizes her romantic relationship with a man who genuinely loves her but does not possess the magnetic macho aura of rap culture. In other words, the affirmative lyricism that empowers Issa's enclosed enclave is also responsible for compromising the enclave's restorative abilities. Like the contradictory function of community as both an ally and aggressor in Beyoncé's *Lemonade*, hip-hop culture plays a contradictory role in Issa's life, a contradiction also echoed in Gay's discussion of rap music in *Bad Feminist*. *Insecure*'s awareness of this contradictory function, I argue, is reflected in the clumsiness of Issa's raps. As hip-hop journalist Stephen Kearse points out, "her raps, always self-written, are bad. The words fumble out, inflected at odd points, and connected by clumsy, simple rhymes" (2017). Although the act of rapping is therapeutic, her clumsiness reveals a state of discomfort, emphasizing, once again, the symbiotic relationship between affirmations and tension.

What are the implications here for the TCT framework? The most obvious implication, already discussed in the previous section of this chapter, is that transformative moments of affirmed resistance and tension often reside in the humdrum of our daily routines and traditions, and like Gay's *Bad Feminist* and *Difficult Women* and Beyoncé's *Lemonade*, there is no convenient resolution to states of discomfort in the post-rupture realms. However, *Insecure*'s exploration of hip-hop culture's conflicting impact on the lives of Issa, Molly, and Lawrence impressively constructs nuanced portraits of its protagonists, portraits that deconstruct and demystify popular culture's rigid understanding of Black identity by imbuing its characters with varying degrees of rage, joy, indifference, and compassion.

Furthermore, the reverberations of the compromised enclosed enclave on Issa, Molly, and Lawrence reinforce the argument that the affirmative post-rupture realm, a temporary reprieve from the external marginalizing forces, remains vulnerable to the hegemonic oppressiveness of outward interference. This explains why Davidson and Deleuze demand an infinite evolution of the subject's subjectivity, an evolution capable of identifying and adapting to the dynamic methods of interference by external marginalizing forces. But as I earlier discussed, the constancy of ordinary objects, settings, and emotions also has the capacity to confront corruptive infiltrations by hegemonic forces. Issa's efforts to mend her relationship with Lawrence, efforts resisting the pestiferous forces that motivated her act of betrayal, reveal a longing for constancy, a desire to maintain and preserve the genuine love she once shared with Lawrence. Throughout the next three seasons, she remains steadfast in her efforts and is eventually rewarded in season 4's gloriously bittersweet reunion between the ex-lovers.

As I conclude this section, I should point out that I have spent a great deal of time describing the enclosed enclaves, their iterations, characteristics, and functionality. I have not, however, said much about the *feeling* of how they look, the textures of their visuality and the illuminating shades of their cinematography. I previously mentioned that the enclosed enclave takes on many forms and figurations, one of them being cinematography. Thus, in the next and final section of this chapter, I turn my focus to the camera lens. I will argue that by illuminating ordinary subjects and objects in extraordinary ways, *Insecure*'s cinematography functions as an enclosed enclave that interrogates and rectifies the inherent color bias of photography. Having said that, the cinematic act of (over) glistening Black bodies must also contend with a familiar sense of tension. Lurking within, behind and beyond the glinted lens is a divergent perspective about the necessity of spectacle, a divergent perspective that complicates and calibrates my analysis on the transformative value of ordinary life. I will begin with a brief overview of the function of cinematography before unpacking the camera's color bias and, finally, addressing the complex implications of how this cinematic shortcoming is confronted by *Insecure*'s use of colored lights.

THE IRIDESCENT VISIONS OF COLORED LIGHTS

The earliest mention in history of using light to reproduce images dates as far back as the era of the ancient Greeks. Aristotle, for example, described "how light waves behave when projected through a small aperture" (Halas 1987, 12). This practice of using a darkened space with a small hole through which light is projected on a wall is called a camera obscura (Halas 1987, 12). Due to continuous innovations in photography, the concept of the camera obscura underwent dramatic transformations in the sixteenth and seventeenth centuries, transformations that culminated into Kodak's revolutionary roll of film, a new photographic technology that refined the art of capturing and preserving images to be developed at a later time (Andrews 2008, 158). The next landmark innovation was photographer Eadweard Muybridge's *The Horse in Motion* (1878), "the first successful serial images" of a man riding a horse (Maxwell 2007, 191). These "kinetic images of animals and humans in motion inspired scientists" like "Thomas Edison . . . and others who, during the late 1890s, went on to develop and refine what would become the picture camera—film as art and business was born" (Maxwell 2007, 191). In the film industry, the art of using the picture camera to capture and light moving images is called cinematography, and the primary goal of this cinematic process is to reflect a film's distinct mood through a series of editing and lighting techniques (Reach 2015, 120). When the motion-picture industry began in the late nineteenth century, the lack of innovative filming styles at the time meant that cinematography was often a straightforward visual documentation of a sequence of events.

This changed in the early twentieth century when cinematography reached new heights of sophistication with the collaboration between filmmaker D. W. Griffith and cinematographer Billy Bitzer. Griffith is best known for his controversial film *The Birth of a Nation* (1915), a cinematic masterpiece, from a technical perspective, which glorifies the Ku Klux Klan. Although *The Birth of a Nation* has rightfully tarnished Griffith's legacy, his contributions to cinema remain noteworthy. His first collaboration with Bitzer began in *A Calamitous Elopement* (1908), and they would go on to make almost five hundred movies together, originating and innovating cinematographic techniques still widely used today. Some examples of these techniques include "the flashback, extreme long shot, traveling shot, split-screen shot, matte shot and various lighting effects . . . backlighting, the iris shot, and the soft-focus shot" (Monaco, Pallot and the editors of BASELINE 1991, 61). Since all forms of photography, including cinematographic images, strive to create a specific narrative mood, lighting is arguably the most instrumental tool in photographic documentation because it has the potential to capture, distort, or reimagine the form and texture of the camera's subjects and settings. Light is thus the "the ghost we all chase" in photography (McFadden 2014).

In 2014, writer and photographer Syreeta McFadden addressed the camera's inherent color bias in what I consider to be a seminal essay on the racial legacy of photography, "Teaching The Camera To See My Skin: Navigating Photography's Inherited Bias Against Dark Skin." McFadden examines how camera technology skews photographic representations of Black skin and, as a result, reproduces false portraits of human experiences. In her recollection of going through a photo album at the age of twelve, McFadden recalls being confused. "In some pictures, I am mud brown, in others I'm blue black," she says. "Some of the pictures were taken within moments of one another" (McFadden 2014). This grave sense of disconnect between who she thinks she is and how she is represented by the camera colors the trajectory of her journey into adulthood by sowing deep-rooted seeds of self-doubt and self-hate (McFadden 2014).[6] A year later, McFadden's mother showed her four proofs from an Olan Mills photo shoot and once again, she could not recognize herself. "I considered each of the images," McFadden says. "I couldn't see my face . . . my eyes looked like sunken holes in a small brown face, and my pupils were invisible. 'I don't even look like me'" (McFadden 2014). The photo shoot's goal was "to create a pastoral scene of domesticity for our rough and ragged family to give to loved ones" (McFadden 2014), implying that photographs are not always about reality; they can also represent a projection of fantasy. But fantasy is not necessarily falsehood, the opposite of truth. Many a time, fantasies evoke aspirations, worlds we long to inhabit and events we wish to manifest. For McFadden's family, the Olan Mills photo shoot was meant to be an aspirational escape from the roughness of their everyday lives by inserting their authentic selves in the setting of pastoral bliss. The camera had other plans.

In addition to McFadden looking unrecognizable, her mother "was kind of blown out on one side" and her father transformed into a "half brown and tan" being, his afro disappearing "into a faux marbled background" (McFadden 2014). As well as misrepresenting their true physical attributes, these photographic misrepresentations in the pastoral imaginary also deny them access to fantasy, the transformative capacity to imagine one's self inhabiting and thriving in other worlds. By denying her Black skin access to this creative ability, young McFadden felt both marginalized and devalued by the camera's skewed lens. The claims in McFadden's personal and heartfelt essay about the psychological impact of the camera's inherent color bias are supported by scholarly research. For example, photography scholar Tanya Sheehan argues that "photographic matter has always been political matter" (2020, 55). Because early photographers in both the United States and Europe "approached black skin as a technical problem" (Sheehan 2020, 56), there was already a consensus at the dawn of photography that white skin was the default color and thus the camera's preferred subject. This argument is also echoed in other contemporary works like Mark Sealy's *Decolonising the Camera: Photography in Racial Time* (2019), a scholarly text that examines the camera's racial politics in the larger context of Western imperialism.

The photographic erasure and distortion of Black skin arguably reached its peak with the introduction of a Kodak-created color reference point called Shirley cards (Harding 2017). In the 1940s, the Kodak company used one of its employees, Shirley, to create a visual template for coloring skin on film (Harding 2017). Shirley, a pale white woman with auburn hair and blue eyes, was placed in a grayish background that heavily contrasted against her skin and white dress and the resulting picture "is used as a metric for skin-color balance, which technicians use to render an image as close as possible to what the human eye recognizes as normal" (McFadden 2014). This is obviously problematic, because when one uses a white subject as a light meter, darker skin tones are prone to gross misrepresentations. In 1977, for example, French New Wave director Jean-Luc Godard infamously rejected Kodak film for an assignment in the African country of Mozambique, decrying the stock as "inherently 'racist'" (Smith D. 2013). Changes were made in the 1970s when makers of chocolate and wood furniture complained that Kodak film was failing to capture the difference in chocolate varieties and wood grains (Zhang 2015). American television was also becoming more diverse during this same period. With the soaring popularity of Black-led television shows like *The Jeffersons* and *Sanford and Son*, Kodak had more convincing reasons to course correct. About a decade later, major breakthroughs were also going on in monochrome movies like Spike Lee's *She's Gotta Have It* (1986). According to Ernest Dickerson, the movie's cinematographer, "the main thing you had to worry about is the reflectivity of African-American skin. I always made sure that the makeup artists I worked with put a moisturizer on black skin so that we [got] some reflections in there" (Harding 2017). Another milestone occurred in 1993 when Kodak created a new diverse color reference featuring a Caucasian woman, an Asian woman and a Black African woman (Zhang 2015), ushering in a new era of awareness about photography's inherent color bias, an awareness evident in *Insecure*'s cinematic aesthetic.

After the critical and commercial acclaim of *Insecure*'s season 1, cinematographer Ava Berkofsky was hired in season 2 as director of photography to elevate the show's cinematic sensibilities (Harding 2017). "When I was in film school, no one ever talked about lighting nonwhite people," she says during an interview with online media platform *Mic*. "There are all these general rules about lighting people of color, like throw green light or amber light at them. It's weird" (Harding 2017). When it comes to cinematic lighting, the unit used to measure composite video signals is called IRE, a name taken from the initials of the Institute of Radio Engineers, the organization responsible for creating the IRE standard (Musburger and Odgen 2014, 37). Discussing the usage of IRE (a scale that ranges from 0 to 100) in cinematic photography, Berkofsky states, "the conventional way of doing things was that if you put the skin tones around 70 IRE, it's going to look right. If you've got black skin, [dialing it] up to 50 or 70 is just going to make the rest of the image look weird" (Harding 2017). Examples of "weird" IRE filtered images of Black bodies can be seen in the murky bright yellow coloring of traditional sitcoms like *The Cosby Show* and *The Fresh Prince of Bel-Air*. This brightness pervades every scene and creates a uniform blandness that misrepresents the unique textures and shades of its subjects. This is what Berkofsky tries to avoid in *Insecure* by, in her own words, "keeping [light] off the walls. If you keep it off the walls, you can expose for the faces and it still has a cinematic look" (Harding 2017). In the subsequent paragraphs, I will discuss two scenes shot under Berkofsky's supervision as director of photography and director, paying close attention to, first, how Black bodies are filtered through colored lights and, most importantly, the complicated implications of these cinematic visions.

The first sequence of shots I will examine is the nightclub scene in episode 4 of season 2. Set a few months after Issa and Lawrence's breakup, both parties have drifted apart and are now navigating the idiosyncrasies of their new lives. Lawrence has finally landed what seems like his dream job and begins dating a bubbly bank teller called Tasha. He also looks considerably more muscular and groomed than in the previous season. However, his past insecurities and unresolved emotions for Issa still linger, threatening to destabilize the perceived stability of his new life. Issa too is experiencing turbulent times. We Got Y'all's after-school initiative is struggling to recruit students, and in the school that partners with the lagging initiative, she is forced to confront racial tensions between Latinos and African Americans. Her love life is equally chaotic. She goes on a string of disastrous dates and becomes both emotionally and sexually frustrated. Seeking reprieve from the brutalities of the external world, Issa decides to retreat into the comfort of an enclosed enclave. This time, in episode 4 of season 2, the enclave takes the form of an outing with her best friends Molly and Kelli. They begin the day at Molly's apartment, drinking, laughing, and getting ready to forget about their troubles and have a good time. With her moisturized skin, refined cheekbones, burgundy crop top, and high-waisted print skirt, Issa is particularly glowing in this scene. Although she retains her ordinary charm from season 1, she is physically more alluring here. I will address the physical transformation of both Issa and Lawrence in a later paragraph but for the time being, let us return to the outing.

The girls finally leave Molly's apartment and head to their destination. They first walk through an outdoor area with green flora before making their way into the nightclub, gorgeously lit with blue lights. As Molly, Issa and Kelli move through the room, the lights reflect differently off their Black bodies, illuminating the specificity of their shades. As writer Xavier Harding bluntly (and hilariously) states, "any brown person who's taken a selfie in the club can tell you cameras aren't made for us" (2017). Darker skin tends to blend in with dimly lit spaces like nightclubs and because the camera lens is often ill equipped at capturing and highlighting various shades of Blackness, pictures of Black people in dark spaces are usually false visual reproductions. This is not the case in episode 4's nightclub scene. All three women have different skin tones: while Issa and Molly are slightly different shades of dark caramel, Kelli is warm yellow. As the three women interact in the dark space of the nightclub, Berkofsky's swirling blue lights flashes over them, keeping the unique authenticity of their individual shades intact. Berkofsky accomplishes this feat by using the *She's Gotta Have It* technique of having a makeup artist apply reflective base on the cast's skin (Collie 2020). And instead of shining the light directly on them, she uses a whiteboard with LED lights inside (S2 LiteMat 4s) to reflect light off the illuminated actors (Collie 2020). Berkofsky also uses a filter called polarizer to train the camera's gaze. "People use them when shooting glass, or cars, or any surface that intensely reflects light," she says during her interview with *Mic*. "The filter affects how much reflection a window, or any surface has. The same principal [sic] works with skin, and this can be a highly effective way to shape the reflected light on an actor[']s face" (Harding 2017).

Returning to the nightclub scene, Issa unexpectedly runs into Daniel, and the moment in which they approach each other is probably one of the most impressive shots in the entire series. With a plaid shirt wrapped around his waist, Daniel is holding a glass and wearing a sleeveless T-shirt. He and Issa are facing each other and, they are both drowning in various shades of blue lights, their dark bodies illuminated in a manner that is magnificently cinematic. The cinematography here is functioning as an enclosed enclave, because unlike the legacy of Kodak's Shirley cards, it, first, truly represents the distinct shades and shine of *Insecure*'s protagonists and, second, it grants these characters the gift of fantasy. This sexier and edgier version of Issa, accurately represented and gloriously lit, is ordinary Issa's attempt to explore life outside of her comfort zone. After the devastating demise of her relationship with Lawrence in season 1, she realizes that in order to pick up the pieces and begin again, she has to take risks and relish in the affirmations of new experiences. She is still clumsy Issa with the bad raps but what her tinier waist and crop top represent is an affirmative indulgence in the exploration of a new persona. In other words, she, once again, resists hegemonic tropes and expectations by allowing herself to fantasize about inhabiting different worlds and experiencing different dimensions of her dynamic personality. The practice of photographically capturing Black skin in an authentic manner, which resonates with its filmic subjects is thus an extraordinarily affirmative counternarrative.

The second cinematic scene I will discuss is in episode 8 of season 4. Written by Natasha Rothwell, the character who plays Kelli, we see Berkofsky taking the helm as director, and her striking visual aesthetic is instantly recognizable. This episode documents the glorious reunion of Issa and Lawrence. After spending two long seasons apart (seasons 2 and 3), working through their traumas, confronting their insecurities, and admitting their shortcomings, they finally reunite and are ready to entertain the possibility of being a couple again. The episode is a beautifully shot catalog of ordinary experiences during a date between Issa and Lawrence. They begin at a crowded bar and despite the seasons apart, the respect they have for each other remains intact. When the bar gets disruptive, they decide to change locations. At the new bar, as they begin to discuss their individual experiences during their period of separation, Lawrence says, "let's not do the tiptoe shit tonight . . . no eggshells. We know each other too well for that" (Rae and Wilmore 2016–2021). Issa nods affirmatively, and they are led to their table by a waiter. What proceeds is a series of comedic and honest moments: they crack jokes through laughs and smiles, reminisce about the past, and have a sincere conversation about the breakup and how it made each of them feel.

Following dinner, they go on a nighttime art walk along a crowded street and like the nightclub scene, they are in a dark setting. After romantically strolling through paintings and clothes hanging on racks, talking about their careers and what makes them happy, they finally stop in front of an art installation. This is arguably the most impressive still in the entire series. The installation is square shaped with lighted vertical lines. One set of vertical lines is glowing red and other beams in blue. Lawrence is standing on the side of the red light and Issa on the side of the blue light and like the nightclub scene, they are both facing each other. The red light brings out the romantic longing on Lawrence's face and the blue light accentuates the intricate curvature of Issa's eyes, exposing a slight worry, perhaps, at the thought that after two emotionally torturous seasons, the beautiful simplicity of this magical reunion might all be a dream. But it is not a dream. Staring at Issa, Lawrence says, "I am pretty happy right now," and the lighting briefly catching Issa's facial transformation from tepid anxiety to pure bliss (Rae and Wilmore 2016–2021). Cinematography, once again, creates an enclosed enclave because it allows its Black subjects to exist in all spaces accurately and authentically (illuminated bars and nighttime streets). Their wide range of expressive emotions can thrive wherever they please and not only in the very limited areas engulfed in the glow of natural light. Berkofsky's lens is thus true and imaginative. She captures the humanity of Issa and Lawrence in its truest form and also gives them the creative license to inhabit any world or location they choose.

Having said that, the affirmative tendencies of Berkofsky's lens must also contend with a familiar sense of tension. During her interview with *Mic*, Berkofsky, according to writer Xavier Harding, admits to wanting "every scene to look like a painting" (2017). While discussing strategies to illuminate darker skin tones on camera, Berkofsky recommends standing "close to a soft light source and turn three quarters to the light, so that it's not filling in everything the same way. Kind of like a Rembrandt painting" (Harding 2017). This ability to capture the authentic glow of Black skin in dark spaces to such an extent that subjects become elevated to the status of acclaimed paintings problematizes my argument about the transformative value of ordinary life. If the subjects are glistened to the point where they become over glistened then they lose the aesthetic simplicity that represents the unremarkable traditions and routines of everyday life. Art historian Simon Schama describes Rembrandt's paintings as "materially present: the looser and rougher the paint handling, the more palpable the flesh; the redness of eyelid rims, the puffball of white hair indicated by the freest brushstrokes" (2019). There is an accomplished sense of visual authenticity in Rembrandt's works, and this rationalizes why Berkofsky looks to him for inspiration while authentically lighting the diversity of Black skin. However, Schama also describes Rembrandt's work as "wonder" and "majestic," fantastical adjectives that elevate his subjects to an otherworldly status (2019). When Berkofsky drowns *Insecure*'s subjects in the glorious glow of colored lights, this vision of Blackness, I argue, tends to elevate the characters from being extraordinarily ordinary to simply being extraordinary. In other words, they, to some extent, lose the everyday/relatable aesthetic of earlier episodes and become illuminated larger than life beings.

There is a glaring contradiction here in the functionality of photography. Photographic images often seek to authentically capture the physicality of specific subjects but, as I previously mentioned, they also offer an indulgence in fantasy. In this pairing, there is little to no conflict because fantasy is a mental gateway that celebrates the vastness of a creative imagination and does not necessarily affect or distort the authenticity of the physical form and the emotional weight it carries. The function of photography at odds with photographic representations of authenticity is a depiction of physical and emotional realism, which becomes so accurate it veers toward the majestic realm and loses its ordinariness. As Schama points out, realist art like the work of Rembrandt is a fastidious endeavor to replicate the physical attributes of a subject and the complex emotions they wear. However, there is something inherently majestic about the artform of painting: the richness of the colors, the meticulous attention to detail, and the nearly religious meditation required during the viewing process. Thus, although one appreciates the gritty authenticity of Rembrandt's commonplace subjects, their existence within the realm of high art inevitably imbues them with an aura of majestic wonder and extraordinary brilliance.

We see a similar tension with *Insecure*'s illuminated subjects. They are not offputtingly bright like the characters on *The Cosby Show* and *The Fresh Prince of Bel-Air*. Rather, Berkofsky uses innovative techniques with colored lights to glisten and emphasize their unique shades of Blackness. Like Rembrandt's art, we see every trace of emotion on their faces and the distinct curvature of their bodies regardless of the setting. Also, like Rembrandt's art, there is something inherently majestic about the art form of cinema.[7]

Although Issa and the other characters remain unabashedly ordinary, the aura of celebrity attached to the acting profession and the usage of expensive camera equipment and inventive shooting techniques inevitably imbues *Insecure* with an aura of majestic wonder and extraordinary brilliance. In the afore discussed nightclub scene, for example, the blue light accentuating Issa's skin becomes so powerful at one point that there is literally a halo resting atop her head. In that moment, she becomes almost otherworldly and transcends the ordinary aesthetic of earlier episodes.

This brings me back to the physical transformation of Issa and Lawrence in season 2 (and beyond). As I stated earlier, they both retain most of their ordinary traditions and behaviors, but they now look like movie stars. They are fitter, their faces more angular and clothes more stylish and expensive. My mentioning of this, I must emphatically state, is not a condemnation. It is human nature to strive to improve one's well-being, both physically and psychologically, and watching a dark-skinned creator like Rae move through the white-dominated televisual/cinematic world of HBO as a beautiful, talented and stylish leading lady is incredibly affirmative. However, this transformation somewhat undercuts the ordinariness of season 1, a plainness that I argue makes the show powerfully relatable. Season 1 is extraordinarily ordinary because it celebrates and normalizes the ordinariness of everyday Black experiences in a manner we have never seen before. Berkofsky's cinematography, on the other hand, is often simply extraordinary because its over glistened subjects evoke a majestic and otherworldly vision of cinematic Black bodies.

Should *Insecure* have stayed with the same aesthetic of the first season? This is my next and final line of inquiry. It would probably surprise the reader (or not) to discover that my answer is no. Every artist strives to creatively progress and evolve. After much thought, I now fervently believe that if the plainness of season 1's televisual aesthetic remained consistent throughout the ensuing four seasons, the show would have lost its charm and visual freshness. There is therefore the argument that due an appetite for artistic evolution, particularly within the innovative format of HBO storytelling, Rae and her creative team were motivated to challenge and affirm audiences in new and unexpected ways. The decision to highlight cinematography does not completely reimagine *Insecure*'s protagonists. They might not be as "plain" as they were in season 1, but they are still quirky and insecure individuals navigating the challenges of everyday life. Moreover, although the emphasis on properly lighting Black bodies tends to veer toward the majestic, the accurate radiance of Berkofsky's colored subjects boldly confronts photography's institutional bias. Her vision as *Insecure*'s director of photography can thus be described as iridescent. From one vantage point, it undercuts the transformative potency of ordinary life but from another, it audaciously defies the white frames of hegemonic lenses and rethinks systematic methods of capturing color on film.

I will conclude this chapter by pointing out that the bold function of Berkofsky's photography has inspired the TCT framework to reexamine the aesthetic function of ordinary life. Despite season 1's affirmative novelty, it cannot match the seismic impact of what Berkofsky's cinematography is doing in the later seasons. Celebrating the ordinary humanity of African Americans, a monoracial ethnic group often burdened by the crushing weight of dehumanizing tropes and stereotypes, is a momentous act of rebellion. However, there is an inherent muteness to the humdrum of everyday life that is unable to emotionally stir audiences in a dramatic fashion. The lavish boldness of Berkofsky's colored lights, on the other hand, underlines a century-long institutional problem and has spawned countless affirmative articles and think pieces on the internet about how the camera lens has historically marginalized and misrepresented bodies of color. For all its strengths, the aesthetic of everyday life arguably cannot provoke such an impassioned response.

This takes us back to the value of spectacle. Like Beyoncé's *Lemonade*, Berkofsky's cinematic visions are spectacular. Her colors are lavish and bright and the impact of her techniques, transgressive and far reaching. What the TCT framework emphasizes here is that during moments on the cusp of profound rethinking, spectacle is often the only appropriate aesthetic response. In *Lemonade*, Beyoncé can only successfully map out the terrain of her new Afrofuturistic and egalitarian world by creating a lavish multimodal spectacle, which shocks the consciousness of viewers, within and beyond her community, into action. Similarly, in both *Bad Feminist* and *Difficult Women*, Gay can only successfully validate her affirmative singularities by creating a lavish literary universe that honors the unique legitimacy of a diversity of individualized experiences. However, I argue that what prevents the spectacular from being dangerously detached from the tactile world of the contemporary is a parallel acknowledgment and celebration of the aesthetics of everyday life, as seen in season 1 of *Insecure*. Spectacle plays a vital role in art but without a reminder of the daily traditions and shared values of ordinary life, it runs the risk of becoming aesthetically esoteric like the obfuscating ruminations of abstract philosophy, an aloof intellectual exercise divorced from the everyday and tactile preoccupations of its audience. Thus, what makes the TCT analytical apparatus necessary and relevant is its ability to create an elastic framework, which allows the aesthetic diversity Gay's, Beyoncé's, and Rae's works to exist alongside each other, addressing each other's limitations while amplifying the multidisciplinary nature of their collective strength. Their tensions do not always find a convenient resolution, but the totality of their emotions and experiences is possibly the truest representation of their unresolved right to both difference and sameness.

NOTES

1. Commonly referred to as *Awkward Black Girl*.
2. Stereotypes such as the mammy, the tragic mulatto, the jezebel, etc.
3. "Issa" from here henceforth refers to the protagonist of *Insecure* and "Rae" denotes Issa Rae, the creator and actress.
4. In recent times, there has been a slow but steady production of research in Western academia about the aesthetics of everyday life. The field of aesthetics of everyday life, an emergent subfield of philosophical aesthetics, is admittedly vast and sometimes convoluted. I am not positioning myself as an expert in this field, and I am certainly not interested in its developing and ongoing debates. Nevertheless, I do want to briefly engage with Saito's text, because she is fixated on the significance of everyday objects and figures.
5. There are two 2006 publications by Austin cited in this manuscript. This citation is from *Getting it Wrong: How Black Public Intellectuals are Failing Black America*, and the previous citations are from *Achieving Blackness: Race, Black Nationalism, and Afrocentrism in the Twentieth Century*.
6. This grave sense of disconnect echoes the chasm in Du Bois's double consciousness between how Black Americans view themselves and how Black Americans are viewed by the dominant white society.
7. Although *Insecure* is a television show, it is an HBO product and, as previously noted, HBO is labeled prestige television due to its cinematic quality.

Conclusion

The philosophical roots of triple consciousness are firmly embedded in Du Bois's seminal concept of double consciousness. Although conceived and extensively articulated in 1903, double consciousness still has a formidable influence on contemporary scholarship about American identity and culture. In articles like "Double Consciousness in the 21st Century" (2021) by T. Joseph and T. Golash-Boza and books like Robert Terrill's *Double-Consciousness and the Rhetoric of Barack Obama* (2015), double consciousness is used to contextualize and culturalize our contemporary understanding of issues surrounding race, identity, and citizenship. Furthermore, a 2021 *New York Times* article about the psychological complexities of interracial relationships compared double consciousness to code-switching (Holt 2021), the practice of a marginalized individual "switching" their speech and behavioral patterns to match the hegemonic code of conduct and linguistic preferences upheld by society's dominant group. And in the arts magazine *Hyperallergic*, the immigrant experience of Chinese mixed-media artist Fei Li is described as "The Double Consciousness of Being a Chinese Woman Living in America" (Yau 2021).

The enduring legacy of Du Bois's double consciousness is a testament to the concept's theoretical dynamism and flexibility. However, as I extensively pointed out in chapter 1, double consciousness is largely informed by patriarchal and imperialist sensibilities, and this invites a legitimate conversation about the concept's contemporary relevance. Although cotemporary narratives about the Black female experience remain influenced by the double consciousness phenomenon, the existential tension between how a Black subject views themselves and how a Black subject is viewed by the antagonistic perceptions of the white world, they are also significantly impacted by other vantage points such as the patriarchal practices of Black hypermasculinity. Building off the rich legacy of Black feminist discourse by scholars and writers like Angela Davis, Alice Walker, Frances M. Beal, Toni Morrison, and Kimberlé Crenshaw, contemporary feminist writers are deciding to reengage with Du Bois's double consciousness by using the term "triple consciousness," a new framework that acknowledges a third female-centric dimension in the Black female consciousness (America, Blackness, and womanhood).

Before proceeding, it is imperative to remind the reader that Du Bois was a product of his time. His preferences and prejudices reflected his era's patriarchal bourgeois sensibilities, sensibilities he adopted and refined as he moved within and through intellectual circles. Furthermore, Du Bois addressed, and in some cases rectified, the shortcomings of double consciousness in his later career. His tenure as the editor of *The Crisis*, for example, sees him radically deconstructing the notion of American exceptionalism by criticizing America's imperial interference in Haiti (Hall 2001, 93). In the 1950s, his frustrations with the injustices of the American democratic project push him toward Marxist theory, and he begins to frame Black American history within a "diasporic . . . vision for a socialist future" (Lynn 2019). He also rebukes his earlier classist prejudices by disavowing his concept of the Talented Tenth (James 2013, 18), the belief that one in ten Black men had the potential to become an elite community leader (Du Bois 1994, 64). In 1948, while delivering a lecture at the Nineteenth Grand Boulé Conclave, Sigma Pi Phi, Du Bois states,

> Some years ago I used the phrase "The Talented Tenth," meaning leadership of the Negro race in America by a trained few. Since then this idea has been criticized. It has been said that I had in mind the building of an aristocracy with neglect of the masses. This criticism has seemed even more valid because of emphasis on the meaning and power of the mass of people to which Karl Marx gave voice in the middle of the nineteenth century, and which has been growing to influence ever since. (James 2013, 18)

Despite these rectifications and clarifications, Du Bois did not, I argue, satisfactorily reengage with double consciousness' gender erasure. Although he "used the pages of *The Crisis* to argue for women's right to vote, the right to work, and the right to pursue a career without having to sacrifice family and motherhood" (Warren 2014, 20), he never unambiguously addressed the silencing of the Black female perspective in his famed double consciousness paradigm, and in his landmark feminist essay "The Damnation of Women" (1920), Black women are primarily defined by reductive stereotypes. This explains the historical efforts by Black feminist scholarship to develop frameworks about the intersectional complexities of a specifically Black female consciousness, historical efforts that most likely influenced contemporary feminist writers like Danielle Moodie-Mills and Sara Lomax-Reese to add a third gendered dimension to Du Bois's double consciousness paradigm.

Unlike these contemporary interpretations and iterations of triple consciousness, there is an interesting assemblage of Black female artists in contemporary American culture such as writer Roxane Gay, popstar Beyoncé, and writer/actress Issa Rae who are engaging with a third lens that I conceptualize as rupture and not a correction and/or completion of the Du Boisian paradigm. Although the works of these women echo the racial and cultural tensions in Du Bois's double consciousness and other "thirdness" concepts like Bhabha's hybridity, their primary preoccupation is the rupture that develops and envelops when the unique orientation of individualized narratives assert their infinite right to difference by simultaneously complementing and complicating the relevance of collective shared histories.

In my discussion of Gay's *Bad Feminist* and *Difficult Women*, I use the counter-actualizing mechanism of Deleuzian philosophy and the theoretical emphasis on singularities in Attridge's idioculture to illustrate how Gay affirms the individual's right to difference by resisting the hegemonic and historic tendency to conceptualize Blackness as a monolithic ethnic identity. But Deleuze's and Attridge's skepticism of community, mostly due to the collective tendency to encroach on individual preferences, is at odds with the more affirmative function of community in Beyoncé's *Lemonade*. To accommodate this variance, I use Ghosh's aesthetic imaginaries, particularly his focus on the dynamism of circular cultural practices and the imaginative process of building new worlds, to examine community's contradictory role in *Lemonade* as ally and aggressor, a contradictory role that radically reimagines ubiquitous concepts such as feminism, traditionalism and Christianity. *Lemonade*'s radical rethinking of religion, for example, undermines the syncretic notion of cultural circulations by exposing spiritual practices that must resist cultural integration with other religious knowledge systems to protect the sanctity of their belief system. This drawback of the aesthetic imaginary, and other associated concepts about cultural hybridity, enables my reworked TCT framework to emphasize the value of protecting the affirmative uniqueness of some marginalized cultures that are at risk of being subsumed into more dominant cultural systems. And finally, in examining Issa Rae's *Insecure*, I use concepts about everyday aesthetics by Ndebele and Saito to analyze how Rae conceptualizes Black womanhood as extraordinarily ordinary and awkwardly insecure, a sharp departure from the self-assured and boastful #BlackGirlMagic discourse in contemporary popular culture. Unlike the spectacular scale of ideas, actions, and declarations in *Bad Feminist*, *Difficult Women*, and *Lemonade*, everyday aesthetics demonstrate TCT's theoretical dynamism by reimagining seemingly trivial aspects of everyday life, such as eating in a restaurant and buying a couch, as defiant episodes of protest.

Although Gay, Beyoncé, and Rae adopt different aesthetic approaches with varying results, they share a significant similarity: a tendency to derive affirmative strength from the unresolved tensions of intersectional conflict by simultaneously rejecting and embracing the notion of community. It was incredibly important for me to use the works of popular artists as my primary materials because, as Stuart Hall eloquently states, by understanding the meanings a people or a society ascribes to popular symbols, practices and activities, the study of popular culture is the study of "shared values" (1997, 2). Hence, by investigating how popular Black female artists simultaneously confront and embrace popular interpretations of universal concepts like race, culture, and identity, my book studies both the shifting and stagnant perceptions of contemporary America's shared values.

The Black female perspective is a particularly fascinating area of study because the affirmative discomforts of its intersectional existence between race and gender speaks to the complex nature of identity formation practices. Not only are Black women marginalized by institutional racism, but they are also victims of Black hypermasculinity, an offshoot of Southern white patriarchy and plantation slavery (Benson 2014, 13). Moreover, the historical, and ongoing, inclination to view Black men as the Black community's natural-born leaders (Delinder 2009, 987), from the Harlem Renaissance to the contemporary Black Lives Matter movement, has often led to the sidelining and silencing of Black women's unique intersectional interests. The concerns of Black men are, for the most part, collectively viewed as the most pressing concerns of the Black community and even the legal system sometimes fails to recognize the concerns of Black women as a unique intersectional experience (Crenshaw 1989, 141). As gender studies scholar and activist Brittney Cooper points out, while referencing the somewhat lackluster reception Breonna Taylor's death generated, the kinds of oppression experienced by Black women do not often fit the "spectacular forms" of racialized violence, such as "America's nefarious lynching past," usually associated with the marginalization of Black men (2020). Thus, in the American imaginary, from Du Bois's double consciousness to the nationwide protests sparked by the murders of Trayvon Martin and George Floyd, racial oppression is often synthesized from the experiential perspective of Black men.

This inability to recognize the multiplicity of perspectives within the African American experience echoes an institutional tendency to view Black Americans as a monolithic ethnic group, a tendency that, I argue, has its roots in the rigidity of America's color line. America was, at its constitutional inception, a nation uncompromisingly divided by the color line. Unlike white-majority European countries, anti-Black racism was literally written into American law. As Pulitzer Prize–winning American historian Carl N. Degler states, "racism ... was translated into law-segregation and rested upon a genetic definition of the Negro" (1973, 757). I am not insinuating here, I must clarify, that European countries were "less racist" than America. After all, during America's infancy, in the eighteenth and nineteenth centuries, European nations were embarking on a mad colonial scramble for territories all over the globe, colonial pursuits largely motivated by white supremacist ideologies. However, because European legal systems were not defined by "a genetic definition of the Negro," perceptions of Blackness in the European imaginary were more fluid. This explains why although most of segregated America shunned African American singer and actress Josephine Baker in the early to mid-twentieth century, she was able to become, in 1927, not only "the highest paid entertainer" in her adopted homeland of France, but also in all of Europe (Martone 2008, 52). While Baker experienced sexism and racism in Europe, the absence of an American-style legal system, wholly drenched in anti-Black racism, gave her access to better legal protection and more avenues in desegregated spaces to negotiate and accrue greater agency (Schroeder and Wagner 2009, 26–33). The rigidity of America's pre-desegregation color line meant the institutional enactment of a restrictive binary: Black versus white. Anyone not legally deemed white was associated with the perceived inhumanity of Blackness, a monoracial group classified as unworthy of constitutional protection and citizenship rights. Blackness thus became a monolithic identity because all Black people were legally deemed unfit for legitimate American citizenship. Unlike in 1920s and 1930s France, where the identity of a Black woman like Josephine Baker could, in certain instances, transcend race and foreground other social markers like social class, profession, citizenship and language, in pre-desegregated America, a Black person could legally be nothing else but a Black person.

Black Americans naturally internalized this perception of their ethnic identity as monolithic and in the works of Black immigrant writers like Jamaican-born Claude McKay, we see differences in perceptions about Blackness. In the novel *Home to Harlem* (1928), McKay's protagonist is Ray, a Haitian immigrant living in the Black "mecca" of Harlem, New York City. Although Ray is enamored with and inspired by Harlem's extraordinary vitality, he becomes increasingly frustrated with America's restrictive characterization of Blackness as a monolithic experience primarily defined by race (McKay 2000, 196). Growing up in Black-majority country such as Haiti, difference is not only primarily defined by race because almost everyone racially looks the same.[1] Thus, in this scenario, other primary identity markers such as language, class, and social mobility also play a significant role in the process of identity formation. The implication here is that Black Americans with immigrant backgrounds, particularly those from Black-majority countries, do not have the same intergenerational experience with the color line as Black American descendants of chattel slavery. This brings us back to the ADOS discourse. Despite the movement's incoherent messaging and alleged xenophobic rhetoric, it is hard to deny that there is some legitimacy to their underlying message. They seem interested in pointing out that America's institutional efforts to conceptualize all Black identities as a monolithic racial experience has historically denied American descendants of chattel slavery opportunities to understand, unpack, and uplift the uniqueness of their ethnic identity. Although the color line is less rigid in the post-segregation era, my book has exhaustively demonstrated that contemporary Black American identity is still oriented by restrictive and reductive racial categorizations. Thus, by denying to legally acknowledge distinctions within America's diverse Black populace, one could argue that America is still propagating, to some extent, the historical practice of characterizing the Black experience as a monolithic identity.

These intersectional, intergenerational, and intercultural tensions are vibrantly reflected in the works of Gay, Beyoncé, and Rae. Gay's attempt to build a fellowship of feminists in both *Bad Feminist* and *Difficult Women* is an acknowledgment that the socio-economic and political advancement of women is dependent on the creation of a community with progressive and egalitarian shared values. However, she must reckon with the fact that communities are flawed because they are movements "powered by people and people are inherently flawed" (Gay 2014, x). Thus, despite community's positive function, it tends to marginalize and eradicate dissenting voices. This is the primary reason Gay's works place the female subject's individualized perspective at the center of every narrative, a bold aesthetic move that rejects hegemonic mandates of rigid community structures. Using Deleuzian terms, Gay's celebration of an affirmative right to difference is a reminder for individuals to be infinitely critical of community leaders and ideologies, a reminder that hegemonic forces and cultures often silence different points of view by characterizing the varied experiences within communities as monolithic.

In *Lemonade*, on the other hand, Beyoncé affirms community's right to sameness. Being an African American woman of Southern and Creole heritage, Beyoncé's existential ruminations are strongly embedded in the cultural specificities and nuances of the nonimmigrant Black American experience. As a marginalized minority Black community within a dominant white society, Black American descendants of chattel slavery have always been primarily defined by race and, as a result, tend to have a strong sense of Black racial solidarity. Moreover, because charismatic community leadership, from the origins of the Black church to the civil rights movement, has always spearheaded anti-racism movements, nonimmigrant Black Americans often view community structures as the epicenter of progressive values. This explains why although Beyoncé affirms her right to difference in *Lemonade*, she ultimately returns to the sameness of community and attempts to find a balance between her individual priorities and her community obligations.

In Rae's *Insecure*, we encounter similar unresolved tensions from both a thematic and aesthetic perspective. For example, although Issa Dee, the protagonist, rejects hegemonic notions of Black womanhood by affirming her awkwardly insecure persona, she is also guilty of perpetuating hegemonic notions of Black masculinity. Moreover, despite *Insecure*'s celebration of ordinary people and their unremarkable routines in the drudgery of everyday life, its cinematic qualities have a propensity to elevate the show's characters from ordinary to extraordinary. For example, compared to season 1's Issa Dee, season 5's Issa Dee is skinnier, prettier, and more fashionable and exudes the aura of a gorgeously lit movie star. Thus, while *Insecure* resists the rhetoric that all Black girls are "magic," as a critically acclaimed show on prestige television, it operates within a cinematic realm of storytelling that requires a few "magical" elements.

The theoretical depth and richness of these artistic engagements have largely been minimized or ignored entirely by existing scholarship. Take Gay for example. Although she is an acclaimed popular writer, her eclectic cross-genre writings on race, identity, and gender are not the subject of the same level of institutional engagement as the works of Black American writers like Ta-Nehisi Coates and Nikole Hannah-Jones. In Beyoncé's case, she is generally regarded as a great performer and an influential pop star. However, beyond the realm of Black feminist scholarship, one can argue that she is not widely recognized as a thought-provoking and innovative artist. This was the impression I got from music and culture scholars while working on this book, an anecdotal impression corroborated by music journalist Jaime Rodriguez, who insinuates that the bias might be due to Beyoncé's more "urban" kind of music (a fusion of R&B, dance pop, and hip hop), a "Black" sound music critics and industry insiders have historically not taken "seriously enough" (2021). There is certainly an intersectional element of racial and gender prejudice at play here as well. Beyoncé is a Black woman who is aesthetically beautiful (in a traditional sense) and artistically sensual. And as popular music scholar Rachel Henry Currans-Sheehan points out, female artists who use sexuality as a form of artistic expression are often not "taken seriously by the public" (2009, 59). With *Insecure*, the HBO show received near universal acclaim but has struggled to profoundly permeate institutional discourse on issues like race, gender, identity, and culture. Because there are very few scholarly texts exclusively dedicated to *Insecure*, conversations about the show's subversive take on ordinary life are mostly relegated to online think pieces, memes, and gifs.

In this book, I identify and amplify the artistic depth of *Bad Feminist, Difficult Women, Lemonade,* and *Insecure* by emphasizing the affirmative counternarratives of marginalized Black American women, uniquely oriented explorations that are largely unshackled from the tenets of hegemonic epistemologies. Using my remodeled triple consciousness framework, I examine how the exploratory counternarratives of these works strive to assert their infinite right to difference by simultaneously embracing and repudiating the shared values of cultural systems. Although this novel reading of triple consciousness originates in and with the syncretic traditions of concepts like Bhabha's hybridity, Ghosh's aesthetic imaginaries, and Davis's noncontradictory oppositions, it is breaking away from these traditions and, hopefully, expanding, continuing and influencing discourses on the profoundly complex nature of identity formation practices.

But there are of course limitations to this expansion. This book admittedly examines the works of Black female artists whose creative emphasis on the aftermath of affirmative rupture can be linked to the almost unprecedented amount of agency they wield in popular culture discourse. For example, although a narrative like *Insecure* subverts hegemonic gendered tropes by celebrating the aesthetic of ordinary life, it accomplishes this goal through the extraordinary medium of prestige television. Thus, for disenfranchised individuals or groups lacking the institutional agency to actualize and affirm momentous moments of rupture, their creative approach to conceptualizing triple consciousness might require a different apparatus. Moreover, because I largely focus on heterosexual narratives, my approach to triple consciousness does not accommodate the complexity of identity formation practices in conversation with gender, race, sexuality, and (dis)ability, practices associated with Black gay authorship, Black ableism narratives, and the Black transgender experience.

While these limitations make a case for further research on the complex variations and dimensions of the third consciousness, they are not necessarily an indictment of my book's theoretical framework. As I underlined earlier, although heterosexual Black women belong to the dominant heteronormative group, they have historically endured, and continue to endure, severe manifestations of systemic marginalization, both from within and beyond the African American community. Despite these obstacles, or, perhaps, because of these obstacles, Black women have a rich but underappreciated history of producing art, which profoundly reflects the anxieties of their times and defies the status quo in interesting and complex ways. From Billie Holiday to Zora Neale Hurston to Nina Simone to Lauryn Hill, Black female authorship has always been oriented by subversive inclinations, and in this book I have demonstrated how this tradition of counterculture manifests in the contemporary works of Roxane Gay, Beyoncé, and Issa Rae. Together, all four selected texts (*Bad Feminist*, *Difficult Women*, *Lemonade*, and *Insecure*) accommodate an exhaustive spectrum of narratives with the assured capacity to rethink hegemonic notions of triple consciousness and ultimately unpack the affirmative discomforts of Black female authorship in contemporary American culture.

NOTES

1. For Black-majority countries, race-based differences are mostly related to colorism.

Bibliography

Abad-Santos, Alex. 2015. "Beyoncé's vocal range and dance ability are a rarity in pop music." *Vox*, May 12, 2015. https://www.vox.com/2014/8/28/18010384/beyonces-vocal-range-and-dance-ability-are-a-rarity-in-pop-music.
Abiodun, Rowland. 2001. "Hidden Power: Osun, the Seventeenth Odu." In *Osun across the Waters: A Yoruba Goddess in Africa and the Americas*, edited by Joseph M Murphy and Mei-Mei Sanford, 10–33. Bloomington: Indiana University Press.
Adell, Sandra. 1994. *Double-Consciousness/Double Bind: Theoretical Issues in Twentieth-century Black Literature*. Champaign: University of Illinois Press.
Ahlgrim, Callie. 2020. "Only 10 Black Artists Have Won Album of the Year at the Grammys—Here They All Are." *Insider*, September 22, 2020. https://www.insider.com/black-grammys-winners-album-of-the-year.
Ahmed, Sara. 2015. "Introduction: Sexism—A Problem with a Name." *new formations: a journal of culture/theory/politics* 86 (2015): 5–13. muse.jhu.edu/article/604486.
Alarcón Jessica M. 2008. "Osun (Oxum/Ochun/Oshun). In *Encyclopedia of the African Diaspora: Origins, Experiences, and Culture*, edited by Carole Elizabeth Boyce Davies, 732–33. Santa Barbara: ABC-CLIO.
Alkana, Joseph. 1997. *The Social Self: Hawthorne, Howells, William James, and Nineteenth-Century Psychology*. Lexington: The University Press of Kentucky.
Alter, Charlotte. 2015. "Sandra Bland's Not the First Black Woman to Experience Police Violence." *TIME*, July 22, 2015. http://time.com/3965032/sandra-bland-arrest-video-police-violence/.
Andrews, Dale. 2008. *Communications & Multimedia Technology*. Burlington: Digital Overdrive.
Ashley, Wendy. 2014. "The Angry Black Woman: The Impact of Pejorative Stereotypes on Psychotherapy with Black Women." *Social Work in Public Health* 29, no. 1 (2014): 27–34. https://doi.org/10.1080/19371918.2011.619449.
Associated Press. 2005. "Women Had Key Roles in Civil Rights Movement." *NBC News*, October 29, 2005. https://www.nbcnews.com/id/wbna9862643#.WyOWy8iFM2w.
Attridge, Derek. 2004. *The Singularity of Literature*. London: Routledge.

Austin, Algernon. 2006. *Achieving Blackness: Race, Black Nationalism, and Afrocentrism in the Twentieth Century*. New York: NYU Press.
———. 2006. *Getting it Wrong: How Black Public Intellectuals are Failing Black America*. Lincoln: iUniverse.
Baldwin, James. 1963. *The Fire Next Time*. New York: Dial.
———. 1985. *The Price of the Ticket: Collected Nonfiction 1948–1985*. New York: St. Martin's/ Marek.
Bankston, Samantha. 2007. *Deleuze and Becoming*. London: Bloomsbury.
Bale, Miriam. 2016. "Beyonce's 'Lemonade' Is a Revolutionary Work of Black Feminism: Critic's Notebook." *Billboard*, April 25, 2016. https://www.billboard.com/articles/news/7341839/beyonce-lemonade-black-feminism.
BBC News. 2016. "Michelle Obama 'ape in heels' post causes outrage." BBC, November 17, 2016. https://www.bbc.com/news/election-us-2016-37985967.
Beach, Christopher. 2015. *A Hidden History of Film Style: Cinematographers, Directors, and the Collaborative Process*. Oakland: University of California Press.
Beal, Frances M. 2008. "Double Jeopardy: To Be Black and Female." *Meridians* 8, no. 2 (2008): 166–76. http://www.jstor.org/stable/40338758.
Beam, Adam. 2016. "GOP Hopeful Not Sorry for Posts Depicting Obamas as Monkeys." Associated Press, September 30, 2016. https://apnews.com/article/barack-obama-ronald-reagan-kentucky-us-news-lexington-90ec82dfca4f45e48628e4ae45b8247f.
Beatty, Paul. 2015. *The Sellout*. New York: Farrar, Straus & Giroux.
Beaulieu, Elizabeth Ann. 2006. *Writing African American Women*. Westport: Greenwood Publishing Group.
Beevor, Anthony. 2009. "Freedom sweeps Europe—but at what cost?" *The Guardian*, September 10, 2009. https://www.theguardian.com/world/2009/sep/10/second-world-war-liberation-europe.
Belkhir, Jean Ait, and Christiane Charlemaine. 2007. "Race, Gender and Class Lessons from Hurricane Katrina." *Race, Gender & Class* 14, no. 1/2 (2007): 120–52. http://www.jstor.org/stable/41675200.
Bell, Bernard W. 1996. "Genealogical Shifts in Du Bois's Discourse on Double Consciousness as the Sign of African American Difference." In *W.E.B. Du Bois on Race and Culture: Philosophy, Politics, and Poetics*, edited by Bernard W. Bell, Emily Grosholz, and James B. Stewart, 87–110. New York: Routledge.
Bellamy, Maria Rice. 2016. *Bridges to Memory: Postmemory in Contemporary Ethnic American Women's Fiction*. Charlottesville, University of Virginia Press.
Benson, Josef. 2014. *Hypermasculinities in the Contemporary Novel: Cormac McCarthy, Toni Morrison, and James Baldwin*. Lanham: Rowman & Littlefield.
Bergson, Henri. 2007. *The Creative Mind: An Introduction to Metaphysics*. Translated by Mabelle L. Andison. New York: Dover Publications.
Beyoncé. 2016. *Lemonade*. Parkwood Entertainment. www.beyonce.com/album/lemonade-visual-album/.
———. 2011. *4*. Parkwood/Columbia.
———. 2013. *Beyoncé*. Parkwood/Columbia.

Bhabha, Homi K. 1995. "Cultural Diversity and Cultural Differences." In *The Post-Colonial Studies Reader*, edited by Bill Ashcroft, Gareth Griffiths, and Helen Tiffin, 206–211. London: Routledge.

Blanco, Lydia. 2018. "The BET Awards Are Still Ours—Support Black Businesses as Much as You Complain About Them." *Black Enterprise*, June 25, 2018. https://www.blackenterprise.com/bet-awards-support-black-business/?test=prebid.

Bogle, Donald. 2015. *Primetime Blues: African Americans on Network Television*. New York: Farrar, Straus and Giroux.

Boyd, Richard. 2009. "Imperial Fathers and Favorite Sons." In *Feminist Interpretations of Alexis de Tocqueville*, edited by Jill Locke and Eileen Hunt Botting, 225–48. University Park: Penn State Press.

Boyd, Svetlana. 2001. "Nostalgia." Monument to Transformation, 2001. http://monumenttotransformation.org/atlas-of-transformation/html/n/nostalgia/nostalgia-svetlana-boym.html.

Brockes, Emily. 2018. "#MeToo founder Tarana Burke." *The Guardian*, January 15, 2018. https://www.theguardian.com/world/2018/jan/15/me-too-founder-tarana-burke-women-sexual-assault.

Brooks, Siobhan. 2010. "Hypersexualization and the Dark Body: Race and Inequality among Black and Latina Women in the Exotic Dance Industry." *Sexuality Research and Social Policy* 7 (2010): 70–80. https://doi.org/10.1007/s13178-010-0010-5.

Brown, Ashley. 2018. "'Least Desirable'? How Racial Discrimination Plays Out In Online Dating." NPR, January 9, 2018. https://www.npr.org/2018/01/09/575352051/least-desirable-how-racial-discrimination-plays-out-in-online-dating?t=1636887124463.

Brown, August. 2018. "With Netflix's 'Roxanne Roxanne,' the Story of Hip-Hop Pioneer Roxanne Shanté Is Finally Told." *Los Angeles Times*, March 23, 2018. http://www.latimes.com/entertainment/music/la-et-ms-roxanne-roxanne-movie-20180323-story.html.

Buck, Kimberlee. 2018. "The History of Black Television." *Los Angeles Sentinel*, February 8, 2018. https://lasentinel.net/the-history-of-black-television.html.

Burawoy, Michael. 2005. "Response: Public Sociology: Populist Fad or Path to Renewal?" *The British Journal of Sociology* 56, no. 3: 417–32. https://doi.org/10.1111/j.1468-4446.2005.00075.x.

Bush, Barbara. 2014. *Imperialism and Postcolonialism*. Milton Park: Routledge.

Bush, Lawrence. 2016. "December 18: Hal Kanter and Diahann Carroll." *Jewish Currents*, December 17, 2016. https://jewishcurrents.org/hal-kanter-and-diahann-carroll.

Butler, Bethonie. 2016. "'Insecure': Everything you need to know about Issa Rae's HBO comedy." *The Washington Post*, October 9, 2016. https://www.washingtonpost.com/news/arts-and-entertainment/wp/2016/10/09/insecure-everything-you-need-to-know-about-issa-raes-hbo-comedy/.

Cannon, Katie Geneva et al. 2011. *Womanist Theological Ethics: A Reader*. Louisville: Westminster John Knox Press.

Carayol, Tumaini. 2021. "Serena Williams Rises Above Tiriac and Co but Misogyny and Racism Take a Toll." *The Guardian*, January 9, 2021. https://www.theguardian.com/sport/blog/2021/jan/09/serena-williams-ion-tiriac-misogyny-racism.

Casey, E. S. 1987. "The World of Nostalgia." *Man and World* 20: 361–84. https://doi.org/10.1007/BF01252103.

Chen, Lizzie. 2021. "Black Television Through the Years." The University of Texas at Austin: Moody College of Communication, 2021. https://moody.utexas.edu/news/black-television-through-years.

Coates, Ta-Nehisi. 2015. *Between the World and Me*. New York: Spiegel & Grau.

Cochrane, Naima. 2019. "Your Musical Guide to the Black of Beyoncé's 'Homecoming.'" *Billboard*, April 19, 2019. https://www.billboard.com/articles/columns/hip-hop/8507911/beyonce-homecoming-musical-guide-blackness/.

Collie, Meghan. 2020. "Here's How the Woman Behind the Camera on Insecure Properly Lights Its Black Actors." *Fashion Magazine*, June 16, 2020. https://fashionmagazine.com/flare/insecure-lighting/.

Conlin, Joseph R. 2014. *The American Past: A Survey of American History, Volume II: Since 1865*. Boston: Cengage Learning.

Cooper, Brittney. 2020. "Why Are Black Women and Girls Still an Afterthought in Our Outrage Over Police Violence?" *Time*, June 4, 2020. https://time.com/5847970/police-brutality-black-women-girls/.

Cosimini, Seth. 2015. "AmeriKKa's Human Sacrifice: Blackness, Gangsta Rap, and Authentic Villainy." In *Violence in American Popular Culture [2 volumes]*, edited by David Schmid, 245–68. Santa Barbara: ABC-CLIO.

Crenshaw, Kimberlé. 1989. "Demarginalizing the Intersection of Race and Sex." *University of Chicago Legal Forum* 1989, no. 1:139–69.

Croce, Paul J. 2018. *Young William James Thinking*. Baltimore: John Hopkins University Press.

Croisille, Valérie. 2021. *Black American Women's Voices and Transgenerational Trauma: Re(-)membering in Neo-Slave Narratives*. Newcastle upon Tyne: Cambridge Scholars Publishing.

Cross, Latoya. 2016. "Beyoncé Flips the 'Formation' Conversation." *JET*, April 05, 2016. https://www.jetmag.com/entertainment/beyonce-flips-formation-conversation/.

Crum, Maddie. 2014. "The Book We're Talking About: 'Bad Feminist' By Roxane Gay." *HuffPost*, August 5, 2014. https://www.huffpost.com/entry/bad-feminist-roxane-gay_n_5638840.

Currans-Sheehan, Rachel Henry. 2009. "From Madonna to Lilith and Back Again: Women, Feminists, and Pop Music in the United States." In *You've Come A Long Way, Baby: Women, Politics, and Popular Culture*, edited by Lilly J. Goren, 53–72. Lexington: University Press of Kentucky.

Dash, Julie, director. 1991. *Daughters of the Dust*. Kino International.

Davidson, Maria del Guadalupe. 2006. *The Rhetoric of Race*. Valencia: Universitat de València.

———. 2010. "Rethinking Black Feminist Subjectivity: Ann duCille and Gilles Deleuze" In *Convergences: Black Feminism and Continental Philosophy*, edited by Maria del Guadalupe et al., 121–34. Albany: SUNY Press.

Davis, Angela Y. 1999. *Blues Legacies and Black Feminism*. New York: Vintage Books.

Davis, Arianna. 2016. "One Awkward Black Girl Interviews Another Awkward Black Girl, Issa Rae." *Refinery29*, October 7, 2016. https://www.refinery29.com/en-us/2016/10/125615/issae-rae-bio-insecure-hbo.

De La Torre, Miguel A. 2004. *Santeria: The Beliefs and Rituals of a Growing Religion in America*. Grand Rapids: W. B. Eerdmans Publishing, 2004.

Degler, Carl N. 1973. "The Problem of the Color-Line." *Journal of Interdisciplinary History* 3, no. 4 (Spring): 757–62. https://www.jstor.org/stable/202694.

Deleuze, Gilles. 1991. *Bergsonism*. Translated by Hugh Tomlinson and Barbara Habberjam. New York: Zone Books.

———. 2004. *Difference and Repetition*. Translated by Paul Patton. New York: Continuum.

———. 1988. *Foucault*. Translated by Seán Hand. Minneapolis: University of Minnesota Press.

———. "How Do We Recognize Structuralism?" Translated by Michael Taormina. In *Desert Islands and Other Texts: 1953–1974*, edited David Lapoujade, 170–92. New York: Semiotexte.

Deleuze, Gilles, and Felix Guattari. 2004. *A Thousand Plateaus*. Translated by Brian Massumi. New York: Continuum.

Delinder, Jean Van. 2009. "Gender and the Civil Rights Movement." *Sociology Compass* 3, no. 6 (December): 986–99. https://doi.org/10.1111/j.1751-9020.2009.00239.x.

Dery, Mark. 1994. "Black to the Future: Interviews with Samuel R. Delany, Greg Tate, and Tricia Rose." In *Flame Wars: The Discourse of Cyberculture*, edited by Mark Dery, 179–222. Durham: Duke University Press.

Destiny's Child featuring Wyclef Jean. 1998. "No, No, No Part 2." *Destiny's Child*. Columbia/Music World.

Dill, Bonnie Thornton. 1979. "The Dialectics of Black Womanhood." *Signs* 4, no. 3 (1979): 543–55. http://www.jstor.org/stable/3173400.

Drexler, Peggy. 2019. "Millennials Are the Therapy Generation." *The Wall Street Journal*, March 1, 2019. https://www.wsj.com/articles/millennials-are-the-therapy-generation-11551452286.

Du Bois, W. E. B. 1994. *The Souls of Black Folk*. New York: Dover Publications.

———. 1897. "The Conversation of the Races." Gutenberg, 1897. http://www.gutenberg.org/files/31254/31254-h/31254-h.htm.

———. 2000. "The Damnation of Women." In *The Crisis* Nov.–Dec. 2000, edited by (editor-in-chief) Ida E. Lewis, 3–8. Baltimore: The Crisis Publishing Company.

———. 1904. *The Suppression of the African Slave-Trade to the United States of America, 1638–1870*. New York: Longmans, Green and Company.

Dunlap, Eloise, Andrew Golub, and Bruce D. Johnson. 2006. "The Severely-Distressed African American Family in the Crack Era: Empowerment Is Not Enough." *Journal of Sociology and Social Welfare* 33, no. 1 (2006): 115–39.

Eaton, Kalenda C. 2010. *Womanism, Literature, and the Transformation of the Black Community, 1965–1980*. Milton Park: Routledge.

Ellison, Ralph. 1980. *Invisible Man*. New York: Random House.

Emba, Christine. 2019. "Black Women Deserve Better." *Washington Post*, January 10, 2019. https://www.washingtonpost.com/opinions/black-women-deserve-better-will-2019-be-the-year-of-change/2019/01/09/fc40e842-1439-11e9-803c-4ef28312c8b9_story.html.

Emerson, Ralph Waldo. 2016. *The Transcendentalist: A Lecture Read at the Masonic Temple*. Scotts Valley: CreateSpace Independent Publishing Platform.

Equal Justice Initiative. 2019. "Racial Double Standard in Drug Laws Persists Today." *ERI*, 2019. https://eji.org/news/racial-double-standard-in-drug-laws-persists-today/.

Fiske, John. 1989. *Understanding Popular Culture*. London: Routledge

———. 1989. *Reading the Popular*. London: Routledge

Fliegelman, Jay. 1982. *Prodigals and Pilgrims*. Cambridge: Cambridge University Press.

Flores, Juan, and Miriam Jimenez Roman. "Triple-Consciousness? Approaches to Afro-Latino Culture in the United States." *Latin American and Caribbean Ethnic Studies* 4, no. 3 (November): 319–28. https://doi.org/10.1080/17442220903331662.

Fobanjong, John. 2001. *Understanding the Backlash Against Affirmative Action*. New York: Nova Publishers.

Freeman, Sarah Wilkinson. 2014. "Politics, Women, 1920 to Present." In *The New Encyclopedia of Southern Culture: Volume 13: Gender*. Vol. 13, edited by Nancy Bercaw and Ted Ownby, 216–23. Chapel Hill: UNC Press Books.

Friedersdorf, Conor. 2016. "Obama's Weak Defense of His Record on Drone Killings." *The Atlantic*, December 23, 2016. https://www.theatlantic.com/politics/archive/2016/12/president-obamas-weak-defense-of-his-record-on-drone-strikes/511454/.

Freire, Paulo. 2018. *Pedagogy of the Oppressed*. New York: Bloomsbury Publishing.

Gallego, Mar. 2003. "Revisiting the Harlem Renaissance: Double Consciousness, Talented Tenth, and the New Negro." In *Nor Shall Diamond Die: American Studies in Honor of Javier Coy*, edited by Carme Manuel and Paul Scott Derrick, 153–66. Valencia: Universitat de Valencia.

Gammage, Marquita Marie. 2015. *Representations of Black Women in the Media: The Damnation of Black Womanhood*. New York: Routledge.

Garraway, Doris L. 2005. *The Libertine Colony: Creolization in the Early French Caribbean*. Durham: Duke University Press.

Gaunt, Kyra D. 2006. *The Games Black Girls Play: Learning the Ropes from Double-Dutch to Hip-Hop*. New York: NYU Press.

Gay, Roxane. 2014. *Bad Feminist*. New York: Harper Perennial.

———. 2017. *Difficult Women*. Greenwich Village: Grove Press.

Gehman, Richard J. 2005. *African Traditional Religion in Biblical Perspective*. Nairobi: East African Publishers.

Ghosh, Ranjan. 2017. "Aesthetic Imaginary: Rethinking the 'Comparative.'" *Canadian Review of Comparative Literature/Revue Canadienne de Littérature Comparée* 44, no. 3 (September): 449–67.

Gibson, Dawn-Marie. 2012. *A History of the Nation of Islam: Race, Islam, and the Quest for Freedom*. Santa Barbara: Praeger.

Ginsberg, Elaine K. 1996. "Introduction: The Politics of Passing." In *Passing and the Fictions of Identity*, edited by Elaine K. Ginsberg and Donald E. Pease, 1–18. Durham: Duke University Press.

Gonzalez, Erica. 2016. "Beyoncé's Stylist Talks Choosing Looks for 'Lemonade.'" *Harper's Bazaar*, April 27, 2016. https://www.harpersbazaar.com/fashion/trends/a15333/beyonce-lemonade-stylist/.

Gonzalez, Gabriel M. and Sally J. Delgado. 2015. "To Each His Own: Deconstructing the Myth of Default Male Pronouns in the Caribbean." In *Caribbean Without Borders: Beyond the Can(n)on's Range*, edited by Maria del Carmen Quintero Aguilo, Gabriel J. Jimenez et al., 221–32. Newcastle upon Tyne: Cambridge Scholars Publishing.

Goodhart, David. 2017. *The Road to Somewhere*. London: Hurst.

Grammy Awards. 2022. "Awards Nominations & Winners." *Grammy*, March 28, 2022. https://www.grammy.com/awards.

Graves Jr., Joseph L. 2013. "Creole (mixed-origin minorities)." In *Encyclopedia of World's Minorities*, edited by Carl Skutsch, 340–41. New York: Routledge.

Green, Aaron. 2018. "A Synopsis of Tchaikovsky's 'Swan Lake' Ballet." *Liveabout*, December 28, 2018. https://www.liveabout.com/swan-lake-acts-i-and-2-synopsis-723768#.

Green, TeResa. 2003. "A Gendered Spirit: Race, Class, and Sex in the African American Church." *Race, Gender & Class* 10, no. 1 (2003): 115–28. www.jstor.org/stable/41675063.

Gregorio-Godeo, Eduardo De, and Maria del Mar Ramón-Torrijos. 2017. "The Study of Popular Culture on the Agenda of Cultural Studies." In *Making Sense of Popular Culture*, edited by Eduardo De Gregorio-Godeo and Maria del Mar Ramón-Torrijos, 3–14. Newcastle upon Tyme: Cambridge Scholars Publishing.

Griffith, Joanne. 2014. "The Cosby Show's hidden power." BBC Culture, October 21, 2014. https://www.bbc.com/culture/article/20140919-was-the-cosby-show-revolutionary.

Grønstad, Asbjørn. 2018. "The Aesthetic Imaginary and the Case of Ernie Gehr." In *Emerging Aesthetic Imaginaries*, edited by Lene Johannessen and Mark Ledbetter, 3–16. Lanham: Lexington Books.

Grosholz, Emily. 1996. "Nature and Culture in *The Souls of Black Folk* and *The Quest of the Silver Fleece*." In *W. E. B. Du Bois on Race and Culture: Philosophy, Politics, and Poetics*, edited by Bernard W. Bell, Emily Grosholz and James B. Stewart, 177–92. New York: Routledge.

Gusterson, Hugh, and Catherine Besteman. 2010. "Introduction." In *The Insecure American*, edited by Hugh Gusterson and Catherine Besteman, 1–20. Berkeley: University of California Press.

Guy-Sheftall, Beverly. 1990. *Daughters of Sorrow*. New York: Carlson Pub.

Haarman, Harald. 2002. "Identity in Translation: Cultural Memory, Language and Symbolic Russianness." In *Beyond Boundaries: Language and Identity in Contemporary Europe*, edited by Paul Gubbins and Mike Holt, 59–72. Clevedon: Multilingual Matters.

Halas, John. 1987. *Masters of Animation*. London: BBC Books.

Hall, Stephen G. 2001. "Haiti." In *W. E. B Du Bois: An Encyclopedia*, edited by Gerald Horne, Mary E. Young, and Mary Young, 93–94. Wesport: Greenwood Press.

Hall, Stuart. 1997. "Introduction." In *Representation: Cultural Representations and Signifying Practices*, edited by Stuart Hall, 1–11. London: Sage/The Open University.

Hamilton, Jack. 2016. "How Rock and Roll Became White." *Slate*, October 6, 2016. https://slate.com/culture/2016/10/race-rock-and-the-rolling-stones-how-the-rock-and-roll-became-white.html.

Harding, Xavier. 2017. "Keeping 'Insecure' lit: HBO cinematographer Ava Berkofsky on properly lighting black faces." *Mic*, September 6, 2017. https://www.mic.com/articles/184244/keeping-insecure-lit-hbo-cinematographer-ava-berkofsky-on-properly-lighting-black-faces#.IrdY52aFu.

Harper, Kimberly C. 2020. *The Ethos of Black Motherhood in America*. Lanham: Lexington Books.

Hatab, Lawrence. 2005. *Nietzsche's Life Sentence: Coming to Terms with Eternal Recurrence*. London: Routledge.

Hattery, Angela J., and Earl Smith. 2007. *African American Families*. Thousand Oaks: SAGE Publications, 2007.

Haywood, Cory Alexander. 2017. "Remembering Our Favorite Black TV Moms." *Our Weekly Los Angeles*, May 11, 2017. http://ourweekly.com/news/2017/may/11/remembering-our-favorite-black-tv-moms/.

Healey, Joseph F. 2011. *Race, Ethnicity, Gender, and Class: The Sociology of Group Conflict and Change*. Thousand Oaks: Pine Forge Press.

Henry, Astrid. 2004. *Not My Mother's Sister: Generational Conflict and Third-Wave Feminism*. Bloomington: Indiana University Press.

Hess, Amanda. 2016. "Warsan Shire, the Woman Who Gave Poetry to Beyoncé's 'Lemonade.'" *The New York Times*, April 27, 2016. https://www.nytimes.com/2016/04/28/arts/music/warsan-shire-who-gave-poetry-to-beyonces-lemonade.html.

Hilfer, Tony. 2014. *American Fiction since 1940*. London: Routledge.

Himes, Chester. 2002. *If He Hollers Let Him Go*. Boston: Da Capo Press.

Hobson, Janell. 2012. *Body as Evidence: Mediating Race, Globalizing Gender*. Albany: SUNY Press.

Holden, George W. 2010. *Parenting: A Dynamic Perspective*. Thousand Oaks: Sage Publications.

Holt, Brianna. 2021. "Do You Hide Your True Self While Dating?" *The New York Times*, November 11, 2021. https://www.nytimes.com/2021/11/11/style/interracial-dating.html.
hooks, bell. 2014. *Feminist Theory: From Margin to Center*. New York: Routledge.
———. 2016. "Beyoncé's Lemonade is capitalist money-making at its best." *The Guardian*, May 16, 2016. https://www.theguardian.com/music/2016/may/11/capitalism-of-beyonce-lemonade-album.
Hunt, Andrea N. 2019. "'TRAPPIN' AIN'T SHIT TO ME'": HOW UNDERGRADUATE STUDENTS CONSTRUCT MEANING AROUND RACE, GENDER, AND SEXUALITY WITHIN HIP-HOP." In *Gender and the Media: Women's places*, edited by Marcia Texler Segal and Vasilikie Demos, 69–85. Bingley: Emerald Group Publishing.
Hurston, Zora Neale. 1990. *Mules and Men*. New York: Harper Perennial.
James, William. 2007. *The Principles of Psychology, Volume 1*. New York: Cosimo, Inc.
James, Joy. 2013. *Transcending the Talented Tenth: Black Leaders and American Intellectuals*. New York: Routledge.
Jay-Z. 1999. "Big Pimpin.'" *Vol. 3 . . . Life and Times of S. Carter*. Roc-A-Fella/Def Jam.
———. 2003. "99 Problems." *The Black Album*. Roc-A-Fella/Island Def Jam.
Johannessen, Lene. 2018. "Introduction: Aesthetic Imaginaries Emerging." In *Emerging Aesthetic Imaginaries*, edited by Lene Johannessen and Mark Ledbetter, xi–xxvi. Lanham: Lexington Books.
Johnson, Eric. 2010. "Nightline Face-Off: Why Can't a Successful Black Woman Find a Man?" *ABC News*, April 20, 2010. https://abcnews.go.com/Nightline/FaceOff/nightline-black-women-single-marriage/story?id=10424979.
Johnson, Todd M., and Gina A. Zurlo. 2015. "The World by Religion." In *Yearbook of International Religious Demography 2015*, edited by Brian J. Grim et al., 3–80. Leiden: Brill.
Jones, Ellen E. 2019. "Why Do Light-Skinned Women Dominate the Pop Charts?" *The Guardian*, July 13, 2019. https://www.theguardian.com/music/2019/jul/13/why-do-light-skinned-women-dominate-the-pop-charts.
Jones, Feminista. 2015. "Why Black Women Are Jumping to Bill Cosby's Defense—and Why They Should Stop." *TIME*, January 9, 2015. https://time.com/3661669/bill-cosby-allegations-black-women-defense/.
Joseph, Delenda. 2016. "Rock Music Is Being Declared Dead After Beyoncé Nabbed A Rock Grammy Nomination." *Uproxx*, December 6, 2016. https://uproxx.com/music/beyonce-rock-grammy-nomination-reactions/.
Joseph, Tiffany, and Tanya Golash-Boza. 2021. "Double Consciousness in the 21st Century: Du Boisian Theory and the Problem of Racialized Legal Status." *Social Sciences* 10, no. 9: 345. https://doi.org/10.3390/socsci10090345.
Joyner, Brian D. 2003. *African Reflections on the American Landscape: Identifying and Interpreting Africanisms*. National Center for Cultural Resources, National Park Service, US Department of the Interior.
Judice, Cheryl Y. 2008. *Interracial Marriages Between Black Women and White Men*. Amherst: Cambria Press.

Jung, Alex E. 2016. "Awkward Black Girl's DNA Is Alive and Well in Issa Rae's HBO Show Insecure." *Vulture*, October 7, 2016. https://www.vulture.com/2016/10/awkward-black-girl-in-insecure.html.

Kearse, Stephen. 2017. "No Reason To Pretend: 'Insecure' Finds Security In Rap." *Uproxx*, February 23, 2017. https://uproxx.com/hiphop/no-reason-to-pretend-insecure-finds-security-in-rap/.

Kennedy, Gerrick D. 2017. "When You're Black You Have to Fight: Tinashe, Kehlani and Other Female R&B Artists Struggle for Attention." *Los Angeles Times*, September 2, 2017. https://www.latimes.com/entertainment/music/la-et-ms-rb-women-20170901-story.html.

Kenny, Kevin. 2003. "Editor's Introduction." In *New Directions in Irish-American History*, edited by Kevin Kenny, 101–4. Madison: University of Wisconsin Press.

Khomani, Nadia. 2017. "#MeToo: how a hashtag became a rallying cry against sexual harassment." *The Guardian*, October 27, 2017. https://www.theguardian.com/world/2017/oct/20/women-worldwide-use-hashtag-metoo-against-sexual-harassment.

Kimmel, Michael. 2017. *Angry White Men*. New York: Bold Type Books.

———. 2001. "Gender Equality: Not for Women Only" (Lecture prepared for International Women's Day Seminar at the European Parliament in Brussels, Belgium). *Europrofem*, March 8, 2001. http://www.europrofem.org/audio/ep_kimmel/kimmel.htm.

Klein, Alyssa. 2015. "An African Spiritual Art Form Caught in Time-Lapse." *Okayafrica*, September 22, 2015. https://www.okayafrica.com/laolu-senbanjo-ori-ritual-body-art/.

Kornhaber, Spencer. 2016. "Kendrick Lamar vs. Capitalism." *The Atlantic*, March 11, 2016. https://www.theatlantic.com/entertainment/archive/2016/03/kendrick-lamar-untitled-unmastered-review-capitalism/472836/.

Lauter, Paul. 1983. "Race and Gender in the Shaping of the American Literary Canon: A Case Study from the Twenties." *Feminist Studies* 9, no. 3 (Autumn): 435–63. https://doi.org/10.2307/3177608.

Lawton, Georgina. 2018. "Kim Kardashian's Cultural Appropriation with Braids Is One Thing, but Let's Leave Her Daughter's Hair out of It." *The Independent*, June 18, 2018. https://www.independent.co.uk/voices/kim-kardashian-north-west-cultural-misappropriation-black-hair-biracial-identity-a8405076.html.

Leahey, Lynn. 2016. "BET's Stephen Hill: Why Black Networks Matter." *Cynopsis Media*, February 8, 2016. https://www.cynopsis.com/cyncity/bets-stephen-hill-why-black-networks-matter/.

Lee, Felicia R. 2019. "To Blacks, Precious Is 'Demeaned' or 'Angelic'" *The New York Times*, November 20, 2019. https://www.nytimes.com/2009/11/21/movies/21precious.html.

Lewis-Giggetts, Tracy M. 2015. "'Black Characters Are Still Revolutionary': Writers Talk About the Complexity of Race." *The Guardian*, September 4, 2015. https://www.theguardian.com/books/2015/sep/04/black-authors-writers-publishers-talk-complexity-race.

Locke, John. 1988. *Locke: Two Treatises of Government*, edited by Peter Laslett. Cambridge: Cambridge University Press.

———. 1836. *An Essay Concerning Human Understanding*. Oxford: Oxford University.

Lockhart, P.R. 2018. "Bill Cosby sentenced to 3 to 10 years in prison for 2004 assault of Andrea Constand." *Vox*, September 25, 2018. https://www.vox.com/2018/9/25/17896250/bill-cosby-andrea-constand-sentence-sexual-assault-prison.

Lomax-Reese, Sara. 2018. "The Triple Weight of Being Black, American, and a Woman." *The Weekly Challenger*, March 29, 2018. http://theweeklychallenger.com/the-triple-weight-of-being-black-american-and-a-woman/.

Loofbourow, Lili. 2018. "The male glance: how we fail to take women's stories seriously." *The Guardian*, March 6, 2018. https://www.theguardian.com/news/2018/mar/06/the-male-glance-how-we-fail-to-take-womens-stories-seriously.

Los Angeles Times. 2018. "Timeline: Bill Cosby: A 50-year Chronicle of Accusations and Accomplishments." *Los Angeles Times*, September 25, 2018. https://www.latimes.com/entertainment/la-et-bill-cosby-timeline-htmlstory.html.

Lowenthal, David. 1985. *The Past is a Foreign Country*. Cambridge: Cambridge University Press.

Lynn, Denise. 2019. "Why W. E. B. Du Bois Went to the Masses." *Jacobin*, December 27, 2019. https://www.jacobinmag.com/2019/12/web-du-bois-jefferson-school-pan-africanism-communist-party.

Lynn, Samara. 2020. "Controversial Group ADOS Divides Black Americans in Fight for Economic Equality." ABC News, January 19, 2020. https://abcnews.go.com/US/controversial-group-ados-divides-black-americans-fight-economic/story?id=66832680.

Maloba, Wunyabari O. 1995. "Decolonization: A Theoretical Perspective." In *Decolonization & Independence in Kenya, 1940–93*, edited by Bethwell A. Ogot and William Robert Ochieng,' 7–24. Athens: Ohio State University Press.

Marable, Manning. 1986. *W. E. B. Du Bois: Black Radical Democrat*. Woodbridge: Twayne Pub.

Martin, Lori Latrice et al. 2015. *Lessons from the Black Working Class: Foreshadowing America's Economic Health*. Santa Barbara: ABC-CLIO.

Martin, Waldo E. 2005. *No Coward Soldiers: Black Cultural Politics in Postwar America*. Cambridge: Harvard University Press.

Martone, Eric. 2008. "Baker, Josephine." In *Encyclopedia of Blacks in European History and Culture* [2 volumes], edited by Eric Martone, 50–53. Westport: Greenwood Publishing Group.

Masci, David, Besheer Mohamed and Gregory A. Smith. 2018. "Black Americans are more likely than overall public to be Christian, Protestant." *Pew Research Center*, April 23, 2018. https://www.pewresearch.org/fact-tank/2018/04/23/black-americans-are-more-likely-than-overall-public-to-be-christian-protestant/.

Massie, Victoria M. 2016. "Beyoncé's 'Daddy Lessons' Is a Reminder of Country Music's Black and West African Roots." *Vox*, November 2, 2016. https://www.vox.com/2016/4/28/11526188/beyonce-country-music-black-roots.

Maxwell, Eden. 2007. *An Artist Empowered: Define and Establish Your Value as an Artist—Now: Triumph over Rejection*. Fair Lawn. Eden Maxwell.

May, Elaine Tyler. 1996. "Rosie the Riveter Gets Married." In *The War in American Culture: Society and Consciousness During World War II*, edited by Lewis A. Erenberg and Susan E. Hirsch, 128–43. Chicago: The University of Chicago Press.

May, Simon. 1999. *Nietzsche's Ethics and His War on 'Morality.'* Oxford: Oxford University Press.

McFadden, Syreeta. 2014. "Teaching The Camera To See My Skin: Navigating Photograph's Inherited Bias Against Dark Skin." *BuzzFeed News*, April 2, 2014. https://www.buzzfeednews.com/article/syreetamcfadden/teaching-the-camera-to-see-my-skin#.pkjZ2lwPOr.

McDonald, Jordan. 2018. "Queen Bey and the Utility of Nefertiti." *Black Praxis*, 2018. https://blackpraxis.com/articles/queen-bey-and-nefertiti.

McDonald, Soraya Nadia. 2018. "From 'Miseducation' to Miss Lauryn Hill." *The Undefeated*, August 23, 2018. https://theundefeated.com/features/from-miseducation-to-miss-lauryn-hill/.

McDonough, Katie. 2013. "I'm Not a Feminist, but . . . " *Salon*, April 6, 2013. https://www.salon.com/2013/04/06/im_not_a_feminist_but/.

McKay, Claude. 2000. *Home to Harlem*. London: X Press.

McKinney, Richard I. 1971. "The Black Church: Its Development and Present Impact." *Harvard Theological Review* 64, no. 4 (October): 452–81. https://www.jstor.org/stable/1509098.

Medien Kunst Netz. 2021. "Pipilotti Rist 'Ever is over All.'" *Medien Kunst Netz*, 2021. http://www.medienkunstnetz.de/works/ever-is-over-all/.

Meer, Nasar. 2019. "W. E. B. Du Bois, Double Consciousness and the 'Spirit' of Recognition." *Sociological Review* 67, no. 1 (January): 47–62. https://doi.org/10.1177/0038026118765370.

Metacritic. 2021. "Best Music and Albums of All Time." *Metacritic*, 2021. https://www.metacritic.com/browse/albums/score/metascore/all/filtered.

Meyers, Donald J. 2005. *And the War Came: The Slavery Quarrel and the American Civil War*. New York: Algora Publishing.

Minestrelli, Chiara. 2017. *Australian Indigenous Hip Hop: The Politics of Culture, Identity, and Spirituality*. New York: Routledge.

Mocombe, Paul. 2010. *The Liberal Black Protestant Heterosexual Bourgeois Male: From W. E. B. Du Bois to Barack Obama*. Lanham: University Press of America.

Mohdin, Aamna. 2017. "INSECURE: The rise of the awkward black girl." *Quartz*, August 27, 2017. https://qz.com/1062383/issa-raeand-michaela-coel-with-insecure-and-chewing-gum-awkward-black-girls-are-finally-having-a-moment-on-tv/.

Monaco, James, James Pallot and the editors of BASELINE. 1991. *The Encyclopedia of Film*. New York: Perigee Books.

Moodie-Mills, Danielle. 2015. "The Burden of Triple Consciousness." NBC News, April 29, 2015. https://www.nbcnews.com/news/nbcblk/oped-burden-triple-consciousness-n350731.

Morris, Aldon. 2015. *The Scholar Denied: W. E. B. Du Bois and the Birth of Modern Sociology*. Berkeley: University of California Press.

Morris, Seren. 2020. "What is American Exceptionalism? Teaching Political Ideology on Trump's Second Term Agenda." *Newsweek*, August 8, 2020. https://www.newsweek.com/american-exceptionalism-teaching-political-ideology-trump-second-term-agenda-1527155.

Morrison, Michael A., and William G. Shade. 2010. *Encyclopedia of U.S. Political History*. Washington, D.C.: SAGE.

Morrison, Toni. 1971. "What the Black Woman Thinks About Women's Lib." *The New York Times*, August 22, 1971. https://www.nytimes.com/1971/08/22/archives/what-the-black-woman-thinks-about-womens-lib-the-black-woman-and.html.

Mura, David. 2018. *A Stranger's Journey: Race, Identity and Narrative Craft in Writing*. Athens: University of Georgia Press.

Murphy, Joseph M., and Mei-Mei Sanford. 2001. "Introduction" in *Osun across the Waters: A Yoruba Goddess in Africa and the Americas*, edited by Joseph M. Murphy and Mei-Mei Sanford, 1–9. Bloomington: Indiana University Press.

Musburger, Robert B., and Michael R. Ogden. 2014. *Single-Camera Video Production*. New York: Focal Press.

MuteRKelly. 2019. "The History of the #MuteRKelly Movement." *MuteRKelly*, 2019. https://www.muterkelly.org/about.

Ndebele, Njabulo S. 1986. "The Rediscovery of the Ordinary: Some New Writings in South Africa." *Journal of Southern African Studies* 12, no. 2 (April): 143–57. https://www.jstor.org/stable/2636740.

Nelson, Charmaine A. 2010. *Representing the Black Female Subject in Western Art*. New York: Routledge.

Nilles, William. 2020. "Beyoncé's 4 Deserved Better." Yahoo, July 5, 2020. https://www.yahoo.com/entertainment/why-beyonc-4-deserved-better-020000365.html.

North, Anna. 2018. "Why Women Are Worried about #MeToo." *Vox*, April 5, 2018. https://www.vox.com/2018/4/5/17157240/me-too-movement-sexual-harassment-aziz-ansari-accusation.

NPR STAFF. 2016. "Jack White on Detroit, Beyoncé And Where Songs Come from." NPR, September 10, 2016. https://www.npr.org/2016/09/10/493177019/jack-white-on-detroit-beyonc-and-where-songs-come-from?sc=tw&t=1616662912940.

Omara, Atima. 2017. "Triple Consciousness: To Be Black and an Immigrant in America." *Salon*, September 17, 2017. https://www.salon.com/2017/09/17/triple-consciousness-to-be-black-and-an-immigrant-in-america/.

O'Neal, Lonnae. 2016. "The 53 Percent Issue." *The Undefeated*, December 20, 2016. https://theundefeated.com/features/black-women-say-white-feminists-have-a-trump-problem/.

Owunna, Mikael. 2017. "From the Sea Islands to Beyonce—The Legacy of the Igbo Landing in Contemporary American Culture." *Spark Reproductive Justice Now*, April 20, 2017. http://www.sparkrj.org/updates/events/from-the-sea-islands-to-beyonce-the-legacy-of-the-igbo-landing-in-contemporary-american-culture/.

OZY Editors. 2018. "Breaking Big: How Roxane Gay Became the Voice of a Movement." *OZY*, July 20, 2018. https://www.ozy.com/true-and-stories/breaking-big-how-roxane-gay-became-the-voice-of-a-movement/88155/.

Patten, Eileen. 2016. "Racial, Gender Wage Gaps Persist in U.S. Despite Some Progress." Pew Research Center, July 1, 2016. https://www.pewresearch.org/fact-tank/2016/07/01/racial-gender-wage-gaps-persist-in-u-s-despite-some-progress/.

PBS/Frontline. 2020. "America's Great Divide." PBS, January 13 and 14, 2020. https://www.pbs.org/wgbh/frontline/film/americas-great-divide-from-obama-to-trump/.

Poisson, Alice. 2018. "Practicing Intersectionality: Against the Colonization of Black Thought in White Feminist Discourse." *Medium*, January 11, 2018. https://medium.com/@arianepoisson/practicing-intersectionality-against-the-colonization-of-black-thought-in-white-feminist-discourse-fa4db9ef96b8.

Pollstar. 2021. "Top Touring Artists of the Decade." *Pollstar*, 2021. https://www.pollstar.com/top-touring-artists.

Rabaka, Reiland. 2010. *Against Epistemic Apartheid: W.E.B Du Bois and the Disciplinary Decadence of Sociology*. Lanham: Lexington Books.

Radford-Hill, Sheila. 2010. "Womanizing Malcolm X." In *The Cambridge Companion to Malcolm X*, edited by Robert E. Terrill, 63–77. Cambridge: Cambridge University Press.

Rae, Issa, and Larry Wilmore, creators. 2016–2021. *Insecure*. HBO Enterprises and Warner Bros. Television Distribution.

Rampersad, Arnold. 2001. *The Life of Langston Hughes: Volume II: 1941–1967, I Dream a World*. Vol. 2. Oxford: Oxford University Press.

Read, Bridget. 2018. "Mute R. Kelly: The Women of Color of Time's Up Say It's Time." *Vogue*, April 30, 2018. https://www.vogue.com/article/mute-r-kelly-times-up.

Roberts, Kamaria, and Kenya Downs. 2016. "What Beyoncé Teaches Us About the African Diaspora in 'Lemonade.'" *PBS NewsHour*, April 29, 2016. https://www.pbs.org/newshour/arts/what-beyonce-teaches-us-about-the-african-diaspora-in-lemonade.

Robinson, Nicholas. 2014. "Beyoncé Named Highest-Earning Black Artist of All time." *Rollingout*, April 30, 2014. https://rollingout.com/2014/04/30/beyonce-named-highest-earning-black-artist-time/.

Rodriguez, Jaime. 2021. "When Beck Beat Beyonce: Grammys Flashback to that Notorious Album of the Year Upset." *Gold Derby*, October 9, 2021. https://www.goldderby.com/article/2021/grammys-beyonce-beck-album-of-the-year/.

Rose, Evan K. 2018. "The Rise and Fall of Female Labor Force Participation During World War II in the United States." *The Journal of Economic History* 78, no. 1 (September): 673–711. https://doi.org/10.1017/S0022050718000323.

Rotten Tomatoes. 2021. "Insecure: Season 1 Reviews." Rotten Tomatoes, 2021. https://www.rottentomatoes.com/tv/insecure/s01/reviews.

Rowles, Duston. 2014. "Ranking The 10 Best Girls Next Door In Television History." *Uproxx*, March 26, 2014. https://uproxx.com/tv/gnds/.

Rowley, Hazel. 2008. *Richard Wright: The Life and Times*. Chicago: University of Chicago Press.

Russ, Valerie. 2018. "Who Is Black in America? Ethnic Tensions Flare Between Black Americans and Black Immigrants." *Philadelphia Inquirer*, October 19, 2018.

https://www.inquirer.com/philly/news/cynthia-erivo-harriet-tubman-movie-luvvie-ajayi-american-descendants-of-slaves-20181018.html.
Sacco, Peter Andrew, and Debra Laino. 2011. *Madonna Complex*. Essex: Chipmunka Publishing ltd.
Saito, Yuriko. 2008. *Everyday Aesthetics*. Oxford: Oxford University Press.
Schama, Simon. 2019. "The Year of Rembrandt with Simon Schama." *The Art Newspaper*, January 30, 2019. https://www.theartnewspaper.com/2019/01/30/the-year-of-rembrandt-with-simon-schama.
Scherer, Lester B. 1997. "Slave Religion" In *Dictionary of Afro-American Slavery*, edited by Randall M. Miller, John David Smith, 626–33. Westport: Praeger.
Schmidt, Alvin. 2001. *Under the Influence: How Christianity Transformed Civilization*. Grand Rapids: Zondervan Publishing House.
Schmitz, Sigrid, and Sara Ahmed. 2014. "Affect/Emotion: Orientation Matters. A Conversation between Sigrid Schmitz and Sara Ahmed." *FZG–Freiburger Zeitschrift für GeschlechterStudien* 20, no. 2 (2014): 13–14. https://elibrary.utb.de/doi/pdf/10.3224/fzg.v20i2.17137.
Schroeder, Alan, and Heather L. Wagner. 2009. *Josephine Baker: Entertainer*. New York: Infobase Publishing.
Schultz, Kevin M. 2018. "Freedom's Just Another Word?" In *American Labyrinth: Intellectual History for Complicated Times*, edited by Raymond Haberski Jr. and Andrew Hartman, 38–50. Ithaca: Cornell University Press, 2018.
Schwarz, Heike. 2013. *Beware of the Other Side(s): Multiple Personality Disorder and Dissociative Identity Disorder in American Fiction*. Bielefeld: Transcript Verlag.
Scott, William. 2004. "The Ethiopian Ethos in African American Thought." *International Journal of Ethiopian Studies* 1, no. 2 (Winter/Spring): 40–57. http://www.jstor.org/stable/27828838.
Sczesny, Sabine, Maga Formanowicz and Franziska Moser. 2016. "Can Gender-Fair Language Reduce Gender Stereotyping and Discrimination?" In *Language, Cognition and Gender*, edited by Alan Garnham et al., 121–31. Frontiers Media SA.
Sealy, Mark. 2019. *Decolonising the Camera: Photography in Racial Time*. London: Lawrence & Wishart.
Shanté, Roxanne. 2008. "Roxanne's Revenge." X-Ray Records. https://open.spotify.com/track/684bQkS2uk2aXa0IMHQE3y?autoplay=true.
Sheehan, Tanya. 2020. "Color Matters: Rethinking Photography and Race." In *The Colors of Photography*, edited by Bettina Gockel et al., 55–72. Berlin/Boston: De Gruyter.
Sheffield, Rob. 2016. "Lemonade: The Queen, in Middle-Fingers-Up Mode, Makes Her Most Powerful, Ambitious Statement Yet." *Rolling Stone*, April 23, 2016. https://www.rollingstone.com/music/music-album-reviews/lemonade-204663/.
Shelden, Randall G et al. 2016. *Crime and Criminal Justice in American Society* (second edition). Long Grove: Waveland Press, Inc.
Sherry, Max. 2020. "Serena Williams Says She Has Been 'Underpaid and Undervalued' For Her Entire Career." *Sport Bible*, October 13, 2020. https://www.sportbible.com

/australia/tennis-serena-williams-says-she-has-been-underpaid-and-undervalued-20201012.

Sims, David. 2016. "Insecure Is Quietly Revolutionary." *The Atlantic*, October 8, 2016. https://www.theatlantic.com/entertainment/archive/2016/10/insecure-hbo-review/503363/.

Smith, David. 2013. "'Racism' of early colour photography explored in art exhibition." *The Guardian*, January 23, 2013. https://www.theguardian.com/artanddesign/2013/jan/25/racism-colour-photography-exhibition.

Smith, Shawn Michelle. 2004. *Photography on the Color Line: W. E. B. Du Bois, Race, and Visual Culture*. Durham: Duke University Press.

Sommers, Kat. 2016. "The Rise of the Visual Album: How 'Lemonade' Stacks Up." BBC America, 2016. https://www.bbcamerica.com/anglophenia/2016/04/the-rise-of-the-visual-album-how-lemonade-stacks-up.

SOPM Editorial Team. 2018. "5 Female Singers with the Largest Vocal Range." *School of Popular Music*, April 3, 2018. https://sopm.gg/blog/5-female-living-singers-largest-vocal-range/.

Staples, Gracie Bonds. 2020. "Why ADOS Is Unapologetic in Seeking Reparations, Black Agenda." *Atlanta News Now* (AJC), February 11, 2020. https://web.archive.org/web/20200604184813/https://www.ajc.com/lifestyles/opinion-why-ados-unapologetic-seeking-reparations-black-agenda/upCHlNX8ldfLqKFxoOxDgN/.

Stewart, Dodai. 2012. "Why We Need to Keep Talking About the White Girls on *Girls*." *Jezebel*, April 19, 2012. https://jezebel.com/why-we-need-to-keep-talking-about-the-white-girls-on-gi-5903382.

Stodghill, Alexis Garrett. 2012. "Beyoncé L'Oreal Ad Controversy Inspires Black Community Backlash." *The Griot*, February 10, 2012. https://thegrio.com/2012/02/10/beyonce-describes-herself-as-african-american-native-american-french-in-new-loreal-ad/.

Stowe, Harriet Beecher. 2001. *Uncle Tom's Cabin*. Bedford: Applewood Books.

Stump, Robert W. 2008. *The Geography of Religion: Faith, Place, and Space*. Lanham: Rowman & Littlefield.

Strong, Tracy B. 1988. *Friedrich Nietzsche and the Politics of Transfiguration*. Berkeley: University of California Press.

Synge, M. B. 2007. *The Growth of the British Empire, Book V of the Story of the World*. New York: Cosimo, Inc.

Terrill, Robert. 2015. *Double-Consciousness and the Rhetoric of Barack Obama: The Price and Promise of Citizenship*. Columbia: University of South Carolina Press.

TIME'S UP. 2021. "TIME'S UP Legal Defense Fund." *TIME'S UP*, 2021. https://timesupfoundation.org/work/times-up-legal-defense-fund/.

Tolentino, Jia. 2017. "The Somehow Controversial Women's March on Washington." *New Yorker*, January 18, 2017. https://www.newyorker.com/culture/jia-tolentino/the-somehow-controversial-womens-march-on-washington.

Toliver, S. R. 2009. "Breaking Binaries: #BlackGirlMagic and the Black Ratchet Imagination." *Journal of Language and Literacy Education* 15, no.1 (Spring): 1–26.

Trier-Bieniek, Adrienne (editor). 2016. *The Beyoncé Effect: Essays on Sexuality, Race and Feminism*. Jefferson: McFarland.

Turner, Richard Brent. 2002. "The Haiti–New Orleans Vodou Connection: Zora Neale Hurston as Initiate Observer." *Journal of Haitian Studies* 8, no. 1 (Spring): 112–33. https://www.jstor.org/stable/41715121.

UTFO. 1996. "Roxanne, Roxanne." Select Records. https://open.spotify.com/track/2j1mCe3bCFx6wzMh6T90i9?autoplay=true.

Vile, M. J. C. 1999. *Politics in the USA*. New York: Routledge.

Volman, Daniel. 2010. "Obama and U.S. Military Engagement in Africa." *Institute for Policy Studies*, May 5, 2010. https://ips-dc.org/obama_and_us_military_engagement_in_africa/.

Waldman, Katy. 2014. "It is Good to be a 'Bad' Feminist." *Slate*, August 5, 2014. https://slate.com/human-interest/2014/08/bad-feminist-by-roxane-gay-reviewed.html.

Walker, Alice. 2001. "*One* Child of One's Own: A Meaningful Digression within the Work(s)" (1979)." In *Mother Reader: Essential Writings on Motherhood*, edited by Moyra Davey, 139–54. New York: Seven Stories Press.

Wall, Cheryl A. 1995. *Women of the Harlem Renaissance*. Bloomington: Indiana University Press.

Ward, Alex. 2021. "Why There's Talk About China Starting a War with Taiwan." *Vox*, May 5, 2021. https://www.vox.com/22405553/taiwan-china-war-joe-biden-strategic-ambiguity.

Ward, Kat. 2016. "Every Look from Beyoncé's Formation Video." *The Cut*, February 07, 2016. https://www.thecut.com/2016/02/every-look-from-beyonces-formation-video.html.

Warren, Nagueyalti. 2014. "His Deep and Abiding Love: W. E. B. Du Bois, Gender Politics, and Black Studies." *Phylon (1960–)* 51, no. 1 (Fall): 18–29. http://www.jstor.org/stable/43199118.

Watercutter, Angela. 2013. "Beyoncé's Surprise Album Was the Year's Most Brilliant Release." *Wired*, December 13, 2013, https://www.wired.com/2013/12/beyonce-album-social-media/.

Watson, Allan. 2016. "'One time I'ma show you how to get rich!' Rap Music, Wealth and the Rise of the Hip-Hop Mogul." In *Handbook on Wealth and the Super-Rich*, edited by Iain Hay and Jonathan V. Beaverstock, 178–98. Cheltenham: Edward Elgar Publishing.

Watson, Elwood. 2015. "The Awkward/Ambiguous Politics of White Millennial Feminism." In *HBO's Girls and the Awkward Politics of Gender, Race, and Privilege*, edited by Elwood Watson et al., 145–66. Lanham: Lexington Books.

Wesley, John. 1833. *The Works of the Reverend John Wesley, A. M. Sometimes Fellow of Lincoln College, Oxford, Volum 2*. Translated by John Emory. New York: B Waugh and T. Mason, for the Methodist Episcopal Church (digitized by University of Chicago).

Wilford, Rick. 1994. "Feminism." In *Political Ideologies: An Introduction*, edited by Robert Eccleshall et al., 252–83. New York: Routledge.

Wollenberg, Skip. 2006. "Viacom Acquires BET." ABC News, January 6, 2006. https://abcnews.go.com/Business/story?id=89100&page=1.

Wright, Richard. 2005. *Native Son*. New York: Harper Perennial Modern Classics.

Wynn, Neil A. 2010. *The African American Experience during World War II*. Lanham: Rowman & Littlefield Publishers.

Yau, John. 2021. "The Double Consciousness of Being a Chinese Woman Living in America." *Hyperallergic*, November 2021. https://hyperallergic.com/693223/the-double-consciousness-of-being-a-chinese-woman-living-in-america/.

Young, Ralph. 2015. *Dissent: The History of an American Idea*. New York: NYU Press.

Zafar, Rafia. 1999. "The Signifying Dish: Autobiography and History in Two Black Women's Cookbooks." *Feminist Studies* 25, no. 2 (Summer): 449–69. https://doi.org/10.2307/3178690.

Zamir, Shamoon. 1995. *Dark Voices: W. E. B. Du Bois and American Thought, 1888–1903*. Chicago: The University of Chicago Press.

Zhang, Ai-min. 2002. *The Origins of the African-American Civil Rights Movement*. New York: Routledge.

Zhang, Michael. 2015. "Here's a Look at How Color Film was Originally Biased Toward White People." *Peta Pixel*, September 19, 2015. https://petapixel.com/2015/09/19/heres-a-look-at-how-color-film-was-originally-biased-toward-white-people/.

Index

abandonment, 71, 72
Achieving Blackness (Austin), 201n5
ADOS. *See* American Descendants of Slavery
aesthetic audacity, 165–66
aestheticization, 174–75
aesthetics, 123, 201n4, 205–6; in iridescent visions of colored lights, 200; of ME/MĒ, 52; in tropes, loops, and spectacle, 179–80; of water and wine weight, 76
"Affect/Emotion" (Ahmed), 59
affirmations: in catharsis, 67; in extraordinarily ordinary *Insecure*, 164; in infinitely becoming, 42, 45–46, 47–48; in *Lemonade* ACT 2, 133
affirmations and tension, 190; in tropes, loops, and spectacle, 175–76, 181, 182
affirmative-action, 64, 92n2
affirmative life force, 94
affirmative rupture, 93
Africa: Black South African literature in, 171; Christianity in, 111–12; Ethiopia, 169; Nigeria, 112, 156n3, 156n5; Pan-Africanism, 169–70; Yoruba in, 112–14, 136, 139, 156n3
African American female artistry, 156n2

African American men leaders, 110, 206
African indigenous spiritual practices, 111, 112–14, 156n3
Africans and America, 27–28
Afrofuturism, 128–29, 200; *Lemonade* ACT 1 related to, 113–14
agency, 16; in configuring contradictions, 88; in *Lemonade* ACT 2, 126, 127
age of Du Bois: Africans and America in, 27–28; American imperialism in, 27, 28–29; award in, 25; Black and American identities in, 26; coworkers in, 27, 28; education in, 26; higher culture in, 26–28, 32; indigenous names in, 28; layered identities in, 29–30, 48n1; liberal Black protestant heterosexual bourgeois male in, 25–26; Obama, B., in, 29–30; political climate in, 29; Spivak in, 28; "Talented Tenth" theory in, 26; TCT in, 25–31; "two world-races" in, 26
aggrieved entitlement, 12–13
Ahmed, Sara, 59
Alkana, Joseph, 24
"All Night" (Beyoncé), 149, 150, 151
American anxiety, working-class, 12–13, 17n6

American Constitution, 6–7; color line related to, 206; Second Amendment of, 8–9
American Descendants of Slavery (ADOS), 120–21, 207–8
Americans, Haitian, 119–20, 207, 211n1
American South, 32–33
"America's Great Divide," 14
angry Black woman stereotype, 115–17
anthropology, 102
Anti-Drug Abuse Act, 145–46
Anywheres, 48n1
"Apathy" (Beyoncé), 132–33
Aristotle, 191
Attridge, Derek, 80–81, 85, 168
Austin, Algernon, 183, 201n5
Awkward Black Girl, 157

Bad Feminist (Gay), 4–5, 56–57, 60–61, 91; "Blurred Lines, Indeed" in, 58–59; Du Bois and, 51–52; flaws related to, 208; folding in, 50; generalized binaries in, 52; generational marginalization in, 119; "good feminism" *versus* "bad feminism" in, 51; "good" *versus* "bad" binary in, 52; Haitian Americans and, 119–20; Jim Crow and, 120; *Lemonade* ACT 1 related to, 118–19, 121–22; messiness of, 59; #MeToo movement related to, 50; oppressed as oppressor in, 51; popular culture and, 49; sexual violence language in, 49–50; skepticism and, 50–51; TCT in, 52, 55, 122; tension in, 51–52, 208; voice in, 50, 92n1; without generalized binaries, 52. *See also* catharsis; ME/MĒ; profits and privilege
Bailey, DeFord, 142
Baker, Josephine, 207
Baldwin, James: *Lemonade* ACT 3 related to, 153–54; on Wright, 172–73

Bambara, Toni Cade, 53
Bambi, 179–80
Bankston, Samantha, 40
Barry, Doug, 76
Beal, Frances M., 48n3
Beatty, Paul, 35
Becky (colloquial term), 135–36
Bell, Bernard W., 25
Bergson, Henri, 40–41
Berkofsky, Ava, 194–95, 196, 197, 198, 199–200
BET. *See* Black Entertainment Television
Beyoncé, 2, 4–5; scholarship related to, 209. *See also* Lemonade
Bhabha, Homi K., 2, 46–47, 57
Bitzer, Billy, 192
Black church: in *Lemonade* ACT 1, 109, 111; in *Lemonade* ACT 2, 137, 140, 141. *See also* Christianity
Black consciousness, 19
Black Entertainment Television (BET), 61–62
Black female agency, 16
Black female authorship, 3, 17n5
Black feminist discourse, 203–4
Black gender relations, 15–16
Black hypermasculinity, 143, 145, 206; in *Lemonade* ACT 1, 108, 115–16
Black Lives Matter, 30–31, 109–10, 206
Black male sexism, 11
Black mother stereotype, 36–37
Blackness, 207
Black South African literature, 171
Black women/female, 17n3
Blake, James, 148
blues, 98–99
"Blurred Lines, Indeed" (Gay), 58–59
Boym, Svetlana, 181
"Breaking Big," 49
Brooks, Siobhan, 82–83
Burawoy, Michael, 25
Burke, Tarana, 15

camera obscura, 191

Carayol, Tumaini, 134
Casey, Edward, 181
catharsis: affirmations in, 67; declaration in, 67; fat camp in, 65–66; "fat-shaming porn" in, 66; obesity trauma in, 66–67, 92n3; TCT in, 67–68; weight-loss surgery in, 66. *See also* interlude
CBS. *See* Columbia Broadcasting System
Census, U.S., 170
Charles, Ray, 142
Christianity, 138; in Africa, 111–12; in *Lemonade* ACT 1, 110–12; Yoruba and, 139–40
cinematography: in iridescent visions of colored lights, 192–95; in *Lemonade* ACT 1, 107; in rap, rage, and restitution, 191
civil rights movement, 10, 12, 109, 186
class privilege, 63–64
Coates, Ta-Nahisi, 35
Cochrane, Naima, 101
code-switching, 203
collective knowledge systems, 3
color line, 56; ADOS related to, 207–8; American Constitution related to, 206; Du Bois on, 21, 31, 34
The Color Purple (Walker), 53–54, 55
Columbia Broadcasting System (CBS), 159
community, 205–6; in *Lemonade* ACT 1, 106–9, 110, 118, 121; in *Lemonade* ACT 2, 142–43; in *Lemonade* ACT 3, 149–50; in *Lemonade* evolution, 94, 117, 208
community gatekeepers, 128, 129, 131–32
configuring contradictions: agency in, 88; code-switching in, 84; collective identities in, 91; college student in, 82, 83; counternarratives in, 86, 87–90; Deleuze related to, 90–91; emasculation in, 89; hairstyles in, 84; idioculture in, 85; 86, 87–88, 91; passing in, 83–84; patriarchal hierarchy in, 89, 90; in post-rupture realm, 88–89, 90, 91; power dynamics in, 88–90; racial hypersexualization in, 82–83; sexual assault in, 84–85; stereotypes in, 82, 86; strip clubs in, 82–83; TCT in, 89, 91; third consciousness in, 83, 85, 87, 90; top-bottom binary in, 89–90; underestimation and marginalization in, 85
Constand, Andrea, 161
contradictions, 205; in water and wine weight, 71–72. *See also* configuring contradictions
"The Conversation of the Races" (Du Bois), 21–22
Cooper, Brittney, 206
Cosby, Bill, 160–62
The Cosby Show, 160–62
couch montage, 178–79, 180, 181–82
counterculture tradition, 210–11
counternarratives, 2, 209–10; in configuring contradictions, 86, 87–90; in infinitely becoming, 44–45; interlude and, 69, 71; in profits and privilege, 63; in water and wine weight, 76–77
country music, 141–42
Crenshaw, Kimberlé, 37–38, 53–54
The Crisis, 204
Croisille, Valérie, 70
Currans-Sheehan, Rachel Henry, 209

"Daddy Lessons" (Beyoncé), 122, 136–37, 141–43, 144
"The Damnation of Women" (Du Bois), 36–37, 204
dating, 195; in rap, rage, and restitution, 185–86; in tropes, loops, and spectacle, 170, 175, 177–78
Daughters of the Dust, 107, 145
Davidson, Maria del Guadalupe, 44–45, 103–4, 189; in rap, rage, and restitution, 190–91

Davis, Angela, 98–99
Declaration of Independence, 5, 7
Decolonising the Camera (Sealy), 193
Dee, Issa (fictional character), 163–64, 209
Degler, Carl. N., 206
Deleuze, Gilles, 3, 189, 190–91, 205, 208; configuring contradictions related to, 90–91; Gay compared to, 47–48; in gendered perspective, 39–40; in infinitely becoming, 40–45, 46–48; tropes, loops, and spectacle related to, 178
Delgado, Sally J., 31
Dery, Mark, 113–14
Desert Islands and Other Texts (Deleuze), 41, 42
Dhlomo, R. R. R., 172
Dickerson, Ernest, 194
Difference and Repetition (Deleuze), 42
Difficult Women (Gay), 4, 68–69, 121–22, 208. *See also* water and wine weight
double consciousness, 20–21, 64; code-switching compared to, 203; from Du Bois, 4, 203–4; *Lemonade* evolution related to, 104; origin of, 23. *See also* triple consciousness; veil
Double-Consciousness and the Rhetoric of Barack Obama (Terrill), 203
"Double Jeopardy" (Beal), 48n3
Dowling, Amber, 157–58
drugs, 145–46
Du Bois, W.E.B., 1–2, 16, 201n6; *Bad Feminist* and, 51–52; "The Conversation of the Races" by, 21–22; double consciousness from, 4, 203–4; "Of Our Spiritual Strivings" by, 19–20, 24, 27, 32–33; "Of the Training of Black Men" by, 20–21, 31; "Of the Wings of Atalanta" by, 32; Talented Tenth by, 204; Washington, B. T., against, 48n2. *See also* age of Du Bois; veil
Due, Tananarive, 79

Dunham, Lena, 59, 60–61, 163

education, 21, 26, 100–101, 156n3
Emba, Christine, 125–26
Emerson, Ralph Waldo, 23
enclaves, 196, 197; in rap, rage, and restitution, 183, 186–88, 190, 191; in tropes, loops, and spectacle, 169–71, 178, 182
Equal Rights Amendment (ERA), 12
Ethiopia, 169
European legal systems, 206–7
"Ever Is Over All," 116–17
Everyday Aesthetics (Saito), 179, 201n4
extraordinarily ordinary *Insecure*: affirmations in, 164; *Amos 'n' Andy* compared to, 159; *Awkward Black Girl* as, 157, 162; Black skin color bias in, 165; *The Cosby Show* related to, 160–62; Dee in, 163–64; *The Fresh Prince of Bel-Air* and, 162; *I Spy* compared to, 160; *The Jeffersons* compared to, 160; *Julia* compared to, 159–60, 201n2; mundanity in, 157–58, 164; "othered" in, 158–59; praise for, 157–58; as prestige television, 162–63; *Roots* compared to, 160; rupture in, 158; serious themes in, 164; sitcoms in, 159–62, 163–64; for television, 157; traditions in, 158

Fanon, Frantz, 28
Fei Li, 203
feminist solidarity, 14–15
Feminist Theory (hooks), 11
53 percent problem, 14–15
Fiske, John, 17n4
Fliegelman, Jay, 5, 7
folding, 50
Fools and Other Stories (Ndebele), 171
Foucault (Deleuze), 43
Foucault, Michel, 43
Freire, Paulo, 7–8, 11, 45, 88
Frontline, 14

Gallego, Mar, 25
gang rape, 49–50
Gay, Roxane, 2, 4–5, 208; Deleuze compared to, 47–48; "In the Event of my Father's Death" by, 85–88; "Open Marriage" by, 88–90; scholarship related to, 209; as second-generation immigrant, 91
gendered perspective: American South in, 32–33; Black mother stereotype in, 36–37; Black women's invisibility in, 38; childhood innocence in, 33; Coates in, 35; Deleuze in, 39–40; gender equality in, 36; gender hierarchy in, 32–33; intersectionality in, 37–38; masculine pronouns in, 31–33; racial rejection in, 33–34; rupture in, 38–39; satire in, 35; singular Black male perspective in, 34–36; Smith in, 34; TCT in, 31–40; twin 'afflictions' in, 37, 48n3; Wright in, 34–35
General Motors (GM), 38
gentrification, 182
geographic locations, 32–33
Getting it Wrong (Austin), 201n5
Ghosh, Ranjan, 123–24, 128, 205
Ginsberg, Elaine K., 83–84
Girls, 59–60, 163
GM. *See* General Motors
Godard, Jean-Luc, 194
González, Gabriel Mejía, 31
Goodhart, David, 48n1
Grammy Awards, 100–101, 131, 156n2
Green, TeResa, 111
Griffith, D. W., 192
Grosholz, Emily, 20
Guattari, Félix, 41
Guy-Sheftall, Beverly, 36

Haile Selassie I, 169
hair, 135–36
Haitian Americans, 119–20, 207, 211n1
Hall, Stuart, 3, 206
Hamilton, Jack, 130–31

Hancock, John, 6
Harding, Xavier, 195
Harper, Kimberly C., 115
Hatab, Lawrence, 42
HBO, 162–63, 201n7
Hegel, Wilhelm Friedrich, 23
"high culture," 2–3, 26–28
Hill, Lauryn, 100–101, 156n2
hip-hop, 57–58, 95; in rap, rage, and restitution, 183, 201n5
"Hold-Up" (Beyoncé), 114–18
Holt, Thomas C., 22
Home to Harlem (McKay), 207
hooks, bell, 11, 100
"How Rock and Roll Became White" (Hamilton), 130–31
Hughes, Langston, 95
Hunt, Andrea A., 185
Hurston, Zora Neale, 53, 102, 126
hypermasculinity, 183, 185, 188–89, 190. *See also* Black hypermasculinity

identities, 26, 29–30, 48n1, 91, 152–53; in Jamesian influences, 25; in *Lemonade* evolution, 93; in veil, 20, 21–22
idioculture, 68; in configuring contradictions, 85, 86, 87–88, 91; *Lemonade* evolution and, 103–4; in tropes, loops, and spectacle, 168; in water and wine weight, 80–81
Igbo Landing, 145, 146, 156n5
immigration, 8, 91
indigenous names, 28
indigenous spiritual practices, 111, 112–14, 156n3
infinitely becoming: affirmations in, 42, 45–46, 47–48; alternate self in, 45; counternarratives in, 44–45; Deleuze in, 40–45, 46–48; duration in, 40–41; foldings in, 43, 44–46; hybridity and, 46–47; power in, 43–44; resistance in, 43–44; self-actualization in, 43; shared values in, 46; structuralism in,

41; substance in, 42–43, 44; TCT in, 40–48; tensions in, 46, 47
Insecure, 4, 75, 154–55, 205, 209; as extraordinarily ordinary, 157–65; as iridescent visions of colored lights, 191–200; as rap, rage, and restitution, 182–91; as tropes, loops, and spectacle, 165–82
interlude: counternarratives and, 69, 71; existential dilemmas in, 68; idioculture in, 68; idiosyncrasies in, 69–70; psychology related to, 70–71; rupture in, 70–71; singularity in, 69; TCT in, 68–69; trauma in, 69–71
internet, 157
"In the Event of my Father's Death" (Gay), 85–88
iridescent visions of colored lights: aesthetics in, 200; art installation in, 197; authenticity in, 196, 197–98; Berkofsky in, 194–95, 196, 197, 198, 199–200; blue light in, 197, 199; camera obscura in, 191; cinematography in, 192–95; color bias in, 192–93, 201n6; dating in, 195; Edison in, 192; enclave in, 196, 197; film industry in, 192; Griffith in, 192; Kodak in, 191, 193–94, 196; makeup artist in, 196; nightclub scene in, 195–96; Olan Mills photo shoot in, 193; paintings in, 197–98; photography functionality in, 198; prestige television in, 198, 201n7; radiance in, 199; reunion in, 196–97; serial images in, 191–92; Shirley cards in, 193–94; spectacle in, 200; transformation in, 199–200

James, William, 23–24
Jamesian influences: Emerson and, 23; Hegel and, 23; identity in, 25; social self in, 24; universal theories in, 24–25; Zamir in, 23
Jay-Z, 147, 151

Jesus Christ, 138–39. *See also* Christianity
Jim Crow, 23, 120
Johannessen, Lene, 123, 128
first John Hancock moment, 5–9
second John Hancock moment, 9–11
third John Hancock moment, 12–16, 55
Jones, Feminista, 161–62
Jung, Alex, 157

Kearse, Stephen, 190
Kimmel, Michael, 12n7, 12–13
Kodak, 191, 193–94, 196

Lamar, Kendrick, 148–49
Lauter, Paul, 75–76
Lemonade (Beyoncé), 4, 92, 208
Lemonade ACT 1: African American men leaders in, 110; African indigenous spiritual practices in, 111, 112–14, 156n3; Afrofuturism related to, 113–14; angry Black woman stereotype in, 115–17; *Bad Feminist* related to, 118–19, 121–22; betrayal in, 105; Black church in, 109, 111; Black hypermasculinity in, 108, 115–16; Black Lives Matter and, 109–10; Black women's marginalization in, 111; cinematography in, 107; civil rights movement related to, 109; community in, 106–9, 110, 118, 121; *Daughters of the Dust* related to, 107; discomfort in, 117; "Hold-Up" in, 114–18; "Intuition" in, 105–6; metaphor in, 106; monologues in, 106–7, 108; Montgomery bus boycott in, 109; opening of, 105; Oshun in, 112–15, 156n3; post-rupture realm in, 110, 117–18, 121; "Pray You Catch Me" in, 105; reincarnation in, 112, 113, 114–15; salvation related to, 138–40; storytelling related to, 105; subservience in, 110; TCT in, 106, 117–18, 122; tension in, 105–6;

third consciousness in, 107–8; trauma in, 106–7; two identical Beyoncés in, 108

Lemonade ACT 2: aesthetic imaginary and, 123; affirmations in, 133; agency in, 126, 127; aggressions in, 134; "Apathy" in, 132–33; Becky in, 135–36; Black Christianity and, 138; Black church in, 137, 140, 141; Black hypermasculinity in, 143; Catholic Church and, 137; community gatekeepers in, 128, 129, 131–32; community in, 142–43; contemporary progressivism in, 122–23; country music in, 141–42; cultural circulations in, 125; cultural hybridity related to, 124; "Daddy Lessons" in, 122, 136–37, 141–43, 144; "Don't Hurt Yourself" in, 122, 124–25, 129–30, 131, 132, 136, 142; Grammy Awards and, 131; imaginaries in, 123, 128–29; independence in, 125; infidelity related to, 143; Malcolm X related to, 125–26, 127, 129; meditative retreat in, 143–44; metamorphosis in, 129–30; monologue in, 132–33; Nefertiti in, 135–36; NOI related to, 126, 127; opposites in, 123–24; Oshun in, 136, 137–38, 139, 140, 141; playfulness in, 133; post-rupture realm in, 124–25, 127; pre-rupture realm in, 127–28; rituals in, 125, 132, 134–35; rock music and, 130–31; The Rolling Stones related to, 130–31; Santeria and, 137–41; self-assurance in, 136; sisterhood in, 133–35; "Sorry" in, 132, 133, 135, 136; soul music related to, 130; space and time in, 123; syncretism and, 137–38; TCT in, 140–41; "undecidability" related to, 140; Williams in, 134; womanist theology and, 138–39

Lemonade ACT 3, 144–56; "All Night" in, 149, 150, 151; apprehension in, 150–51; Baldwin related to, 153–54; community in, 149–50; crack epidemic, 145–46; DNA in, 152; feminist resistance in, 145; football field in, 144, 151, 156n4; forgiveness in, 147; "Formation" in, 151, 152–53; "Forward" in, 148; "Freedom" in, 148–49; Hurricane Katrina in, 151; Igbo Landing related to, 145, 146, 156n5; individualism in, 150; *Insecure* and, 154–55; intersectional interests in, 148–49; Lamar in, 148–49; "Love Drought" in, 144–45; monologue in, 144; mournfulness in, 144; plantation mansion in, 152; polytheism and, 153; reconciliation in, 148; "Redemption" in, 149, 150; religious identity in, 152–53; reunion in, 155–56; sacrilegious acts and, 153; "Sandcastles" in, 146–47; syncretism related to, 148, 153–54; traditionalism in, 147–48, 153; true love in, 150, 153–54; vulnerability in, 147; wealth related to, 151–52

Lemonade evolution: affirmative life force in, 94; affirmative rupture in, 93; *artist* in, 104; belief systems in, 102–3; *Beyoncé* release strategy in, 97; *Beyoncé* theme and music in, 97–98; Black feminism in, 99–100, 156n1; blues in, 98–99; box-office data on, 95; collaborative team in, 102; commodities in, 100; community in, 94, 117, 208; crossover in, 94–95, 101; Davis in, 98–99; description in, 101; double consciousness related to, 104; ethnic heritage in, 95–96; feminism in, 97–99; fluidity in, 104; *4* in, 96–97; genres in, 101; Harlem Renaissance in, 99; hip-hop in, 95; historical documentary in, 101; hooks in, 100; identities in, 93; idioculture

and, 103–4; lead single and, 96–97; money-making in, 100; music cohesion in, 98; music industry racism in, 94–95; octave vocal range in, 96; oppositions in, 99; personal life in, 104; precedents related to, 103; premier and review in, 98; privilege in, 96; R&B and dance pop in, 95; research on, 93; solo career in, 94; symbiosis in, 93; syncretism in, 102–3; TCT related to, 104
Locke, John, 5–6, 17n6
Lomax-Reese, Sara, 1–2, 39
Los Angeles Times, 161
"Love Drought" (Beyoncé), 144–45
Lowenthal, David, 5, 7–8
Lynn, Samara, 120–21

Make America Great Again, 13–14
makeup artist, 196
Malcolm X, 125–26, 127
Maloba, Wunyabari O., 111
"Man Against Himself" (Matou), 173, 180–81
marginalization, 85, 111; in rap, rage, and restitution, 188–89, 190–91
"The Mark of Cain" (Gay), 73–75, 76–79, 92n4
Martin, Trayvon, 151
Marvel Comics, 92n2
Marx, Karl, 204
masculine pronouns, 31–33
Massie, Victoria M., 141–42
Matou, Joel, 173, 180–81
McFadden, Syreeta, 192–93
McKay, Claude, 207, 211n1
ME/MĒ, 63, 64, 118–19; accusation related to, 55–56; aesthetic of, 52; from Bambara, 53; belonging in, 55–56; Crenshaw on, 53–54; Dunham on, 59, 60–61; empathy and, 61; *Girls* related to, 59–60; Harlem Renaissance writers compared to, 52–53; hip-hop in, 57–58; *inter*-national culture in,

57; interracial marriages and, 56; third John Hancock moment in, 55; privilege and, 61; stereotypes of, 60; symbiosis in, 57–58; TCT in, 55, 57; tension in, 56–57; from Walker, 53–54, 55
#MeToo movement, 15–16, 50, 161
mental health, 63–64, 119
Merkato, 169–71, 174–75, 183, 187–88
Milano, Alyssa, 15
The Misadventures of Awkward Black Girl (Awkward Black Girl), 157
The Miseducation of Lauryn Hill, 100–101, 156n3
Mocombe, Paul, 19, 25–26
monologues, 144; in *Lemonade* ACT 1, 106–7, 108; in *Lemonade* ACT 2, 132–33
Moodie-Mills, Danielle, 1–2, 39
Morris, Aldon, 25
Morrison, Toni, 10–11, 53
Mules and Men (Hurston), 102
#MuteRKelly, 15–16, 17n8
Mura, David, 80

Nation of Islam (NOI), 126
Ndebele, Njabulo, 164, 171–74, 176, 205
Nefertiti (queen), 135–36
New York Times, 49–50, 203
Nigeria, 112, 156n3, 156n5
Nilles, William, 95
NOI. *See* Nation of Islam
nostalgia, 13, 181

Obama, Barack, 14; in age of Du Bois, 29–30; in profits and privilege, 64
Obama, Michelle, 64
Odeleye, Oronike, 16, 17n8
"Of Our Spiritual Strivings" (Du Bois), 19–20, 24, 27, 32–33
"Of the Training of Black Men" (Du Bois), 20–21, 31
"Of the Wings of Atalanta" (Du Bois), 32

Omara, Atima, 39
"Open Marriage" (Gay), 88–90, 116
Oshun, 136, 137–38, 139, 140, 141, 149; in *Lemonade* ACT 1, 112–15, 156n3
OZY, 49–50

Pan-Africanism, 169–70
passing, 83–84
The Past Is a Foreign Country (Lowenthal), 5, 7–8
patriarchal hierarchy, 89, 90
patriarchal pyramid, 9
Pedagogy of the Oppressed (Freire), 7–8, 11, 45, 88
Peterson, Lataya, 54
Poisson, Ariane, 37–38
political climate, 29
popular culture, 2–3, 17n4
popular literary culture. *See Bad Feminist;* catharsis; configuring contradictions; interlude; ME/MĒ; profits and privilege; water and wine weight
popular music culture. *See Lemonade*
post-rupture realm: configuring contradictions in, 88–89, 90, 91; in *Lemonade* ACT 1, 110, 117–18, 121; in *Lemonade* ACT 2, 124–25, 127
Precious, 54–55
pregnancy, 79
prestige television, 198, 201n7; extraordinarily ordinary *Insecure* as, 162–63
Principles of Psychology (James), 24
Prodigals and Pilgrims (Fliegelman), 5, 7
profits and privilege: acknowledgment of, 64–65; affirmative-action in, 64, 92n2; BET in, 61–62; categorizations in, 62; class privilege in, 63–64; corporate interests in, 62; counternarrative in, 63; "ME" in, 63, 64; mental health in, 63–64; Obama, B., in, 64; Obama, M., in, 64; stereotypes in, 62; TCT related to, 65; third consciousness in, 64–65; *Toya* in, 62
protest literature, 172–73
psychology, 24, 70–71
pussy, 170–71, 187–88

queer, 59

Rabaka, Reiland, 37
race, 79–80, 81. *See also specific topics*
Radford-Hill, Sheila, 127
Rae, Issa, 2, 3–5, 71, 201n3. *See also Insecure*
Rampersad, Arnold, 94–95
rap, rage, and restitution: affirmations and tension in, 190; breakup in, 189–90; broken pussy in, 187–88; cinematography in, 191; civil rights activism in, 186; conspiracy in, 188–89; corruption in, 187; dating in, 185–86; depression in, 183–84; enclaves in, 183, 186–88, 190, 191; feminism in, 186–87; frustration in, 184; hip-hop in, 183, 201n5; hypermasculinity in, 183, 185, 188–89, 190; insecurity in, 184–85; marginalization in, 188–89, 190–91; "punks" in, 185; Shanté in, 186; social justice in, 182–83; subjectivities in, 189–90; TCT in, 190–91; UTFO in, 186
Rashad, Phylicia, 161
Reconstruction era, 12
"The Rediscovery of the Ordinary" (Ndebele), 171
Rembrandt, 197–98
resource mobilization theory (RMT), 10
Rist, Pipilotti, 116–17
rituals, 125, 132, 134–35
R. Kelly, 15–16, 17n8, 161
RMT. *See* resource mobilization theory
The Road to Somewhere (Goodhart), 48n1
rock music, 130–31

Rodriguez, Jaime, 209
The Rolling Stones, 130–31
Roots, 160
rupture, 158; in gendered perspective, 38–39; in interlude, 70–71; in *Lemonade* evolution, 93. *See also* post-rupture realm
rupture and tension, 74–75

Saito, Yuriko, 164, 179, 201n4
"Sandcastles" (Beyoncé), 146–47
Santeria, 137–41
satire, 35
Schama, Simon, 198
Sealy, Mark, 193
Sebro, Adrien, 158–59
Second Amendment, 8–9
The Second Treatise of Government (2T), 6, 17n6
second-wave feminism, 10
sexual assault, 49–50, 84–85
sexuality, 11, 25–26, 209, 210
sexual swap, 77, 92n4
sexual violence language, 49–50
Shanté, Roxanne, 186
Sheehan, Tanya, 193
Shirley cards, 193–94
sitcoms, 159–62, 163–64
"*Skinny*" (Spechler), 65
Smith, Shawn Michelle, 23, 34
social justice, 182–83
social self, 24
Somewheres *versus* Anywheres, 48n1
Sommers, Kat, 103
"Sorry" (Beyoncé), 132, 133, 135, 136
The Souls of Black Folk (Du Bois). *See* veil
Spechler, Diana, 65–68
Spivak, Gayatri Chakravorty, 28
stereotypes, 115–17, 200, 204; Black mother as, 36–37; in configuring contradictions, 82, 86; of ME/MĒ, 60; omission of, 159, 201n2; in profits and privilege, 62; in tropes, loops, and spectacle, 167

Stewart, Dodai, 59–60
Stowe, Harriet Beecher, 171, 172
Strawberry, Darryl, 146
strip clubs, 82–83
Strong, Tracy B., 42
structuralism, 41, 72–73
syncretism, 205, 210; *Lemonade* ACT 2 and, 137–38; *Lemonade* ACT 3 related to, 148, 153–54; in *Lemonade* evolution, 102–3

Talented Tenth, 26, 204
Tanner, Leslie, 10
TCT. *See* triple consciousness theory
television. *See Insecure*
tensions, 74–75, 175–76, 181, 182, 190; in infinitely becoming, 46, 47; in *Lemonade* ACT 1, 105–6; in ME/MĒ, 56–57
Terrill, Robert, 203
third consciousness, 64–65; in configuring contradictions, 83, 85, 87, 90; in *Lemonade* ACT 1, 107–8. *See also* triple consciousness
Thompson, CaShawn, 167
A Thousand Plateaus (Deleuze), 40
TIME'S UP movement, 15
De La Torre, Miguel A., 139
Toya, 62
traditionalism, 147–48, 153
traditions, 158, 168
traumas, 66–67, 92n3, 114; in interlude, 69–71; in *Lemonade* ACT 1, 106–7; in water and wine weight, 75, 77–79, 81
triple consciousness, 39, 203–4
triple consciousness theory (TCT), 16; in age of Du Bois, 25–31; in *Bad Feminist,* 52, 55, 122; from Black feminist discourse, 203–4; in catharsis, 67–68; in configuring contradictions, 89, 91; counternarratives of, 2; description of, 1–2, 17nn2–3; in gendered perspective, 31–40; infinitely

becoming in, 40–48; in interlude, 68–69; Jamesian influences in, 23–25; in *Lemonade* ACT 1, 106, 117–18, 122; in *Lemonade* ACT 2, 140–41; *Lemonade* evolution related to, 104; in ME/MĒ, 55, 57; profits and privilege related to, 65; in rap, rage, and restitution, 190–91; rethinking of, 2; veil in, 19–23

tropes, loops, and spectacle: aesthetic audacity in, 165–66; aestheticization in, 174–75; aesthetics in, 179–80; affirmations and tension in, 175–76, 181, 182; appearance in, 165–66, 201n3; Baldwin in, 172–73; betrayal in, 180; #BlackGirlMagic in, 167; Black South African literature in, 171; couch montage in, 178–79, 180, 181–82; cultural circulations in, 182; dating in, 170, 175, 177–78; defense in, 166, 177–78; Deleuze related to, 178; Dhlomo related to, 172; diversity in, 167–68; enclave in, 169–71, 175–76, 178, 182; Ethiopia related to, 169–70; fiction and exposition in, 172–73; gentrification in, 182; girl next door archetype in, 166–67; idioculture in, 168; insecurity in, 166; "Lowkey Trying" in, 176–77; Matou in, 173; Merkato in, 169–71, 174–75, 183, 187–88; Ndebele on, 171–74; ordinary in, 166, 168, 173–75, 176, 181; Pan-Africanism in, 169–70; preferences in, 179–80; privilege in, 167; protest literature in, 172–73; pussy in, 170–71; rethinking in, 174; spaces in, 176; "spectacle" in, 174; stereotypes in, 167; therapy in, 176–77, 178; traditions in, 168; unemployment in, 175; U.S. Census on, 170

Trump, Donald, 13–14, 48n1

2T. *See The Second Treatise of Government*

unemployment, 9, 38, 175
United States, 170; Trump related to, 13–14, 48n1. *See also* Obama, Barack
universal theories, 24–25
An Untamed State (Gay), 49

veil: Black consciousness in, 19; differences in, 22–23; dilemma of, 21–22; education in, 21; endowments in, 22; "gift" in, 20; Grosholz in, 20; identities in, 20, 21–22; Mocombe in, 19; nationality in, 21–22; "Of Our Spiritual Strivings" and, 19–20; "Of the Training of Black Men" in, 20–21; polarizing lenses in, 20; racist antagonism of, 20–21; relevance in, 19; subhuman self in, 20–21; White society and, 20

Voices from Women's Liberation (Tanner), 10

Walker, Alice, 48n3, 53–54, 55
Walt, Stephen M., 28
Washington, Booker T., 48n2
Washington, George, 6
water and wine weight: abandonment in, 71, 72; abuse in, 74; aesthetics of, 76; alienation in, 72, 74–75; broken marriage in, 73–74; Cain and Abel related to, 78–79; contradictions in, 71–72; counternarrative in, 76–77; cultural systems in, 80–81; *difficult* man in, 75–76; *difficult* women in, 75–76, 80; dissolution in, 74; fate in, 71; hope in, 73; idioculture in, 80–81; infrastructures in, 72–73; Lauter related to, 75–76; liberation in, 73; post-rupture realm in, 78–79; pregnancy in, 79; psyche in, 75; race in, 79–80, 81; rupture and tension in, 74–75; sexual swap in, 77, 92n4; third consciousness in, 77–78; toxicity in, 74; traumas in, 75, 77–79, 81; unpredictability in,

76–77; victims in, 73–74; white writers in, 80
weight-loss surgery, 66–67
Weinstein, Harvey, 15
West, Kanye, 57–58
White, Armond, 54
White, Jack, 131
white female racism, 11
white women, 116
white writers, 80
Wilkins, Roy, 9
Williams, Serena, 134

womanist theology, 138–39
working-class American anxiety, 12–13, 17n6
World of Wakanda, 92n1
World War II, 9
Wright, Richard, 34–35, 52, 53, 171; Baldwin on, 172–73

Yoruba, 112–14, 136, 139, 156n3
YouTube, 157

Zamir, Shamoon, 23

About the Author

Nahum N. Welang received his PhD in American Literature and Culture from the University of Bergen (Norway), and he is a currently an assistant professor in English Language-Literature at the University of Stavanger (Norway). His work has appeared in edited collections such as *Aesthetic Apprehensions: Silence and Absence in False Familiarities* and in journals including *The Journal of Popular Culture* and the *Canadian Review of North American Studies*.

www.ingramcontent.com/pod-product-compliance
Lightning Source LLC
Chambersburg PA
CBHW020742020526
44115CB00030B/838